A Guide
to Chinese Literature

by
Wilt Idema and Lloyd Haft

CENTER FOR CHINESE STUDIES
THE UNIVERSITY OF MICHIGAN
ANN ARBOR
1997

MICHIGAN MONOGRAPHS IN CHINESE STUDIES
ISSN 1081-9053
SERIES ESTABLISHED 1968
VOLUME 74

Originally published as *Chinese letterkunde*
by Uitgeverij Het Spectrum in 1985
© 1985 by Het Spectrum B. V.
New edition published
by Amsterdam University Press in 1996
© Amsterdam University Press, Amsterdam, 1996

Library of Congress Cataloging-in-Publication Data

Idema, W. L. (Wilt L.)
[Chinese letterkunde. English]
A guide to Chinese literature / by Wilt Idema and Lloyd Haft.
p.   cm. —
(Michigan monographs in Chinese Studies, ISSN 1081-9053 ; no. 74)
Original published: Chinese letterkunde. Uitgeverij Het Spectrum, 1985.
Includes bibliographical references and index.
ISBN 10: 0-89264-123-1 (pbk.) (alk. paper)
ISBN 13: 978-0-89264-123-9 (pbk.) (alk. paper)
1. Chinese literature—History and criticism.
2. Chinese literature—Bibliography.
I. Haft, Lloyd. II. Title. III. Series.
PL2271.I3413   1997
895.1'09—dc20   96-42978
CIP

CONTENTS

and other fantastic novels. The *Jin Ping Mei* and other social novels. Chapbooks.

PREFACE

For at least three thousand years literature has played a central role in Chinese culture. Even in the most recent times, literary works and their authors have stood in the spotlight of social and political debates which affected the lives of millions. This great respect for literature, together with China's long history of writing and printing techniques, has resulted in a vast body of writings from past eras, while present-day literary production is so extensive that even the specialist can hardly keep abreast. A one-volume history of Chinese literature merely sketches this vast terrain, inevitably tending to be one-sided or oversimplified at many points.

As this book is intended for the general reader as well as for students of Chinese culture, we have chosen a somewhat unusual structure. In the first six chapters we analyze specific features that characterized the Chinese literary tradition from its beginnings until the early twentieth century, with one chapter devoted to the study of Chinese literature in the West. The remaining chapters present a concise overview of the literature itself. The bibliography, arranged by chapter and subject, represents a selection of the most relevant studies and translations in English, French, German, and Dutch.

By using the term "Chinese literature," we imply that Chinese literature presents at least some points of comparison with Western literature. But we believe that it would be misleading to approach Chinese literature with the usual Western expectations. Though a literary text is, of course, the product of its individual author, it is also decisively shaped by certain features of the social milieu. Without meaning to be overly deterministic, we assert that the development of literature is influenced by levels of material affluence, economic and social structures, prevailing value systems, and so forth. We feel that some understanding of this background is indispensable for comprehending and appreciating the unique qualities and tendencies of Chinese literature. For this reason we continually stress such background features.

In view of the long history of our subject, we have been forced to keep our historical outline as brief as possible. This book is not an anthology; nor have we included excerpts in translation. Fortunately a wide range of Chinese literature is now available in Western languages.

Unlike many other chroniclers of Chinese literary and general history, we do not feel changes of dynasty to be the most meaningful turning points. Rather, we have divided literary history into periods according to the material changes that decisively affected the face of literature, such as the invention of paper and the general adoption of book printing. Within these larger periods, we follow the changing configuration of genres. The questions that interest us are: when do new genres arise? Does the relative prestige or status of genres change?

Within each period and subperiod, we discuss each genre separately, observing the same structure wherever possible. After a brief description of the formal features of the genre, its use, and its development within the given period, we go on to mention the most important authors and works. Needless to say, we can only briefly describe most writers and works, although we have singled out a few for more detailed discussion. Some authors excelled in more than one genre, creating awkwardness in our discussion, and we have been forced to omit many of the most colorful and appreciative remarks that could have been made about Chinese writers.

The bibliography is limited to works in English, French, German, and Dutch. Except for English-language titles, the list is extremely selective, attempting only to point the way toward the most initially important books and articles. Most of these works contain bibliographies of their own. We concentrate mainly on publications appearing after 1945, including earlier publications only if they have remained standard or are especially interesting for other reasons. Within each section we have arranged the titles in chronological order by date of publication; they can thus also be read as a concise history of the study of that subject by Western Sinologists. If a title is reasonably self-explanatory, we give no comment, but for others we give a brief indication of their content, sometimes including our evaluation of their worth.

This book began as a set of lectures that Wilt Idema prepared in the early 1980s. For several years the series was used in mimeographed form as the textbook for a survey course in Chinese literature at Leiden University. Lloyd Haft wrote some additional material and the authors together revised the entire text. The result was *Chinese letterkunde*, published by Uitgeverij Het Spectrum in 1985. The present book is an extensively revised and expanded version of Lloyd Haft's translation of the 1985 Dutch edition.

Among the many friends and colleagues whose assistance helped make this book possible, special thanks are due to Ank Merens, Francisca Bijkerk, Elly Hagenaar, Michel Hockx, Anne Sytske Keyser, Jeroen Wiedenhof, Maghiel van Crevel, David Rolston, and William Tay. Acknowledgment is also made to the Amsterdam University Press for valuable technical assistance.

We know that it is at best a hazardous undertaking for two authors to attempt a general history of Chinese literature. Though our text undoubtedly reflects the biases and limitations imposed by our own specializations and background, we have tried to maintain a uniform approach to all periods and genres, and we hope to have done at least some measure of justice to the immense, superb, and ever-vital tradition of Chinese literature.

W.I. and L.H.

Transcription and pronunciation

In this book we spell Chinese words (including proper names) according to the *pinyin* system, which is in official use in the People's Republic of China. In a few cases (e.g., "Peking," "Canton," "Chiang Kai-shek") we have chosen to retain older English spellings which are still probably more familiar to many readers.

In the *pinyin* system, the pronunciation of many letters is very different from what an English speaker might expect. The following table is no more than a rough approximation for the general reader.

b, d, g	as in English (g as in *girl*)
p, t, k	as in English
c	as ts in *tsetse fly*
ch	as in *charcoal*
j	as in *jingle* (*not* as sh in *Pershing*!)
q	as ch in *cheese*
r	as r in *American*
sh	as in *sharp*
x	as sh in *she*
y	as in *year*
z	as dz in *adze*
zh	as J in *John*
a	as e in *pen* in the combinations yan, -ian, juan, quan and xuan; otherwise as a in *father*
ai	as aye in *aye*
ao	as ow in *now*
e	as e in *yet* in the combinations ye, -ie, -üe, and -ue; otherwise as e in *the* or o in *Milton*
ei	as in *neigh*
en	as un in *stun*
eng	as ung in *sung*
er	as in American *her*, or as *are*
i	after s-, z-, c-, ch-, zh-, sh- and r- as i in American *sir*; otherwise as in *thing* or *machine*
ie	as ye in *yet*
iu	as yo in *yoyo*
o	as in *long*
ong	as German ung in *Achtung*
ou	as ow in *slow*
u	after j-, q-, x- and y- as French u in *lune* or German ü in *grün*; otherwise as u in *rule*
uai	as wi in *wild*
ue	as French ue in *duet*
ui	as way in *sway*

Occasionally an apostrophe is used to clarify syllable boundaries. For example, *Chang'an* is to be read as *Chang* followed by *an*, not as *Chan* followed by *gan*.

Readers of this book who wish to consult somewhat older literature on China will often find Chinese words and names spelled according to the so-called Wade (or Wade-Giles) system. The main differences are in the spellings of the consonants:

Pinyin	*Wade-Giles*
b, d, g	p, t, k
p, t, k	p', t', k'
c	ts'/tz'
ch	ch'
j	ch
q	ch'
r	j
x	hs
y	y, i
z	ts/tz
zh	ch

There are a few differences in the vowel conventions. In Wade-Giles spelling the sound of French u in *lune* is always spelled with two dots; e.g., pinyin *qu* is equivalent to Wade-Giles *ch'ü*. Wade-Giles *yen* rhymes approximately with English *men*. The most obvious differences are in the following group:

Pinyin	*Wade-Giles*
chi	ch'ih
ci	tz'u
ri	jih
si	ssu
shi	shih
zi	tzu
zhi	chih

Chinese Dynasties

Xia	ca. 2000–ca. 1500 B.C.
Shang (or Yin)	ca. 1500–ca. 1100 B.C.
Zhou	ca. 1100–256 B.C.
Qin	221–206 B.C.
Han	206 B.C.–A.D. 220
Western Han	206 B.C.–A.D. 8
Eastern Han	A.D. 23–220
The Three Kingdoms	
(Wei, Wu and Shu–Han)	221–265/280
Jin	265–420
Southern and Northern Dynasties	316–589
Sui	589–618
Tang	618–906
The Five Dynasties	906–960
Song	960–1279
Northern Song	960–1126
Southern Song	1126–1279
Jin	1122–1234
Yuan	1260–1368
Ming	1368–1644
Qing	1644–1911
Republic	1912–1949 (continuing in Taiwan)
People's Republic	1949–

Part I.
Introduction

Chapter 1.
THE CONCEPT OF LITERATURE

The word "literature" has a long history, during which its meaning has undergone many changes. Nowadays the word is used in a wide variety of meanings—a fact which can cause considerable confusion. That confusion has not been much relieved by the emergence of general or comparative literary theory as an academic discipline, and even if specialists all agreed on the definition of their terms, it is doubtful whether their theoretical consensus would have much effect outside scholarly circles. In practice, then, if we wish to make serious use of the term "literature," we must first make clear the sense in which we intend to use it.

THE MODERN WESTERN CONCEPT OF LITERATURE

The modern Western concept of literature has its artistic roots in Romanticism and its socioeconomic origins in the Industrial Revolution. (Actually, of course, there is more than one "modern" or "Western" concept of literature, but this discussion focuses on what seems the dominant contemporary tendency.) This concept views literature as a form of language use which primarily emphasizes the aesthetic function rather than the communicative function. Whatever else it is, literature can be seen as a particular use of language. Language can be described as a system of signs (a code) with which the speaker or writer (the sender) communicates a message (information) to a listener or reader (the receiver). Language is a medium for the transmission of information, but the medium can become a goal in itself if the receiver's attention is focused not on the information but on the enjoyment of the specific way in which it is presented. That enjoyment can be of many kinds; it need not at all imply the perception of "beauty."

The literariness of a text, its value as literature as perceived by the reader, may be just as the author intended it to be. In that case, the author is likely to work within the conventions of existing literary genres—and, by helping to exhaust the possibilities offered by those genres, to contribute to their ongoing development. The shattering of all existing conventions may become a convention in itself; modern literature abounds with examples.

3

But the author's intentions are no sure guide to the presence or absence of literary quality. Many works fail to gain recognition as literature exactly because of their overly rigid adherence to conventions. Other texts, though they may not have been intended as literature and may show no observance of conventions, may be enjoyed as literature long after their original (extraliterary) relevance has passed. There are no hard-and-fast formal or stylistic criteria by which the literariness of a text can be judged with certainty: doggerel and great poetry may exhibit striking formal similarity. Ultimately it is readers who determine whether or not a work can be regarded as literature. In other words, the body of "literature" comprises those texts which are read as "literature." And the taste of readers—including professional, well-read, or deeply interested readers—is liable to change. What one generation regards as literature may be rejected by a later generation. We can safely assume that our descendants will read a limited selection of our own contemporary writings, and their choice will probably include works that we do not now regard as belonging to "literature."

We have said that in the case of literature the aesthetic function of language takes precedence over the communicative function, but of course this does not imply that literary works have no serious message to communicate. True, much modern literature is written primarily to amuse the reader, but there are also many authors whose intention is to inform, to move, to convince, to influence, or even to convert the reader. Marxist critics, in particular, have repeatedly emphasized that an author, by making use of the language (and the ideology they claim is embodied in that language) of a given society, is inevitably, consciously or unconsciously, communicating values and exerting influence upon readers.

The distinction between "literature" and "rhetoric" has always been vague. We may describe rhetoric as the technique of structuring linguistic expression so that the message will be transmitted as effectively as possible. The linguistic means and stylistic devices that a nonliterary writer or speaker uses for rhetorical purposes are frequently identical with those employed in literary works. Consequently many rhetorical texts are read as literature, not only in later centuries but even upon their first appearance. In such cases the rhetoric may even be self-defeating. The Dutch writer Gerrit Komrij once complained that his polemic essays were apparently so stylistically charming that few readers paid much attention to the concrete points he was trying to make: it was the prose itself that they admired, and they read it for amusement, not as a source of relevant remarks on anything outside the printed page.

A complicating factor in all of this is that in the Western literary tradition the fictional forms (epic, novel, drama, etc.) have always played a prominent role. This fact has led some critics to posit fictionality as the essential feature of all literature. The term "fictionality" implies that a literary text is to be regarded as a self-contained "world of words" having no direct reference to the world of historical reality as we know it. In this view, whatever one reads in the literary work is not to be taken as a message from author to reader regarding concrete reality. This definition, like all other definitions which attempt to make the concept of literature dependent upon formal criteria, is too rigid in practice. There is much fiction in literature, but not all literature—witness the time-honored genre of essay—is fiction.

ORAL LITERATURE AND WRITTEN TEXTS

The modern concept of literature as a form of language use helps remind us that literature, despite its etymology, includes more than written texts. In every society an oral literature exists side by side with the written. Even in our modern society, with its near-complete literacy, there is an oral literature in the form of jokes, riddles, humorous and bawdy verse, cheerleaders' yells, traditional auctioneers' phrases, etc. In a literate society, oral literature is inevitably influenced by written literature. The scope of that influence depends on the general level of literacy and the variety and availability of written literature. Standing in sharp contrast are societies which have no written tradition and whose literature is exclusively oral. In such cases, oral literature often shows much formal variety, including a rich tradition of myths, sagas, legends, and epics. Where writing does not exist, memory becomes an especially important vehicle of transmission. Researchers have described astounding examples of lengthy texts coming down in virtually unchanged form through centuries of time, but in general oral literature is characterized by a high degree of fluidity. This is true of almost all stories, songs, and the like, no matter how short, which are handed down from generation to generation. Many traditional jokes, for example, reappear perennially in slightly altered form. Long epic poems are seldom memorized in their entirety. Rather, there is a specific technique of oral composition which enables the trained singer of epics to reconstruct a traditional story at will, making use of a fixed rhythm and an enormous repertoire of standard formulas, transitional passages, and episodes. No two performances of the same epic, even by the same singer, are likely to be identical. Oral literature employs the colloquial language of its audience, but this language often includes a specifically literary register characterized by special vocabulary and turns of phrase; sometimes the pronunciation shows unusual features as well.

Oral literature has always played an important role in Chinese society. Despite the great importance attached to writing and literature in Chinese civilization, the level of literacy remained extremely low until well into the twentieth century. The great majority of the population had no direct access to written literature, except in the case of texts that could be performed. For the bulk of the populace until very recent times, literature meant oral literature.

Oral literature thrived in China in a wide variety of forms, ranging from jokes to myths, from proverbs to prosimetric ballads of enormous length. Owing to the fluidity of oral literature, it is hazardous to attempt to draw conclusions about the state of oral literature in earlier periods. Those elements of oral literature which have been absorbed into the written tradition are ipso facto preserved in a distorted form, often with strong concessions to the conventions of written literature. At the same time it is certain that oral literature has often provided the impetus for new developments in written literature, particularly poetry.

A text, whether it is a prayer, a genealogy, a chronicle of kingly reigns, or a song, must be recorded if it is to be handed down indefinitely without change. Until Edison's invention of the phonograph, writing was the only means of recording. A written text is resilient: it can be read and reread, copied and reproduced. It can even be forgotten for centuries and then rediscovered intact. Compared to oral "texts" with their high instability, written texts offer great advantages for the study of a tradition. Accordingly, the term "literature" is often used to designate the entire body of extant written texts in a given language. This usage is especially common where the entire body of such texts is rather limited. For example, many handbooks of Greek and Latin literature still use the term in this sense. As the corpus of texts becomes larger, it is increasingly difficult to employ the word "literature" in such a broad meaning. "Chinese literature," conceived as the totality of existing texts written in Chinese, would be impossibly vast as a subject for meaningful study. To the extent that nineteenth-century Sinology intended or pretended to do so, it was possible only because of the very limited stock of Chinese books available in Europe at the time.

THE LANGUAGE OF TEXTS

If a large audience is to understand a written text, the text must, of course, employ the contemporary spoken language. If a text is primarily intended for silent reading, or if it need be comprehensible to no more than a select circle of readers, a specific written style may develop. Such a written medium may differ markedly from the contemporary vernacular in grammar, idiom, and stylistic complexity. An example in our own society would be the language of legal documents. Once a written style of language has gained a certain prestige among the literati, they may well continue to use it despite changes in the vernacular. The preservation and use of a normative literary language can have many practical advantages when a language spreads over a wide area and gives rise to dialects which become mutually incomprehensible languages. An obvious example is Latin in the Middle Ages. Though Latin was a "dead" language in the sense of being nobody's native tongue, it could still be spoken and understood. In China, too, a distinct written language developed. But because of the nature of the Chinese writing system and the particular looseness of its relation to the vernacular, this literary language eventually became more or less incomprehensible when spoken or read aloud.

Evidence from historical linguistics suggests that until somewhere in the third century B.C., the language of Chinese texts runs closely parallel to the spoken language of the period. Then from the fourth and third centuries B.C., a distinct written style begins to emerge. On the basis of these texts, during the Western Han dynasty (206 B.C.–A.D. 48), a specifically written language developed. This is the so-called classical Chinese or *wenyan* (language of texts, civilized or cultured language). During the Eastern Han (26–220) there was already a considerable difference between *wenyan* and the vernacular, and in later centuries the distinction grew steadily more pronounced. By far the greater part of traditional Chinese literature (in the most general sense of the word) is written in this "classical" Chinese. In addition to *wenyan* literature, from the second century A.D. onward there have been preserved a gradually increasing number of texts written wholly or partly in the spoken language (*baihua*, plain language) current in their time. In some cases *baihua* was used because the author's command of *wenyan* was inadequate. For example, many of the earliest translations of Buddhist works are in a language that is presumably late-Han vernacular; later many of these texts were translated again into impeccable *wenyan*. Other texts were deliberately written in the contemporary vernacular in order to preserve the spoken word with precision, as in the case of testimonials, anecdotes, and sayings of Chan (Zen) masters. The novels, plays, and stories of the last three dynasties (Yuan 1260–1368, Ming 1368–1644, Qing 1644–1911) are mainly in the vernacular. There are also numerous hybrid forms of *wenyan* and the spoken language. While classical Chinese prose was never much influenced by the vernacular, down through the centuries *wenyan* poetry absorbed numerous elements from the spoken language. Modern Chinese literature since 1917 (again, taking literature in the broad sense) is predominantly in the modern standard language, which is relatively close to the modern spoken language, but often it still shows strong *wenyan* influence. Even today, classical Chinese is still being written, though the practice is diminishing as fewer and fewer people have a sure grasp of this demanding medium.

THE DEVELOPMENT OF THE TRADITIONAL CHINESE CONCEPT OF LITERATURE

Learning to read and write is expensive in many ways. Texts and other material supplies are necessary, and neither teachers nor students can devote their time to direct, material forms of productive activity. Assuming that the time necessary to acquire literacy remains roughly constant as long as a given system of writing remains in use and that the cost of reading and writing materials remains more or less constant, socioeconomic conditions will set the limits as to the percentage of the population who can become literate. That percentage can be increased only by improvements in the overall socioeconomic situation—a difficult proposition in a pretechnological, agrarian society—or by a decisive reduction in the cost of reading and writing materials, as by the invention of paper, the invention of the printed book, or the mechanization of the graphic industry. Whether or not the maximum economically feasible literacy level is actually attained depends on the value system of a given society. There are, after all, other things to be learned besides reading and writing, and every society includes groups besides teachers and students who have to be fed and clothed by the productive sectors of the population. For these reasons the literacy percentage is very low in almost all premodern societies, and the farther back we go in history, the smaller that percentage tends to become. Universal (primary) education was unknown before the Industrial Revolution, and even in the twentieth century it has remained a luxury restricted to more affluent countries. Socioeconomic factors also determine the volume of writings that a given society can support: a limited number of copies can be made of a limited number of texts. In this case, too, the earlier in history, the smaller the volume of writings. It is the literati who decide which particular works are to be written and handed down. Needless to say, modern literary criteria did not guide the choices of the literati in traditional societies. They selected texts which appeared most valuable according to their philosophy of life. Different value systems led (and lead) to very different choices. The differences are especially striking when we consider those texts which were the first to be regarded as important enough to be recorded in written form and passed on to future generations. There is a vast difference between the Bible and the *Iliad*. The earliest Chinese writings are neither creation myths nor heroic epics, but very different texts which contrast sharply with the former two. The *Shijing* (Book of odes) is a collection of 305 poems, mostly quite short and in the nature of folk poetry; the *Shujing* (Book of documents) consists of addresses and expostulations attributed to rulers and their aides. The content of both collections dates from 1000 to 600 B.C. The *Yijing* (Book of changes) comprises 64 hexagrams and their cryptic commentaries, together forming a handbook of divination.

As long as no more than a few written works are in circulation in a given society, all texts are more or less equally important and valuable. If there is a dramatic increase in the number of writings, with a corresponding differentiation in their content and character, the texts are likely to be subdivided into the categories of "high" literature, professional literature, and popular literature. "Literature" (or high literature) is then the term for texts which are felt to be of general educational value and which are, accordingly, regarded as part of the necessary intellectual baggage of every cultured person. When literature is regarded in this light, the literary canon constitutes the basic curriculum of all education. Literature is then regarded as having its nucleus in important writings from an earlier period, which enjoy a special status. Literature is expected to combine utility with pleasure and to exert upon readers an influence that is simultaneously intellectual, moral, and aesthetic. Works which contain useful knowledge but remain limited to one specific area, such as medicine or military science, are classified as professional literature. Works intended only to amuse, and which have (or are considered to have) no educational value, fall outside the scope of "literature." Such dubious "reading matter," to the extent that it is distracting or misleading from the official point of view, may even be considered a threat to society. We may call these more or less despised writings "trivial literature." (It should be remembered that we are using the term "trivial" in a technical sense; it would be incorrect to equate "trivial" with "popular" or "mass" literature. Though what we are calling "trivial" literature had less status, it was, like "high" literature, mostly written and read by members of a highly educated elite.)

Within the Western tradition, such a concept of literature was strongly promulgated not only in Hellenistic Alexandria and Horace's Rome after the introduction of papyrus as a writing material, but also in Renaissance Europe after the more or less simultaneous introduction of paper and of printed books. A similar concept of literature arose in China in the third century A.D. following the adoption of paper in the second century. Though the invention of book printing in China (in the eighth century) led to a tremendous increase in the volume of high, professional, and popular literature, it did not change the concept of literature decisively.

Cultures vary enormously in their definition of educational value. From the time of Aristotle the Western tradition has accorded a high place, often the very highest, to fiction. Unlike factual history, which remains tied to the incidental or "accidental" features of real events, fiction was thought to provide better demonstrations of general or "essential" truths. In the Chinese tradition, on the other hand, history has always been regarded as the highest embodiment of truth; fiction has been anathema. During the centuries when the traditional concept of literature held sway, the literary masterpieces of each culture would have been regarded by the other as popular literature at best. Prior to the twentieth century China would have dismissed the *Iliad* and *Odyssey* as popular amusements; in Europe before the Romantic period it is doubtful whether the *Shijing* would have attracted much attention.

THE INTRODUCTION OF THE WESTERN CONCEPT OF LITERATURE INTO CHINA

Beginning with the Age of Romanticism, the West increasingly abandoned the traditional concept of literature that demanded the union of utility with pleasure in works of educational value. Literature is no longer expected to have an educational function in addition to its aesthetic value, so genres previously regarded as popular, such as the novel, have been incorporated into the body of high literature, whereas other genres, such as the sermon, have been relegated to the status of professional literature. This modern concept of literature has not, however, gained universal acceptance in the West. Many Marxist critics, for example, not only insist that all texts inevitably have a communicative function, but demand in addition that the communicative function should be applied in socially progressive directions and should raise the reader's level of consciousness.

In China, the modern Western concept of literature as a more or less autonomous field of endeavor, though at times rather in vogue, has never been generally accepted. The great majority of writers, regardless of their political convictions, have continued to demand a didactic role for literature. Nearly all Chinese writers have hoped that their work would contribute directly or indirectly to the establishment of a strong, modern, and morally just China. Traditional notions of the social and political function of literature were reinforced by the coming of Marxism, which has been widely influential in modern intellectual circles since the 1920s. The concept of the mission of literature remained more or less comparable with traditional thinking in these matters, but there were some strikingly new ideas as to how literature could best fulfill its function in the twentieth century. China abandoned the use of the classical written language (*wenyan*) on the grounds that it was no longer adequate for the representation of modern consciousness and would, in any case, impede communication with the mass of the population. New genres, such as the (Western) novel and the (spoken) drama, were borrowed from the West. At the same time China's traditional literature was reevaluated in the light of the new trends; numerous works previously considered trivial were elevated to the status of classics.

In our study of Chinese literature we shall take the modern Western concept of literature as our guide. Some of the works we examine have not been regarded as masterpieces by Chinese normative criticism whether traditional or modern. Nevertheless, though we will choose works to be studied, we will try to show the status and role of these works within their own literary tradition and to demonstrate how literature functioned (and still does function) in Chinese society. We must consciously ask what kind of texts were written, by whom, for what purpose, and how and by whom they were read. Even a rough and tentative answer to these questions will help to prevent misconceptions and to improve our understanding of the texts.

Chapter 2.
LANGUAGE AND WRITING, PAPER AND PRINTING, EDUCATION AND LITERACY

LANGUAGE AND WRITING

The Chinese Language

The oldest extant fragments of Chinese writing are oracle bone inscriptions dating from the Shang or Yin dynasty, which is thought to have ruled over the North China Plain during the second half of the second millenium B.C. These inscriptions, carved in tortoise shells or sheep's scapulae, were used for divination. To the extent that they can still be deciphered, they comprise questions posed to the oracle, often followed by the answers (and occasionally by the subsequent outcome). These earliest inscriptions are in a form of Chinese that can be called monosyllabic. Nearly all the words consist of a single syllable; there are no case endings or verb conjugations; grammatical relations between words in a sentence are indicated by word order and function words. Whether this earliest form of Chinese was already a tone language is a matter of dispute among linguists; modern theories suggest that the tones originated in specific word-endings (e.g., a final -s, a final glottal stop) that were later dropped.

For a long time written Chinese probably more or less kept pace with changes in the spoken language, but starting about the second or third century B.C., a distinct written language—*wenyan*—evolved which remained in use until the twentieth century.

Spoken Chinese, however, underwent striking changes largely unrelated to the writing system. It changed in sound. Consonant clusters, which had been prominent, disappeared almost entirely. If Chinese had remained monosyllabic, the resulting great number of homophones would have made aural comprehension difficult. But a continual increase in the number of polysyllabic words compensated for the simplification of the sound system. Rudiments of morphology also appeared: plural suffixes like *-men*, nominalizing suffixes like *-tou*, etc.

From an early date, spoken Chinese evolved along several distinct lines called *fangyan* ("regional languages" or dialects). Texts as old as the fifth century B.C. show clear evidence of dialect differences. The oldest Chinese dictionary of dialects, the *Fang yan* (Regional words), dates from about the beginning of our era. On strict linguistic grounds, it might be more accurate to refer to some Chinese "dialects" as separate languages. Cantonese and Hakka, for example, differ from spoken Mandarin at least as much as German does from Dutch or Italian from French. Within the dialects, further distinctions can be made into subdialects and the *tuhua* (patois or "locality language") of specific places.

Alongside the dialects there developed a sort of lingua franca, *guanhua* (officials' language). It was spoken at court, by members of the bureaucracy, and in associated circles. *Guanhua* was primarily based on North Chinese features, since in most periods the capital was located in North China. For a long time the pronunciation of Henan province was used as a standard. Modern standard chinese (*guoyu* "national language" or *putong hua* "general language"), as taught and promoted since the early years of this century, is a sort of modern *guanhua* enriched with countless modern terms and new expressions. The standard pronunciation is that of educated speakers from Peking.

The Chinese Writing System

The monosyllabic nature of the Chinese language in those early days made possible the development of a writing system in which each individual word was represented by a single symbol or character (*zi*). Since word form was invariable regardless of grammatical context, no need was felt for a syllabic or alphabetic script.

All Chinese characters belong to one of a small number of distinct types. Even the earliest preserved forms of the writing system employ the same principles of character structure that are still in use. Traditionally these were known as the *liu shu* (six types of written signs), though the older commentaries do not always agree as to the exact designation of the types.

By far the majority of characters belong to one of the following types:

1) Pictograms: stylized illustrations of an object or action.

2) Ideograms: simple symbolizations of an abstract concept. For example, the character for "sweet" is traditionally explained as a picture of a mouth with something in it.

3) Compound ideograms: two or more existing characters are combined to symbolize an abstract idea. For example, the combination of the characters for "man" and "speak" becomes the character for "trust(worthiness)."

4) Loan characters: the character for a rarely used word may be substituted for another word of different meaning but identical pronunciation.

5) Phonetic compounds: characters formed by the combination of two other characters, one of which (the so-called "phonetic") indicates the pronunciation while the other gives at least a broad clue to the meaning. For example, a character for the word *liang* meaning "roof beam" is composed of the phonetic element *liang*, itself in use as the character for a common surname, combined with the character for "wood."

A sixth category, the so-called "mutually defining" type, is often mentioned, but there is much debate as to whether it is really distinct from the others. The classical example is the pair of characters *kao* (examination) and *lao* (old), both of which originally signified "elder." They are said to be semantically related because older people naturally administer examinations to the young. In practice, this category is unimportant.

In the earliest examples of Chinese writing, the great majority of characters belong to the first three categories. Then in the second and third centuries B.C., large numbers of loan characters were used. In still later versions of the same texts, many of the loan characters were changed to phonetic compounds by the addition of a meaning element or "radical."

In the long run the phonetic compound proved the most productive and versatile way to form new characters, and of the more than 50,000 characters now in existence, probably more than 90 percent are phonetic compounds. Unfortunately for students of Chinese, however, the "phonetic" element in phonetic compounds does not reliably indicate present-day pronunciation of the character. Once a given phonetic compound gained acceptance as the standard character for a given word, it remained standard regardless of subsequent changes in pronunciation.

Words of more than one syllable are written with as many characters as there are syllables. Normally each syllable can be said to be a meaningful morpheme, but occasionally one or more syllables of a word are of unclear etymology. In such cases, as with borrowings from foreign languages, characters are often used purely for their phonetic value. As early as the Han dynasty (206 B.C.–A.D. 220), non-Chinese botanical names were systematically transliterated through the use of a particular group of characters which rarely occurred in other contexts.

The visual appearance of the characters has changed markedly through time, the general tendency being toward simplification and formalization. The present-day standard written style, *kaishu* (regular script), is an adaptation of the older *lishu* (clerks' script) style to the characteristics of paper as a writing material; *lishu* had been widely used for writing on wood or bamboo. *Lishu*, in its turn, had come into vogue during the Qin dynasty (221–206 B.C.). The *lishu* characters were simpler and more streamlined than those of the still older *dazhuan* and *xiaozhuan shu* (large and small seal scripts). For special decorative and calligraphic purposes, both *lishu* and the seal styles have remained in use up to the present.

Popular written styles include various types of cursive script. Of these, *xingshu* (running script) is still relatively similar to *kaishu*, but *caoshu* ("grass" or "draft-version") characters are often so abbreviated as to be legible only in context (if then!).

In the People's Republic of China, a system of simplified characters (*jianti zi*) has been officially in use since the 1950s. These characters, the significance of which is often exaggerated by foreigners struggling to learn Chinese, basically represent nothing much more than the official approval for public use of simplified versions which have long been used for informal and personal purposes. Many of the *jianti zi* are identical with forms used in *xingshu*, *caoshu*, or the so-called *suzi* (popular or vulgar characters). But the nature of the writing system, including the existence of various written and printed letters or typefaces, remains unchanged.

Though the number of Chinese characters theoretically exceeds 50,000, most are rarely used. In pre-Han texts, no more than several thousand discrete characters occur. Pupils in modern Chinese primary schools learn about 3,000 characters. Even a very well-read scholar would rarely know more than 10,000. Many characters in dictionaries are in fact historical variants, characters for obsolete or dialect terms, etc.

THE REPRODUCTION OF TEXTS

Writing Brush and Ink

If the oracle bone inscriptions are the oldest surviving examples of written Chinese, another important early source are the bronze inscriptions dating from the Western Zhou dynasty (1126?–774 B.C.). In later periods, too, texts were sometimes cast in bronze to ensure their preservation. These bronze inscriptions include official decrees of enfeoffment, treaties, etc.

Even in ancient times, however, neither bronze nor bone was the most common writing material. Undoubtedly the most common procedure was to write characters with brush and ink on strips of wood or bamboo, or on pieces of silk, but because these materials are less durable than bronze, the oldest preserved documents in wood and silk date from the second and third centuries B.C.

Tradition has it that the writing brush was invented by General Meng Tian, the builder of the Great Wall, sometime before his death in 209 B.C. But archaeological evidence indicates that the brush must have been in use long before Meng Tian's time. Scholars believe that even some of the oracle bone inscriptions show signs of having been painted over with a brush after carving. It is possible, of course, that Meng Tian did in fact invent a technically improved version of the writing brush, perhaps thereby making possible the development of Clerks' Script under the Qin.

The traditional Chinese ink, referred to in the West as India ink, is compounded of soot and glue. It is manufactured in the form of solid sticks; the writer must rub the ink on a specially shaped "inkstone," mixing it with water to the desired consistency.

Originally, most writing seems to have been done on wooden or bamboo strips about an inch wide and somewhat more than a foot long. For important texts, longer strips might be used. Incorrect characters were simply scraped off with a knife. Sometimes, whole texts were scraped clean so that the strips could be re-used. Understandably, both the writing brush and the knife became traditional attributes of the clerk.

The inscribed strips were perforated and strung together to form a book that could be rolled up: the so-called *juan* or "roll." In the case of longer books, the rolls were heavy and difficult to transport. The fifth-century B.C. philosopher Mozi, who took his books with him on his travels, claimed to need five full carts to carry them in, while the daily work load of the First Emperor (r. 221–210 B.C.) was 120 pounds of documents.

Though the wooden or bamboo strips lent themselves well enough to ordinary writing, for drawing purposes they were much less handy than silk, which provided a larger unbroken surface. Silk was often used for illustrated manuscripts and for maps. Like all textiles prior to the Industrial Revolution, however, silk was much too expensive to use for ordinary writing. Silk was, in fact, so rare that it was used as a kind of money as late as the Tang dynasty (618–906).

No doubt owing to the clumsiness of the strips and the rarity of silk, the total number of texts that have come down to us prior to the invention of paper is actually very small. From the invention of writing to about A.D. 100, practically nothing more remains, aside from the Classics, than the works of several philosophers, a number of histories, and one book of poetry (the *Chuci*, songs of Chu). Of specialized professional or popular literature, nothing has been preserved save scattered and very recent archaeological finds.

The Invention of Paper

This situation improved decidedly with the introduction of paper (*zhi*). It is not clear exactly when and where paper was invented; *zhi* was in use as a wrapping material before it was sufficiently improved for writing purposes. Writing paper became widespread in the first century A.D., and in 105 the head of the imperial factories, the eunuch Cai Lun (d. 114), wrote a memorial to the throne in which he mentioned the invention of paper. Though the manufacture of paper was a rather complicated process, the raw materials—bark, straw, rags—were readily available. And the product was, of course, much lighter and more convenient in use than any previous writing material. During the second century there were notable improvements in the manufacturing process, and the customary style of writing was adapted to the new material. Ink of high quality was developed; the names of superior ink makers of this period, such as Wei Dan (179–253), have come down to us.

It was not long before the use of wooden and bamboo strips was abandoned entirely. Silk, being more durable than paper, remained in limited use, but by the Tang dynasty it too had become practically obsolete as a writing material.

Though the period from the end of the Han to the founding of the Tang was one of warfare and civil disturbance, the use of paper led to a tremendous increase in the number and variety of preserved texts. The first anthologies were compiled, and people began to reflect on the role and nature of litera-ture, which eventually led (in the third century) to the first Chinese writings on literature.

Needless to say, this period witnessed intense growth in the number and variety of high texts. Extant texts from the second and third centuries include commentaries on the Classics, new histories and notes on their predecessors, new philosophers and many more commentaries on the old, and even the collected works of individual authors.

Military, medical, alchemical and religious—Taoist and Buddhist—texts were written and preserved in great numbers, and the earliest known examples of popular literature also date from shortly after the introduction of paper.

From the earliest times there had been an Imperial Library, and undoubtedly there were always individuals who owned books, but not until the second century B.C. do we read about extensive private libraries. Previously, private book collections were so unusual that the writer of an anonymous memorial could be identified on the basis of the quotes he used.

The invention of paper also made possible the making of "rubbings"—exact copies of stone inscriptions. As early as 175 B.C., the order was given to prepare a correct, integral text of the Classics in stone for this purpose. Similar projects were also undertaken in later dynasties.

The Invention of Book Printing

In fifteenth-century Europe paper and book printing were introduced almost simultaneously, but in China several centuries intervened. Buddhism played a significant role in the invention of book printing because of the great importance it attached to the reproduction of the scriptures. The use of large seals to print amulets gradually evolved into book printing by means of carved wooden blocks. At first the individual pages were glued together in sequence, forming a long strip which could then be rolled up. Later it became customary to fold the strip in accordion fashion. As the paper was printed on one side only, it was an easy matter to sew the folded accordion along one side. Glue was unnecessary. These folded-and-sewn strips of pages became the standard book form in traditional China and their use persisted into the twentieth century. The oldest preserved examples of printing date from the early eighth century; in the ninth century book printing became widespread, and in the tenth century government authorities commissioned the first printing of a complete set of the Classics.

In China the system of block printing remained in general use, so that the insertion of text in various styles or of illustrations required no additional facilities for printing. Printing with movable type was not unknown; the first description of the process occurs in the *Mengqi bitan* (Writing-brush chats of the dream stream) by Shen Gua (1031–1095); the procedure is said to have been invented by a certain Bi Sheng. Owing to the vast number of distinct characters in Chinese, however, movable-type printing requires a substantial initial investment and is profitable only if large numbers of copies are to be printed. In traditional China books were normally printed in quite small editions of several hundred, or at most several thousand copies.

In addition, Chinese ink does not "take" well on porcelain or bronze, the materials from which movable Chinese types were manufactured, whereas it is eminently suitable for use with wooden blocks. Wooden type, however, would not last long enough to justify its use. For these reasons movable-type printing was never adopted for general purposes, though it continued to be used occasionally.

Needless to say, traditional craftsmen-printers produced very little by modern standards, but in their day their industry represented a phenomenal technical and economic breakthrough. It has been estimated that from the eighth until the eighteenth centuries, the price of a printed book averaged no more than one-tenth that of a handwritten copy. This meant a much larger number of potential buyers. Commercial printer-publishers came to exist side by side with the various governmental agencies that produced printed books. In addition to high literature and professional publications, there was a growing market for trivial literature, originally in *wenyan* but later, especially after the economic boom of the sixteenth century, in the spoken language as well.

The general introduction of printing led to a vast increase in the number of preserved books of all kinds. Massive compilations and encyclopedias were cut on blocks and printed. Both the Buddhist canon and the Taoist canon were cut and printed a number of times. However, some government compilation projects were so huge that monetary considerations prohibited printing before the advent of modern printing techniques.

About 1875 Western mechanized printing techniques were introduced in China. Movable type was adopted for books, newspapers, and magazines. In addition, between about 1875 and 1920 lithography was widely used in China for book printing. Lithography made the production of small editions much cheaper than was possible with block printing, as the page format could be dramatically reduced and there was no more need for the relatively expensive services of the block carvers. Within a few years wood-block printing effectively disappeared from the scene. In the twentieth century further printing improvements made possible massive editions to meet the growing demand of modernizing China. Mao Zedong's "Little Red Book" was printed in millions of copies.

The various technical developments which we have discussed, and which so decisively influenced the size and composition of the preserved body of Chinese literature, suggest an overall division of the history of Chinese literature into four periods:

1) from the earliest days to the invention of paper (ca. 100 B.C.);

2) from the invention of paper to the general introduction of printed books (ca. A.D. 1000);

3) from the general introduction of printed books to the coming of modern printing techniques, ca. 1875;

4) the modern period.

EDUCATION AND LITERACY

Education and Literacy before ca. A.D. 1000

Formal training in reading and writing has a very long history in China, but it is impossible to say exactly what percentage of the population was literate in the various historical periods. In pre-Han times, the young nobleman was expected to be educated in the Six Arts (*liu yi*): ritual, music, archery, charioteering, arithmetic, and reading and writing (*shu*). Reading and writing was by no means regarded as the most important subject, and it is probable that the main emphasis was on reading, writing being considered the occupation of "clerks with brush and knife." We can safely assume that before the invention of paper, very few men and almost no women were literate.

The appearance of a convenient and relatively cheap writing material like paper, together with the drastic reduction in book prices which printing made possible, resulted in much more widespread literacy. Reading and writing played an ever more central role in education, and the educated man was expected to produce texts of his own instead of merely copying, as a competent craftsman, existing writings. Among the literati, calligraphy became a prized art; the works of the first great master, Wang Xizhi (303–361), are admired and studied to the present day. Education was mostly in the hands of the private tutors hired by well-to-do families, but in later centuries Buddhist monasteries, with their libraries, also functioned as schools.

Though the percentage of literate men increased, it remained small by modern standards. Starting in the first century A.D., literate women, even women scholars, are occasionally mentioned. During the Tang many literate courtesans wrote poetry; one of them, Xue Tao (770–832), even had a popular type of letter paper named after her.

Education and Literacy from 1000 to 1900

Besides the introduction of book printing, the period of transition from the Tang to the Song saw a number of significant changes in Chinese society. During the Song, society as a whole was remarkably education-minded, largely because of the "democratic" ideal of scholarship. It was theoretically possible (though in practice pretty much a myth) that any intelligent male pupil who really applied himself, be he ever so poor, stood a fair chance of earning the title of *zhuangyuan* (top of the list in the state examinations at the capital), with all that implied in terms of a splendid subsequent career and marriage. This "poor-boy-makes-good" theme, endlessly varied and embellished, became a standard subject for short stories, novels, and the performing arts.

While better-off families continued to make use of private tutors, a wide variety of local schools also provided elementary education. These might be organized and run by a village, a neighborhood, a lineage, or a group of families. Typically, a single teacher might be charged with the education of from ten to thirty pupils of all ages, differing vastly as regards talent and educational level.

The exact percentage of literacy prior to the eighteenth century remains unclear. It has been estimated that in the eighteenth and nineteenth centuries, in peaceful periods, perhaps 30 to 45 percent of all boys received some form of primary education; for girls the percentage ranged from 2 to 10 percent. The percentage of boys attending school was much higher in the cities than in the countryside, but rural areas varied widely in educational opportunities, depending on the area's prosperity, tradition, and social expectations. In general, the Southern and Eastern provinces engaged in education more intensively than the rest of the country.

The percentage of boys attending school or studying with tutors does not, however, indicate the overall percentage of literacy. Learning to read, for example, was usually a matter of brute memorization of texts in *wenyan*. In many cases pupils would not have been able to explain, or even to translate correctly into spoken Chinese, the texts they had supposedly learned. Writing, too, was often learned through the medium of classical texts containing obsolete or abstruse characters. Students regarded education as horribly tedious, and many quit within a couple of years without having learned much that was of practical use. Better educational methods were known, but probably never found wide application.

We should also ask how literacy should be defined in the Chinese context. For those with an alphabetic language, the term "literate" could conceivably be applied to anyone who knows the letters and, hence, can spell out and recognize words, even if with difficulty. But how many characters must a Chinese know to be considered minimally "literate"? Is it enough to know enough characters to get along in one's daily work as, say, a government clerk, a bookkeeper, a shopkeeper, or a foreman? Or should the criterion be the ability to read with substantial understanding texts in a number of different fields?

However liberal the norm applied, in the eighteenth and nineteenth centuries it seems clear that even minimal literacy did not extend to more than 20 or 30 percent of the male population. At the turn of the twentieth century, illiteracy among the population as a whole was often estimated at 85 percent. And of those regarded as literate, the number at home with all texts and genres could not have exceeded a quarter of that theoretically literate 20 or 30 percent.

But however small the *percentage* of high-level literacy, in a country with a population as large as China's, the absolute *number* of well-educated people was of course huge. They included, first and foremost, those who had gone beyond the primary level to a true mastery of *wenyan*, virtually always in the hope of sooner or later passing the state examinations. Already in Song times, the examinations represented the royal road to a career in government, and in the Ming and Qing their importance was even more pronounced.

The number of highly literate women was very small in all periods, even though not all Chinese would have endorsed such traditional proverbs as "for a woman, to have no talent is a virtue." Only a single woman, Li Qingzhao (1084–ca. 1151?), ever attained a literary reputation on a par with that of the leading male writers. From the viewpoint of literary history, by far the most influential group of readers and potential writers was that of the male scholars and examination students.

Education and Literacy in the Twentieth Century

Since 1900 the various Chinese governments have made efforts to achieve general or universal primary education of a truly modern sort. In the beginning, this usually meant replacing traditional-style education with modern primary schools in the most prosperous areas. In other words, the content of education was changed for the more or less elite students, while the situation of the general population remained unchanged. Before 1949, it was probably girls who achieved the most significant practical increase in literacy.

After the founding of the People's Republic, great efforts were made to expand primary education. In 1965, roughly 70 percent of school-age children attended some form of primary school, but the Cultural Revolution (1966–1969) disrupted formal education throughout the People's Republic for years.

Even today education is far from uniform, especially in rural areas. Not all children can or do attend school. In rural areas, it is often difficult to combine the rigidity of a modern school system with the seasonal exigencies of agriculture, and this has reinforced many parents' traditional doubts as to the usefulness of book-learning. Rural folk tend to believe that girls, especially, have no real need for education. Truancy is widespread, and many children leave school as soon as they can contribute to the family income. The 1964 census described 38 percent of the total population as "illiterate or semi-literate." By the 1982 census that category had shrunk to 23 percent, but experts suspect this figure is far too optimistic.

In Taiwan, where an extensive educational system had already been built up during the period of Japanese rule (1895–1945), primary education is universal. Secondary and university education have also been highly developed.

Both in the People's Republic and in other Chinese-speaking areas, the reading public for modern Chinese literature consists mainly of college graduates, students, and others who have had at least a secondary-level education. Of course, a wider audience exists for popular literature.

Chapter 3.
TRADITIONAL CHINESE SOCIETY, ESPECIALLY IN THE PERIOD FROM THE HAN TO THE QING

GREAT TRADITION AND LITTLE TRADITIONS

Sociologists and anthropologists have devised many different conceptual approaches to the study of traditional societies and their historical development. In setting out to discuss Chinese society, we think it best to make clear at the outset which theoretical framework we will be applying and why we think it is appropriate to the material.

We think that one can most profitably study the functioning or "behavior" of literature in Chinese society in terms of concepts developed by the American sociologist Robert Redfield. In his studies of Central American societies, Redfield was struck by the persistence of widely varying local cultures side by side with a uniform urban-based culture of lawyers, doctors, and Catholic priests. A local culture would typically be limited to a small area. It would have produced few if any written records. The local villages would be aware of the differences between their "own" traditions and the Catholic tradition, recognizing the latter as in some sense superior.

The Roman Catholic faith, on the other hand, applies to the entirety of a large geographic region; it has an extensive written tradition in which continuity with the past is consciously maintained, and its practice and promulgation are in the hands of a distinctly trained professional group, the clergy. The Roman Catholic Church claims universal validity for its teachings and the attendant behaviors.

To apply Redfield's insights to traditional Chinese society, we need to make certain modifications. In traditional Chinese society, vastly divergent local cultures, representing individual village or market communities, existed side by side with other cultures which extended across the entire Chinese-speaking world and were represented by distinct groups within society. These more or less nationwide and uniform cultures, however, by no means enjoyed equal prestige, and the corresponding social groups were of widely unequal status. The various professional groups were far overshadowed by a universal

24

culture, often referred to by the general term *Confucianism*, which was identified with the government and the *gentry*. Erik Zürcher has called this universal culture the "Central Tradition," applying the term "peripheral traditions" to the professional cultures. As both "central" and "peripheral" cultures had the advantages of a written tradition, they both enjoyed a great measure of uniformity and continuity throughout the Chinese-speaking world.

What were the peripheral professional cultures? Starting at least as early as the second century A.D., we can trace the existence of a medical culture represented by specialized physicians and a military culture upheld by professional officers. But certainly the most important professional cultures were the religious ones—Taoism and Buddhism—with their monks and priests and their very extensive written traditions. While the Taoist priesthood was at times a hereditary function, the celibate Buddhist clergy was recruited entirely from other segments of the population.

The Central Tradition claimed universal and unlimited validity. It theoretically had the answers to all meaningful questions about man, society, and the cosmos. Accordingly, the Central Tradition regarded itself as competent to judge the other cultures—the professional traditions—as their importance in each case was limited to a single, specialized field of human activity. The superiority and authority of the Central Tradition was accepted without complaint by the medical and military cultures, but others, like the Buddhist culture, yielded only after putting up long and significant resistance.

The Central Tradition was based on a formidable written tradition going back to antiquity. Its cultural dominance was reinforced by the social position of its exponents: government officials and gentry, who in turn could justify their place in society on the grounds that they were the defenders and agents of the universal culture. They consciously thought of themselves as more important than all other groups in society, including the specialized professions.

THE DEVELOPMENT OF THE CENTRAL TRADITION

Neither the Central Tradition nor its social base remained unchanged down through the centuries. Calling the Central Tradition of China "Confucian" is comparable to calling that of Europe "Christian": in both cases the developed and codified teachings of later ages contained many elements that were not to be found in the original records of the founder and his disciples.

In the last few centuries before the Han, drastic political and social changes had led members of the nobility to debate with keen interest the question of how the sovereign could bring about order and stability. Originally Confucianism, old and influential though it was, was no more than one of various components of the Central Tradition, which also included such other schools as Mohism, Taoism, and Legalism. The "Confucianism" which ultimately became the official state ideology under the Western Han dynasty (206 B.C.–A.D. 8) was actually a comprehensive synthesis. In it the older Confucianism was integrated with the canonical Classics of antiquity and with various elements taken from rival schools. The result was a Central Tradition in which both Confucian writings and those of the other philosophers continued to play a role, though the latter were regarded as being of somewhat lesser validity.

Despite numerous reformulations, this "synthetic" Confucianism remained the Central Tradition throughout later ages, even in the periods when Buddhism was probably more vital and creative as a philosophy. Histories of Chinese philosophy are often somewhat misleading in this respect; their authors often concentrate on the development of new ideas, judging them purely on their philosophical merits. They seldom provide a historical survey of the most prominent opinions held by specific groups.

There were several main stages in the long-term reformulation of "Confucianism." During the Eastern Han the great commentaries on the individual Classics were compiled. Starting in the second century A.D., Taoist philosophical works, especially the *Zhuangzi*, came into wider circulation than before. Together with the *Yijing*, they became one of the main sources of inspiration and influence on the third-century reformulation of the Central Tradition, in which the official cosmology was streamlined and rationalized. This particular reformulation of Confucianism is known by the lamentably misleading name of "Neo-Taoism."

In the seventh century, under the Tang dynasty (618–906), the great subcommentaries were compiled. They represented an attempt to reduce all canonical writings to a single tightly integrated system without internal discrepancies.

The last great reformulation took place in the eleventh and twelfth centuries, during the Song dynasty (960–1279); it is known in the West as *Neo-Confucianism*. Whereas the Confucianism of the preceding Tang dynasty had been rather scholastic in nature, stressing the role of Confucianism as a state institution, Song dynasty Neo-Confucianism stressed the role of Confucianism as a moral philosophy for personal life. It proceeded to formulate increasingly strict rules for the personal behavior of men and women, and insisted on one's utmost sincerity in the performance of one's social duties inside and outside the family. Stimulated by Buddhism, Neo-Confucianism also systematized its ontology. To the extent that such comparisons are meaningful, Neo-Confucianism can be characterized as a "Protestant," even a "Puritan" version of Confucianism. Neo-Confucianism, as systematized by Zhu Xi (1130–1200), remained the orthodox interpretation of the Classics that was used in the state examinations from the fourteenth century until the fall of the Qing dynasty in 1911, despite numerous attempts by individual thinkers to challenge certain aspects of it.

On the whole the Central Tradition remained remarkably self-contained; in its many centuries of existence it assimilated almost nothing of importance from outside traditions. Even Buddhism and religious Taoism, which both played significant roles in society from the second century A.D. onward, enriching the Chinese vocabulary with countless words and concepts, had little demonstrable direct influence on the successive revisions of Confucianism. Though the term the Three Teachings (*san jiao*) was often used in Song times and later to refer collectively to Confucianism, Taoism, and Buddhism, in practice neither Buddhism nor Taoism could claim equal status with Confucianism.

The Representatives of the Central Tradition: Gentry and Literati

In pre-Han times the exponents par excellence of the Central Tradition were the noblemen, "the gentlemen" (*shi*). In traditional Chinese thought, society was seen as a harmoniously functioning system of four main groups:

1) the *shi*, who provided leadership;
2) the *nong* (peasants), who provided sustenance;
3) the *gong* (craftsmen), who saw to the provision of implements; and
4) the *shang* (merchants), who distributed necessary supplies.

Down through the centuries the representatives of the Central Tradition always identified themselves as *shi*, though this term actually had quite different meanings in different periods. Under the Han, the "gentlemen" were in fact major landowners; starting in the second century A.D. this group evolved into a new aristocracy, whose members obtained governmental posts by virtue of their birth. Some of these families continued to provide members of the Son of Heaven's administrative apparatus for as long as eight centuries. For many families, government office gradually became a more important source of income than their often dwindling landholdings. For nonaristocrats, a career in government service was virtually unthinkable. For members of the aristocratic families to champion the Central Tradition seemed a natural part of their role as the social elite: one was a Confucianist because one was a gentleman.

All this changed in the Song, when far-reaching social and economic changes led to the emergence of a new type of elite. This was what historians have often termed the *gentry*. The gentry was much larger than the old aristocracy had been. On the local level elite status was mainly dependent on land ownership, but the national elite—the bureaucracy—was theoretically open to anyone who could pass the examinations, thereby demonstrating mastery of the orthodox tradition. In other words, one became a gentleman by being a Confucianist.

The examination system made elite status seem mostly a matter of intelligence and diligent study. The Central Tradition was no longer in the hands of self-assured aristocrats who regarded their status as a matter of course. Despite later social changes, this situation of an open and fluid elite, at least in theory constituting an "aristocracy of merit," remained basically in effect until the abolition of the examination system—and the last examinations at the capital were held in 1905.

In practice, the representative group of the Central Tradition, the literati, was far from homogenous. Socioeconomically, its members varied from dwellers in truly opulent luxury to hard-pressed schoolmasters and clerks eking out an unenviable existence. From Song times on, however, the majority were probably landowners of at least some means.

Intellectually, literati varied from struggling students who had barely mastered a few partly understood texts, to sensationally erudite scholars who were familiar with virtually the whole literature of Confucianism in addition to being well read in the specialized professional literature of their day.

Literati also differed greatly with regard to the importance they attached to the *content* of the orthodox texts which they had studied. The narrower spirits among them might try to put the teachings into practice with fundamentalist literalness, while the more liberal minds might or might not behave as seemed fitting for "Confucianists."

Central and Peripheral Cultures

In their attitude toward the professional cultures, the literati showed great personal differences, but over time a general shift seems to have occurred in the degree to which the "peripheral" traditions were taken seriously. The exponents of the Central Tradition always felt themselves collectively superior to those of the professional cultures: physicians and officers, priests and monks. Members of the Confucian elite were perfectly free to take a personal interest in a professional culture, for example in medicine or Buddhism. In fact well-trained Confucians, by virtue of their knowledge of the universally applicable tradition, expected to be able to attain greater insights into a "peripheral" field than its professional exponents, since the latter could not but have narrower vision.

In any case the Central Tradition tended not to engage in serious dialog with the professional cultures. It preferred to instruct them. But in the days when the Confucian elite was taken from the aristocracy and the number of literati was still small—until about the tenth century and the spread of book printing—the elite Confucians seem to have been more receptive to the professional cultures. Mention is frequently made of contacts between literati and priests or monks, and formal debates were held at court between the proponents of the Three Teachings.

Later, when membership in the elite became a matter of being a master of orthodoxy and the number of literati had greatly increased, even this rather condescending interchange grew less common. Confucianism took pains to dissociate itself from the peripheral traditions, especially Buddhism and Taoism. Buddhism and Taoism tried to strengthen their own positions by presenting themselves to literati as complements to Confucianism—a strategy later adopted by the Jesuit missionaries to China in the seventeenth century. The military and medical sciences were accorded somewhat more respect on account of their practical usefulness, but a Confucian gentleman who dabbled .in medicine was often thought of as a better doctor than a professional physician.

Though the traditional view distinguished "high" from "trivial" literature, nearly always it was the representatives of the Central Tradition who wrote both types of literature, and the Central Tradition that classified texts into high, professional, and trivial. High literature was the written corpus of the Central Tradition itself. As commonly used today, the term Chinese literature typically encompasses a more or less extensive selection from the traditional high and trivial literatures. The professional literatures are usually ignored, with the very serious consequence that the vast religious literatures of the Buddhist and Taoist traditions are disqualified from consideration.

In the light of Western literary history this is very strange, to say the least. In the West, religious literature has been the source of numerous texts that are regarded as literary masterpieces—hymns, visions, allegories, sermons, and songs. Though China's Buddhist literature has been studied by philosophers and historians of religion, it has received very little attention from a literary point of view. And the literature of religious Taoism, though almost equally extensive, has only recently attracted serious scholarly attention.

In the history of Chinese literature, Buddhism and Taoism are chiefly important as influences on trivial literature. Many literati authors omitted Buddhist and Taoist writings from their collected works and deliberately avoided Buddhist or Taoist terminology in their regular compositions. Even authors who are known to have been devout Buddhists or Taoists in their private lives rarely include blatantly Buddhist or Taoist elements in their writings. Trivial literature, however, was always ready to assimilate new ideas, forms, and figures—miracles and horrors, fairies, gods, and demons.

LITERATI AND LITERATURE: WRITER AND BUREAUCRAT

Chinese literature was created by a specific subgroup within the very small literate population of traditional China: the *literati*. And within this group it was the upper stratum that produced the greatest volume of writings. There were exceptions, but on the whole a writer's success was based on a background of wide reading and study, which was economically feasible only for the few.

Those who could not buy books had to borrow them from friends or find their way to one of the private libraries where books were guarded as rare treasures. For many, a job as private secretary or tutor was the only way to stay in contact with the world of letters. Public libraries were rare. The imperial libraries were not open to the general public. During the Tang dynasty some of the larger Buddhist monasteries had extensive libraries, which often included Confucian texts. Starting in the Song, the *shuyuan* (academies where young literati prepared for the state examinations) sometimes had libraries. In more recent centuries, commercial lending libraries specializing in trivial literature are said to have existed in a few of the very largest cities.

Certainly until the end of the Tang, nearly all authors whose names have come down to us belonged to the highly select group of literati who managed to gain employment as government officials. High or low in rank, successful or unsuccessful in office, practically all had some kind of career in the bureaucracy. Starting in Song times, the number of authors who were not government officials increased, but even in the late nineteenth century the majority of well-known authors had at least some experience in the bureaucracy. Quite a few authors of trivial literature never attained to office (which is not to say that they would not have wished to), but even "trivial" authors often had bureaucratic careers.

The Uniformity of Chinese Literature

Traditional Chinese writers nearly always addressed themselves to their social and intellectual peers. As a result, much of Chinese literature seems curiously monotonous from a Western point of view. The subjects are limited to those of interest to the elite strata. Though this narrow focus is especially evident in high literature, much trivial literature shows the same tendency. (It must be said, however, that from the sixteenth century on, writers of novels and novellas in particular show more interest in previously neglected subjects.) Discussions usually range no further than specific differences of opinion within the Central Tradition. Literature is not seen as a forum in which various equally important cultures engage in dialog or debate. If anything, a major aim is to subject "incorrect" ideas to a sort of excommunication—a tendency that has persisted into the twentieth century. Changes in the composition of the social base of the Central Tradition did have identifiable effects on literature, but to the new student of Chinese literature, these are no more than details.

China is a vast geographic entity, comparable in size to Europe. Nevertheless, although there were considerable differences in the daily life led by literati in different areas, the remarkable uniformity of bureaucratic practice, beginning with the standardized examinations, had a strong determining influence on Chinese literature. In Europe, especially after the breakup of the Carolingian Empire, a number of distinctive national literatures emerged which eventually contributed to each other's development. In China the nationwide uniformity of the writing system tended to minimize the importance of dialect differences, while the rise of book printing helped to ensure the homogeneity of the Chinese intellectual world just at a time when European culture was beginning its long process of diversification. Over the past millennium, while European culture broke up more and more clearly into national variants, the Chinese Central Tradition became more monolithic despite increases in the geographic area over which it held sway.

And just as the Central Tradition resisted influence from the professional cultures, the Chinese literati rarely took much interest in the cultures that were developing along the borders of the Chinese world—Korea, Japan, Vietnam—not to speak of cultures beyond Chinese influence. The only exception, Buddhist monks, for whom South Asia was the holy land of their religion, had only an extremely limited knowledge of foreign languages. Most translations of Buddhist sutras were made by teams of translators, with bilingual foreigners as intermediaries. Only a few Chinese monks acquired a knowledge of Sanskrit or other Indian languages sufficient for extensive reading and original translation. Some acquired this knowledge during pilgrimages to the holy sites in India, where they often stayed for many years. A few wrote substantial descriptions of the many countries and cities through which they had traveled. All this, however, seems only to have strengthened the awareness of the foreign origin of Buddhism, which discredited it in the eyes of both Taoists and Confucians.

As a result of this disdain for peripheral cultural traditions inside China and for foreign cultures, traditional Chinese literature, especially high literature, developed to a large extent in self-imposed splendid isolation. This very specific literary tradition cannot be understood without some familiarity with the worldview of its practitioners—the basic philosophy of the Central Tradition.

Chapter 4.
THE CENTRAL TRADITION IN TRADITIONAL SOCIETY

Although the Chinese Central Tradition continued to develop over the centuries, practically none of that development was due to external influences. The successive reformulations continued to be based on the same underlying assumptions that had always served as this culture's guidelines for thinking about man, society, and the cosmos.

THE WAY

The Bible begins with the creation of the world. As a consequence, in traditional Western thought the world of time and space is assumed to have been created by an eternal God, and a clear division is felt to exist between earthly and heavenly realms. The earth is associated with whatever is transitory, impermanent, imperfect, bodily—and sinful. Heaven is the sphere of the eternal, permanent, perfect, spiritual, and holy.

Traditional Chinese thought has no place for the idea of a creation. What exists has always existed and shall always do so. Accordingly, there is no concept of necessary "development" or "improvement" or "correction" of the creation through such means as a Fall, the birth of a Savior, a Last Judgment. Nor, on the other hand, is the existent world taken to be hopelessly engaged in continual degeneration. Chinese thought did not find it necessary to look outside this world for a First Cause. In the Chinese view there is no fundamental dualism: gods and demons belong to the same continuum as humans and animals; they obey laws that are similar or parallel to those governing the thoughts and actions of human beings. They are not denizens of a radically other or higher world unknowable in principle by men.

To be sure, there do exist Chinese creation myths, such as that of Pangu, out of whose body the world was supposed to have been formed. But these ideas are peripheral to the Central Tradition, functioning mainly as occasional sources of poetic imagery. And in the absence of any strong concept of a Creator, the traditional Chinese writer does not assume the role or pose of a god-like "creator" in his own right, as many Western authors have done. The

Chinese writer does not have the pretension of creating a world of words out of nothing. Rather, he weaves or reworks given, existing words and ideas into a new text.

Since all that exists is regarded as constituting a single, integrated whole, there is no external realm or dimension in which supposedly higher truth can be sought. In the Chinese Central Tradition, an ordering principle is inherent in all that exists. It is not, as in some Western philosophies, a sort of inferior shadow or distortion of an Idea; nor is it an imperfectly glimpsed sign, symbol, or allegory of something else. In Chinese thought, although persons, things, or events are often regarded as exemplary or typical, they are never seen as mere reflections of supposedly transcendental realities.

Things are as they are simply because that is the way they are. The inherent principle of order, common to all that exists, is called the Way (*dao*). The Way is not some sort of law or pattern that any higher power imposed on what exists. And since the Way is not so foreign to everyday human reality as to be past man's finding it out, it was never necessary for the Way to be revealed either by a God or by prophets. The Way reveals itself in the ongoing process of historical existence, and human beings who apply themselves to discovering the pattern or recurrent regularities in that process are perfectly able to do so.

The present is understandable as the instance of a pattern only if it can be interpreted as the recurrence of a similar situation in the past. Since it is vitally important to be able to compare present and past, very great value is attached to the writing of history. Written history makes the present meaningful and "workable." In all forms of Chinese literature, historical precedent is what is most authoritative. A given situation is not described in terms of myths, gods, or fictive abstractions, but in terms of concrete historical examples. Only what is typical has value. The unique, the individual, is a curiosity without meaning: a freak. The Way is knowable to man thanks to the accumulation of experience: Shennong (the Divine Husbandman), one of China's emperors in predynastic times, is said to have discovered the characteristics of the various plants by tasting them himself.

In Chinese literature there are no texts, like the Bible or the Koran, which enjoy the unique status of being considered the word of God. The Chinese writer did not aspire to prophetic stature, nor did he appeal to a Muse to inspire him. However exceptional the understanding of the Way attained by Confucius, or by his great model, the duke of Zhou, these great figures were and remained of human proportions.

The Way is present not only in the physical world of nature—where it expresses itself in the alternation of the seasons and in the growth cycle of plants and animals—but also and preeminently in the life of human society.

As part of the Way that inheres in all that exists, there is also a Way in society: a normal system of mutual relations between humans. It implies loyalty of the subject to the ruler, obedience of children to their parents, mutual reliability between friends, and so on. Ethical rules and the norms of morality are regarded as no more than the explicit formulation of natural tendencies that are in all persons from birth. There is only one Way, and for every relationship or situation that can develop, there is only one correct procedure. Every deviation from the one correct Way is incorrect and should be avoided.

There is, however, no such thing as an anti-Way, actively operating to seduce mankind into error. There is no such thing as a struggle between a saving Redeemer and a tempting Devil, between Light and Darkness, or between Good and Evil. Whatever deviates from the straight Way is crooked, deformed, heterodox. Crimes and misdeeds are seen as the result of defective understanding—a sort of evil arising from stupidity, caused by the confusing influence of desires. There is no antagonism between body and soul or spirit; desires are normal, but must be kept under control.

As long as all people conduct themselves in accordance with the one correct and normal Way, order (*zhi*) will prevail in society. Otherwise disorder (*luan*) will result. The Central Tradition is acutely aware of how precarious and fragile a thing an orderly society is. People easily let themselves be seduced into forgetting morality in search of their own private aims, thereby obscuring the "difference between human beings and wild beasts." Chinese thinkers were strongly preoccupied with the horrors of misused and arbitrary power, of violence and of war. For them these things were Hell enough. Disorder and anarchy were anathema, while order, rare as it was, seemed to them a Heaven on earth. Blessedness, for Chinese thinkers, is not a condition to be hoped for in a hereafter, but in life on earth in a well-ordered society. There is no Paradise other than what is brought about here and now by man on earth.

Order and disorder in society are so important that they actually have influence on all that exists. When disorder prevails in society, rains can be expected to fall out of season, crops to fail, and famines and natural catastrophes to follow. When there is order in society, nature also flows along lines of regularity, making prosperity and happiness possible. Heaven and earth themselves are an accurate barometer of social processes.

Not surprisingly, the question of paramount interest to early Chinese philosophers was how to establish order in a disorderly world, and this same question remained the principal preoccupation of the Central Tradition down through the centuries. Students of comparative religion have sometimes described religion as an approach to issues of ultimate concern. The West has tended to contrast religion, as a field of the high and the pure, with worldly and "impure" matters like politics. Indeed, it has often been thought improper for the church to become involved in politics. In China, however, the ordering of society—that is, politics—was itself the issue of ultimate concern. Religion, as the quest for personal enlightenment, physical immortality, or eternal bliss, was, from the viewpoint of the Central Tradition, a private affair at best—which could easily degenerate into antisocial behavior. Owing to the concrete, this-worldly attitude of the Central Tradition, much Chinese literature strikes a first-time Western reader as rather superficial. On the other hand, tangible problems were treated with a seriousness that has sometimes been lacking in Western literature. Rather than speculating on how many angels could sit on the point of a needle, Chinese writers preferred to calculate how much seed refugees needed in order to make a new start as farmers. In high Chinese literature, at least, this seriousness resulted in a striking lack of humor.

Of course, even within the Central Tradition, there was more than one style of thinking about the Way. The older Confucianism always held that the Way, as present in society, is good, and that it can be known and formulated by man—for example, in the *li* (the rules for correct behavior, etiquette, and ceremonial). In the philosophical Taoism of the *Laozi* and *Zhuangzi*, by contrast, it is often stated that the Way in its totality can only be experienced through mystical contemplation; it cannot be formulated in words. These Taoist texts also describe the Way as amoral: as the foundation of all that exists, the Way is in the nature of an abstract principle and does not concern itself with the fate of individual humans. Numerous passages in *Zhuangzi* ridicule the Confucians and their constant striving to combat disorder by formulating norms for behavior.

Nevertheless, there is no fundamental antagonism between the two schools: both agree that there is one true Way and that order prevails if man lives in accordance with it. So it was possible for third-century Confucianism (Neo-Taoism) to gloss over the most obvious differences by asserting that the Way, inherent in all things, is to be experienced in its totality through mystical contemplation; it is one *and* moral. The Way as a whole expresses itself in the primary, complementary aspects of rest and movement, most clearly expressed in the undistorted forms of nature: rocks and streams, mountains and rivers. Starting in the third and fourth centuries A.D., nature mysticism, in which the contemplating spirit merges with the contemplated landscape and attains union with the Way, became an important element in Chinese literature and painting. Of philosophical schools, only Legalism (third century B.C.) challenged the idea of a single unchanging Way, claiming that each historical period has its own specific qualities and requires equally specific reactions and behaviors from man. But this iconoclastic view had no lasting influence and has always been decried as the ultimate heresy.

THE RULER AND HIS VIRTUE

All ancient Chinese philosophical schools (including Legalism) agreed that the primary responsibility for ensuring the propagation and observance of the Way and for bringing about an ordered and properly hierarchical society, rests with the ruler—the king or emperor. This remained one of the most fundamental axioms of the Central Tradition. The idea of society as a republic or an association of equal citizens was entirely foreign to Chinese thought, and Chinese history is entirely without examples of any such thing. It went without saying that the structure of society should be hierarchical; Chinese thinkers could conceive of a leaderless society as resulting only in total anarchy, the war of all against all. The self-evident nature of the hierarchical order of society in Chinese thought has been linked by some scholars to the universal practice of ancestor worship in Chinese culture, as ancestor worship insists on the subordination of the younger to the older.

The ideal situation is for human society to be united under a single ruler, whose power extends to the entire world. The ruler should fulfill his awesome responsibility by being a living exemplar of the Way, spontaneously displaying the behavior and speech appropriate to every context. His exemplary behavior toward his subordinates will induce similarly correct behavior in them; their own subordinates will then be likewise inspired, and so on, so that eventually all levels of society will function harmoniously and the whole world will be brought into a condition of order.

If the ruler succeeds in inspiring the appropriate behavior in his subjects, he is said to have *de*—a word which has been variously translated as virtue, force, *virtu*, and *mana*. The greater his virtue or *de*, the greater the social and cosmic order that will radiate outward from his court, permeating society and cosmos. The ruler is personally responsible for natural catastrophes; Chinese censors did not hesitate to attribute droughts or floods to culpable private behavior on the part of the emperor.

The ideally perfect ruler is said to "do nothing" (*wu wei*—no doing, nothing to attain). In other words he fulfills his ritual responsibilities, such as performing the yearly sacrifices to Heaven and Earth, but does not need to take more concrete steps to interfere in the course of events. The reason is that his *de* exerts such strong influence that all members of society automatically comport themselves in ways appropriate to their positions; there is no need for explicit correction. He is like the Pole Star, which remains stationary while the other stars turn in their orbits around it. Forcefulness in a ruler is laudable only as long as order is still to be established. Resort to force of arms is a sign of weakness. In practice, of course, war has played a prominent role in China's history, but at least in theory the Central Tradition has always regarded military matters as a necessary evil. Though soldiers were to be duly rewarded for their services, the Chinese Central Tradition has never known the romantic idealization of warfare that was a feature, for example, of Western chivalric culture. Narrative celebration of martial prowess developed in China only as a form of oral literature, subsequently having some influence on trivial literature (novels, the drama). But the deeds and words of the ruler, being important on a cosmic scale, were matters of intense interest at all levels of society. Historiography centered on the chronicles of the successive rulers, and the lives of the emperors continued to be a favorite subject of both high and trivial literature.

The ruler's responsibility for the world's well-being is unlimited. Aided by the apparatus of government, the ruler is to see that in every situation, every person shall think, act, and speak correctly. No distinction is made between state and society. In contradistinction to the West, where limitation of the powers of government was formulated in legal terms from an early date, in China there were in principle no limits to the legitimate scope of governmental authority: the individual had no rights vis-à-vis the government.

In practice, the government lacked the technical means to enforce its will directly on more than a few specific sectors of social life. Nevertheless, the government regarded itself as obliged and entitled to intervene wherever it deemed necessary. The citizen had no right to resist this influence, which presented itself in terms of paternalistic instruction and benevolent guidance. There was no division between the individual's rights and those of society (as represented by the government). Nor was there an equivalent of the Western distinction of church and state, whereby individuals, in certain matters of conscience, might claim to be under a different jurisdiction than that of the temporal authority. The Chinese government, for example, not only regulated concrete facets of the life of Buddhist monks but also intervened in matters of doctrine. In sum, the ruler united in his person the highest spiritual and worldly authority—which the Chinese tradition did not regard as separable—over the wide realm referred to as "all-under-Heaven."

THE BUREAUCRATIC CAREER

The life of an individual, especially a gentleman, acquires its value from the contribution the person makes to the ruler's sacred enterprise of ordering the world. It is potentially within every person's power to exude civilizing influence; one's *de* can have a positive effect within one's own milieu. This effect is predominantly on one's inferiors, but superiors are also susceptible to it. The higher a person's position in society, the more far-reaching the influence of that person's virtue. The greatest influence of all is exercised by those who fill posts in the government bureaucracy. Within government circles, in turn, it is those of the highest rank whose *de* is potentially the most widely efficacious. And the very greatest potential resides with those who serve at the ruler's side. A career in government service is the most noble calling possible for man. It also represents the only realistic chance of immortality, in the form of the lasting fame which one can acquire for the meritorious role one plays in the sacred work of ordering all-under-Heaven.

Though a career in government was extremely lucrative, the thought of financial gain was supposed to play no role in one's motivation. Only when severe poverty made it impossible to care appropriately for one's parents was it allowable to seek a modest government post specifically for the emolument.

Of all the gentlemen in the realm, the ruler is expected to select the most virtuous to be his helpers. Some are to fill specialized posts in the capital; others will represent the emperor in outlying areas. During the reign of a good ruler it is considered shameful to live in poverty because one has failed to be selected for a post. Ideally, one's rank in the bureaucracy is supposed to be proportional to one's *de*, and it is on grounds of their virtue that the ruler promotes his subordinates. In choosing his gentleman-helpers and evaluating their performance in office, the ruler and his representatives are supposed to attend only to their capacities or lack thereof; personal feelings or family ties are to be irrelevant. Whether the ruler appoints men as vassals or as bureaucratic office holders, the principles are the same. In choosing successors, the perfect rulers of antiquity bypassed even their own sons, giving preference instead to the most capable administrators. Appointment to office and promotion from one office to another are both taken as proofs of one's virtue. It is the most natural thing in the world for the holder of a high rank to regard his status as indicative of both his own virtue and that of the ruler; the countless self-satisfied eulogies were undoubtedly meant in all sincerity.

Since a career in government is to be the highest calling of man, there can be no greater evil than the presence of slanderers and flatterers who becloud the ruler's judgment. Speaking ill of others merely to better their own position, they keep the ruler ignorant of the qualities of those whom they slander. Good men fail to gain the appointments they deserve, play no part in the sacred work of ordering the empire, and are deprived of their chance at eternal fame. In theory, a perfect ruler will naturally see through the machinations of such schemers and punish them severely. Alas, not every ruler is perfect.

One of the oldest Chinese poems is the plaint of a dismissed administrator, who has been victimized by slanderers, unjustly banished from court, and thereby evicted from the sphere of blessedness. This plaint—the "Lisao" (Encountering sorrows) attributed to Qu Yuan (ca. 339–ca. 278 B.C.) and included in the *Chuci* (Songs of Chu)—makes heavy use of the erotic imagery of the shaman songs that were current in Chu. The ruler is presented, among other things, as the passionately desired but unattainable loved one; the misunderstood administrator appears in the role of the eager suitor. The plaint of the insufficiently appreciated gentleman persisted as a central theme in traditional Chinese poetry.

If it is shameful not to serve during a good ruler's reign, it is equally shameful to be in office under a bad ruler. Since a ruler will seldom be ideally perfect, even if his errors are many and serious, a gentleman should be ready and willing to serve under him as long as there is hope that he may mend his ways. If the gentleman becomes aware of abuses in the functioning of the empire, he is to report them immediately. He is not to hesitate to censure the ruler, preferably indirectly, but if necessary in strong language, even at the risk of putting his own life in jeopardy. Only after all attempts to reform the ruler have failed, and the ruler has revealed himself as thoroughly and hopelessly corrupt, must one give up one's post, or refuse a new one if offered. Such refusal in itself amounts to a denunciation of the regime, an impeachment of the sovereign. It also implies criticism of all those who do remain in office, suggesting that they are but evil flatterers, lacking in virtue, motivated only by the lust for money and fame. It is a condemnation of contemporary political activity as nothing but a vulgar power struggle.

Such a decision is not to be taken lightly. In the interest of maintaining one's moral integrity, one is deliberately excluding oneself from participation in the work of blessedness and from the hope of eternal eminence. Considering the weighty implications and consequences, it may be advisable to disguise one's true motives by pleading one's own lack of talent, one's unsuitability for service—yet in itself, such modesty is a sign of virtue.

A gentleman who has withdrawn from government service is supposed to apply himself to the improvement of his own *de*—for example, through study or contemplation—and to wait for better times. Meanwhile, he is only too aware of the irreversible passage of time and the shortness of his own life. No matter how charming or enjoyable the retired life of the "hermit" may be, or how idyllically it is often portrayed in literature and the arts, it remains a last-ditch measure. The true vocation of the gentleman is a career in government.

The Study of Literature

One prepares for a career in government by study, which is a never-ending process of self-cultivation. The goal of study is not the amassing of knowledge but the perfection of behavior. Through education man can be brought to full knowledge of the Way, so that in every situation that can arise in society he will spontaneously exhibit the correct behavior and speech. Though the norms are innate, man needs practice if he is to react normally at all times. The human mind is often compared to a (bronze) mirror, which must be polished until it reflects all phenomena completely and without distortion, allowing man to act entirely in accord with the moral situation. Mental growth is not a goal in itself. It becomes valuable only when it is substantiated in social relations. In principle, action does not have to be preceded by a weighing of alternatives, since in every situation there is but one correct action. Hesitation is a symptom of imperfection. A person's value does not depend on the heights or depths of his subjective experience or psychological processes, but on the way in which he fulfills his social role as father, son, friend, bureaucrat, and so on. Virtue is evident in deeds and words; one is judged on the basis of one's comportment.

Chinese biographers are not much interested in the supposed man behind the public figure. They nearly always confine themselves to a survey of the main events in the person's public life (especially the bureaucratic career); the comportment is sketched in a few bold strokes by citing typical acts and characteristic quotes. No attention is given to private life or inner experience.

Study is to be carried out on the basis of literature, and under the direction of a teacher. The Chinese teacher does not merely instruct his pupil in matters of knowledge or skills, but more importantly he guides the pupil in his continual rehearsal of self-perfection. The true teacher is an exemplar who does not merely expound the Way, but actually reveals it in his living.

Literature, upon which study is based, consists of writings that record the deeds and words of the holy rulers and their wise advisors—the formulations of the Way. Needless to say, within the body of literature, the highest importance attaches to those writings which record the deeds and words of the *holiest* rulers and the *wisest* advisors of antiquity. These are known as "The Classics" (*jing*, literally "warp of the fabric"). There is, however, no absolute boundary between these writings and those which embody the deeds and texts of rulers and dignitaries of later ages. As time goes on, the body of literature to be studied grows larger. By continually immersing himself in the words and deeds of those who embodied the Way, the student tries to assimilate himself to their ways of thinking and doing so that his behavior in comparable situations will be similar.

The Practice of Literature

The practice of literature—the writing of texts—is an aspect of behavior. In fact, it *is* the behavior! To write a text is to formulate the situation in which one finds oneself: the correct formulation of the correct perception, which must inevitably lead to the correct actions. To write a text is to put into words the feelings that a given situation calls up. Chinese literature testifies: the prose is historical or argumentative, and the poetry is lyrical. But the Chinese writer certainly does not, like the Dutch art-for-art's-sake poet Willem Kloos, strive for "the very most individual expression of the very most individual emotion." His goal is to formulate correctly the spontaneously normal feelings in a given situation in which such formulation is necessary or desirable. He is confident that the formulation of those feelings will evoke similar feelings in the hearer or reader. The traditional Chinese literary critic, naturally enough, uses one and the same term for the aspect of reality under consideration (the "subject"), the inner state of the writer, the style of his work, and the reader's response.

The literature of traditional China can be described as a sort of mathematics of society. Every situation permits but one moral evaluation. With regard to any matter whatsoever, the writer's standpoint and the feelings he experiences are supposed to be entirely appropriate to the situation. The formulation of his own judgment then coincides exactly with the description of the situation; and this formulation, being the correct interpretation, shall be utterly convincing. The writer's activity can be compared to that of a scientist: the scientist applies to a given process a specific mathematical formula which is both an adequate description of the process and a demonstration of the scientist's understanding of that process. Once the scientist has come up with the proper formula, it is entirely reasonable that he should rely on it for practical applications, and the elegant concision of the formula, recognizable as correct by others having the necessary expertise, wins confidence in its reliability.

A text is an act, a deed. The traditional Chinese reader approaches a text as both the description of a situation and an expression of the character of the author. Though he may well admire the internal structure of the text aesthetically, the text is never divorced from its referential and expressive functions. Also, the reader makes no distinction between the *persona* assumed by the writer in the text and the writer's actual personality. The "I" in the text is taken to refer to the writer himself.

The State Examinations

Since texts are regarded as directly revealing the character of their authors, the ruler can choose his administrators on the basis of texts they have produced—in practice, of written examinations. Once examinations have become institutionalized as the royal road to the coveted blessedness of a career in government, skill in writing and the mastery of existing literature take on an added aura of importance in society. The study of literature becomes more than just the pursuit of wisdom: it is the way to get rich. Before long the examinations become a mechanical formality, and the students devote their attention primarily to the types of text they will need to know to pass. Being the supreme embodiment of the belief that the text reveals the virtue of its writer, the examinations incited frequent travesty of that principle. Texts were often little more than impersonal demonstrations of technical ability and were criticized accordingly. Nevertheless, the idea that literary merit cannot exist in the absence of moral virtue has remained pervasive.

Notwithstanding frequent criticism of the examinations as overly formalistic, in one form or another they continued in use until the twentieth century. The traditional admiration for literary talent (*cai*) never diminished; the ability to improvise well on a given subject was especially prized and became itself a well-loved theme treated in countless literary anecdotes, plays, and fiction.

Despite the very high prestige it enjoyed in society, being a writer or a poet was never a goal in itself. To be famous only as a poet was to have failed as a responsible member of society. A great writing talent finds its crowning glory in a bureaucratic career: literature, after all, is practiced as a way of attaining virtue. High administrators, and the ruler himself, should also be the best writers. Writers and poets are not bohemians. Far from regarding themselves as at odds with society, they are actually the ideal types within society. The writer is a government official or hopes to become one. The modern Western reader is surprised if an ordinary well-behaved citizen, not even to mention a high executive, turns out to be a great writer. The traditional Chinese point of view reverses these terms: how is it possible that such a great poet as Li Bai (701–762) failed to attain prominence in government?

LITERATURE AND GENDER IN CHINA

By now it must have become abundantly clear that most authors in traditional China were men. Moreover they wrote for other men about the affairs of men. The ability to read and write was a precondition for a successful official career, and the act of writing was an act of participation in public life. In traditional Chinese society, the elite maintained strict separation of the sexes. While their menfolk pursued careers in society, in schools, and in the bureaucracy, the women of the aristocracy and of the gentry lived their lives secluded in the inner quarters. Before marriage a woman was expected to obey her father; following her marriage and entrance into a different family she was to obey her husband; upon the husband's death she was to obey the eldest son. Ideally, even a young widow was not supposed to remarry.

In the hierarchical order of society, women were subordinated to men at every level. While there was little explicit opposition to literacy for women as such, many men expressed concern that wide reading might well make women dissatisfied with their societal role. The very act of a woman's writing—let alone the desire to see her writings published!—was seen by many men as an unbecoming transgression of the limits imposed upon her. "For a woman, to have no talent is a virtue" was a proverb current in the Ming (1368–1644) and Qing (1644–1911). It is perhaps no accident that Li Qingzhao (1084–ca.1151), the only woman poet to achieve status fully equal to male poets', lived at a moment in history when on the one hand books had become widely available (she has left us a detailed description of the rise and fall of her and her husband's library), while on the other hand the increasing strictness of the Neo-Confucianist rules for personal behavior had not yet become institutionalized. Outside the home the only classes of educated women men encountered were courtesans and nuns. As courtesans were trained to entertain men by their wit and skills, many were literate and able to versify. Some were actually famous for their verse. Nuns needed literacy in order to be able to recite the scriptures.

Women with an inclination to write encountered another difficulty: traditional literature offered scarcely a single form or genre that fitted their circumstances, as the forms and subject matter of literature were determined by the social life of men. There existed a limited body of writings, usually by women, concerning the duties and tasks of women, but these urged against any literary ambition and hardly provided models for emulation. The earliest of these tracts is the *Nüjie* (Rules for women), written by the learned woman historian Ban Zhao (ca. 48–ca. 116), who ended her life as a teacher of women in the emperor's seraglio. Whenever literacy for women was defended, one of the most-heard arguments was that reading these texts on ritual and personal behavior would teach women their place. The impossibility of a woman's pursuing a higher education and venturing out into the world of men was dramatized in the very old and perennially popular story of Liang Shanbo and Zhu Yingtai. Zhu Yingtai insists on leaving her parents' home in order to study, and her parents eventually allow her to do so dressed as a boy. While studying, she falls in love with a fellow student, Liang Shanbo, who does not suspect she is a girl. Zhu Yingtai urges him to visit her parents and ask for the hand of "her sister"—i.e., herself—in marriage. When she herself returns home, she discovers that her parents have already promised her in marriage to someone else. When Liang Shanbo visits the Zhus, his request is denied, and soon afterward he dies. Zhu Yingtai requests that her wedding procession pass by his grave. The grave opens up and she jumps into it, after which it closes and a pair of butterflies are seen fluttering about.

Only a few subgenres of literature were more hospitable to women. Men often affected the persona of a lady pining in her boudoir, lamenting the absence and faithlessness of her lover but utterly devoted and loyal to him. The figure of the woman abandoned by her lover was an analogue of the official neglected by his emperor, and the use of the persona of a woman emphasized the humility of the author toward his prospective patron. Many women wrote boudoir laments using the settings and vocabulary developed in this tradition. Li Qingzhao is a case in point. She and other women poets infused their poems with a poignancy and authenticity all their own; some went further and (though very rarely until the end of the nineteenth century) questioned the social rules that excluded them from full and meaningful participation in literary life and contemporary politics. Another genre of writing popular among women under the last dynasty was the *tanci* ("songs for picking"), long and involved narrative ballads in prosimetric form. One of the earliest preserved works in this genre by a woman relates the tale of a girl who, dressed as a boy, succeeds in the highest examinations and achieves the highest position in the bureaucracy.

Most authors in traditional China, whether male or female, accepted the hierarchical structure of society and the separation of the sexes as self-evident and unquestionable. Tales of women eloping with exceptional students who later pursue brilliant careers were probably not written or read as attacks on conventional gender roles, but rather as affirmations of the exceptional qualities of the male heroes. Traditional Chinese literature, both high and low, reflects male fantasies, male fears, and a male view of society and culture. While sex was never considered sinful, and marriage was regarded as the only normal condition of adult men and women, traditional physiology taught that a man possessed a strictly limited amount of vital force, which he might easily squander by overindulging in sex. He might even be robbed of his precious vital force by immoral women, fox spirits, female ghosts, or demons. Many visions of women in male writings reflect the same male anxieties found in other cultures. Typically, women are either glorified as self-sacrificing wives and mothers or vilified as insatiable temptresses. The more male society insisted upon the rigid application of the rules governing separation of the sexes, the stronger the fear of the dangerous woman seemed to become. On the one hand, stories of female suicides and virtuous courtesans abound. On the other hand, the figure of the female swordfighter becomes more and more prominent, perhaps reflecting an archetypical castration anxiety.

Not all male authors were completely blind to the injustices involved in the subordination of women. One way in which male authors in later centuries addressed these issues was through sex-role reversal, setting their stories in some mythical country where women, rather than men, have more than one spouse, and where the men are subjected to such painful practices as footbinding. Eighteenth- and nineteenth-century authors also show a distinct interest in the theme of the effeminate man and the masculine woman, and at least one lengthy novel describes a colorful assortment of homosexual relations. The first to question fundamentally the position of women in society were the reformers of the last years of the nineteenth century; yet their persistent male perspective is betrayed by the fact that they wanted society to produce healthier and better-educated mothers, who would raise stronger and more intelligent offspring. The first decade of the twentieth century saw the appearance of the first Chinese feminist, Qiu Jin (1875–1907), who dressed as a man, went to Japan for study, and insisted on full equality and economic independence for women.

All in all, whereas many other aspects of traditional culture have been swept away by the reforms and revolutions of the twentieth century, traditional ideas of gender have proven extremely resistant to change. Despite undeniable improvements in the position of women in Chinese society, equality of the sexes and female rights are still often seen as a gift bestowed on women by the government or the Party, rather than as their birthright.

Chapter 5.
THE WAY AND THE GOVERNMENT: TRUTH AND LITERATURE

LITERATURE AND GOVERNMENT

The Way is formulated in literature, and the ruler and his ministers are expected, after studying the literature, to seek actively to bring about the realization of the Way in society. In China the Way, literature and government form a close-knit trinity. The Central Tradition assumes that literature is intimately related to government: the quality of a given regime determines the quality of the texts produced under that regime. The ruler and his governmental apparatus are responsible for ensuring the correctness of the thoughts and actions of all their subjects—hence also, especially, for the correctness of all texts in circulation.

Literature as a Reflection and Criticism of Government

Since texts are to consist of formulations of the writer's sincere feelings in a given situation, under a good regime the writer cannot but sing praises of the order and peace which the ruler and his government have established. If, under the leadership of a good ruler, society seems clearly to be in process of transition from chaos to order, the writer will be struck by all manner of good omens. If chaos reigns, the writer can only give voice to his lament and despair—or, making himself a living symbol of disorder, abandon himself to dissolution, of which his works will then be a testimonial. If society seems to be drifting from order toward chaos, the writer will use his texts to point out numerous abuses in the hope that the ruler and his representatives may take notice in time to improve their ways and save the situation. In short, the text indicates not only the moral state of its author, but also the degree to which the Way was in effect during his life and times.

As early as the Han dynasty it was quite generally believed that some of the songs in China's oldest anthology of poetry, the *Shijing*, had been collected under official auspices during the first centuries of the Zhou dynasty (trad. 1126–256 B.C.). The king was supposed to have sent special agents to travel throughout the realm in search of songs, so that by studying the texts they collected, he could get an impression of the quality of government implemented by his vassals in the various localities.

Of course, the writer who intends to criticize his superiors often finds it prudent, for reasons of personal safety, to cast his writing in an allegorical mold. Political allegory, in which social evils and abuses are attacked in disguised form, is one of the very few forms of fiction allowed in traditional high literature. Since it seemed unimaginable that the songs in a canonical collection like the *Shijing* could be concerned with such a trivial and personal matter as love, rather than with the more fundamental problem of ordering society, it was assumed they did in fact address this issue in a subtle, indirect way. The political import of the songs was laid bare by a tradition of historical-allegorical exegesis, at times truly astounding in its inventiveness, that was fully developed well before the Han.

Once it was accepted that earlier poems were to be interpreted allegorically, later writers deliberately wrote allegories, so that readers also came to look for an allegorical meaning. In time practically every well-known work whose subject was not overtly political came to be interpreted as referring to a particular political situation. This topical allegory usually was limited to a specific situation; it rarely took the form of an extended narrative—there was no *Faerie Queene* in Chinese literature, although the trivial literature from the sixteenth to eighteenth centuries does include a few allegorical novels.

In later centuries some emperors felt called to follow the example of the Zhou kings by collecting songs, and poets often tried to present themselves as speaking for the people. They could hope for no greater honor and fortune than to be chosen by a virtuous ruler to compose the texts for new hymns to be used in the imperial rituals. If the ruler and his ministers were insufficiently virtuous, it was the poet's solemn duty to write about social evils in the hope that his words would reach the ruler's ears and inspire him to improve his *de*. The poetry of social criticism is an important subcategory of the Chinese poetic tradition through the ages.

If a poet did not take refuge in allegory, he might imitate anonymous folk songs or pretend merely to have written down the words of someone else, for example, an illiterate person of low social standing. The actual subjects of criticism tend to be stereotyped: the ruler succumbs to excessive luxury, spends his time drinking and womanizing, or falls prey to swindlers and charlatans who lead him on a superstitious occult quest for physical immortality; the holders of high office are chosen for reasons other than their virtue, ignore the problems of the people, and seek nothing but personal advantage; wealthy merchants, in league with corrupt officials, make fortunes through speculation without contributing to the ordering and improvement of society; office-holders, eager to realize profits by whatever means, give their subordinates a free hand, allowing clerks, crooks, and tax collectors to ride roughshod over the common people. Ultimately the people must pay the price for these social ills, and as that price becomes intolerable—prohibitively high taxes, long corvée duty, arbitrary conscription for senseless military campaigns in far-off areas—banditry and rebellion are sure to follow.

The State as Patron of the Arts

The state is responsible not only for the quality of the literature produced under its rule, but it is also supposed to guarantee its correctness. Incorrect writings will mislead readers into false ideas about the Way, with the result that they will not fulfill their roles in the sacred social order. The state must encourage correct and forbid incorrect literature. (Its attitude toward trivial literature is at best one of suspicious tolerance.)

Ruler and state always took this responsibility very seriously, even if later emperors seldom followed the drastic example of the First Emperor of the Qin dynasty (r. 221–210 B.C.), who commanded that all books except legal texts and necessary professional works should be burned and that dissenting scholars should be buried alive. In later centuries the First Emperor was strongly criticized, not so much for having burned books and silenced dissidents as for having burned the wrong books and buried the wrong dissidents. The highly respected Confucian stalwart Han Yu (768–824) ends a diatribe against Buddhism and Taoism—a highly popular anthology piece—with the demand to put the torch to their writings. The Central Tradition never questioned the duty and the right of the state to regulate literature.

The state carried out its task of regulation in various ways. It took pains to ensure that the texts and interpretations of the Classics were correct, organizing conferences, where necessary, to establish a standard reading and interpretation of disputed passages. After the invention of paper the text of the Classics was carved in stone so that anyone could obtain a rubbing of the correct text. First done in A.D. 175, the stones suffered war damage and other forms of deterioration, so that this formidable project was repeated several times. After the introduction of book printing, the government oversaw dissemination of the Classics and their commentaries in printed form.

The compilation of histories was another important task of government. From antiquity special functionaries recorded the ruler's words and deeds, and each dynasty kept its own official archives. Anyone wishing to use them to write a history needed to obtain the emperor's permission, and the finished work could be released only with his approval. Because reliability determined the usefulness of histories, the emperor had to ensure their truthfulness. However, emperors were expected not to tamper with the records of their own reign; those who gave in to the temptation were criticized for their interference. Starting with the Tang dynasty, a standard feature of government was a state commission charged with writing a history of the previous dynasty or sometimes of a longer period.

The work of writing the history of the current dynasty was entrusted to a special staff. The avalanche of bureaucratic documents was regularly edited to produce the *qijuzhu* (records of activities), which in turn were the basis for the *shilu* (true accounts of the period of each ruler's reign, compiled after his death). From time to time the state ordered a *guoshi* (history of the [current] dynasty) to be prepared on the basis of these *shilu*. All compilations required approval at the very highest levels, and if necessary they were revised numerous times. The finished works were kept in the archives and considered secret documents. Private historiography did exist, but it was normally of more limited scope: commentaries, studies of specialized subjects, and so on. The government regarded private dynastic histories with great suspicion.

All levels of government also played an active role in compiling, revising, and publishing other books. They published dictionaries, compiled huge thesauri, and prepared gigantic encyclopedias that attempted to systematize all existing knowledge by means of excerpts from the entire body of extant writings. The zeal for completeness could be so extreme that when the *Yongle dadian* (Great canon of the Yongle period), for example, was completed in 1407, its bulk—more than 22,000 "books" (*juan*)—made publication in printed form impossible. The government commissioned anthologies, as well as collected editions like the *Quan Tang shi* (Complete poems of the Tang). It also undertook the editing and publication of the collected works of important authors, sometimes with extensive commentaries.

There is hardly a single area of traditional high literature in which the state was not actively involved at one time or another. The government also published numerous handbooks for its officials in such fields as medicine, agriculture, and military affairs, and at times took an active part in the compilation and printing of both the Buddhist and the Taoist canon.

Clearly the state was the most important patron and publisher of literature. Although some rulers and high bureaucrats were inevitably more interested in literature than others and used their positions to help authors, their patronage flowed through bureaucratic channels. Private patronage was, by comparison, negligible. Commercial publishers played practically no role as patrons of scholarship. From the sixteenth century on they were involved to some degree in the development of trivial literature. Some employed the hack writers who prepared text editions of plays and novels, and some, though usually not with much success, were authors in their own right.

The State as Censor

The state also had a duty to combat incorrect literature. The government was not equally effective in all periods in enforcing official policy, and at times the nature of forbidden texts was such that officials were not strongly motivated to take seriously their duty of suppressing them. But if the government was really determined to destroy a given text, it was fully capable of extirpating it. Although various rebellious movements are known to have disseminated texts of their own, practically nothing was preserved apart from fragments quoted by Central Tradition writers as iniquitous illustrations of the movement in question. Only with the Taiping Rebellion (1849–1864) were a large number of rebel writings preserved, not least because the movement, being partly of Christian inspiration, attracted the attention of foreign missionaries.

The government's authority extended also to the literatures of the professional cultures, including Buddhism and Taoism. Emperors pronounced judgment in cases of dispute between Buddhists and Taoists and proscribed the texts that could give rise to such disharmony. During the Tang dynasty, for example, the *Huahu jing* (The book of the conversion of the barbarians) was banned. This Taoist book claimed that Buddhism was a simplified form of Taoism that Laozi had preached to the ignorant barbarians after his departure from China.

Of course, the state was most vigilant in its concern for the orthodoxy of the literature of the Central Tradition: Confucianism. The most dreaded evil was heresy, the false presentation of the Way. In this connection, not only individual books but even whole groups of texts could come under suspicion. During the Sui dynasty (589–618), for example, the so-called *weishu* ("weft books") were successfully banned. *Weishu* had been written since the Han dynasty; they were books in which the Classics were interpreted as oracle texts. Today no trace of them survives except in the form of quotes in other books.

Individual writers, too, might be proscribed as heretical. Even the works of Zhu Xi (1130–1200) were forbidden for a while on the grounds that they contained dangerous heresies, though in this case the proscription had little effect: his interpretations became the backbone of the orthodoxy in which examination candidates had to school themselves during the Ming (1368–1644) and Qing (1644–1911).

It was the state's duty to suppress all writings at variance with the Way— in other words, which misrepresented the facts. And the state, of course, decided what the facts were. A notorious inquisition was carried out under the Qianlong Emperor (r. 1736–1795); all texts containing criticism of the Manchu regime and its ancestors (the Jin dynasty, 1122–1234), or even passages which could conceivably be construed as critical, were forbidden. The authors were subjected to extreme punishments; if they were already dead, their remains were desecrated and their descendants executed or banished. Many of the texts were never seen again. Another ruler who mercilessly punished whatever could possibly be read as criticism of his person was the founder of the Ming dynasty, the Hongwu Emperor (r. 1368–1398).

Later Chinese writers had much to say about these witch-hunts. But their censure was directed at the supposedly unfortunate choice of texts, and not at the principle of suppression itself. In the Chinese tradition, when the state acts to regulate the thoughts of its subjects, it is not arrogating to itself unreasonable rights: it is merely doing its duty.

THE CLASSIFICATION OF TEXTS

In traditional China, literature was supposed to be *true*: to be a correct depiction of the moral situation and the feelings it evoked. Literature could fulfill its task of general edification only if what it taught was the truth. Teaching the truth, in turn, was possible only through correct reflection of the Way as multifariously present in all that exists.

In the Chinese language, the most general term for the concept of literature is *wen*. The word has a wide range of meanings, but they all derive from the root sense of a regularly recurrent pattern, for example in a woven fabric. *Wen* is the visible form of an immanent structure. *Li* is the word for this principle or immanent structure that is present in every aspect of reality. Each written character (which can also be called *wen*) conveys the essential features of the object it represents (at least in the case of pictograms and ideograms). In this sense the character *is* the object it means, and Chinese lexicographers often seek to derive the meaning of the word from the form of its written character.

By formulating an occurrence or situation and the feelings it evokes, the text (*wen*) reveals the *li* that is present in each detail of historical reality. The text makes the world understandable. As the embodiment of *li*, the text itself also has internal structure and order. Literature is the ordered expression in words of the Way that is immanent in the seeming chaos of reality. Accordingly, literature cannot but be didactic. Nevertheless, in the Chinese tradition there is a perennial controversy between critics who take as their slogan *wen yi zai dao* (texts serve as vehicle for the Way), favoring an explicit moralism in literature, and those who prefer the formula *shi yan zhi ye* (poetry is the expression of feelings), trusting that the formulation of spontaneous normal feelings will inevitably be suitably edifying.

High Literature

If literature is to reliably express the Way that is present in all that exists, the events it describes must truly have happened. Truth is the essence of literature. The best of all texts are the Classics. They comprise faultless formulations of the Way by the holy rulers and sage administrators of antiquity, whose continual self-perfection brought them full knowledge of the Way. All other literature is regarded as continuing the tradition of the Classics in form and content. As the Classics do include examples of historical and philosophical texts, the Histories (*shi*) and Philosophers (*zi*) of later centuries could logically be regarded as continuing these aspects of the Classics.

Classics, Histories, and Philosophers constitute three of the four main categories into which traditional bibliographers divide the writings of the Central Tradition. (To the extent that professional literatures were included, these were classed as Philosophers.) In the case of the fourth category, that of *ji* or Collections, the idea of continuity with the Classics is somewhat less obvious. The Collections comprise anthologies of poems and short prose pieces in various genres, as well as the collected works of individual authors. All poetry, however, was traditionally regarded as a continuation of the *Shijing*, and each of the short prose forms—memorial, letter, funerary oration and so on—was traced back, sometimes with great ingenuity, to a prototype in one of the Classics. Literature in its totality was seen as a single Holy Writ of ever-growing proportions and variety.

The Five Classics and the Four Books

When reference is made to the Five Classics, the following works are intended: the *Shujing* (Book of documents), the *Shijing* (Book of odes), the *Yijing* (Book of changes), the *Chunqiu* (Annals of spring and autumn), and the *Li* (Rites). These texts are extremely varied in content: a handbook on divination (the *Yijing*), a collection of ritual songs (the *Shijing*), a collection of fastidious rules for all aspects of public behavior (the *Li*), a motley collection of war speeches and other princely pronouncements (the *Shujing*), and a dry-as-dust chronicle of a minor state (the *Chunqiu*). The dates of composition of the texts vary from the tenth to the first century B.C. (or even later, in the case of the *Shujing*). Practically all these texts are themselves compilations that took centuries to develop into their present form. They contain materials of widely divergent background—chronologically, regionally, intellectually, and stylistically.

In later centuries, reference was often made to the Nine or the Thirteen Classics. These differences in count were partly a matter of taking each ritual book as a Classic in its own right or of according autonomous status to each of the three canonical commentaries to the *Chunqiu*. At times, additional works were reckoned as belonging to the Classics: for example, the *Er Ya*, an ancient glossary, the *Lunyu* (Selected sayings), containing the dialogs of Confucius, or the *Mengzi* (Mencius), which records the dialogs of his outstanding follower Meng Ke (372–289 B.C.). When the *Lunyu* and *Mengzi* are not reckoned Classics, they are grouped with the Philosophers. The bibliographic category of Classics also includes the almost endless stream of relevant commentaries, subcommentaries, exegeses, and studies.

In Neo-Confucianism a special place was given to the *Sishu* (Four books), and it became customary to speak of the "Four Books and Five Classics." The Four Books include, besides the *Lunyu* and the *Mengzi*, the *Zhongyong* (The central mean) and the *Daxue* (The great learning). The last two originally were chapters of the *Liji*, one of the three texts collectively designated as the *Li*. They were given the status of independent works by Zhu Xi, as they gave outstanding support to his insistence on personal moral cultivation as the basis of societal order.

From a modern point of view the Classics as a whole are not of great interest as literature, with the important exceptions of the poetry of the *Shijing* and the historical prose of the *Zuo zhuan* (Zuo's commentary), one of the commentaries on the *Chunqiu*. They are, however, of great importance for the history of Chinese literature. Having supposedly been written by the holy rulers, wise statesmen, and infallible masters of antiquity, the Classics were regarded as a perfect expression of the Way in both form and content. The Classics contained the highest truth in the most felicitous wording. Obscurity of phrasing was interpreted as indicative of profundity. Down through the ages, Chinese education was centered on memorization of the Classics. The Classics not only determined the literati's attitudes on man, society, and the cosmos (and on the place of literature therein); they were also an inexhaustible source of examples, sayings, quotations, and allusions.

The Art of Writing and Literary Criticism.

The Classics, for all practical purposes, cannot be added to. While later generations might possibly come to regard the work of a given writer as belonging to the Classics, no writer would have the arrogance to claim such status for his own work. After Han times few writers presented their ideas on man, society, and the cosmos in the form of single large-scale philosophical works. Most preferred the commentary, the letter, or the essay. As for historiography, it was primarily the responsibility of the government; in any case it made steep methodological demands on the writer. In practice, from the second century A.D. on, the most frequently written forms of literature were poetry and the shorter prose forms, both classified under Collections. In making their pronouncements on literature, therefore, many traditional Chinese writers were referring only to the genres included in Collections. It should be remembered, however, that they did continue to regard the other three categories as literature.

By studying literature, one not only learned the Way, but also how to put the Way into words. By studying the works of great writers, one assimilated their styles of reaction and expression as a preparation for similar reactions of one's own in comparable situations. Actually, it is not so much that one "assimilated" anything from outside; rather, through study, one polished the mirror of one's own spirit until its perfection was as complete as that of the models studied. At this stage, one would be capable at all times of putting normal feelings faultlessly into words. The imitation of examples was intended to result in the spontaneous and therefore perfect formulation of one's own—correct—emotions.

In the history of Chinese poetics, periods which stress imitation alternate with others which emphasize spontaneity. In the latter phases, the tendency is to condemn rigid convention as an impediment to the expression of honest, hence normal, feelings. The formulation of honest feelings is said to arise spontaneously in a moment of sudden insight which defies rational analysis. Though study is indispensable as a background to writing, the attainment of sudden insight, like the experience of the Way in its totality, is an experience that cannot be deliberately learned. The source perennially quoted in this connection is the *Zhuangzi*, in which the wheelwright and the carver explain that the fine points of their technique have evolved in the course of diligent practice over many years and cannot be taught to others, not even to their own sons.

On the whole, Chinese writers on literature were not overly interested in technical problems. The belief that there was only one correct behavior available in each given situation was incompatible with the development of a science of rhetoric, a system of purely technical devices for winning an undecided audience over to one's own point of view. Critical writings tend to be appreciative rather than prescriptive. Though systematic treatises on literature are not lacking, many of the most influential critical writings took the form of prefaces and afterwords, anecdotal records of conversations, and short poems. The function of prescriptive handbook was fulfilled to a large extent by the anthology, which provided selected models for imitation and emulation. As such, the anthology probably played a much larger role in the development of Chinese literature than it did in other traditions. Much critical writing first strikes the Western reader as unsystematic and impressionistic. Chinese critics often tried to illustrate the essential characteristics of an author by quoting a single illustrative couplet or by summarizing his most typical features in a two- or four-character phrase. They delighted in rating poets, often according to a ninefold classification of upper, middle, and lower, each category subdivided again into upper, middle, and lower. Many texts were published with the critical comments of a later reader added in the upper margin of the page. These marginalia might range from simple expressions of admiration to more extended considerations on all conceivable aspects of the text. The later editor of a text might also draw the reader's attention to commendable phrases and passages by placing little circles or other marks beside the characters concerned, a practice known as *pingdian* (appreciative dotting). These styles of criticism, developed in the field of high literature, were later also applied to drama and fiction.

Trivial Literature

Texts which are *untrue* because the events they describe never really happened, because the feelings they express were not really felt, or because the line of reasoning is absurd—cannot, with the important exception of topical allegory, make any positive contribution to the study of the Way. The Chinese tradition does not value fiction as being a way to express higher truths that lie beyond the realm of mere fact. On the contrary, fiction is condemned as by definition misleading and inciting to moral corruption. Accordingly, all forms of fiction (story, novel, novella, narrative ballad, play) are traditionally excluded *ipso facto* from the realm of literature. There is room in true literature for anecdotes, myths, sagas, and legends only if they can be presented as actually historical. When Chinese myths and legends were put into written form, they tended to be sobered up into dry "factual" accounts.

Trivial literature in *wenyan* had its origin in texts which the original authors regarded as historical, but which later historians rejected as being too full of the supernatural, insufficiently credible, or whatever. Trivial literature in the vernacular spoken language, being mainly rooted in older trivial literature or in recent folk tales, could lay even less claim to being good history. Authors of fiction continued to base their work heavily on existing stories, however many liberties they took in the retelling. A genuine made-up story was to be read as topical allegory.

Fiction—stories whose truth was but partial—was at best tolerated as muddled history. There could be no question of its active promotion by the government. And if the state found it had been encouraging fiction unawares, measures were taken to correct the situation. A striking example is the fate that befell the *Taiping guangji* (Extensive records of the Taiping Xingguo period). This work, a thematically ordered compendium of the *xiaoshuo* ("insignificant tellings," fiction) of the preceding millennium in 500 *juan*, had been completed in 978 on imperial order as one of the numerous compilation projects in the early years of the Song dynasty. Suddenly objections were raised (the collection was said to be "of no use to young students"), and though the printing blocks had already been cut, publication was suspended. Fortunately for contemporary editors and publishers, the text was preserved in manuscript; it was finally published in the Ming dynasty.

Trivial literature struggled to exist, depending on enthusiastic readers and commercial publishers. Of the objections raised against trivial literature, the easiest to refute was the charge that the occurrences depicted in fiction lacked credibility. After all, the Classics and Histories also occasionally mentioned the supernatural, and Confucianism by no means denied the possible existence of gods, ghosts, dragons, and other fabulous beings. The charge of inciting to immorality, too, could be answered: in fiction as in life, in the long run virtue was ultimately rewarded and evil punished. And at the very least, one could always appeal to one of the sayings of Confucius: that even board games are less dangerous than idleness. Fiction might well be in itself useless, but it could distract from worse temptations.

Very rarely—for example, in the late sixteenth and early seventeenth centuries—cautious attempts were made to defend certain works of fiction on grounds of their intrinsic literary merits. But as long as the Central Tradition determined the intellectual framework of the literati, such ideas stood no chance of general acceptance. But while trivial literature was not considered literature, it was certainly written and read, performed and enjoyed. Forms that rulers, bureaucrats, and literati barely tolerated officially were in practice written and consumed by these same paragons of virtue.

From the second century A.D. on literature grew increasingly, and after the coming of the printed book and the economic boom in the sixteenth century, its growth was truly explosive.

The Language and Functions of Trivial Literature

The distinction between trivial and high literature largely coincides with that between *baihua* and *wenyan* literature. Nearly all texts in *baihua* prior to the twentieth century belong to trivial literature, though there are exceptions—for example, the Song dynasty *yulu* of the various Neo-Confucian schools, or the lyrical folk poetry written in the vernacular. And some *wenyan* texts are considered trivial. One of the most important forms of trivial literature, for example, was the short story in the classical written idiom (*chuanqi*), which evolved from the jokes, anecdotes, supernatural stories, and legends of the period from about the second to the sixth century A.D. This genre finally came into its own during the Tang dynasty, especially from the second half of the eighth century. Thereafter, the *chuanqi* was partially eclipsed by *biji* ("writing-brush notes"), collections of short notes on a practically unlimited range of subjects, depending on the author's interests and whim. The *chuanqi* made an impressive comeback, however, in the first century of the Ming, and again in the initial century of the Qing.

Chuanqi show great variety in their subject matter, but they nearly always involve love or the supernatural, often in combination. This is true of the Tang *chuanqi* and also of the most famous later collection, the *Liaozhai zhiyi* (Notes on strange matters from the Studio of Idleness) by Pu Songling (1640–1715), which contains nearly 500 stories and anecdotes.

Within trivial literature a distinction can be drawn between texts written to be read and those intended for performance. The first category includes not only the *wenyan* genres of *chuanqi* and *biji*, but also the vernacular novel and novella as they were printed from the sixteenth century on. The second comprises the various forms of drama as well as narrative ballads (*shuochang wenxue*). *Shuochang wenxue* includes many forms of narrative text, in prose and verse, which the performing artist was to tell, declaim, or sing according to the specific conventions of the form concerned. The oldest preserved drama texts date from the thirteenth century. The oldest extant narrative ballads date from the eighth century. These so-called *bianwen* (transformation texts) of the Tang are edifying tales in alternating prose and verse. Drama and *shuochang wenxue* include both written and oral literature. By no means could all actors and actresses, storytellers, and singers read and write; often they learned their repertoire directly from their teachers with no written text whatsoever. Besides the oral literature performed by professional artists, there was also a folk oral literature including fairy tales, folk tales, jokes, songs, sayings, and proverbs.

Trivial Literature and Popular Literature

There was much mutual influence between various forms of trivial literature, as well as between trivial and oral literature. Folk tales might be expanded into story cycles which provided the material for *shuochang wenxue*, drama, novel, and short story. Short stories in *wenyan* were sometimes adapted for the novella, drama, or *shuochang wenxue*, whence they found their way into oral literature. In the later dynasties, especially the Ming and Qing, some story cycles were known all over China and served as inexhaustible sources of material for all forms of trivial literature. Examples are the civil wars from A.D. 180 onward that led to the tripartition of the Han Empire in A.D. 220/221; the adventures of the monk Xuanzang and his disciples Monkey and Pigsy on their pilgrimage to the Western Paradise; the adventures of a group of noble robbers in the early years of the twelfth century; the gruesome crimes solved by the incorruptible Judge Bao; and the love story of Zhang Gong and Cui Yingying.

Trivial literature, however, was not identical with popular literature. The various forms of trivial literature undoubtedly had their fans in various social strata, but if the forms involved written texts, only people with some degree of literacy could read or write them. To be sure, trivial literature assimilated much material from the professional cultures and other less prestigious sources, but it was actually written—and read—mostly by representatives of the Central Tradition. This is certainly true of forms like the *chuanqi*, the novel, the novella, and the various forms of drama, but also of *shuochang wenxue*, even if the latter also owes some of its texts to monks, priests, and literate performing artists. To a large extent, the texts of trivial literature were expressions, albeit in somewhat modified form, of the philosophy of the same Central Tradition that was the basis of high literature.

Of course, what traditional China regarded as trivial need not seem so to the modern reader. Many traditional trivial works were written with great verve and skill. Numerous cases are on record of an author devoting his entire lifetime to the writing of a single novel. Contemporary readers were well aware that many trivial works were of outstanding literary value. In public, however, they could only lament the fact. The more attractive a trivial work was, the greater the danger it posed to established morality. In the twentieth century, many plays, short stories, novels, and novellas underwent a spectacular change of status that would have been unthinkable in the old days. Far from being dismissed as "books that incite to vice," they became classic masterpieces.

Chapter 6.
THE STUDY AND TRANSLATION OF CHINESE LITERATURE IN THE WEST

Though it has been nearly four centuries since the Western world first took cognizance of some form of Chinese literature, the process of familiarization has been almost unbelievably slow and unsystematic. Matteo Ricci prepared a Latin translation of the Confucian *Sishu* (Four books) in 1594, but it was not until the second half of the nineteenth century that full translations of the Chinese Classics appeared in the modern European languages.

For a long time, Westerners were mainly interested in philosophical and historical texts; Chinese belles-lettres were more or less ignored. Until the second half of the twentieth century, the West's image of Chinese literature was virtually limited to the Classics and Histories, classical *shi* poetry, and a few classical novels. Translations were of widely varying quality, and on most genres no reliable secondary literature was available. In the preface to his *Topics in Chinese Literature*, first published in 1950, James R. Hightower could still say, " . . . the few existing Western language studies on purely literary topics are seldom of any use" (p. vii).

This situation has changed radically since the 1960s. Partly owing to the American military presence in the Far East, more and more dictionaries and textbooks of modern Chinese have been published. An increasing number of universities offer programs in Chinese, and Classical Chinese culture is no longer the exclusive focus of interest. In the past few decades the approach to Chinese culture has become increasingly differentiated, including in its scope the vernacular literature of earlier centuries, modern and contemporary Chinese literature, and other cultural forms that had been neglected by earlier generations of Sinologists. While the Western academic's concept of Chinese literature has changed beyond all recognition within the past forty years, for much of the general public, Chinese literature still remains pretty much what it always was: exotic, potentially fascinating, but practically unknown.

BEFORE 1800

Early in the sixteenth century, Europe began to receive reports on China from Spanish and Portuguese travelers. Aside from attracting some attention from humanists such as Montaigne and Scaliger, these early fragments had little effect. In 1582 the Jesuit missionary Matteo Ricci was sent to China, where he spent more than a quarter century. Ricci developed an outstanding command of the Chinese language; thanks to his efforts, some members of the highest Chinese court circles became interested not only in Western science, but also in Christianity. Ricci's Latin version of the Four Books was completed in 1594 and was followed by works of other missionaries dealing with various aspects of Chinese society.

Starting in the seventeenth century, knowledge of China began to spread through Europe. On the one hand, there was a great deal of serious (though naively idealistic) intellectual interest in Chinese philosophy and society. Western thinkers like Leibniz, Spinoza, Rousseau, and Voltaire were influenced by such images of China as seemed plausible in their day, and they in turn gained an audience for their ideas of China. At the same time, in the arts there arose the phenomenon of *chinoiserie*: stylized, often pathetically inept imitations of Chinese art as the artist had seen it or imagined it to be. The combination of ignorance and idealism resulted in a fragmented vision of China which unfortunately has continued to influence the West until very recently.

In *philosophy* this vision includes the idea that the Confucian philosophy of China's Central Tradition is a close relative of European humanism or the philosophy of the Enlightenment, but with the additional advantages of being still more rational or "reasonable," and of not being contaminated with Christian ideas. In *aesthetics*, the vision encompasses the notion that the main features of China's cultural tradition find their most characteristic expression in the stereotyped and idyllically romanticized elements which Europeans of a bygone day found exotic and charming. The fragmentary character of this vision of China was all the more enhanced by the deep gulf between academic Sinology (such as it was) and the interest in China shown by other elements of society.

In the eighteenth century the Western Sinology that Ricci established was carried on mainly by other Jesuits. Like their predecessors these writers usually regarded belles-lettres as unimportant or even objectionable. Nevertheless, the eighteenth century did see the translation of a number of Chinese literary works. In about 1733 the French missionary Lacharme completed a paraphrase (in Latin prose!) of the *Shijing*. A century later this version was to bear fruit in German poetic adaptations by Friedrich Rückert, which in turn influenced various twentieth-century German poets.

In 1735 Jean-Baptiste du Halde published his *Description de la Chine*, which contained many texts and data collected by the Jesuits. This book, which throughout the eighteenth century was regarded as an authoritative source, included several novellas and a Yuan dynasty play, *Zhao shi gu'er* (The orphan of the Zhaos) by Ji Junxiang. The translation of the play was by Joseph de Prémare, who was also the author of one of the best early grammars of Chinese. Prémare's translation inspired several later European adaptations, most notably Voltaire's *Orphelin de la Chine* (1755). The first Chinese novel to be translated into a European language was the *Haoqiu zhuan* (The fortunate union), a twenty-chapter melodramatic romance, which was published in 1761 in an English version. Quickly retranslated into several other European languages, it attracted the attention of Goethe.

Antoine Gaubil (1689–1759) has been called the greatest French Sinologist of the eighteenth century. His publications included a translation of the *Shujing* that appeared in 1770. He also completed translations of the *Yijing* and the *Liji*, but they were never published.

The thirteen-volume *Histoire générale de la Chine*, by J. A. M. de Moyriac de Mailla (1669–1748), was published between 1777 and 1785. Mailla's history, which relied heavily on Chinese sources (especially the *Tongjian gangmu*) was used until well into the twentieth century and did much to encourage the simplistic image of an "unchanging" China which long dominated the West's conception of Chinese history.

THE NINETEENTH CENTURY

During the nineteenth century the West's knowledge of China grew by leaps and bounds. For the first time reasonably complete dictionaries of Chinese were compiled in Western languages. Sinology became a recognized field of study at universities in various countries. Though China remained practically closed to foreigners during the first decades of the century, Europeans began to apply themselves seriously to the study of available written sources. The Chinese novel and drama began to attract attention, partly because of the insights they afforded into the language and customs of contemporary China.

After the Opium War of 1839–1842, China became increasingly accessible to foreigners. The years to 1900 saw the publication of several Western translations of the Chinese Classics that have remained standard works in the field to the present day. Art and literature continued to receive less attention than history and philosophy—areas of crucial importance for the missionary effort. Nevertheless, a number of literary works appeared in translation. It was especially classical Chinese poetry, of which French translations were published from the 1860s on, that eventually attracted notice in serious literary circles in the West.

In 1814 the *Collège de France* established a chair of Sinology. The second man to hold this post, Stanislas Julien (1797–1873), became a truly legendary Sinologist who greatly influenced further developments both by his own writings and through the accomplishments of his students. In addition to his philosophical concerns (he published, for example, a Latin translation of the *Mengzi* in 1824), Julien took real interest in popular and trivial literature. He translated several Yuan dynasty plays, including the *Huilan ji* (Chalk circle), which later made a lasting impression on Bertolt Brecht, and the *Xixiang ji* (Dream of the Western Chamber). His interest in Chinese fiction resulted, among other things, in a full translation of the *Ping Shan Leng Yan* (the title is made up of the names of the four main characters).

Julien's interest in nonclassical Chinese literature was not exceptional in his day. It undoubtedly stemmed from a desire to enter into the spirit of living Chinese culture despite all physical barriers. Owing in no small part to Julien's influence, in the first half of the nineteenth century Paris became the undisputed hub of European Sinology. In 1836 one translator of popular literature who had studied in Paris, Heinrich Kurz (1805–1873), published a German translation of the novel-in-verse *Huajian ji* (The floral-patterned letter paper). In the classical field, an outstanding product of this early French school was the translation of the *Zhou li* (Rites of Zhou) by Eduard Biot (1803–1850), which has never been superseded in a Western language since its publication in 1851.

In the second half of the nineteenth century, the Western countries forced an entry into China. After the Treaty of Tientsin (1858), which established additional treaty ports and opened all China to Western missionaries, the Western political, commercial, and religious presence grew steadily. The propagators of Christianity in China felt a great need for knowledge of the indigenous philosophical and religious traditions. Western diplomats wished to establish dialog with the representatives of China's Central Tradition and to gain some acquaintance with the literary basis of that tradition. The requirements of these groups were met by the first complete and fully annotated translations of the Confucian Classics in Western languages.

The missionary James Legge (1815–1895) produced English translations which, while not impeccably reliable, have remained highly useful to the present day. In his accompanying notes and introductions, however, Legge could not always resist adding rather bold personal comments on the quality of the original texts and their spiritual content.

The French translations by Séraphin Couvreur (1835–1919) were based consistently on the Neo-Confucian interpretations that were the official Chinese reading of the Classics at the time. Couvreur also compiled a famous Chinese-French dictionary. His fellow missionary Léon Wieger (1856–1933) published, in addition to historical and philological works, important translations and adaptations of Taoist texts.

While missionaries addressed themselves to the Chinese Classics and to the indigenous popular religion, diplomatic and colonial-administrative circles turned their attention to Chinese law, customs, and morals. Indigenous literature was a major source of information and examples. A British consular official, Herbert Giles (1845–1935), wrote the first Western history of Chinese literature. He was one of the few early Western Sinologists to take a specific interest in Chinese belles-lettres. His numerous translations of poetry, short stories, and other prose genres were followed by his *History of Chinese Literature*, which appeared in 1901. Giles's book was followed a year later by *Geschichte der chinesischen Literatur*, written by the German ethnologist Wilhelm Grube (1855–1908).

While Western translators in China toiled over their translations of the Classics, in Europe translators began to attempt classical Chinese poetry. The 1862 anthology *Poésies de l'époque des Thang* was compiled and translated by Marquis d'Hervey de Saint-Denis, the successor to Julien's chair in the *Collège de France*. In addition to poems by Li Bai and Du Fu, it included an introductory essay on the nature of Chinese poetry. In 1867 Judith Gautier, daughter of the famous poet Théophile Gautier, published her free verse translations in *Le livre de jade*; she had taken some lessons in Chinese from a Chinese domestic. The works of d'Hervey de Saint-Denis and Judith Gautier were direct influences on Hans Bethge and Klabund (pseudonym of Alfred Henschke, 1890–1928), who in the early years of the twentieth century won a certain following for their German adaptations. These very free versions in turn had considerable influence on the poetry of several minor European languages including Dutch.

THE FIRST HALF OF THE TWENTIETH CENTURY

In the early years of the twentieth century academic Sinology was mainly interested in the philological study of early Chinese history and philosophy. A few short decades saw enormous progress in making reliable knowledge of the language and the older texts more widely available. Equipped with a grammar like *Grammatik der chinesischen Schriftsprache* (1881) by Georg von der Gabelentz, and with dictionaries like those by Couvreur (1890), Giles (1892), and F. W. Baller (1900), Western scholars could learn written Chinese faster and more accurately than ever before. By applying to Chinese material the techniques and analytic strategies that had been developed in European comparative and historical linguistics, Bernhard Karlgren (1889–1978) was able to make great strides toward elucidating the historical origins and dialectal features of the underlying spoken strata of the language.

Of the many Sinological publications prior to the Second World War, those especially relevant to the study of literature include the partial translation, with commentary, of the *Shiji* by Eduard Chavannes (1865–1918), the studies on the *Shijing* by Marcel Granet (1884–1940), the translation with commentary of the *Qian Han shu* by Homer H. Dubs (1892–), and the translations of Chinese philosophical works by J. J. L. Duyvendak (1889–1954).

Other translators took up the challenge of Chinese literature. The years of the First World War saw publication of the first collections by two translators into English who were much followed in later years: Arthur Waley (1889–1966) and Ezra Pound (1885–1972). Waley was entirely self-taught in Chinese and never set foot on Chinese soil. He once turned down an invitation to visit China, saying he was really only interested in the culture of an era which no longer existed geographically. Waley combined a sound knowledge of Chinese with considerable literary gifts. His translations, in which high reliability went together with memorable and elegant phrasing, have continued to be admired both within and outside the world of scholarship. His translations from the Classics included the *Lunyu* and the *Shijing*, but he was by far most famous for his translations of *shi* poetry, especially that of Bai Juyi (Po Chü-i).

The technical features of Waley's *shi* translations, which have been adopted by many later translators, may be summarized as follows:

1) The translation respects the form and content of the original. Usually no attempt is made to "improve" the poem by deletions, alterations in sequence, etc.

2) The rhyme schemes of the original are ignored in translation. Waley considered that rhyme would impose a far too unnatural choice of words and lead too far from the meaning of the original.

3) In most cases the identity of the lines in the original is respected. In the English translation, the number of stressed syllables corresponds to the number of written characters in the Chinese line. This principle in particular has been much imitated by later translators, not all of whom have been able to match Waley's happy combinations of rhythm and meaning. This technique preserves, albeit on a rather theoretical level, a certain structural

resemblance to the Chinese text despite the loss of the original rhymes. But with the rhythmic length of the lines being fixed in advance, the translator may be tempted to choose words mainly for the metrical space they occupy.

Ezra Pound, a founder of modern American poetry, studied and translated the poetry of various exotic languages and tried to apply in his own poetry some of the techniques he had observed. Pound could not read Chinese, but working from annotations prepared by the art historian Ernest Fenellosa, he published in 1915 the collection *Cathay*, in which poems by Li Bai, Wang Wei, and others were rendered into English free verse. Influenced by Fenollosa's writings on the subject, Pound became an outspoken champion of the theory that the translator should regard the Chinese script as a series of "ideograms"—in other words, that the original pictographic meaning of each character (or part of a character, even if that is no more than the phonetic element in a phonetic compound!) should find expression in the translation whenever possible. Pound also felt that any attempt at direct literal translation was pointless: even if the translator succeeded in incorporating all the formal features of the original, the emotional weight and implication of those same features would inevitably be different in their new context. The translator, he suggested, was far better advised to attempt a sort of close rewriting in the idiom of his own contemporaries. The translator should feel free to change or even delete "mere words" in the original if they seemed superfluous or to have been used to fill out metrical patterns.

In Sinological circles Pound was never taken quite seriously, but his influence in the literary world has been enormous. His imaginative renderings of the poems from the *Shijing*, in his *The Classical Anthology Defined by Confucius*, have found many admirers, even among Sinologists. In the work of many younger American translators, including Gary Snyder (*Riprap and Cold Mountain Poems*, 1958), Pound's influence is modulated, and the more dubious features of the ideogram theory have been abandoned.

The degree to which different translations of the same text may vary is perhaps most evident in translations of poetry, but every literary translation, of whatever genre, bears the stamp of its maker's approach to the original. Those translators who wish to accent the exotic quality of the original will not hesitate to use words, turns of phrase, or grammatical structures that are not customary in the target language. On the other hand, those translators who regard their work as a serious contribution to the modern literature of their own language are liable to reduce jarringly exotic elements—sometimes by deleting outright passages that seem incompatible with contemporary aesthetic standards.

As examples of very free translations which were well received in the Western milieu, we may mention the simplified and abridged versions of

Chinese novels by the German writer Franz Kuhn (1884–1961). Kuhn's German versions of novels like the *Jin Ping Mei* and *Honglou meng* were not only much read and repeatedly reprinted in Germany, but many were retranslated into other European languages.

THE SITUATION SINCE THE 1950s

Since the Second World War an increasing number of excellent Western books on Chinese literature have appeared. The terrain rather unevenly staked out by pioneers like Giles and Grube was given systematic if brief treatment in J. R. Hightower's *Topics in Chinese Literature* (1950). Good translations from various Chinese genres were provided with informative commentaries and collected in such anthologies as *Sources of Chinese Tradition* (W. T. de Bary, W. T. Chan, and B. Watson, 1960), *Anthology of Chinese Literature* (Cyril Birch, 1965–72), and *A Treasury of Chinese Literature* (C. and W. Chai, 1965). C. T. Hsia's *A History of Modern Chinese Fiction* (1961) went well beyond its announced field of fiction; it is actually a highly illuminating introduction to the nature and origins of modern Chinese literature, in which the concepts and values of modern Western literary criticism were usefully applied.

In the decades since these studies, the literature in the field has expanded tremendously, and there has been a trend toward increasing specialization. American translators produced annotated versions of many works not previously studied in the West. The techniques of the New Criticism, in which the text is approached as an autonomous entity and studied without recourse to biographical, historical, or social contexts, began to be applied in Sinology. Since the 1970s a similar specializing tendency has also been evident in Europe.

In recent years a very wide range of modern and contemporary Chinese authors has been published in translation series issued by Panda Books (Peking) and Renditions Paperbacks (Hong Kong). Reaching beyond a strictly Sinological readership, these publications are helping to dissolve the rigid distinction between academic and literary interest in Chinese authors. Western publishers have taken an interest in such Chinese fiction writers as Wang Anyi (1954–), Zhang Jie (1937–), and Zhang Xianliang (1936–). All in all, since the 1980s the Western reader has been able as never before to obtain at least readable translations of twentieth-century Chinese literature. It remains lamentable that many works of real literary merit have not been translated, whether because for linguistic reasons they do not lend themselves easily to attractive translation or because their authors have not managed to get themselves promoted as aggressively in Sinological or commercial circles.

Besides the studies and translations which have appeared in book form, much secondary literary has been published in scholarly journals. Sinological journals in which contributions on literature have figured prominently include *Asia Major, Bulletin of the School of Oriental and African Studies, Harvard Journal of Asiatic Studies, Journal Asiatique, Journal of Oriental Studies, Monumenta Serica, Oriens Extremus,* and *T'oung Pao.* More recently established journals dealing specifically with Chinese literature include *C.L.E.A.R. (Chinese Literature—Essays, Articles and Reviews)* and *Modern Chinese Literature. Literature East and West* has often published comparative studies. *Renditions* focuses especially on translations.

In addition to the Sinological journals in Western countries, important English-language periodicals are published in various parts of the Chinese-speaking world. *Chinese Literature* (Peking) publishes translations from and articles on Chinese literature of all periods. A growing interest in comparative literature in the People's Republic of China has resulted in the establishment of *Cowrie. The Chinese Pen* (Taipei) is useful for the present-day literature of Taiwan. *Tamkang Review,* another Taiwanese journal, presents studies of a literary-technical or comparative sort.

In bibliographic matters the modern student has access to resources barely dreamed of by Sinologists forty years ago. The very important early bibliography *Bibliotheca Sinica* (1924) by Henri Cordier included Western publications on China up to 1924. The need for a sequel was met by two works: *China in Western Literature* (1958) by Yuan Tung-li, which includes books published from 1921 to 1957 in Western languages, and *Index Sinicus* (1964) by John Lust, covering the periodical literature in Western languages from 1920 to 1940. Meanwhile, the *Bibliography of Asian Studies,* appearing annually from 1936 on, became an internationally recognized standard bibliography on Sinological subjects. From 1936 to 1940 it was called *Bulletin of Far Eastern Bibliography.* Starting in 1941 it was published under the title *Far Eastern Bibliography,* first as a supplement to the *Far Eastern Quarterly,* and from 1965, when the name of the *Far Eastern Quarterly* was changed to *Journal of Asian Studies,* to the latter.

Specifically on Chinese literature Martha Davidson published *A List of Published Translations from Chinese into English, French and German* between 1952 and 1957. Two important bibliographies by Li Tien-yi appeared in 1968: *The History of Chinese Literature: A Selected Bibliography* and *Chinese Fiction: A Bibliography of Books and Articles in Chinese and English.* Richard John Lynn's *Chinese Literature: A Draft Bibliography in Western European Languages* (1979) lists books and monographs (no articles) dealing with all areas of Chinese literature old and new.

In recent years a number of excellent bibliographies have appeared which give more specialized coverage of specific periods, genres, and so on. These will be listed in the bibliographies to the chapters concerned.

For traditional Chinese literature, the student now has at his disposal the *Indiana Companion to Traditional Chinese Literature* (1986), edited by William H. Nienhauser, Jr. Introductory essays cover the major genres; the individual entries on authors and titles also include good bibliographies. The literature of the first half of the twentieth century is introduced in the four volumes of *A Selective Guide to Chinese Literature, 1900–1949* (1988–1990), dealing respectively with novels, short stories, poetry, and drama. Each volume in this series provides summaries of about one hundred well-known works or collections, with relevant bibliographic information.

Part II.
From the Earliest Times
to the Invention of Paper

CHINESE POLITICAL HISTORY
BEFORE A.D. 100

Traditional chronology places the reign of China's mythical earliest rulers, such as Huangdi (the Yellow Emperor) and Shennong (the Divine Husbandman), near the beginning of the third millennium B.C. Legends credit these rulers with the invention of many of the basic necessities of human civilization. Legend also has it that these rulers passed the throne on not to their sons but to deserving ministers. Yao supposedly passed the throne on to Shun and Shun in turn to Yu, who as his minister had relieved a flood of nine years' duration by draining the rivers off into the sea.

Yu, however, was succeeded by his son. The dynasty thus established, the Xia, is supposed to have ruled China during the first half of the second millennium B.C. So far no archaeological finds have positively been identified as remains of the Xia. The Xia gave way to the Shang dynasty when Jie, the evil last Xia king, was overthrown by King Tang with the assistance of the wise minister Yi Yin. The Shang, which later changed its name to Yin, ruled the Central Plain during the second half of the second millennium B.C. The historicity of this dynasty, which had long been doubted, has been amply confirmed by archaeological finds in the twentieth century.

During the reign of Zhou, the notorious last king of the Shang, the people flocked to the domain of the lords of Zhou, in the western part of modern Shaanxi. King Wen of Zhou remained loyal to the Shang throughout his life, but his son and successor King Wu, helped by the wise old minister Lü Wang, led his troops against the Shang and became the founder of the Zhou empire. Traditional chronology places this event in 1122 B.C., but modern scholarship favors an eleventh-century date. During the minority of King Wu's son and successor King Cheng, the government was led by his younger brother Dan, the duke of Zhou. The Zhou kings appointed their younger siblings and meritorious officers as rulers of fiefs throughout the conquered territories.

In later years the central authority of the Zhou kings steadily declined. In 770 B.C. they had to relocate their capital from Hao (near modern Xi'an) to Luoyang. The power of individual fiefs continued to increase as they warred not only against each other but against non-Chinese peoples. States situated on what were the borders of the Chinese world expanded spectacularly. During the seventh and sixth centuries B.C. the state of Jin, based in modern

Shanxi, held a dominant position, but in the course of the fifth century B.C. it disintegrated into the independent states of Han, Wei, and Zhao. During the sixth and fifth centuries B.C. the southern states of Chu, Wu, and Yue were engaged in a complex series of wars, from which Chu eventually emerged victorious. In the Northeast, the state of Qi (modern Shandong) at one time occupied the state of Yan, only to be almost annihilated by Yan in turn. One after another, the rulers of these states arrogated to themselves the title *wang* (king), which had originally been the prerogative of the kings of Zhou.

In the early years of the third century B.C. it looked as though the Chinese world would be divided between Qi in the East and Qin in the West. The state of Qin was based in the Wei River valley in modern Shaanxi. In the fourth century B.C. Qin had annexed what is now Sichuan; it also adopted the ruthless Legalist policies of the statesman Shang Yang. After the formal termination of the Zhou dynasty in 256 B.C. Qin quickly occupied the territory of the other states. In 221 B.C. upon the completion of his conquest of the Chinese world, the reigning king of Qin adopted the new title of *huangdi* (emperor), calling himself First Emperor. A number of important measures were taken to ensure the permanent political and cultural unification of the realm: uniform bureaucratic administration was imposed throughout the empire, weights and measures and the written language were standardized, and the writings of rival philosophical schools were destroyed. General Meng Tian was ordered to strengthen the walls and fortifications along the northern border.

Almost immediately after the death of the First Emperor in 210 B.C., rebellions broke out all over China, and Qin authority collapsed. Initially, the most powerful contender for the throne appeared to be the redoubtable general Xiang Yu, but he eventually lost out to Liu Bang, who was of humble origin but who won the loyalty of an effective group of capable commanders and advisors. Liu Bang became the founder of the Han dynasty (206 B.C.–A.D. 220). He established its capital at Chang'an, the modern Xi'an. The dynasty enjoyed its greatest power during the reign of Emperor Wu (r. 141–87 B.C.), who extended its authority far into Central Asia. In the long run, however, even his persistent military efforts proved inadequate to the threat posed by the inhabitants of the steppe country along China's northern border, who were at this time known as the Xiongnu.

By the end of the first century B.C. effective power in the central government was monopolized by the imperial family's relatives by marriage. One of these, the prime minister Wang Mang (r. A.D. 9–23), took over the imperial throne and proclaimed the Xin (new) dynasty, but he did not manage to gain lasting control of the provinces, and civil war broke out. The ultimate winner, known to history as Emperor Guangwu, relocated the capital to Luoyang. The first two centuries of Han rule are referred to as the Western or Early Han; the last two are called Eastern or Later Han. After the unification of the Chinese heartland, Chinese power was again extended into Central Asia.

Chapter 7.
HISTORICAL PROSE

We have already made much reference to the importance the Central Tradition attached to history as an indispensable aid to grasping the present. Historiography has always been one of the most prominent elements in the Chinese literary tradition. The earliest rulers had court historians who recorded the words and deeds of the ruler, whose behavior was supposed to be the main determinant of order or chaos in society and in the world of nature. In later centuries also, the main focus of historiography was on the ups and downs of the ruler and his administration. Traditional Chinese historical writing is a veritable ocean of information for the modern student of political or institutional history; by contrast, the social–economic historian must be satisfied with a few scattered scraps.

THE *SHUJING*

The earliest preserved example of Chinese historiography is the *Shujing* (Book of documents), also known as the *Shangshu* (Documents of high antiquity). In its present form the *Shujing* consists of fifty texts (or fifty-six, if some of the texts are regarded as two independent texts). They are arranged in chronological order of the events to which they refer. Many take the form of addresses attributed to the holy rulers (and their wise ministers) in high antiquity or in the early years of the Zhou dynasty. The last text refers to an event that occurred in the state of Qin in 626 B.C. No attempt is made to link the various texts into an integrated whole.

Of the texts in the preserved version of the *Shujing* eighteen are certainly and four are very probably falsifications ("reconstructions") dating from early in the fourth century A.D. The majority of these refer to events in the Xia/Yin dynasty. In the second century A.D., after the burning of the books under the Qin, only twenty-eight texts were known to exist. Within this body of twenty-eight texts, two groups can be distinguished. Some, referring to the history of the early Zhou dynasty, were probably written soon after the events concerned (for example, the various texts in which the early Zhou rulers address the conquered Xia/Yin subjects, in which the doctrine of the

76

Mandate of Heaven is set forth). The other group, texts associated with the holy rulers of early antiquity but actually mostly dating from the fourth and third centuries B.C., deal with such subjects as government, jurisprudence, or the ideal ruler. This group also includes a geographical description of the ancient Chinese world. In traditional China the entire *Shujing* was believed to be an authentic record of the words and deeds of the ancient rulers. The language of the *Shujing* is terse and difficult at many points; some use is made of parallelism.

From the earliest times the *Shujing* was regarded as one of the Classics. In pre-Han times, when the notion of the Five Classics did not yet exist, the ancient texts which everyone was expected to study were often referred to simply as the *Shishu* (Odes and documents).

THE *CHUNQIU* AND *ZUO ZHUAN*

The next historical work, chronologically speaking, is the *Chunqiu* (Annals of spring and autumn). It is a chronicle of the state of Lu, covering the period from 722 to 479 B.C. It records important events in Lu in strict order of occurrence, year by year, month by month, sometimes even day by day. Also included are major happenings in other states that were relevant for Lu. The style of the entries is succinct, as shown in the following example from the first year of the reign of Duke Yin (722 B.C):

First year. Spring, first month of the King.
Third month: the Duke and Yifu of Zhu concluded a treaty in Mi.
Summer. Fifth month: the count of Zheng defeated Duan in Yan.
Autumn. Seventh month: the celestial King caused the assistant Huan to
   bring the burial gifts for Duke Hui and Zhongzi.
Ninth month: a pact was made in Shu with the people of Song.
Winter. Twelfth month: the Duke of Ji came; Gongzi Yishi died.

Soon after the completion of the *Chunqiu* the belief arose that it had been written by Confucius himself. It was thought that Confucius had employed a meticulously exact choice of words as a way of implying moral judgment upon the persons described. For example, by describing a ruler's death in terms other than those which would customarily have been used on such occasions, Confucius was indicating that this particular ruler had not conducted himself in ways worthy of his role. Before long, commentaries were written to explain the deeper meanings implicit in the formulations of the *Chunqiu*. Two of the three ancient commentaries on the *Chunqiu*—the

Gongyang zhuan (Gongyang's commentary) and *Guliang zhuan* (Guliang's commentary)—are specifically concerned with this kind of exegesis.

The third commentary, the *Zuo zhuan* (Zuo's commentary), is composed of two parts. Like the *Gongyang zhuan* and *Guliang zhuan* it contains textual exegesis, but it also provides concise yet detailed descriptions of the events mentioned in the *Chunqiu* and of certain other events in the same period. The *Zuo zhuan* gives us a lively and varied picture of Chinese knightly society— and the attendant wars—from the eighth to the fifth century B.C. The main focus of the descriptions in *Zuo zhuan* is not Lu but another state, Jin. It is generally assumed that the *Zuo zhuan* was originally written as an independent work (probably in the second half of the fourth century B.C) and was later rearranged as a commentary on the *Chunqiu*. *Zuo zhuan* has, on very shaky grounds, been ascribed to a certain Zuo Qiuming, who is described as a blind disciple of Confucius.

The *Chunqiu* and the three commentaries are all regarded as belonging to the Classics. Some systems of classification lump them together as one Classic, but others count them as three separate Classics (in each case the *Chunqiu* is counted with one of the commentaries).

Another text concerned with roughly the same period and events as the *Zuo zhuan* (though it is not considered a Classic) is the *Guoyu* (Conversations of the states). The *Guoyu* purports to be a record of conversations and speeches held on the occasion of important events in the various states, especially at court. The items are grouped into books named after the states to which the contents refer. Within each book the items are arranged chronologically, though there is no running historical narrative.

The *Guoyu* was probably compiled partly on the basis of the same sources as the *Zuo zhuan*, and it dates from roughly the same period. The dialogs and treatises in the *Guoyu* are highly didactic and often long-winded. Zuo Qiuming has been credited with the authorship of this work also.

THE *ZHANGUO CE*

The period from the fifth to the third century B.C. is treated in the *Zhanguo ce* (Intrigues of the Warring States; the period of the Warring States extends from the formal recognition of the tripartition of the old state of Jin in 403 B.C. to the unification of China by Qin in 221 B.C). The *Zhanguo ce* comprises 452 texts of varying length; the main feature is usually a speech or letter intended to convince a ruler or high minister to pursue or to avoid a certain course of action. The emphasis is on the persuasiveness of the argument rather than the rightness of the action. The style is clever and at times humorous. The argument is occasionally supported by an appeal to fables or anecdotes.

The historical reliability of many of the texts in the *Zhanguo ce* is very slight. Many are believed to have been exercises in persuasive argument based on hypothetical scenarios: given situation *x*, which arguments could be used to induce ruler *y* to choose course of action *z*? The present *Zhanguo ce* was compiled by Liu Xiang (79–8 B.C), the imperial librarian, from several then-extant collections of similar exercises. (Other materials of this kind, not included in the *Zhanguo ce*, have been unearthed in recent years.) Following the model of the *Guoyu*, the texts are arranged in books according to the states to which they refer; within the individual books, the texts are in rough chronological order. Though the style of the *Zhanguo ce* was admired in later centuries, the book was often criticized for the blatantly amoral political opportunism of certain passages.

Liu Xiang also compiled other works, including the *Shuoyuan* (Garden of persuasion), a collection of historical anecdotes arranged thematically according to the virtues they describe, and the *Lienü zhuan* (Biographies of exemplary women). Owing to his prestige, other works were later incorrectly attributed to him; one of these was the *Liexian zhuan* (Biographies of immortals).

SIMA QIAN AND THE *SHIJI*

The *Shiji* (Records of the Grand Historiographer) was begun by Sima Tan and completed by his son Sima Qian (145–87? B.C). It is a history of China from the earliest times until the reign of Emperor Wu (r. 140–87 B.C). It is based on various sources, including those already described in this chapter, texts of similar nature which have since been lost, and oral traditions which Sima Qian collected during his extensive travels through China.

The *Shiji* consists of 130 books or chapters. The first twelve are the "annals" (*benji*), providing a chronological outline of the most important events in the Empire as viewed from the court of the kings of Zhou and later of the Han emperors. The next ten books are the "tables" (*biao*), containing, in tabular form, a summary of the successive reigns and rulers in the independent states (under the Zhou) or fiefs (under the Han), including the most important events occurring in the periods concerned. The third group, comprising eight books, is composed of "treatises" (*shu*, in later dynastic histories also often called *zhi*). Each treatise deals with a single subject, such as music, rites, or political economy. The fourth group of chapters (thirty books) is that of the "hereditary houses" (*shijia*), detailing the histories of the various states under the Zhou and of the most important Han fiefs; this section also contains the biography of Confucius. The last and largest group, containing seventy books, is the collection of "exemplary traditions" (*liezhuan*). This section is often designated as the "biographies," because most of the books deal with the lives of individuals. However, the section also contains a number of chapters dealing with the relations of the court with various foreign peoples.

The biographies in the *Shiji* and in later historical works did not attempt to portray individuals from the viewpoint of their psychological development or personal uniqueness. Rather, a biography was intended as a description of a person's exemplary fulfillment of a social role. A biographer often chose to write only about those incidents in a person's life which seemed especially appropriate as examples of the type of character being portrayed. Hence the biographies in later historical works are often highly stereotyped. In the *Shiji* biographies this process is not yet fully in evidence, and the *liezhuan* include a gallery of fascinating figures. In several cases these descriptions undoubtedly owe some of their color and vividness to a background in legendary source material. In the *liezhuan*, an individual book is not necessarily limited to the description of a single person, but may treat two or more individuals of similar type, such as court jesters, terrorists, millionaires.

THE *HAN SHU* AND OTHER DYNASTIC HISTORIES

The model of the *Shiji* was adopted by Ban Gu (A.D. 32–92), the chief compiler of the *Han shu* (The Book of the Han; often also known as the *Qian Han shu*, The Book of the Former Han). Ban Gu's father Ban Biao (3–54) had begun this work as a sequel to the *Shiji*, but Ban Gu imparted a rather different character to the book by limiting its focus, as no previous historian had done, to a single dynasty. The *Han shu* covers the Han dynasty from its founding in 209 B.C. to the fall of Wang Mang in A.D. 23. After Ban Gu's death, the *Han shu* was completed by his sister Ban Zhao. The hundred books of the *Han shu* fall into four, not five, groups: the category of hereditary houses is absent. The *Han shu* is much more solidly based on preserved written sources than is the *Shiji* but, unfortunately, this gain in historical accuracy often entails a loss of liveliness.

The *Han shu* served as the model for the dynastic histories (*zhengshi*) written in later centuries. From the Tang onward, there existed an important government bureau charged with compiling the history of the previous dynasty. This bureau had at its disposal the previous dynasty's archives, which had often already been edited during that dynasty. It was, for example, customary after the death of a ruler to compile "true notes" (*shilu*) on his reign, based on the very extensive "court journals" (*qijuzhu*). The *shilu* were lengthy chronicles which included excerpts from the most important documents and biographies of major personages dated according to the time at which their death had been announced at court. (The complete Ming and Qing *shilu* have been preserved.) In the course of time the dynastic histories came to be collated excerpts with explanatory text, despite the fact that the compilers included the most highly regarded of Chinese writers. Most dynastic histories were compiled by committees. A rare exception is the *Xin Wudai shi* (New history of the Five Dynasties) by the famous stateman, poet, and prose writer Ouyang Xiu (1007–1072). This work, written by Ouyang Xiu out of dissatisfaction with the previous so-called *Jiu Wudai shi* (Old history of the Five Dynasties), which had been prepared earlier under the Song, has stood as a much-praised example of style. Later, a government committee also compiled a new version of the history of the Tang; it is generally known as the *Xin Tang shu* (New history of the Tang), in contradistinction to the so-called *Jiu Tang shu* (Old history of the Tang), which had been compiled during the Later Zhou dynasty (951–960).

OTHER FORMS OF HISTORICAL WRITING
IN LATER PERIODS

Another form of historical writing was the continuing chronicle, a history wholly in the form of annals that was not limited to a single dynasty. The most famous, a work from a much later period, the *Zizhi tongjian* (Ongoing mirror as an aid to government) by Sima Guang (1019–1086), covers the period from 405 B.C. to A.D. 959. Its title again indicates the function of history for traditional China: the purpose of studying the past was to obtain guidelines for present-day politics. Under the guidance of their master the disciples of Zhu Xi made an abridgement of the *Zizhi tongjian* entitled *Tongjian gangmu* (Main lines and details in the continuing mirror). It was modeled upon the *Chunqiu*, so the moral lessons stood out clearly, and it enjoyed a great popularity. It was reworked into French by J. A. M. de Moyriac de Mailla as *Histoire générale de la Chine*. Published in twelve volumes from 1777 to 1785, it long contributed to the European notions of a supposedly unchanging Chinese history. In later centuries sequels appeared to both *Zizhi tongjian* and *Tongjian gangmu*.

An additional form of historical writing derived from the *Zizhi tongjian* was the *jishi benmo* (records of affairs in their beginnings and ends). This form was introduced by Yuan Shu (1131–1205), who grouped together by subject the information provided by the *Zizhi tongjian* on important events which had occurred more or less concurrently, giving the finished work the title *Tongjian jishi benmo.*

There were also histories in essay form dealing with the development of the various governmental institutions over many centuries. The oldest work in this genre is the *Tong dian* (Continuing canon) by Du You (735–812). The form continued to be practiced in later periods.

It goes without saying that there were a vast number of specialized studies on specific subjects relating to chronology and historical geography. Histories also included *difang zhi* (local gazetteers), historical and geographical handbooks on specific regions. A *difang zhi* included material on the local administrative structure, government buildings, crops, taxes, biographies of local notables, scenic attractions, and much else. Collections of anecdotes were classed under Histories.

BIOGRAPHY AND AUTOBIOGRAPHY

Biography was by no means limited to the "exemplary traditions." Innumerable collections of biographies have been preserved which contain material relating to a specific region or period, or to a particular social role. A modern reader would probably call them character sketches rather than biographies. The traditional Chinese biography is usually very short. It has a highly stereotyped structure, since the subjects were not important for their individuality, but for their success in fulfilling rigidly defined social roles. A sketch would typically comprise the name of the subject, his geographical and familial background, an anecdote from his youth that foreshadowed his later comportment, a brief summary of his career in government (which might include no more than the circumstances of entering government service and the final rank attained), one or more incidents during his career that illustrated his character, one or more illustrative excerpts from his memorials to the throne or other writings, and finally his posthumous title.

There later developed the genre of *nianpu* (annalistic biography), in which all known facts of a person's life from birth to death were related in strict chronological order of occurrence. Some persons wrote *nianpu* of their own lives. The *nianpu*, too, is different from the modern Western concept of biography or autobiography. It can best be thought of as a systematic card file. As always, the main emphasis is on the public side of the person's life.

Another somewhat later genre, preserved from as far back as the Song dynasty, is that of *riji* (daily notes, diaries). These, too, tend to impress the modern reader as remarkably impersonal, but in the Chinese context there was little place for "confessional" autobiography since in China a gentleman's public behavior was not to be taken as deliberate role playing that had little to do with the "real" person behind it. On the contrary, in his public behavior the man was truly himself, and his words were to be the expression of sincere feeling. In this sense, it could even be said that all literature, and especially poetry, was autobiographical, so that no distinct genre of autobiography was necessary. Whereas a British elder statesman might spend his last years writing his memoirs, his Chinese counterpart turned his attention to the editing of his own collected works, perhaps taking care to delete certain items.

The Chinese genre that most closely approaches Western autobiography is the *xu* (explanation, apologia; usually translated as preface, though in older texts it is actually the last item in a book), in which the author of a book explains why and under what circumstances he wrote the book. A famous example of a *xu* is the one written by Sima Qian for his *Shiji*.

HISTORICAL FICTION AND HISTORICAL ROMANCE

History was rarely written in the form of a connected story. The epic, which served as a model for the early Greek historians, was unknown in ancient China. In traditional Chinese historical literature, the facts relevant to a given event or development are scattered over various sections and chapters of a book. Biographical facts relating to a given historical figure are often to be found in biographies of his contemporaries in the same work.

Texts did exist, especially from the sixteenth century on, in which history, though based on disparate sources, was told as a connected story. These works, however, were regarded as novels—in other words, as fiction not history. They were written in the vernacular and often made at least some use of material from oral traditions. Called in English *historical romances*, these works never won entry into the traditional corpus of histories, though their scope came to cover the whole of Chinese history. Owing to their considerable quantity of legendary material, they cannot claim to be reliable, let alone scholarly, though their manner of presentation is at times excellent. Nevertheless, in practice they were often undoubtedly more influential in shaping their readers' conception of Chinese history than all other forms of historical writing.

THE PLACE OF THE HISTORIES IN CHINESE LITERATURE

Despite their biases traditional Chinese histories represent an immense body of useful material for modern historians. But what is of interest to the historian may not be so to the reader of literature. Traditional Chinese historical writing is *official* in every sense of the word: substantial and reliable, but dry and drab. Only the earliest historical works, like the *Shiji* and *Han shu*, whose authors could make but limited use of existing texts and archives and were forced to come up with their own interpretations, have great literary value. The *Shiji* is unanimously regarded as one of the masterworks of Chinese literature.

The Histories were, however, of tremendous importance for Chinese literature. Probably no other civilization has had such a strong consciousness of history as the Central Tradition in China. The present, in its constantly shifting configurations, was the repetition of a continually recurrent past. The present was understandable only to the extent that it could be seen as a reflection of history. Describing the present in terms of the past was not an idle display of erudition; it was simply the only possible form of understanding. If the relevant historical precedent could be identified, the apparent randomness of the present could become comprehensible as one phase in the cyclic transformation of the Way. The historical allusion, the description of current events as if one were speaking of their distant precedents, the characterization of a person in terms of a historical figure—these were not frills, not mere stylistic tricks, but necessities. Writers and readers of traditional high literature shared a common knowledge of history as it had taken form in traditional historiography: a virtually inexhaustible fund of events and figures through which every conceivable contemporary situation could be typified and evaluated.

Chapter 8.
THE PHILOSOPHERS

THE PHILOSOPHICAL SCHOOLS

Against a background of dramatic political and social change, the period from the sixth century B.C. onward saw the growth of philosophical speculation on the nature and functioning of the cosmos, of society, and of man. This philosophical interest is reflected in the *Shujing*, the *Guoyu*, and the *Zuo zhuan*, but it comes into its own in the so-called philosophical works, traditionally regarded as the teaching of one particular master but in fact seldom written by a single author. The intellectual life of this period was characterized by the coexistence of distinct schools which, however bitterly opposed to each other's ideas, sometimes showed curious cross-relationships: the "Legalist" Li Si was a pupil of the "Confucianist" Xun Qing, and the "Legalist" Han Fei quoted the "Taoist" *Daode jing* with approval. The nature of the schools also varied considerably. Some appear to have had a very strict internal organization; others, a loose teacher-disciple network. Some "schools" may even reflect the bibliographers' need for systematization rather than any social reality. Writers of the third and second centuries B.C., not surprisingly, show considerable differences in their classification of schools.

The division of the Philosophers into nine schools (*jiu jia*) goes back to the *Yiwen zhi* (Treatise on letters) in Ban Gu's *Han shu*. The nine schools are:
1) the Confucianists (*ru jia*),
2) the Taoists (*dao jia*),
3) the Naturalists (*yinyang jia*),
4) the Legalists (*fa jia*),
5) the Logicians (*ming jia*),
6) the Mohists (*mo jia*),
7) the Diplomats (*zongheng jia*),
8) the Eclectics (*za jia*), and
9) the Agriculturalists (*nong jia*).
The "tellers of fables" (*xiaoshuo jia*) are mentioned as a tenth school.

Some of the schools are known to us on the basis of preserved texts; for others, such as the Naturalists and Agriculturalists, there is no single extant text associated with the school. The *Zhanguo ce* could be regarded as a text of the Diplomats school. Of some philosophical works, only fragments remain. Recent archaeological digs have unearthed nearly contemporary manuscripts of several known texts, as well as some manuscripts of previously unknown or lost works, enabling us to fill out the picture of the development of Chinese philosophy in this period. Some of these recently recovered writings are associated with the Huang-Lao branch of political philosophy (named after the Yellow Emperor and Laozi), which flourished at the Han dynasty court during the first half of the second century B.C.

Forms of Philosophical Writing

China's oldest philosophical works are in dialog form. But unlike Plato's dialogs, a fictional literary form which the writer used as a framework to develop his own ideas, Chinese philosophical dialogs theoretically record real conversations which a master's disciples wrote down from memory after his death.

In the oldest of these works, the *Lunyu*, the dialogs are often very short. Some are simply isolated remarks by Confucius or one of his disciples. Moreover, the *Lunyu* has little discernible order in the sayings. In the somewhat later *Mengzi*, the dialogs tend to be longer, and those dealing with a given subject are grouped together where possible.

Later works abandon the dialog form and collate the sayings according to subject. Often, however, this still produces no continuous argument. Examples can be found in the third important work of early Confucianism, the *Xunzi*, which is supposed to contain the teachings of Xun Qing (?–ca. 238 B.C.).

A similar form is evident in the *Zhuangzi*, the most important Taoist work, said to have been written in part by Zhuang Zhou (ca. 369–ca. 286 B.C.). Every chapter consists of a long exposition, whether technical or lyrical—sometimes in allegorical form—followed by a number of short anecdotes and sayings on the same subject.

The next stylistic development is a structure in which each chapter is a coherent treatise in itself. This is the case, for example, in the most important Legalist book, the *Han Feizi*, which probably was actually written for the most part by Han Fei (280–233 B.C.) himself. In the Han and later, a collection of essays became the usual philosophical form, a tradition which probably reached its pinnacle in the erudite, astute essays by Wang Chong (27–97?) as collected under the title *Lun heng* (Steelyard of expositions).

On occasion philosophical writings also made use of verse. The *Daode jing* (Book of the Way and virtue), a Taoist work of perhaps the fourth century

B.C. which is attributed to the legendary Laozi, uses gnomic verse; wisdom of a strongly paradoxical cast is put into rhyme. The *Zhuangzi*, too, contains a number of passages in poetic form.

Since the oldest philosophical works were collections of texts and sayings of and about the master that were in circulation among his disciples, one can discern various layers in these compilations. The absence of a single author gives some of these works structural or compositional features that would be unacceptable in a modern context. In the *Mozi*, which is based on the thought of Mo Di (?–392 B.C.), many of Mo Di's ponderous sermons are repeated in three practically identical versions.

The second and third centuries B.C. also saw the composition of philosophical works by groups of scholars which resemble eclectic encyclopedias, though they bear the name of the eminent gentleman whose patronage made publication possible. An example is the *Huainanzi*, written under the patronage of the prince of Huainan, Liu An (179–122 B.C.).

THE CONFUCIANISTS

The most important philosophical school is that of the Confucianists. The oldest preserved work, the *Lunyu* (Selected sayings), consists of sayings of Confucius, sayings of his disciples, and brief dialogs. It was compiled during the two or three generations following the death of the master in 479 B.C. The sayings and dialogs, nearly 500 in all, are often extremely short and pithy. They are divided, in no clear order, into twenty books put together in various periods. The sayings and dialogs are often strongly anecdotal and some make lively reading, but there is no attempt at systematic recording of dialog.

The *Mengzi* (Mencius) records the exchanges between Meng Ke (372–289 B.C.) and rulers or other contemporaries. These dialogs, probably compiled by Master Meng's pupils not long after his death, are grouped into seven books, each of two parts. The dialogs are much more extensive than those in the *Lunyu* and include detailed argumentation and development of ideas. The writing shows notable clarity and variety, and similar subjects are grouped together.

One of Mencius's basic ideas—that man is naturally good—is diametrically opposed in the *Xunzi*, where we read that man is naturally bad and can function in society only by virtue of the correcting influence of education and ritual. The *Xunzi* comprises thirty-two independent essays. Some may have been written by Xun Qing (Xun Kuang, ?–ca. 238 B.C.), but others date from the second century B.C. The *Xunzi* employs few anecdotes and practically no dialogs. The essays contain strictly rational attacks on many forms of belief and superstition. Some chapters are in verse.

Certain passages from the *Xunzi* recur almost verbatim in the *Liji* (Notes on the rites). Together with the *Zhou li* (Rites of Zhou) and the *Yi li* (rules and rites), this work shares the collective designation *Li* (Rites), traditionally regarded as a single one of the Five Classics. The *Zhou li*, also known as the *Zhou guan* (Officials of the Zhou), is a dry, detailed description of the hypothetical structure of government under the earliest Zhou kings. Traditionally attributed to the duke of Zhou (Zhou Gong), it was at various times used as a pretext for drastic reform proposals. For this reason some have suggested that the *Zhou li* was originally written for Wang Mang by the imperial librarian Liu Xin, the son of Liu Xiang. The *Zhou li* probably dates from the fourth or third century B.C.

The *Yi li* exhaustively describes the rules and prescriptions governing important events in the lives of rulers and nobles under the Zhou. Like the *Zhou li*, it is probably idealization after the fact.

The *Liji*, a collection of forty-nine texts of widely varying date and content, was compiled in its present form by Dai Sheng in the early years of the first century B.C. Some of the texts, like those in the *Yi li*, are concerned with detailed rules; others are in the form of essays (e.g., on music) like those in the *Xunzi*. Still others are collections of pronouncements on the Confucian rites. Two of the chapters, *Daxue* (The great learning) and *Zhongyong* (The central mean), were later designated by Zhu Xi (A.D. 1130–1200) as two of the Four Books (*sishu*) that were to serve as a general introduction to Confucianism (the other two Books were the *Lunyu* and the *Mengzi*). From the Ming dynasty on, these Four Books were among the most important materials studied by all participants for the state examinations.

The *Liji* was compiled by Dai Sheng on the basis of a more extensive effort by his uncle Dai De. The texts from the latter work which do not appear in the *Liji* are preserved under the title *Da Dai Liji* (Notes of the elder Dai concerning rites). Most of the *Da Dai Liji* texts probably date from the first century of the Han.

The *Xiaojing* (Book of filial piety), a short text in the form of a dialog between Confucius and a disciple, stresses the importance of *xiao*, the Chinese traditional virtue of reverence and obedience to be observed by the young toward their elders.

The *Chunqiu fanlu* (Abundant dew of the Annals of spring and autumn), a work in eighty-two sections ascribed to Dong Zhongshu (179-104 B.C.), is important for its treatment of the relations between Heaven, Earth, and Man. Through this work many of the speculations of the Naturalists on such subjects as *yin* and *yang* and the Five Phases (*wu xing*) found their way into Confucianism.

In the *Fayan* (Exemplary words) by Yang Xiong (53 B.C.–A.D. 18), each chapter treats one subject in dialog form. The style is highly archaic. Yang Xiong condemns various heresies prevalent in his day, even going so far as to attack his own poetry.

From the Han on, the *Yijing* was also regarded as one of the Five Classics. The *Yijing* (Book of changes; also known as the *Zhouyi* or "Changes of Zhou") presents sixty-four hexagrams with their cryptic interpretations; this part of the book is probably of very ancient origin. It also includes a number of essays filled with cosmological speculations, which probably date from the fifth to the second century B.C.

The *Kongzi jiayu* (Sayings from the school of Master Kong) is a compilation of traditional material related or attributed to Confucius but not included in the *Lunyu*. It probably dates from the Earlier Han but was published anew in the first half of the third century A.D. by Wang Su, who added new material to the collection.

THE MOHISTS AND THE LOGICIANS

The philosopher Mo Di (?–392 B.C.) is famous for his defense of universal love and pacifism. His doctrine of universal love, his plea for austerity in the matter of burials, and his condemnation of music were all sharply opposed by Mencius. The writings of the Mohist school are collected in the *Mozi*. This work must have been compiled at a time when the school was already divided into three branches for a fair number of the texts are presented in two or three slightly different versions. Some of the oldest books contain dialogs; there are also essays written in a cumbersome, repetitive style. Chapters of relatively late date treat such subjects as defense technology, strategy, and logic.

The only preserved work specifically on logic is the *Gongsun Longzi* (master Gongsun Long). The oldest preserved full-length treatise on warfare is the *Sunzi* (Master Sun).

THE LEGALISTS

The most important works of the Legalist school are the *Shangjun shu* (writings of the Lord of Shang) and the *Han Feizi* (Master Han Fei). The *Shangjun shu* is thought to comprise the teaching of Wei Yang (d. 338 B.C.), an advisor of the Qin ruler, who was enfeoffed with Shang. Like the *Han Feizi*, it is mostly in essay form.

The *Han Feizi*, which consists of fifty-five books, was probably written in large part by Han Fei (d. 233 B.C.) himself. The essays are famous for their clarity and liveliness and owe much to their apt use of fable and anecdote, as does the *Zhanguo ce*. From a literary point of view, the *Han Feizi* is one of the most important philosophical works.

THE TAOISTS

The most important Taoist writings are the *Daode jing*, the *Zhuangzi*, and the *Liezi*. The *Daode jing* (Book of the Way and Virtue) is attributed to Laozi (the Old Master), who was, according to legend, an older contemporary of Confucius. Some scholars place the origin of the *Daode jing* in the sixth century B.C. and others in the third. This short book, in eighty-one sections, consists for the most part of suggestions for the ideal ruler, formulated in aphoristic verses with interspersed ancient glosses. In later centuries, it was often read as a mystical text.

Most important of all the Taoist writings is the thirty-three-book *Zhuangzi* (Master Zhuang). It is possible that the first seven books were actually written by Zhuang Zhou (369–286 B.C.); the others date from the third and second centuries B.C. Most of the books consist of a rather long discussion of a specific subject, followed by a number of thematically relevant anecdotes and fables. The essay or discussion sections are sometimes very technical, sometimes brilliantly poetic. Occasional use is made of the dialog and the allegorical dialogs are famous. The *Zhuangzi* is outspoken in its attacks on Confucianism, and Confucius is often made to appear ridiculous. And whereas most philosophical works are at least theoretically meant to be read by the ruler, the *Zhuangzi* is addressed to the "'hermit." In terms of literary value, the *Zhuangzi* is unquestionably the most important of the philosophical books.

Comparable to the *Zhuangzi* in some respects, the *Liezi* (Master Lie) is shorter, simpler in style, and less imaginative. Though this eight-book work did not attain its present form until the fourth century A.D., it includes much older material.

The *Baopuzi* (The Master who cherishes simplicity), by Ge Hong (284–364), includes much discussion of the various methods of gaining physical immortality.

THE ECLECTICS

A number of philosophical works are too heterogenous to classify with any particular school; they are more in the nature of compendia. The *Guanzi* (Master Guan) takes its name from Guan Zhong (early seventh century B.C.), the chief advisor to Duke Huan of Qi (the first of the Five Hegemons), but most of its content probably dates from the fourth and third centuries B.C. It includes notable chapters on fiscal and economic policies. The *Guanzi* is sometimes regarded as a Legalist work.

The *Yanzi chunqiu* (Master Yan's Spring and Autumn) presents advice for rulers in the form of dialogues between Yan Ying (?–500 B.C.) and successive dukes of Qi. This work, in eight books, consists mostly of sermons but includes an occasional humorous anecdote.

The *Lüshi chunqiu* (Lord Lü's Spring and Autumn) was compiled by scholars under the patronage of Lü Buwei (d. 235 B.C.), chancellor of Qin. It is intended as a comprehensive outline of human knowledge. The same is true of the *Huainanzi* (Master Huainan), compiled by scholars under the patronage of the prince of Huainan, Liu An (d. 122 B.C.). The *Huainanzi* is often classified as Taoist.

The *Yantie lun* (Debate on salt and iron), by Huan Kuan (early first century B.C.), reports on a debate held at court in 81 B.C. This discussion of economic policy occasioned a sharp clash between proponents of Confucianist and Legalist policies.

In the *Baihu tong(yi)* (Debate in the White Tiger Hall), Ban Gu reports on a debate at court in A.D. 79 on the subject of the correct interpretation of the Classics, especially as regards ritual matters.

Roughly contemporary with this work is the *Lun heng* (Steelyard of expositions), an original Han philosophical work in eighty-five chapters by Wang Chong (A.D. 27–97?). The essays in the *Lun heng* are noted for their stylistic clarity and for the virulence of their attacks on widespread conventional forms of superstition.

PHILOSOPHICAL WRITINGS FROM THE SECOND CENTURY ON

From the second century A.D. on, the number of new philosophical books written in the Central Tradition declined strikingly. Authors became more attracted to commenting on existing texts or expressing their ideas in essays or letters which later became part of their collected works. The relative lack of philosophical works certainly did not indicate any diminution in philosophical activity, though the modern student of the period might wish it had been recorded in more neatly organized form.

In the Song dynasty, the Central Tradition borrowed from Chan (Zen) Buddhism the use of *yulu* (records of conversations). *Yulu* originally were word-for-word accounts of conversations between master and disciple; they also include students' notes on the master's sermons and lectures. As verbatim accounts they are, of course, written in the contemporary vernacular. The *yulu* of some Neo-Confucian philosophers, such as Zhu Xi, are very extensive and give what seems to be an accurate impression of the form and content of their instruction.

PROFESSIONAL LITERATURES

If the Philosophers attempt to formulate general rules applicable to man, society, and cosmos, the professional literatures attempt to apply these regularities in the concrete terms of a specific field. In other words, they are Philosophers with a specialty. It is understandable, therefore, that traditional bibliographers classify professional literature as belonging to the Philosophers. This holds true of Buddhist and religious-Taoist literature as well, though such works were included less frequently than literature on medical, military, and agricultural subjects.

THE PLACE OF THE PHILOSOPHERS
IN CHINESE LITERATURE

The Philosophers are of varying interest to the modern reader. If they include tedious orations and sermons, they also feature the lively dialogs of the *Lunyu* and especially the *Mengzi*, as well as the bright, well-written essays of Han Fei and Wang Chong. The high point of Chinese philosophical literature, and by universal agreement one of the masterpieces of world literature, is the *Zhuangzi* with its wealth of allegories and anecdotes, its brilliant humor and satire. For Chinese literary history, it is especially the Confucian and Taoist works that are relevant. As we have already seen, the *Lunyu* and *Mengzi* were later often considered to belong to the Classics; until the early years of the twentieth century they were regarded as the sources of all wisdom and formed the indispensable core of all forms of education. Within the Central Tradition, Taoist works never attained a comparable degree of importance, but all well-educated and reasonably liberal literati were familiar with the *Daode jing* and *Zhuangzi*, seeing them as a sort of useful appendix to the primary texts. Chinese literature is replete with references and quotes relating to these texts; they were especially well-loved by authors writing on nature mysticism or on the satisfactions of a life in retirement.

From the Confucian Philosophers a gentleman gained an understanding of the Way in its diversity; from the Taoist writings, if he wished, he could learn to contemplate the Way in its totality. If the former codified the norms for behavior in public life, the latter could be consulted when normal participation in public life was impossible because of circumstances or personal character. In this sense the Taoist books played a modest role in the Central Tradition by virtue of their usefulness as complement or counterfoil. The philosophical works of the other schools were much less widely read and studied, at least before book printing, but they were never entirely forgotten.

Chapter 9.
POETRY

THE *SHIJING*

The oldest preserved collection of Chinese poetry, the *Shijing* (Book of odes), consists of 305 poems dating from roughly 1000 to 600 B.C. The collection probably attained its present form not long after 600 B.C. Sima Qian and later writers named Confucius as the editor of the *Shijing*; the tradition was that he had selected the poems from an original body of about 3,000. Whatever its exact origin, the collection is referred to and quoted in the *Lunyu*.

The *Shijing* has four main sections: *(guo)feng, xiaoya, daya,* and *song*. Though it is possible that the terms originally referred to the type of musical performance associated with the songs in each section, they are now taken to be descriptions of the poems' contents. The 160 poems in the *guofeng* (tunes from the states) are divided among 15 small states in the North China Plain. They may well have been folk songs originally, but it is clear that they were edited and revised, probably at the court of Zhou. Their subject matter is extremely varied, touching every aspect of contemporary life. Most are very short. In the *Shijing* as a whole the characteristic poetic line consists of four syllables; in the *guofeng*, four or six such lines are often combined into a stanza, the poem frequently comprising only two or three stanzas.

The *xiaoya* (smaller odes) section contains seventy-four poems; the *daya* (greater odes), thirty-one. The poems often concern the life of the nobility, and most were probably written by aristocrats. In general, they are longer than the poems in the *guofeng*. The *daya* include a number of poems praising memorable deeds of the great Zhou rulers and describing the origins of the ruling house. These poems are long by *Shijing* standards (e.g., eight stanzas of eight lines), but despite their narrative qualities, it would be going too far to describe them as epic poems. The *song* (hymns) comprise forty poems, presumably hymns which were sung or recited during religious ceremonies at the Zhou court. (A few hymns from Song and Lu are also included.) In the other three divisions of the *Shijing* the even lines rhyme, but in the *song* there are some unrhymed poems. The *song* poems are the oldest in the *Shijing*; the *guofeng* are the most recent.

Many poems in the *song*, *daya*, and *xiaoya* are concerned with important matters of state. Besides songs of praise, the *daya* and *xiaoya* include undisguised poems of complaint; political satire may also be present. The traditional commentators read all the poems, even in the *guofeng*, as political statements. Practically every poem was taken to refer to a specific historical situation, and putative authors were named—sometimes just "the people" of a particular state, sometimes an individual like the duke of Zhou. The poems were subjected to interpretations that seem highly far-fetched to the modern mind. But for the traditional commentators, it went without saying that a poem, and certainly a poem included in such a classic as the *Shijing*, must be a statement of the author's feelings about the ruler and his administration. Beginning in the Han dynasty, it was believed that the poems in the *Shijing* had originally been collected by officials specially sent out from the Zhou court. It was supposed that the Son of Heaven read the songs produced by the people of the various states in order to get an impression of the quality of government in their areas. Some of the ancient interpretations were so obviously unbelievable as to draw condemnation from later Chinese scholars. Zhu Xi (1130–1200), among others, took a stand against certain bizarre, though time-honored, allegorical readings.

After the burning of the books under the Qin, the *Shijing* was preserved and transmitted under the Earlier Han in four slightly varying versions, each with its own tradition of commentary. The version that ultimately supplanted the others and was transmitted to posterity was the version preserved and interpreted by members of the Mao family. Accordingly, the *Shijing* is often referred to as the *Mao Shi*. One of the other versions, the incompletely preserved Han version, seems to have devoted particular attention to the art, already well-attested in the *Zuo zhuan*, of producing apt quotes from the *Shijing* on specific occasions. This Han school has left us a collection of anecdotes, the *Han Shi waizhuan*, in which each item is validated with a quote from the *Shijing*.

Poems from the *Shijing* are frequently quoted in early historical and philosophical texts. These works also contain a small number of poems in the same vein that are not included in the presently preserved *Shijing*.

THE *CHUCI*

The *Chuci* (Songs of Chu) is an anthology of entirely different character. It is said to have been compiled originally by Liu Xiang (76–5 B.C.); it was later provided with commentary by Wang Yi (d. A.D. 158), who also added his own work to the collection.

The oldest parts of the *Chuci* are from the state of Chu and may date from the fourth century B.C. The collection contains, first of all, a number of religious songs. These include the "Tianwen" (Heavenly questionings), a catechism-in-verse of ancient Chinese mythology (but without the answers to the questions), the "Zhaohun" (Summons to the soul), and the "Dazhao" (Great summons). In the "Zhaohun" and the "Dazhao," the soul of a deceased king is called back into his body by the expedient of first listing the terrors likely to be encountered in all possible directions (east, west, north, south, heaven, and underworld) and then cataloging in detail the pleasures available at the palace. Other examples of religious poetry are found in the section called "Jiuge" (Nine songs). The "Jiuge" contains shaman songs, usually consisting of two parts. In the first part, the shaman or shamanka describes the preparations for a journey in search of a god and the subsequent journey; in the second part, he or she expresses disappointment that the god could not be found or has since departed. The relation between the shaman (whether male or female) and the god or spirit is strongly erotic. It is not known whether or not these songs played a secular role at the Chu court.

The opening poem of the *Chuci*, the "Lisao" (Encountering sorrows), is ascribed to Qu Yuan, who is supposed to have lived in the late fourth and early third centuries B.C. Owing to slander by jealous rivals at court, he fell into disfavor with the king of Chu and—so the legend continues—was banished; subsequently, fearing that his sincerity and loyalty would never be recognized, he committed suicide. In later centuries Qu Yuan became the archetypical model of the loyal but unrecognized official, while in modern times he has been taken as the type of the patriot. The famous dragon-boat races, still held yearly on the fifth day of the fifth lunar month, are said to have originated in attempts to rescue Qu Yuan.

The "Lisao" is a long poem (374 lines), in which two themes predominate. The first laments a degenerate age in which values have been reversed: contemptible persons are raised to prominence while the worthy are banished. The plaint is sometimes direct, sometimes allegorical. The second theme is the poet's journey through the cosmos in search of the beloved; the search fails. The treatment of this second theme shows clear influence of shaman songs like those in the "Jiuge," but in the "Lisao" the quest for the beloved, and the ultimate disappointment, allegorically represent the minister's loyalty to the ruler and his fall from favor owing to the influence of slanderers.

Other songs in the *Chuci* treat various episodes in the legend of Qu Yuan, such as "Buju" (The consulting of the oracle) and "Yufu" (The fisherman). Still others, written in imitation of the "Lisao," represent the authors' frustration at their failure to gain recognition for their talents. This last group includes works by Jia Yi (200–168 B.C.), Dongfang Shuo (154–93 B.C.), and Liu Xiang (ca. 76–5 B.C.).

Some of the older songs in the *Chuci* are often ascribed to Song Yu, who is supposed to have lived in Chu in the third century BC. Later anecdotes portray Song Yu as the ideal courtier: a handsome man and witty speaker who broke women's hearts through no fault of his own. In the "Jiubian" (Nine pleas), usually attributed to Song Yu, a prominent theme is the quick passage of time and the consequent end of youth and hope.

The form of the poems in the *Chuci* is different from that of the *Shijing* poems. For one thing, the *Chuci* poems are often longer, without division into stanzas (though the concluding section is sometimes designated as a *luan*, or *envoi*). Some of the *Chuci* poems have four-syllable lines; the even lines rhyme, while the odd lines are followed by the meaningless syllable *xi*. In the "Lisao" and certain other poems, use is made of a six-syllable line in which the antepenultimate syllable is unstressed, a grammatical particle usually occupying this position. Here, too, even lines rhyme and odd lines are followed by the syllable *xi*.

THE *FU* OF SIMA XIANGRU AND OTHERS

The *fu* has, on the one hand, clear affinities with the poetry of the *Chuci*. At the same time, it clearly shows the influence of rhetoric as practiced by the Diplomats (*zongheng jia*) and recorded in the *Zhanguo ce*. The *fu* is a type of poem in which an object, action, or feeling is described in exhaustive detail. The author not only tries to deal with all aspects of his subject matter, he also tries to exhaust all relevant resources of the language. It is probably no accident that some of the earliest *fu* poets are also known as lexicographers. At times they show such a predilection for lists and catalogs that their work is perhaps better characterized as "enumerative" than "descriptive." What may well be the oldest *fu*, occurring as a chapter in the *Xunzi*, are actually riddles.

The *fu* was intended to be read aloud, not sung; in this respect it differs from all other genres of traditional Chinese poetry, as these all originated in song. Accordingly, a fixed line-length was less essential in *fu* than in other poetic forms. The lines in the *fu* may vary with each couplet, lines of four or six syllables being the most frequent. The even lines rhyme, and a change of subject often goes together with a change of rhyme. The length of a *fu* depends on its subject. Prose passages may occur as an introduction to the *fu* or as insertions providing variety. In Chinese anthologies *fu* are usually grouped together with the various prose genres, because *fu* cannot be classified as *shi*; a general category of "poetry" is unknown. But this does not mean that we should not treat the *fu* as a genre of poetry. Translations of the word *fu* as "rhymed prose," "prose poem," or "poetic essay" are misleading.

Song Yu is credited with the authorship of a large number of *fu*, most of which actually date from the second century B.C. or later. Some of these have considerable literary value. Examples are the "Feng fu" (The wind), in which the wind as experienced by the king is contrasted with the wind in the lives of the commoners, the wind representing lifestyle and influence; the "Gaotang fu" (Mt. Gaotang), describing Mt. Gaotang, where the Goddess of Mt. Wu was supposed to have offered herself to a king of Chu in a dream; and the "Nüshen fu" (The goddess), describing the apparition of the Goddess of Mt. Wu herself.

The oldest preserved and definitely datable *fu* is the "Funiao fu" (The owl), composed by Jia Yi (200–168 B.C.) after his exile to Changsha. It is a rather unusual *fu* in that it devotes much space to philosophical reflection, expressing an attitude of resignation that clearly harks back to the *Zhuangzi*. The poet Mei Cheng (d. 140 B.C.?) is the author of the "Qi fa" (Seven stimuli). This poem, addressed to "a sick prince of Chu," seeks to arouse the sick man to activity by presenting an attractive description of seven delights: zither music, exquisite foods, a pleasant ride, a feast at the palace, a hunt, a victory celebration, and a visit to the seashore—but in the end the only thing that can revive the prince from his lethargy is the prospect of enjoying a discussion with scholars. Imitations of this *fu*, in which not one but seven subjects are attempted, were so many as to constitute a distinct subgenre, the *qi* (seven).

Unquestionably the most famous *fu* poet is Sima Xiangru (179–118 B.C.), a native of Chengdu. Failing in his first attempts to find employment at court, he returned penniless to Sichuan, where he carried off the young widow Zhuo Wenjun after first seducing her with his zither playing. Her rich father refused to support the couple financially. They began operating a wineshop at the market—but meanwhile, Sima's "Zixu fu" (Sir Fantasy) had been brought to the attention of Emperor Wu, who summoned him to court on its merits. The "Zixu fu" describes the hunting parks of the princes of Qi and Chu. Later Sima Xiangru wrote for Emperor Wu his greatest work, an expansion of the "Zixu fu" called the "Shanglin fu" (The Imperial Park). It describes in superlatives the Imperial hunting preserve. "Zixu fu" and "Shanglin fu" are often classed together as a single work under the title "Shanglin fu." The "Shanglin fu" is noted not only for its length but also for the richness of its vocabulary. The "Shanglin fu" was preserved because it was included in Sima Xiangru's biography in the *Shiji* (and in the *Han shu*), which also includes two other, shorter *fu*.

The erudite scholar Yang Xiong (53 B.C.-A.D. 18) is the author of six extant *fu*. The most famous, the "Changyang fu" (Tall poplars), is a virtuoso description of an imperial hunt in the vicinity of the Changyang palace. In his later work *Fayan* (Exemplary words), Yang turned against the *fu* on the grounds that whereas the legitimate function of the *fu* should be *feng* (disguised criticism), the luxurious descriptions common in *fu* more often encouraged rather than censured improper conduct.

The historian Ban Gu (32–92) also wrote *fu*. The best-known is the "Liang du fu" (The two capitals), in which the capital of the Western Han, Chang'an, is compared unfavorably with the Eastern Han capital, Luoyang. Zhang Heng (78–139), a famous statesman and scholar who was, among other things, the inventor of a type of seismograph, wrote the "Liang jing fu" (The two metropolises), in which the simplicity of Chang'an appears in stark contrast to the luxury of Luoyang.

The *fu* described so far are, on the whole, relatively long. But there are also a few attractive short *fu* from Later Han times, including the "Guitian fu" (Back to the fields) by Zhang Heng and the "Meng fu" (The nightmare) and "Wangsun fu" (The orangutan), both by the short-lived Wang Yanshou (second century A.D.). Of many *fu* from the Earlier and Later Han periods, only fragments remain.

Part III.
From the Invention of Paper
to the Spread of Book Printing

CHINESE POLITICAL HISTORY, 100–700

Popular rebellions rocked the Han dynasty in A.D. 184. They were quickly suppressed, but the generals assigned to the task soon turned against each other, robbing the central court of all its power. Eventually northern China became the domain of the warlord Cao Cao (155–220). In the Southeast Sun Quan held sway, while the Southwest was occupied by Liu Bei, who claimed to be a member of the imperial family. Upon the death of Cao Cao, his son Cao Pi accepted the abdication of the last Han emperor, thereby becoming the first emperor of the Wei dynasty (220–264). Sun Quan now declared himself emperor of the Wu dynasty (221–280), while Liu Bei ascended the throne as heir to the Han. His dynasty is usually referred to as the Shu-Han (221–263): "Shu" is an old name for western Sichuan.

At the court of the Wei, real power soon came into the hands of the generals of the Sima family. Following their conquest of the territory of Shu-Han, they accepted the abdication of the last Wei emperor and established the Jin dynasty (265–419). The Jin succeeded in reunifying the Chinese world by their conquest of Wu in 280, but after the turn of the century the Jin itself was plagued by internal warfare among the imperial princes, and the capital city of Luoyang went up in flames. One of the princes set himself up as emperor in Jianye (the modern Nanjing), and from there the Jin continued to rule southern China for another century. Northern China was ruled during the fourth century by a quick succession of short-lived dynasties; many of the ruling families were from non-Chinese backgrounds. During the troubled early decades of the fourth century, many elite families from North China moved to the South.

At Jianye the Jin was eventually displaced by the Song dynasty (420–479); to distinguish it from the much more famous later Song dynasty, this one is often referred to as the Liu Song, because Liu was the family name of the ruling house. This dynasty in turn gave way to the Qi (479–501), which eventually was succeeded by the Liang (502–556). The Liang dynasty lavishly supported Buddhism, which had entered China during the Later Han and acquired a wide following from the fourth century on. Upon the collapse of the Liang, the Chen dynasty (557–589) took power.

During these centuries in the North the most long-lasting dynasty was the Wei (386–534), which had been established by the non-Chinese Toba. Their capital, originally at Datong, was eventually moved to Luoyang. In the second

103

half of the sixth century, all of northern China was again unified by the Sui dynasty (589–618). During the reign of its second emperor, Emperor Yang (r. 605–617), great public works (e.g., the Grand Canal) and long but unsuccessful military campaigns against Korea exhausted the population and caused widespread rebellion. The ensuing civil war resulted in the victory of Li Yuan, who proceeded to found the Tang dynasty (618–906). Later tradition attributes the virtual founding of the dynasty to his son Li Shimin, who in 627 killed his elder brother the crown prince and supplanted his father on the throne. The Tang took over the capital of the Sui (the modern Xi'an) but renamed it Chang'an. The court, however, also frequently stayed at the secondary capital of Luoyang.

During the long reign of Li Shimin's son and successor Emperor Gaozong (r. 649–683), real power at court gravitated to his consort Lady Wu and her relatives. After his death Lady Wu became the only woman in history to ascend the throne herself; she is known as Empress Wu Zetian (r. 690–705). She changed the name of the dynasty to Zhou, had many of the Li princes killed, and was a great patron of Buddhism. In the end, however, she was persuaded to restore the Tang dynasty.

Chapter 10.
FU, PROSE, AND LITERARY CRITICISM

THE INVENTION OF PAPER AND THE GROWING
CORPUS OF LITERATURE

The perfection of paper as a suitable material for writing by the end of the first century marks a watershed in the development of Chinese literature. Prior to the first century A.D., no collected works by individual Chinese authors are still extant. Only the great historical and philosophical works have come down to us. Letters, memorials, and other short prose forms were preserved if they happened to be included in historical works such as the *Shiji* and the *Han shu*. The *Shiji* is also an important source of early poetry; the works of Sima Xiangru, for example, owe their preservation to the *Shiji*. There are also the two great early poetry anthologies, *Shijing* and *Chuci*.

Starting in the second century A.D., we begin to encounter the "collected works" (*ji*) of an increasing number of authors, and the collections are more and more extensive as time goes by. In the first few centuries after the year 100, these preserved works were usually not compiled by the authors themselves or by others during or soon after their lifetimes. They are compilations based on later anthologies and encyclopedias. In later periods, the author or close descendants edited an author's collected works.

Works of individual authors have been preserved in a wide variety of forms, bound and free, *fu* and *shi*, memorials (*biao*), treatises (*lun*), letters (*shu*), biographical writings, etc. As *shi* poetry is treated separately in chapter 11 it will not be discussed here.

THE SHORT PROSE GENRES

Within the vast field of prose, a large number of distinct genres came to be recognized. Early in the third century no more than six were mentioned; by early in the sixth century nearly twenty were recognized, and in the eighteenth century more than a hundred genres were distinguished. The nomenclature of the genres was based only in part on formal characteristics.

The classification was most fundamentally a matter of the function the texts fulfilled in society, especially in government: who was addressing whom, and to what purpose? Texts dealing with the same subject, but in different forms (e.g., the memorial, the letter, and the treatise) might at times differ only as regards their preamble and conclusion, not in the manner in which the subject was treated in the main body of the text. By contrast, definition of poetic genres is very much centered on formal criteria like rhyme structure and line length.

Among the prose genres, many of the most prominent were those frequently used in the bureaucracy. If a career in government was the highest calling possible for a gentleman, it was logical for him to regard the texts he wrote in office, contributing to society's well-being, as the most important of all his works. The bureaucratic piece, especially the memorial to the throne in which the writer put into words—to be read by the ruler!—his feelings on a given social issue, was one of the most important forms of literature. Many a writer's collected works consist mainly or wholly of bureaucratic pieces, with memorials predominant. The memorial was subdivided into various types depending on whether the writer thanks the ruler for a favor, proclaims his agreement with a measure or policy, expresses his disapproval of a decision, makes a proposal of his own, or congratulates the ruler on the appearance of a good omen.

Other bureaucratic prose genres were used for communication with colleagues or subordinates. There were various forms used by the ruler to issue edicts, depending on the occasion on which and the person or persons to whom the proclamation was made. Akin to these were the texts used for certain sacrificial rites, declarations of war, and oaths. Needless to say, some of these genres were much more frequently used than others.

The government represented a limited, even if uniquely important, sector of public life. Outside the bureaucracy, there were countless occasions for individuals to express their feelings and ideas in writing. One of the most common genres was the letter to a friend or relative. Others included the preface to a book (whether one's own or another's), the afterword for a newly acquired book or work of art, the appreciative note on a painting or its subject, the report on or description of a noteworthy event, or the essay on a controversial subject.

Another important group includes the various sorts of texts written on the occasion of a person's death and burial. In traditional China mourning and burial were accompanied by extensive rituals for which appropriate texts were required. To name just a few, there were the lament (the expression of one's initial pain upon hearing of the decease), the sacrificial text (in which one addresses the deceased), the epitaph (which is carved in stone and buried with the coffin to enable descendants to determine the rank and position of the deceased), and the biographical sketch (containing an outline of the deceased's career).

The customary subjects of the various prose genres were intimately related to their functions. Memorials deal with the tasks of the government and the problems arising in the pursuance thereof. Prefaces give an impression of a book and its author. Epitaphs eulogize the deceased. Some genres, like the letter and the essay, allow a wider choice of subjects, though here also the most frequent subjects were those the Central Tradition regarded as primary. The letters which an author included in his collected works were usually those to friends and colleagues on matters of public interest. Gossipy letters to family and intimates are notably absent.

All the short Chinese prose genres are remarkably brief. Many comprise no more than a couple of lines; seldom is one longer than a few pages. Though some memorials were much longer, owing to the complexity of their subject or the number of distinct issues treated, their unusual length was an exception and was clearly felt as such. The important thing in all the prose forms was after all the conclusion, the judgment, the feeling and opinion of the writer. With the exception of the fable, fictional prose forms, such as the story or novel, the fairy tale, the legend, the myth, or the saga, have no place in traditional high literature.

THE RISE OF PARALLEL PROSE

Parallel prose (*pianwen*) includes all texts which, though belonging to a wide variety of short prose forms, are wholly written in parallel style. In other words the text from beginning to end is characterized by the stylistic device of parallelism or antithesis. Where this device is employed in pure form, two successive lines of equal length show an identical structure both syntactically and semantically. A simple example in English might be: "White birds fly through the air/ Black fish swim in the water." Not only is the grammatical pattern the same in both lines, but words of similar grammatical function in both lines also belong to a similar meaning category ("white" and "black" are both colors, "birds" and "fish" are both types of animals, "fly" and "swim" are both verbs of motion, and so on).

The monosyllabic nature of *wenyan* makes it eminently well suited for the use of parallellism. Unlike the Indo-European languages, it has no case endings or conjugational variants to disrupt the exact symmetry of the corresponding words. Occasional applications of parallellism can be found even in the oldest preserved texts of the Central Tradition, like the *Shujing* and *Shijing*. Parallellism is not limited to use in prose; it is widely employed in poetry. As a stylistic device it lends itself especially well to descriptive passages.

In later centuries a prominent feature of traditional Chinese education was training in the construction of pairs of parallel lines. The teacher would begin by naming any one-syllable word, whereupon the pupil was expected to produce a contrasting word of the same semantic category. For example, if the teacher said "heaven," the pupil might answer "earth." Once the student had grasped the basic principle, he would be confronted with combinations of two characters, such as "blue heaven" or "setting sun," to which he might answer "yellow earth" or "rising moon." The number of syllables assigned was gradually increased until the student had no trouble coming up with parallel lines of three, four, six, or more syllables (as usual in prose), or with couplets of five- or seven-syllable lines as used in poetry. The couplet (*dui* or *duilian*) itself became a modest literary genre and was a frequent choice for inscriptions and the like.

The ability to produce unhesitatingly a suitable parallel to a difficult line was regarded as a proof of great literary talent. There were also some notoriously difficult lines for which it was said that no one had ever succeeded in finding a satisfactory antithetical line. Parallel lines were admired still more intensely if their author managed to include in them suitably antithetical allusions or quotations. One is almost led to wonder whether the immense and perennial popularity of parallellism was a result of the philosophy of the Central Tradition, which encouraged the recognition of a Pattern far more than the search for a Cause.

From about 100 on, the stylistic device of parallelism became increasingly prominent in prose as well as in *fu*. At first it was mainly used in *fu*, but gradually it extended to the memorial, the letter, and the essay. Parallelism was never much used, however, in the writing of histories.

The high point of parallel prose came in the first half of the sixth century, during the Liang dynasty. The great literary theorist Liu Xie (466?–539?) even wrote his *Wenxin diaolong* (The literary mind and the carving of dragons), a systematic fifty-chapter treatise on high literature, in parallel style. (The contents of this work will be discussed below.) But even afterward parallel style remained customary for certain prose genres.

In later centuries, and in the modern era, the parallel style met with much criticism for being rhetorical fireworks without real depth. While the style does tend in that direction, one should certainly not write off as mere word-play all texts sharing this feature. The great masters of this complex style succeeded in expressing their thoughts with both wit and clarity. Unfortunately the modern Chinese reader often lacks the familiarity with the Classics and with other early literature that would make possible an adequate appreciation of their virtuosity. Where these early writers were "dancing in their chains," the modern reader sighs under the dull burden of footnotes, reference books, and indexes.

THE *FU* IN THE LATE SECOND CENTURY AND AFTER

The *fu* remained one of the most favored forms of poetry in this period despite the gradual rise of the *shi*. Many poets from this era are famous for both *shi* and *fu*. In general, the *fu* are shorter than those from earlier times. Perhaps this is because poets tended to choose more modest subjects (animals, musical instruments, etc.); the higher technical demands involved in composing a work entirely in parallel couplets may also have been a factor. In this period there is no longer a clear distinction between lyrical and more purely descriptive *fu*. A good example of a strongly lyrical *fu* is the "Denglou fu" (Climbing the tower) by Wang Can (177–217), in which the poet, residing in Chu as a refugee, expresses his homesickness. In many cases the poem presents an allegorical description of the poet, as in the "Yingwu fu" (The parrot) by Mi Heng (173–198): the caged parrot symbolizes the gentleman of high ability whose gifts and talents lead to the loss of his freedom.

Cao Zhi (192–232), a younger son of the redoubtable warlord Cao Cao, is famous not only as a *shi* poet but also as the author of the "Luoshen fu" (The goddess of the Luo River). This work, clearly influenced by the *fu* of Song Yu, shows the poet crossing the Luo River and catching a momentary glimpse of the river goddess, who does not, however, grant him her favors. This *fu* has been interpreted as an expression of Cao Zhi's unfulfilled love for an older sister-in-law, but also as a protest at his failure to attain a prominent government position.

Xi Kang (223–262) was related to the imperial house of the Wei dynasty. An iconoclastic character, he was, among other things, a famous zither (*qin*) player, and his "Qin fu" (The zither) describes the origin, construction, and technique of playing the instrument. It is, at the same time, a lament on the difficulty of finding a friend who "understands one's music" (*zhiyin*)—i.e., who can appreciate the talents of a gentleman.

One of the most important *fu* poets of the second half of the third century was Pan Yue (247–300). He too frequently lamented the lack of recognition for his abilities. In "Qiu xing fu" (Autumn reflections), after detailing his failures and the hazards of a bureaucratic career, the poet decides to retire to the country and enjoy an untrammeled life.

The best known *fu* of Zuo Si (d. ca. 306), a contemporary of Pan Yue, is the "San du fu" (The three capitals, i.e., of Wei, Wu, and Shu-Han). Zuo Si is said to have spent ten years working on this *fu*, and legend has it that after the poem's publication it became so popular that the price of paper rose in Luoyang! One interesting feature is Zuo Si's preface, in which he claims to have verified personally all the statements in the poem. (It was not unusual for *fu* writers to be accused of fantastic exaggeration.)

The "Wen fu" (The text), by Lu Ji (261–303), which describes the process of writing a text, is a milestone in the development of Chinese literary criticism; it will be discussed in more detail below.

The "You Tiantai shan fu" (Roaming the Celestial Terrace Mountains), by Sun Chuo (314–371), describes a journey over a narrow stone bridge across a deep ravine to the top of Mt. Tiantai, a paradise inhabited by immortals and arhats. The same journey stands for the development of mystical insight in which the ego becomes one with the universe. This *fu* represents a fuller formulation of the same idea that is expressed in many landscape poems in the more succinct *shi* form, such as those by Xie Lingyun (385–443).

The famous *shi* poet Tao Qian (365–427) also wrote *fu*. Most of them are not very original, but his "Guiqulai ci" (Song of the return home) has remained a well-loved favorite.

The *shi* poet Bao Zhao (?–466) was also famous for *fu*. Best known is the "Wucheng fu" (The ruined city), in which the contemplation of the blossoming and decay of a city leads the poet to realize the inevitable transitoriness of all human striving.

The last great *fu* poet, Yu Xin (513–581), was also renowned during his youth in Nanjing as a writer of *shi* and parallel prose. Having been sent to the North as an emissary, he was detained and forced to serve under various northern dynasties. His "Ai Jiangnan fu" (Lament for the South) describes the violent end of the Liang dynasty in highly allusive language.

During the Tang dynasty, when the *fu* was a required subject for the state examinations, there was a form of composition known as the *lüfu* (regular *fu*). Written on a prescribed subject, the *lüfu* used designated rhymes and observed very strict rules for parallelism and tone contrast. As a reaction against the *lüfu*, in the eleventh century the so-called *wenfu* (prose *fu*) enjoyed a modest vogue. It is a fairly short poem in which the poet is completely free in matters of line length, rhyme, parallelism, and tone contrast. The most famous *wenfu* are the "Qiusheng fu" (The sounds of autumn) by Ouyang Xiu (1007–1072) and the two "Chibi fu" (The red cliff) by Su Shi (1037–1101).

TEXTS ON TEXTS

In earlier periods the evaluation of literature had been concerned almost exclusively with a text's correctness or lack thereof. But by the third century, the abundance and variety of works by individual authors led to systematic reflection on the nature of literature and the relative value of specific texts and authors. This reflection resulted in theoretical treatises and the compilation of anthologies.

Literary criticism begins to appear in the early years of the third century. Cao Zhi and his elder brother Cao Pi (187?–226?) focused on the evaluation of their contemporaries; Cao Pi also emphasized the value of "texts" as a means of gaining eternal fame.

Lu Ji's Wen fu

Lu Ji's "Wen fu" describes the process of writing. This poem consists of nineteen stanzas marked by the use of distinctive rhymes. The opening stanza describes the author's previous education and subjective preparation; the final stanza tells of the civilizing influence of texts. The other seventeen stanzas can be arranged in two groups. The first nine concern inspiration, the joy of writing, the choice of genre and style, and five specific techniques (writing is compared in each case with weaving). The following eight discuss five common faults in writing (the effect of the text being compared with that of ceremonial music) and the author's sorrow at his inability to achieve full adequacy of expression.

The Wenxin diaolong *and the* Wenxuan

The grand synthesis of literary theory and criticism in this period was achieved by Liu Xie (d. ca. 520) in his *Wenxin diaolong* (The literary heart and the carving of dragons, i.e., the form and content of a literary work). Liu Xie occupied modest bureaucratic posts, and during the last years of his life he enjoyed the patronage of Xiao Tong (501–531), the eldest son of Emperor Wu of the Liang dynasty. The *Wenxin diaolong* consists of fifty chapters, the last being a brief autobiography of the author and an introduction to the text and its title.   .

The first twenty-five chapters deal with the origins of literature and of individual genres. In his discussion of the origins of literature, Liu Xie defines *wen* as the outward manifestation of the *dao*. The *dao* is nowhere better expressed than in the *jing* (Classics). With regard to the various genres, Liu Xie first traces each back to a point of origin in the Classics, then describes the genre's features, follows its historical development, and evaluates its most important exponents. Chapters 5 through 8 deal with the *Chuci*, *shi*, *yuefu* and *fu*; chapters 9 to 25 discuss prose genres, usually two per chapter. The following twenty-four chapters are concerned with a variety of general literary subjects: form, content, style, organization, etc. The *Wenxin diaolong* is written entirely in parallel prose and is regarded as one of the finest examples of that style.

Soon after the completion of the *Wenxin diaolong*, an anthology of poetry and prose was compiled under Xiao Tong's supervision. This work, which superseded all previous compilations and represents a distillation of the belles-lettres of the Han dynasties and the following period, is known as the *Wenxuan* (Choice of texts) or the *Zhaoming wenxuan* (Zhaoming's choice of texts; Zhaoming was Xiao Tong's posthumous title). In many ways the *Wenxuan* can be seen as a concrete illustration of the critical judgments expressed in the *Wenxin diaolong*.

STORIES AND SUPERNATURAL ANECDOTES

Also dating from these centuries are a number of collections of supernatural stories and anecdotes, most of which survive only in fragmentary form. In the tales of the miraculous (*zhiguai xiaoshuo*), evidence is presented for the existence of gods, ghosts, and spirits. The most important work in this category, the *Soushen ji* (Investigations of the supernatural) by Gan Bao (early fourth century), contains the earliest known versions of many familiar Chinese folk legends. Some of the miracle stories from these centuries are of Indian origin, and a number of collections of supernatural stories were clearly written as propaganda for Buddhist concepts, such as reincarnation.

The most famous book of anecdotes, the *Shishuo xinyu* (A new account of well-known tales), compiled by Liu Yiqing (403–444), contains several hundred anecdotes and *bons mots* of leading personalities of the third and fourth centuries arranged thematically according to virtues and vices. It presents a fascinating panorama of aristocratic society in a turbulent period.

NORTH CHINESE WRITERS OF THE FIFTH
AND SIXTH CENTURIES

The extant literature of the second and third centuries is almost exclusively of North Chinese origin; that of the three subsequent centuries (following the transfer in 317 of the Jin dynasty's capital to Jianye, now called Nanjing) is mostly from the Yangzi valley, the domain of the so-called Southern Dynasties. Not until the sixth century do noteworthy writers appear again in North China.

The *Shuijing zhu* (Commentary on the book of streams), by Li Daoyuan (d. 527), is famous for its descriptions of nature, which are regarded as an important influence on the later landscape essays by Liu Zongyuan (773–819). The *Luoyang qielan ji* (Monasteries of Luoyang), written by Yang Xuanzhi after a visit to the ruins of Luoyang in 547, evokes the lost glories of that city in its former role as capital of the Northern Wei in the early sixth century. The description of the Buddhist monasteries is interlarded with legendary material.

The statesman Yan Zhitui (531–after 590) owes his literary fame mostly to the *Yanshi jiaxun* (Admonitions to the members of the Yan family), a collection of essays on philosophical and philological topics. Yan Zhitui is also credited with the authorship of a book of supernatural stories, the *Yuanhun ji* (Wronged souls).

Chapter 11.
POETRY: *SHI* AND *YUEFU*

THE RISE OF *SHI* POETRY

During the Eastern Han there arose a new form of poetry called by the old name *shi*. *Shi* poems are characterized by lines of fixed length and by rhyme at the end of the even-numbered lines. The lines are usually of five or seven syllables, with a caesura after the second syllable of five or the fourth syllable of seven. In the third century, many *shi* poems were still written in a four-syllable line. The number of couplets is potentially unlimited; a change of subject is often signaled by a change in rhyme. As *shi* are almost always lyrical in nature, they tend to be short. In the Tang dynasty, technically stricter forms of *shi* were developed. These are collectively referred to as *jinti shi* (modern-style poetry); by contrast, the looser and older forms came to be called *gu(ti)shi* (ancient-style poetry). Both "ancient" and "modern" forms of *shi* have continued to be written down to the present day.

The Themes of Shi *Poetry*

The bulk of *shi* poetry is occasional verse. Sometimes the poems bear a title indicating the subject, but usually no more is mentioned than the person for whom and the occasion on which the poem was written.

In all forms of Chinese literature the author is expected to produce sincere feelings appropriate to the situation, but in no other form is the requirement for unity of situation and feelings (*jing* and *qing*) so stringent and explicit as in poetry. The description of an event or a landscape *is* also the description of the feelings it evokes.

What occasions in public life called for poetry? First of all, there were the various aspects of life in government. Important happenings at court or in the bureaucracy, such as the appearance of good omens, the offering of important sacrifices, the conclusion of military campaigns, the completion of new palaces, hunts and feasts, were recorded by one or more of those present. For such major events, the *fu* was the most suitable form, though later other forms, including the *shi* and *ci*, were also used.

The activities of the ruler and the government might also inspire the poet, whether to praise or to censure. As we have already seen, the poetry of social criticism occupied a prominent place in Chinese literature. Here the form of choice was the *yuefu*. Another means of criticizing ruler and government in terms clear only to the elect was the allegorical poem. Poems on historical subjects were often employed to censure contemporary abuses.

Friendship was also a prime source of poetic inspiration. Through the centuries, most poets were government officials whose careers entailed frequent transfer from one out-of-the-way post to another, so that meetings with friends were a rarity. Not surprisingly, many poems were written on these precious occasions. Others were written on the parting of friends, whether the writer himself was departing or was seeing a friend off to a far post. Leaving a friend was doubly poignant if it also meant leaving the capital, the site of the emperor's sacred work of ordering society, with all the attendant pleasant and worthy companionship. Moreover leaving the capital often represented a failed attempt to gain an official post, or a demotion to a post in the provinces. The most trivial scene encountered en route to a provincial post could evoke homesickness for the capital and the poet's friends there. A poet who had retired from bureaucratic life was likely to extol the pleasures of a quiet life in the country as a way of quelling lingering doubts as to the wisdom of his decision.

In many of these poems, the authors express their awareness of the brevity of life, the insignificance of man in time and space, and the irrevocability of parting and death. Autumn and evening evoke melancholy because they remind the poet of the approaching evening of his own life. But spring, too, makes him sad, for the annual return of buds and blooms reminds him all the more that he has but one life to live. The resulting poems are replete with exhortations to himself and his friends to grasp every chance, let no opportunity slip by. The poet often turns to drink to ease his cares. And if he is profoundly saddened by the evanescence of his life amidst the endless relativity and change of the cosmos, he can try—with or without the aid of wine—to transcend it through mystical union with the Way.

The Marginal Role of Religious and Love Poetry

With the exception of the descriptive *fu*, traditional Chinese poetry is predominantly lyrical. Narrative poems are comparatively rare. Some lyrical poems contain short narrative passages, but they are seldom the poet's focus.

In *shi* poetry, narrative examples are limited to the categories of *gushi* and *yuefu*. The few famous narrative poems, like Bai Juyi's (772–846) "Changhen ge" (Song of eternal regret), which tells of the disastrous passion of Emperor Xuanzong (r. 712–756) for High Consort Yang, are famous partly because they are so unusual within the tradition. "Changhen ge," at 120 lines, is considered a long poem!

An epic, in the sense of a poem born of a chivalric culture and praising the military feats of heroes, could not arise in China because the Central Tradition always regarded the use of force as inferior to the transforming power of true virtue. War was seen as a necessary evil. There are, of course, poems in praise of successful generals, but normally more attention is paid to the suffering and deprivations caused by war. The knightly warrior is not idealized in high literature, but he is in oral literature, and from there evolves into a stock figure in trivial literature.

In principle the subjects of Chinese lyric poetry are unlimited: every situation evokes feelings which a writer could conceivably express in poetic form. And for some poets, especially in the Song dynasty, no subject was too trivial. Their poetry at times seems almost like diary entries in verse form.

In practice, however, the choice of subjects remained rather limited down through the centuries, in part because private subjects, especially family life, were avoided almost entirely. The poet wrote mainly in response to events in society at large and to landscapes outside the home; only very rarely did he mention the homely realities of his life with wife and children. The reader gets to know the writer as a participant in society, not as a private person. Religious verse and love poetry, both of which figure so prominently in the Western lyrical tradition, are notably absent in China.

More exactly, religious poetry is absent in its usual Western sense. The Chinese Central Tradition makes no fundamental distinction between heavenly and earthy, religious and secular, soul and flesh. For the Chinese writer, socially oriented action in this world is itself the highest value; the social order, as embodied par excellence in ruler and government, itself has a sacral character.

Religious poetry in the Western sense, fundamental to which is belief in a personal God, is absent save for a few sacrificial hymns in the *Shijing* and shaman songs in the *Chuci*. In Chinese poetry there is no place for despair over one's supposed sinfulness, any more than for praises of a God of salvation. Western mystical poetry, in which the poet expresses love for a Savior, enjoys intimations of transfiguration or blessedness, and is the recipient of special visions, has no nearer Chinese equivalent than the nature mysticism in which the poet, in a condition of stillness, feels at one with all existents in the Way.

There are, of course, Chinese love poems, but by comparison with the Western tradition they represent a very small part of the poetry that has been preserved. In families of high status, women were kept strictly isolated from casual social contacts. Marriages were contracted between families, not individuals; the young bride and bridegroom saw each other for the first time on their wedding day. Marriage and family life were regarded as private matters and only very exceptionally became subjects for poetry. No poems in the high tradition were written for one's own future marriage partner, although there are poems in memory of a deceased wife.

Since the social life of high-class women was segregated from that of men, there was no room for the development of a poetry of courtly love in which a man of low standing, like the European troubadour, could have expressed unfulfillable longing for a married lady of the nobility.

What Chinese poetry does contain are many poems on the plight of jilted courtesans and neglected palace ladies. The rejected woman, however, actually stands for any unrecognized talent, especially the virtuous gentleman who fails to be called to a position in government. Sensuous though many of these poems are, it would be incorrect to read them as love poetry. When gentlemen wished to enliven their meetings—outside the home!—with female company, they turned to courtesans. If they happened to fall in love with the ladies of pleasure, they (or their descendants) seldom saw fit to include the relevant poems in their collected works.

It is only in folk poetry, or in poems clearly associated with the folk tradition (such as *yuefu* or the songs in the *Shijing*), that amorous matters feature prominently. Genres like the *ci* and *qu*, which originated in the milieu of the houses of pleasure and never attained the respectability of the *shi*, also allowed considerable scope for these themes. But although various aspects of love might be mentioned, in these forms also the poet is usually concerned to describe the feelings of the abandoned woman.

YUEFU POETRY AND THE *GUSHI SHIJIU SHOU*

Within the category of "ancient-style" poetry is a body of poems called *yuefu* (bureau of music). The name goes back to the *Yuefu* (Bureau of Music) established under Emperor Wu of Han (r. 140–87 B.C.) to provide music for court rituals and feasts and to collect appropriate melodies. The only *yuefu* texts still preserved from that period are hymns. It is an open question whether Emperor Wu's *Yuefu* did in fact collect contemporary folk songs. In later centuries the word *yuefu* was used as a general term for songs meant to be sung, whether they were folk songs or hymns composed at court. It is unclear to what extent the earliest preserved versions of such folk songs are actually revisions by literary specialists. In any case the name *yuefu* is applied both to these early versions and to imitations by later writers in which title, subject, and even significant phrasing recall a *yuefu* poem of the older period. Formally speaking, *yuefu* are scarcely distinguishable from other ancient-style *shi*; occasionally *yuefu* show somewhat more variation in line length.

Though most *yuefu* are lyrical, the genre also includes two famous long narrative poems. "Kongque dongnan fei" (The peacocks fly southeast) tells the sad story of spouses who, being forced to separate, commit suicide. The heroine of "Mulan shi" (The song of Mulan) is a young girl who secretly takes her father's place when he is called up for military service. "Kongque dongnan fei" may date from the third century; "Mulan shi" is probably of fourth- or fifth-century origin.

Among the earliest *shi* poems are the *Gushi shijiu shou* (Nineteen ancient poems). Of anonymous authorship, they probably date from the first and second centuries A.D. Subjects treated include the sorrow of the abandoned woman, the loneliness of the traveler, feasts at court, and graves beyond the city walls. Characteristic of these poems are a pessimistic, somber view of life, despair at separation and death, and an attitude of *carpe diem*. These poems were much imitated by later authors.

SHI POETS OF THE THIRD CENTURY

The first individually identifiable *shi* poets lived during the last years of the Han dynasty. Their names are associated with the Jian'an Period (196–219). The most important is Cao Zhi (192–232). Cao Zhi's father Cao Cao (155–220) is also remembered as a poet, and his older brother Cao Pi (187–226) was not only the first emperor of the Wei dynasty but also a poet and literary theorist. Cao Zhi's *shi* are mostly occasional poems written in connection with important events in his life, such as court feasts and partings with relatives. His *shi* reveal his disappointment at being denied a significant role in politics. He is particularly remembered for his "Luoshen fu" (The goddess of the Luo River). A well-loved anecdote has it that Cao Zhi was able to compose a poem in the time it took to walk seven paces.

The most important poet of the Wei dynasty was Ruan Ji (210–263). He is famous, among other things, as the author of a group of eighty-five poems known as *Yonghuai shi* (Poems in which I sing of my deepest feelings). Most of these poems are not easily comprehensible at a first reading, and the traditional commentaries treat them as allegorical satires on the political situation toward the end of the Wei. In certain cases this approach is undoubtedly valid, but at times the attempt to relate individual poems to specific events seems extremely far-fetched. The persistent search for a political message is, however, thoroughly consistent with the traditional idea that poetry is the expression of feelings on the subject of the ruler and the government.

Noteworthy among the poets of the second half of the third century are Pan Yue (247–300), Lu Ji (261–303), and Zuo Si (d. ca. 306). Pan Yue, also famous for his *fu*, wrote well-known *shi* poems in memory of his deceased wife. Lu Ji was regarded as the best *shi* poet of his time, but his lasting fame is due to his "Wen fu." Zuo Si was famous in his own time for his "San du fu" (The three capitals). He created the genre of *yongshi shi* (poems on historical subjects) and used it as a vehicle for political criticism.

SHI POETS OF THE PERIOD 350–450

The political disturbances of the early fourth century were followed, culturally speaking, by a relatively barren period. When literature again began to flourish, Central China, with its capital at what is now Nanjing, had replaced North China as cultural center. The most important poets of the late fourth and early fifth centuries are Tao Qian, Xie Lingyun and Bao Zhao.

Tao Qian (365–427), also known as Tao Yuanming, was not much of a success as a bureaucrat. Legend has it that he lost his last official post, as magistrate of Pengze, after an incident in which he knelt before a visiting inspector with the words: "Am I supposed to bow down to such a bumpkin just to earn my five bushels of rice?" He eventually lived in retirement in the country. In his *shi* he sings the joys of rural life and the pleasures of wine as consolation for his despair over his inability to contribute to the improvement of the times. A few poems show the rare quality of self-ridicule. The style of Tao's poems is relatively simple. A perennial favorite in prose anthologies is his "Taohuayuan ji" (Record of peach blossom spring), which tells the story of a lost fisherman who stumbles on an opening in a cliff leading to a blissful world of peace and plenty, which, once he leaves it, he never again can find. This piece is actually the preface to a poem on the same subject, which has not achieved the same popularity. As a poet, Tao Yuanming was not recognized as a truly great figure until Tang and Song times.

Xie Lingyun (385–443) was descended from one of the leading families of the Southern Dynasties. His checkered career ended with his decapitation as a rebel. Throughout his life Xie had a keen interest in Buddhism. He is regarded as China's first landscape poet— that is, a poet in whose works the description of uncivilized nature, "mountains and rivers," plays a major part. This aspect of his poetry can be seen as the culmination of a process of change in customary attitudes toward nature: nature is no longer a terrifying, threatening element but a direct manifestation of the Way or the Buddha Nature.

The poet Bao Zhao (d. 466) had a modest official career, despite his renowned literary gifts. Not surprisingly, dissapointment is a prominent theme in his poetry. He is highly regarded for his *yuefu* imitations and for his mastery of the seven-syllable verse line. Somewhat unusual in the context of Chinese poetry is his frequent use of personification. Bao Zhao is also famous for his *fu*, including the "Wucheng fu" (The ruined city).

PALACE-STYLE POETRY

In the late fifth and early sixth centuries, cultural life came to be dominated by what we may call literary salons—that is, groups of writers centered about certain people at court. In particular, the members of the Xiao family, the ruling house of the Liang dynasty, were patrons of salons in which a technically refined but thematically narrow type of poetry was written. This came to be known as palace-style poetry (*gongti shi*), so called because its subject matter is mostly taken from various aspects of luxurious palace life, especially in the women's quarters. One favorite subject, for example, is the ennui of the palace lady neglected by the emperor. Whereas the work of older poets was anthologized in the *Wenxuan*, the palace-style poetry was collected in the *Yutai xinyong* (New songs from a jade terrace). From mid-Tang times on, this kind of poetry has been almost unanimously condemned as frivolous. The most important poet of the sixth century is Yu Xin (513–581); in addition to his *shi*, he is famous as the last great *fu* poet. Thematically the poetry of the first century of the Tang is mostly a continuation of the preceding century's court poetry.

TONE CONTRAST

Contact with the Sanskrit language and Buddhist chanting, together with centuries of experience with the *shi* form, led Chinese poets to realize the effects that they could attain through regular alternation of tones. The earliest formulation of rules for the application of tones in *shi* is attributed to Shen Yue (441–513), one of the leading poets of his day. In the fifth and sixth centuries four tones were distinguished. The tones were designated "level" (*ping*) or "oblique" (*ze*) according to a simple formula: the first or Even tone was considered level, while the second, third and fourth tones, called Rising, Going and Entering respectively, were oblique. (Owing to changes that have occurred over the intervening centuries, these tone categories no longer correspond exactly to the four tones of modern standard Chinese. The category of words having the ancient Even tone has been divided into the first and second tones of modern Chinese; the ancient Rising tone has become the modern third; the ancient Going tone has become the modern fourth; and the Entering tone, comprising words ending in -p, -t, or -k, has been lost entirely as a distinct category. These final consonants disappeared from the northern vernacular by the thirteenth century, and the words formerly having the Entering tone have been redistributed among the four modern tones.)

Though nothing is now known with certainty about how the ancient tones were pronounced, a long tradition says that the level tone sounded somewhat longer or more drawn out in time, the oblique tones, by contrast, having a shorter, more clipped sound. Whatever the exact aural effect, the alternation of level and oblique tones imparts a certain rhythm to the line. In general, excessive repetition of the same tone is avoided. Where tone contrast is applied, the patterns of alternation of level and oblique tones within two successive lines are each other's mirror image: the syllables having a level tone in the first line have an oblique tone in the second, and vice versa.

Tone contrast is seldom applied with absolute consistency. In practice the contrast must be correct at least as regards the even-numbered syllables of the two successive lines. Tone contrast may be combined with parallellism, but need not be. Either of these two stylistic devices may be employed in the absence of the other. When tone contrast is used, it is normal for the pattern of level and oblique tones in the first line of a couplet to be identical with that in the second line of the previous couplet. This phenomenon is called "sticking" (*nian*). Where parallelism is in force, on the contrary, the first line of a new pair is definitely not supposed to echo the syntactic and semantic patterns of the previous line.

Eventually, in the course of the sixth and seventh century, further codification of tonal rules resulted in the emergence of the so-called "modern poetry" (*jinti shi*), which could take three forms: *jueju*, *lüshi*, and *pailü*. These forms will be discussed in the next chapter.

CHINESE POLITICAL HISTORY, 700–1000

The Tang dynasty was at the height of its glory during the long reign of Emperor Xuanzong (r. 713–756). An expansionist military policy again projected Chinese power far into Central Asia, despite fierce opposition from the expanding Tibetan empire. This era came to a sudden end in the autumn of 755 when armies under An Lushan, commander of China's northern frontier, rebelled in Youzhou (the area of modern Peking) and marched south. An Lushan's troops quickly took Luoyang; Chang'an fell to them the following year. Fleeing the capital, the emperor was forced by his own escort to order the suicide of Yang Guifei (High Consort Yang), who had dominated the palace during the preceding decade. While the emperor continued his westward journey across the mountains toward Chengdu, military opposition to the rebellion was organized by his son and successor, Emperor Suzong, who obtained the help of Uighur troops.

An Lushan was soon killed by his own son, and the rebellion was subdued in 763. Nevertheless, the central government had to grant *de facto* independence to the northeastern generals. Throughout the second half of the eighth century, the capital area continued to be plagued by coups and countercoups, rebellions and incursions. In retrospect, the two long reign periods of Emperor Xuanzong, Kaiyuan (713–741) and Tianbao (742–756), came to be seen as an outstanding time of undisturbed peace, economic glory, and national prestige. It was not until early in the ninth century that the central government again partly succeeded in reasserting its authority. At the same time, however, eunuchs became increasingly important in court politics. Attempts to deprive them of their power backfired and resulted in major purges of the bureaucracy. Government persecution of Buddhism (842–845) had long-term effects on that religion's strength as an institution.

The power of the Tang was definitively broken by the rebellion of Huang Chao, which lasted from 874 to 884. Huang Chao's peasant armies ravaged the country from North to South; after pillaging the rich international merchant port of Canton in 879, they trekked through China and occupied Chang'an for several years. Though hunger eventually forced them to move on, the Tang government was able to suppress the rebellion only when some of Huang Chao's former commanders switched sides. One of these, Zhu Quanzhong, rose to become the most powerful warlord in northern China.

Accepting the abdication of the last Tang emperor, he founded the Liang dynasty (907–922), with its capital at Kaifeng.

Intermittent warfare continued to ravage northern China for more than half a century, a hectic period usually referred to as the Five Dynasties. The most important opponent of Zhu Quanzhong was Li Keyong, leader of the Shatuo Turks. He eventually defeated the Liang and supplanted that dynasty with his own Later Tang dynasty (923–935). The Later Tang was in turn followed by the Later Jin dynasty (936–946), founded by Shi Jingtang. Following the collapse of this dynasty, Liu Zhiyuan proclaimed the Later Han dynasty (947–950), which existed for only four years before it was supplanted by the Later Zhou dynasty (951–960) of Guo Wei, who managed to unify almost all of northern China. An important contestant in the North Chinese arena during these years was the Liao dynasty (916–1122), founded by the Khitan in southern Manchuria. In exchange for their support of the Jin (936–946), they were given control over sixteen prefectures in northeastern China, including the area of modern Peking.

At the same time southern China was divided into a great number of states. The courts of some of these southern states became important cultural centers, including the Former Shu and Later Shu dynasties, with their capital city of Chengdu, and the Southern Tang, with its capital in what is now Nanjing.

In 960 the Later Zhou dynasty (951–960) was succeeded by the Song dynasty (960–1279) when troops about to leave the capital for a campaign against the Khitan Liao dynasty put their commander Zhao Kuangyin on the throne. Kaifeng remained the capital of the new dynasty. Gradually the other states were brought under Song control; the reunification of the Chinese world was completed with the conquest of the Northern Han (modern Shanxi) in 979. However, the Song dynasty never succeeded in recovering the Sixteen Prefectures, and the situation at the border between the Song and the Liao remained tense.

Chapter 12
POETRY: *SHI*

ANCIENT-STYLE POETRY AND MODERN-STYLE POETRY

The increasing deliberate use of tones as a poetic element led to the development, in the sixth and seventh centuries, of three new subtypes of *shi*, distinguished primarily on the basis of strict rules governing tone placement. These three are referred to collectively as *jinti shi* (modern-style poetry).

The Forms of Modern-Style Poetry

The three distinct types of modern-style poetry are the *jueju* (stopped-short lines), the *lüshi* (regulated poem), and the *pailü* (linked regulated). A *jueju* consists of four lines, usually of five or seven syllables. If the seven-syllable line is used, the first line usually rhymes with the second and fourth. Later critics assigned a function to each of the four lines of a *jueju*: opening, development, turnabout, and conclusion.

The regulated poem has eight lines of five or seven syllables. The two internal couplets (that is, lines 3 and 4 and lines 5 and 6) must show parallelism—a fact which often makes this form immediately recognizable even in translation. In the opening couplet, parallelism is allowed but is seldom used in practice. Enjambement often occurs in the closing couplet. Change of rhyme is not allowed in the regulated poem.

If more than two parallel couplets intervene between the opening and closing couplets, the poem is said to belong to the linked regulated type. Linked regulated poems of thirty to forty couplets are not uncommon, but in this type also, change of rhyme is avoided as much as possible.

The Themes of Tang Poetry

Whether modern-style or ancient-style in form, Tang poetry has little to add to the previously existing palette of subjects. The vast bulk of poetry

124

remains occasional verse, expressing the author's feelings on significant events in his social life as an official: important feasts at court, parties and meetings with colleagues, saying farewell to colleagues, journeys taken to assume duties at far-off posts, return journeys to the capital, a visit to a hermit (who is, typically, not at home), etc. The poem's occasion and the person for whom it is written are often included in the title. Many of these poems were written on request or in reply to a colleague's poem, in which case the rhymes or even the rhyming words of that poem were taken over intact. The feelings expressed are often utterly conventional: at court feasts, joy at the virtuousness of the ruling house; at parties among friends, the *carpe diem* attitude; at farewells, lamentation over the transitoriness of human life; on journeys into the provinces, depression and homesickness; admiration for the purity of the hermit who has retired from the world; and in general, regrets that one's own talents or those of friends remain unrecognized.

Political criticism is usually phrased in conventional, allegorical terms; poets often chose the *yuefu* form so that the author's complaints could be stylized as the words of peasants, soldiers, and others low down on the social ladder. Love poems are rare, though there are many about palace ladies once loved but later neglected by the emperor. This had been a much-used theme in the court poetry of the sixth century. Landscape poetry occupies a modest place; more often, a conventionally described spring or autumn landscape functions as the background and correlative of the author's emotional state. Only a few poets showed significant originality of subject or imagery, and even their collected works consist mostly of conventional verse.

The Periodization of Tang Poetry

Traditional Chinese critics distinguish four periods in the development of *shi* during the Tang dynasty: *Chu Tang* (Early Tang, i.e., the seventh century), *Sheng Tang* (High Tang, 700–785), *Zhong Tang* (Middle Tang, 785–835), and *Wan Tang* (Late Tang, 835–900). The poetry of the Early Tang is basically a continuation of the court poetry of preceding centuries. The High Tang coincides largely with the long reign of Xuanzong (712–756) and the rebellion of An Lushan; this is the period in which modern-style poetry first blossomed. The ravages of the An Lushan rebellion led to a reconsideration of the nature and value of literature, resulting in renewed emphasis on the moral mission of poetry. The poetry of the Late Tang is described as refined, sometimes to the point of artificiality. The *shi* poetry of the tenth century is mostly a weaker continuation of Late Tang poetry.

Tang poetry was eventually published almost in its entirety in the collection *Quan Tang shi* (Complete Tang poems). This work, compiled in the early years of the eighteenth century, contains more than 49,000 poems by some 2,200 authors. An anthology on which many Western studies and translations were based is the *Tang shi sanbai shou* (Three hundred Tang poems), which has remained a proverbial favorite in China since its compilation in the mid-eighteenth century.

THE EARLY TANG

The poetry of the Early Tang has been briefly characterized above; important names associated with this period are Chen Ziang and Zhang Ruoxu. Chen Zi'ang (ca. 659–700) urged poets to return to the style of the Wei and Jin dynasties (i.e., of third-century poetry); his influence is said to be a major cause of the sudden flowering of *shi* poetry in the following century. Only two poems by Zhang Ruoxu (660–720) have been preserved; he is famous for the poem "Chunjiang huayue ye" (A river in spring, a night of blossoms and moonlight), a satire on the growing power of Empress Wu Zetian.

THE HIGH TANG

The most famous poets of the High Tang are Wang Wei (?–761), Li Bai (701–762) and Du Fu (712–770).

Wang Wei

Wang Wei had a successful career in the bureaucracy; aside from a few short interruptions he spent almost his entire adult life in the capital city of Chang'an. His works include many occasional poems on happenings at court. He is most famous, however, for his landscape poetry. Like Xie Lingyun, Wang Wei was a believing Buddhist. For the poet, the contemplation of nature is a way of participating in its peace and serenity: landscape and emotion are one. Wang Wei is also remembered as a painter, though no extant paintings can be attributed to him with certainty.

Li Bai (Li Po, Li Tai-p'e)

Li Bai (Li Taibai, better known in the West as Li Po) lived a rather footloose life, drifting from one patron to another. He gained early recognition as a major poet, but the road to officialdom remained closed to him, perhaps because he was the son of a merchant trading with Central Asia. He was present at court only in the period 742–744, when he was a member of the Hanlin (Forest of writing brushes) Academy. At that time the Hanlin was not yet the prestigious Imperial Secretariat, but rather the emperor's personal circle of poets and other entertaining characters. According to legend Li Bai died attempting, while drunk, to seize the moon's reflection in water. Though he did write in the various genres of modern-style poetry, his preference was for the ancient-style *shi*, including the *yuefu*. His poems, characterized by simple diction and frequent variation in line length, make a strong impression of spontaneity. Other features are playful exaggeration and personification. Though his works include occasional poems full of conventional flattery, he also wrote poems of social consciousness. His poems are full of the longing to escape from this world to the carefree and permanent realm of Taoist immortals—or to the consolations of wine. His frequently declared passion for drinking, together with the many anecdotes telling how he wrote his best poems while thoroughly drunk, have given him the reputation of a bohemian—which may account, in turn, for his disproportionate popularity among Western readers. In China he is often affectionately referred to as a *zhexian*—that is, an immortal undergoing temporary exile from heaven.

Du Fu

Li Bai is often contrasted with his younger contemporary Du Fu. Though Du Fu did meet Li Bai and deeply admired his works, in his own poetry he showed a strong preference for modern-style forms. The regulated poem became a perfect instrument in his hands. His poems are stylistically complex, and at times his search for striking expressions led him to the conscious use of ambiguity. Du Fu had a modest career in officialdom and experienced the rebellion of An Lushan at close hand. His best poems are those from the last twenty years of his life, including the famous and often-translated cycle of eight poems called *Qiuxing* (Autumn meditations). Also remarkable are a number of poems addressed to his wife. His work bears witness to his direct personal involvement in the problems of his age, which he describes very realistically. His personal bearing in public life and his poetry of sociopolitical awareness earned for him in later centuries the title of *shi sheng* (the saint of poetry).

Other Poets

Meng Haoran (689–740) is known for his landscape poems and for verse in which he laments his lack of recognition. Gao Shi (ca. 702–765) and Cen Shen (ca. 715–770) are both famous for poems on the life of soldiers stationed on China's northern borders. Wei Yingwu (737–792 or 793) is remembered primarily for his landscape poetry, which deals largely with cultivated landscapes.

THE MIDDLE TANG

The most famous poets of the Middle Tang are Bai Juyi (772–846)—better known in the West as Po Chü-i—and his friend Yuan Zhen (779–831), and Han Yu (768–824) and his friend Meng Jiao (751–814).

Bai Juyi (Po Chü-i) and Yuan Zhen

On the whole, Bai Juyi had a successful career. Originally outspoken in his opinions, as time went by he became more cautious, shying away from the factional struggles that rocked the Tang bureaucracy in the ninth century. He repeatedly stressed the political and moral value of literature, as, for example, in a famous letter to Yuan Zhen (*Yu Yuan Jiu shu*) dating from 815. He deliberately wrote most of his poetry in uncomplicated language that was supposed to be understandable, according to legend, even to uneducated old women. Yet he also wrote a number of *pailü* each of 200 lines. He greatly admired Du Fu, and among his own works he considered his poems of social criticism to be the most important. In 809 he wrote, for example, in imitation of Yuan Jie (719–772), fifty *xin yuefu* (new *yuefu*) poems in a popular manner satirizing contemporary social and political ills. (*Xin yuefu* differ from the traditional *yuefu* in that the writer of *xin yuefu* chooses his own subject rather than producing a new variant on an established one.)

In contrast to Bai Juyi's own preference, contemporaries and later readers attached more importance to the poems addressed to his bosom friend Yuan Zhen or to those dealing with domestic life. Some of his poems include humor and self-ridicule. Two perennial favorites are his long narrative poems

"Changhen ge" (The song of eternal regret) and "Pipa xing" (The ballad of the lute). "Changhen ge," which dates from 809, tells the story of Xuanzong's disastrous love for High Consort Yang, the rebellion of An Lushan, their escape and her death, and a shaman's efforts, at Xuanzong's desperate instigation, to track her down in heaven. "Pipa xing" (816) tells of Bai's encounter in Jiujiang with a merchant's wife, a former courtesan, who reveals the details of her unhappy life; the poet, in exile at the time of writing, identifies her fate with his.

Yuan Zhen was involved in many obscure adventures and had a checkered career as a bureaucrat. During his lifetime his poetry was almost as popular as Bai Juyi's and he was praised for his virtuoso use of rhyme. With the passage of centuries, however, his reputation as a poet has diminished. His short story "Yingying zhuan" (The story of Yingying) has remained one of the very best-known *chuanqi* (short stories in the classical language).

Liu Yuxi (772–842) wrote poetry in a simple style, often imitating contemporary folk poetry. After Yuan Zhen's death, Liu Yuxi became Bai Juyi's main correspondent-in-verse.

Han Yu and Others

Han Yu was not only a leading prose writer but a major poet. His official career was uneven, owing to his sharp attacks on Buddhism and his advocacy of a renewed, purified Confucianism. At first he wrote heavily didactic, linguistically uncomplicated poems which his contemporaries found rather prosaic. In the years of his professional eclipse, however, he wrote very difficult poetry characterized by technical virtuosity; a famous example is the "Nanshan shi" (Poem of the Southern Mountains). When he once again became successful, he mostly wrote facile occasional verse.

His somewhat older friend Meng Jiao, who was never successful in public life, is another poet whose work shows a clear development from relatively simple poetry toward hermetic verse and strikingly original, sometimes far-fetched vocabulary.

Li He (790–816), a protégé of Han Yu, lived only a short time. His poetry abounds with shamans, ghosts, and the miraculous and macabre. Its unconventional, intense imagery makes it curiously appealing to the modern Western reader.

THE LATE TANG

The outstanding exponent of Late Tang poetry is Li Shangyin (ca. 813–ca. 858). Success in officialdom eluded him; he occupied staff posts under various semi-independent provincial governors. His poems on historical subjects are satires in disguise. His untitled poems may refer to a secret love affair, and their elusively intimate mood has inspired widely varying Western translations. Much of his work is dense and difficult to understand, obscure allusions and quotations making various interpretations possible.

Du Mu (803–852, often referred to as Xiao Du or "little Du" to distinguish him from Du Fu) was rather more successful in his career and was a legendary *bon vivant*. He is especially famous for his *jueju*. His "Ebang gong fu" (The Ebang Palace) describes the craving for luxury of the Qin emperor, who brought his dynasty to rack and ruin.

Wen Tingyun's (812?–866) outrageous lifestyle cost him his official career. He wrote memorable poems on abandoned women. Wei Zhuang (ca. 836–910) eventually attained to high office in the state of Shu. His long narrative poem "Qinfu yin" (Plaint of the woman of Qin) describes the horrors of the occupation of Chang'an (881-883) by the forces of the rebel Huang Chao. Wen Tingyun and Wei Zhuang are also the first important *ci* poets (see Chapter 16).

POETRY CRITICISM

Not much poetry criticism has been preserved from Tang times. The monk Jiaoran (d. 789) compiled the *Shi shi* (Norms for poems), in which a number of formal rules are stated. The poet Sikong Tu (837–908) wrote the *(Ershisi) shi pin* (Classification of the [twenty-four styles of] poems), in which twenty-four two-character designations are applied to a like number of poetic styles; each style, with its associated subjects and appropriate emotional states, is described in a rhymed verse of twelve four-character lines.

The Japanese monk Kūkai is the author of the *Bunkyō hifuron* (Treatises from the secret storehouse of the mirror of literature), a collection of texts on, and examples of, parallelism and tone contrast—for the use of Japanese practitioners of Chinese poetry. The texts are mostly taken from the works of sixth- and seventh-century Chinese writers.

POETRY OF BUDDHIST INSPIRATION

Working in a rather different direction from that of the poets just described, a few poets of lasting fame took their central inspiration from Buddhism. Wang Fanzhi (Zealot Wang), whose very existence is probably no more than legendary, is the traditional author of a number of starkly worded poems on the transience of human life, but also of a rhymed collection of rules of etiquette.

Hanshan(zi) (Master of the Cold Mountain), who may also be legendary, is credited with a collection of more than 300 poems including nature poems, bitter satires, and sermons in verse form. The leading poet-monk of the ninth century was Guanxiu (d. 903). Both Hanshan and Guanxiu make extensive use of Taoist terminology in their poetry.

Chapter 13.
TANG PROSE: ANCIENT-STYLE PROSE
AND SHORT STORIES

ANCIENT-STYLE PROSE

The prose of the first half of the Tang dynasty mostly continues the parallel prose of earlier centuries, though occasional protests called for a return to a simpler style. It was only after the rebellion of An Lushan that literature was subjected to a more general reevaluation, leading to widespread condemnation of stylistic artificiality and to renewed emphasis on the didactic function of literature.

Han Yu

The most vociferous spokesman for the reform in prose style and content, the so-called *guwen yundong* (ancient-style prose movement), was Han Yu (768–824). He was fiercely opposed to Buddhism both as a philosophy and as a social institution; his own ideal was a newly purified form of Confucianism. More than once, his opposition to Buddhist observances at court earned him demotion. Han Yu believed that the content should determine the form of literature. Opposing parallel prose on the grounds that its form dominated its content, he took as his model the ancient prose (*guwen*) of the Philosophers and the *Shiji*. At first he considered originality a prime requirement of prose texts; later he placed more emphasis on the Confucian correctness of the content. In his final period he held that correct content can convince readers only through the medium of correct form. Han Yu did not reject any and all use of parallelism; in fact, parallel sentences occur frequently in his own work. He did, however, oppose obligatory parallelism as an excessively formalistic device.

Han Yu's most famous prose works are in miscellaneous forms such as essays, letters, and prefaces. His *Yuandao* (Inquiry into the Way) presents his views as to the orthodox lineage of the Confucian tradition—Mencius is given precedence above *Xunzi*—and condemns Buddhism and Taoism in no uncer-

132

tain terms. *Shishuo* (Explanation of the concept of "teacher") stresses that no student of the Way can succeed without a teacher. In *Song Meng Dongye xu* (Preface to send off Meng Dongye, i.e., Meng Jiao), Han Yu takes saying goodbye to his friend Meng Jiao as an occasion to relate his opinions on the nature and development of poetry. (A *xu* is a short prose piece expressing the writer's feelings about himself or others; the form lent itself well to use as a preface or postscript to a longer work. In Tang times many *xu* were written on the occasion of parting from friends.) The *Ji Shi'erlang wen* (Text for the sacrifice for Shi'erlang) was written for his short-lived nephew, with whom he had grown up. The *Liu Zihou muzhiming* (Tomb inscription for Liu Zihou, i.e., Liu Zongyuan) is a biography of Liu Zongyuan that includes an evaluation of his prose.

Han Yu also wrote parodies and fables, for which he was occasionally criticized by his friends. One of these texts, the *Mao Ying zhuan* (Biography of Hair Point, i.e., the writing brush), describes the career of a writing brush in the clichéd terminology of an official's biography. In *Ji eyu wen* (Text for the sacrifice to the alligators), Han Yu, as prefect of Chaozhou, asks the alligators to depart from his precinct. This work may not have been a parody. He had been banished to Chaozhou in 819 after writing a strongly-worded memorial, the *Jian ying Fogu biao* (Memorial against the welcoming of the Buddha bone), condemning the reception and worship of a Buddhist relic at the palace.

Liu Zongyuan

Liu Zongyuan (773–819) early gained fame as a writer. His official career was unremarkable until, during the short reign of Emperor Shunzong in 805, he was quickly promoted. After the emperor's forced abdication and subsequent death, all the members of Liu's faction were banned. Accordingly, Liu spent the years from 806 to 815 in Yongzhou, in the south of what is now Hunan Province. In 815 he was named prefect of Liuzhou (in modern Guangxi), and there he died in 819.

Liu Zongyuan has none of the virulent anti-Buddhism of Han Yu. His most famous works date from the Yongzhou period. Regarded as the creator of the genre of the landscape essay, he described, in eight short essays collectively called the *Yongzhou ba youji* (Reports on eight Yongzhou wanderings), the various aspects of Yongzhou's scenic beauty. He is also the author of a number of fables.

Liu Zongyuan also wrote biographies, which may or may not be fictional, of selected common people. The most famous of these are *Zhongshu Guo Duotuo zhuan* (Biography of the gardener Camel Guo), in which he warns against government burdened with excessive regulations; *Ziren zhuan*

(Biography of the carpenter), in which he compares the work of the chancellor to that of an architect; and *Bushezhe shuo* (Explanation of the phenomenon of the snake catcher), an attack on excessive taxation of the common people.

Liu Zongyuan is much praised for the acuity of the essays in which he attacked, among other things, the belief in omens. In his own day he was admired for his *Chuci* imitations, and he still enjoys a certain reputation as a landscape poet, but his place in the history of poetry is much more modest than Han Yu's. In prose, however, the two men have been mentioned in the same breath since the eleventh century.

During the Tang dynasty the *guwen yundong* failed to put an end to the popularity of parallel prose, though Yuan Zhen (779–831) is said to have made contributions toward a simplification of the language used in chancellery documents. It was not until the eleventh century, with the rediscovery of Han Yu and Liu Zongyuan, that the *guwen yundong* again emerged into the spotlight.

THE SHORT STORY IN THE CLASSICAL LANGUAGE

The Tang period also saw the flowering of the short story in the classical literary language. The Chinese name of this genre is *chuanqi* (traditions relating to strange matters). This expression, originally the title of a ninth-century collection of such stories, soon passed into more general use. Emerging gradually from its predecessors in the form of anecdotes, jokes, legends, and tales of the supernatural, this type of short story flourished in the second half of the eighth century and later.

The authors of *chuanqi* were just as reluctant as their literary forebears to invent stories and present them frankly as fiction. Consequently, they often named specific people as their informants, giving details as to their relation to the characters in the stories. But whereas writers in earlier times had tended to tell only the bare facts in a rather terse style, the *chuanqi* authors gave more attention to the formal and artistic possibilities of their stories. Many of the preserved stories are re-tellings of material of widely varying credibility. A number are clearly designed as fables, and a few may have been written to show existing persons in a bad light.

The Form and Content of Chuanqi

The new interest in the art of storytelling is evident in the way the authors of *chuanqi*, in contrast to earlier writers, give detailed descriptions of the background, motives, and behavior of the characters. Many *chuanqi* are of rather limited scope, treating no more than one or two events, typically of a supernatural or private nature: they deal with miracles or love. Quite a few, however, comprise a whole chain of events linked by a well developed plot. The technical interests of *chuanqi* writers extended not only to the form and structure but also to prose style. They write in a simple, unadorned style obviously influenced by historical prose. The structure of many *chuanqi* resembles that of the biographies in dynastic histories and comparable sources. The main text is often interlarded with samples of other literary genres, especially poems and letters supposedly written by the characters.

One of the most famous *chuanqi*, "Yingying zhuan" (The story of Yingying; also known as "Huizhen ji," "Report on encountering a fairy"), by Bai Juyi's close friend Yuan Zhen (779–831), concerns a certain Zhang, who happens to be staying at a monastery where the other lodgers include the widow Cui and her daughter Yingying. Zhang falls in love with Yingying. At first she rejects him, but eventually he enjoys her favors—only to abandon her. In the end each marries a different partner. In this *chuanqi* we find, in addition to the main narrative, several poems in the *jueju* form, a letter written by Yingying to Zhang after he has left her, and a *pailü* in thirty couplets by Yuan Zhen in which, following established poetic conventions, he describes Yingying's nocturnal visit to Zhang as a visit paid by an immortal fairy to a mortal man.

In many *chuanqi*, the story itself is little more than a connecting framework for various letters, poems, etc. A few, however, are written wholly or mostly in parallel prose. For example, "You xianku" (A visit to the cave of the fairies), a long *chuanqi* traditionally attributed to Zhang Zu (early eighth century), is written in a kind of parallel prose that includes elements of the contemporary spoken language. Despite its length "You xianku" tells a simple story: a young traveler loses his way; night finds him in the dwelling place of immortal fairies who receive him with great hospitality, entertain him with music and poetry, and let him spend the night with one of their number. But the next morning, after his departure, the place turns out to have vanished without a trace.

The subjects of *chuanqi* lean heavily toward the supernatural or miraculous—encounters with ghosts, demons, immortals, fairies, gods, or supernatural animals. Other stories tell of weird or unusual love affairs—the relationship between a literary man and a *ji* (geisha, courtesan), a fairy, a dragon's daughter, or a fox. A frequently occurring character is the *xiake* (knight-errant), whose brave and selfless feats of arms bring the lovers together.

The Best-Known chuanqi

"Gujing ji" (Report on the old mirror), attributed to Wang Du (early seventh century), is a sequence of short supernatural tales about an old bronze mirror having magical powers. This work represents a kind of transitional link between the older, pithier *zhiguai xiaoshuo* tradition and the newer, longer *chuanqi*.

Another work supposedly dating from the same period, the anonymous "(Bu Jiang Zong) Baiyuan zhuan" (Story of the white monkey; a supplement to the [biography of] Jiang Zong), tells the story of Ouyang Ge's wife. During a campaign in the far South, she is abducted by a white gibbon, but in the end her husband succeeds in freeing her. This story was said to have been written to slander Ouyang's son.

The most important *chuanqi* of the first half of the eighth century is "You xianku," described in the previous section.

Shen Jiji (ca. 800) is the author of both "Renshi zhuan" (The story of Lady Ren) and "Zhenzhong ji" (Report on [what occurred] within the cushion). "Renshi zhuan" is about a certain Zheng who falls in love with a woman in the city of Chang'an. He continues to love her even after discovering that she is actually a fox, and they set up a household together. The fox-fairy helps her husband to become rich and his patron to obtain the women he desires. But when she accompanies her husband on his journey to take up an official post, they run into the emperor's hounds, whereupon she reverts to her true identity, tries to escape, and is finally killed.

"Zhenzhong ji" tells of a student on his way to the capital to take part in the examinations. Staying at an inn, he falls asleep on a headrest which he has been able to borrow from an immortal. He experiences, in dream, a fabulous career. But when he wakes up, the millet porridge that had been put on the stove before he fell asleep is still not ready to be served—whereupon the student awakens to the fact that earthly life is but a dream.

A similar motif is present in "Nanke taishou zhuan" (The story of the prefect of South Branch), by Li Gongzuo (ca. 800). In this story also, the main character dreams of a splendid career, only to discover on waking up that during sleep his soul has reigned over an anthill. "Xie Xiao'e zhuan" (The story of Xie Xiao'e), by the same author, is about a woman of humble background who finally succeeds in taking revenge on robbers who have murdered her father and her husband.

In "Liu Yi," by Li Chaowei (late eighth century), the student Liu Yi, having failed in the examinations, is returning home when he meets, on the shore of the river Jing, a girl who is tending sheep. The girl tells him that she is a daughter of the Dragon King of Lake Dongting. She asks him to deliver to her parents a letter in which she informs them that her husband is mistreating her. Liu Yi duly delivers the letter, and the girl is brought back home by her furious family. The family wishes to reward Liu Yi by giving her to him in marriage. Declining the offer, he resumes his journey. Years later, however, he ends up marrying her.

"Liushi zhuan" (The story of woman Liu), by Xu Yaozuo (ca. 800), tells of the love between the courtesan Liu and the poor poet Han Yi. Liu's patron, having heard her praise Han Yi, presents her to him as a gift. When Han eventually goes to take up a post in the provinces, however, he has to leave her behind in Chang'an. They exchange poems in which she swears loyalty to him. Subsequently she is forced to become the concubine of a Turkish general in Chinese service. When Han Yi returns to Chang'an, they happen to catch sight of each other. One of Han's friends succeeds in kidnapping her, and the couple are reunited.

"Huo Xiaoyu zhuan" (The story of Huo Xiaoyu), by Jiang Fang (early ninth century), is about the courtesan Huo Xiaoyu, whose lover, the minor poet Li Yi (748–829), abandons her so as to be able to make a good marriage. She finally dies of despair; her erstwhile lover, in the meantime, has become incurably mad with jealousy.

Of all the *chuanqi* about love affairs between students and courtesans, the most famous is undoubtedly "Li Wa zhuan" (The story of Li Wa), by Bai Xingjian (ca. 776–826), a younger brother of the poet Bai Juyi. "Li Wa zhuan" is about the son of a provincial governor. The young man squanders all his wealth on the courtesan Li Wa, who finally connives with her mother to throw him out of the house. Now destitute, he becomes a paid mourner at funerals. His father, happening to see him in this role during a visit to the capital, beats him so severely that he is at first abandoned for dead. Sick and covered with sores, the young man can only take to begging. On a winter's day he happens to come to Li Wa's house. Taking pity on him, she helps him to recover his health and makes it possible for him to study. He passes the examinations, gains an official post, is reconciled with his father, and marries Li Wa.

"Yingying zhuan," by Bai Juyi's friend Yuan Zhen, has already been mentioned. In or about 813, Chen Hong wrote a companion piece in prose called "Changhen ge zhuan" (Story of the Song of eternal regret), to Bai Juyi's "Changhen ge." Chen's "Dongcheng laofu zhuan" (Story of the old man east of the city) is also set against the background of the An Lushan rebellion and describes the hero's reversal of fortune: once favored by Xuanzong as a trainer of fighting cocks, he eventually becomes a monk.

"Wushuang zhuan" (The story of Wushuang), by Xue Diao (ca. 829–872), is set in the turbulent years after the suppression of the An Lushan rebellion; the heroine is finally reunited with her lover through the heroic self-sacrifice of another character.

"Qiuranke zhuan" (The story of the curly-bearded foreigner), by Du Guangting (850–933), is the story of a mysterious hero who lays aside his own ambition to be emperor after meeting Li Shimin (who was, in the traditional view, the actual founder of the Tang dynasty).

Collections of Short Stories

Ninth-century *chuanqi* authors usually published their works in collections. The original collections are no longer known to us, the present versions being reconstructions made on the basis of later compilations.

The oldest known collection is the *Xuanguai lu* (Records of mysterious and remarkable things), compiled by Niu Sengru (780–848). Li Fuyan produced a sequel to this work: *Xu Xuanguai lu* (Continued records of mysterious and remarkable things). It contains numerous popular fairy tales, an example being "Dinghun dian" (The inn where marriages are determined), which presents the legend of an old man in the moon who ties future marriage partners together with a red thread.

The collection entitled *Chuanqi*, by Pei Xing (ca. 860), is composed mostly of legends of immortals centering about the Canton region. It also contains the story "Kunlunnu" (the dark slave), in which the hero, who unites the two lovers, is a dark-skinned slave from Southeast Asia.

Ben shi shi (Poems traceable to events), by Meng Qi (late ninth century), is a collection of anecdotes and *chuanqi* which purport to describe the circumstances under which then-popular poems were composed.

Besides the *chuanqi* that have come down to us, the Tang period also saw the compilation of various collections of anecdotes. Most are more important from an historical (or literary-historical) point of view than as literature. A few, however, also include substantial stories. The best-known collection of miscellanea, anecdotes, and stories is the *Youyang zazu* (Variety dishes from Youyang), by Duan Chengshi (803–863).

Ancient-Style Prose *and* Chuanqi

Some scholars have postulated a close relation between the *guwen yundong* and the rise of *chuanqi*. Those who support this view point to the concurrent emergence of *guwen* and *chuanqi*, arguing that the ancient-style prose movement, by throwing off the straitjacket of parallel prose, made possible a freer style of narrative prose. It is also claimed that young literati included *chuanqi* in the selections they sent to high officials in the hope of winning patronage.

In recent years, this view has been disputed. There is not much evidence that *chuanqi* were in fact so used. An unencumbered narrative style had been continually employed in historical works down through the centuries and was therefore theoretically available even without the coming of the *guwen yundong*. At the same time the artful storytelling would seem to go badly with the didactic intent which the *guwen yundong* prescribed for prose.

The Preservation of Chuanqi

Virtually the entire body of Tang *chuanqi* is preserved, together with the *zhiguai xiaoshuo* of the preceding period, in the *Taiping guangji* (Inclusive records from the chronological period Taiping Xingguo), a thematically arranged collection of supernatural stories, legends, and *chuanqi* in 500 *juan*, compiled on imperial order and completed in 978. Many *chuanqi* owe their preservation to inclusion in this work. In subsequent centuries *chuanqi* have been an inexhaustible source of inspiration and material for vernacular literature: fiction, drama, and narrative ballads.

Chapter 14.
POPULAR LITERATURE: *CI* AND *BIANWEN*

Besides the poetry (*shi* and *fu*) and prose written by high officials and those of their immediate circle, there have come down to us from Tang times a number of texts, in various genres, written by authors not belonging to the elite. These are written in language at least heavily influenced by the contemporary spoken language, and some are in more or less pure vernacular. These texts are often referred to as "popular literature," but it should be remembered that these texts, too, had their origin among the very small percentage of the population who could read and write, even if the texts were designed to be read or performed for a largely illiterate audience. The relation between this popular literature and the literature in *wenyan* can perhaps be compared to that between vernacular and Latin literature in the late Middle Ages.

THE DUNHUANG MANUSCRIPTS

One of the main sources of our knowledge of this popular literature has been the discovery, in the vicinity of Dunhuang in northwestern Gansu, of a sealed cave full of paper. For centuries Dunhuang was an important post along the trade route running from China through Central Asia to India and the Near East—the fabled Silk Route. Buddhism took hold early in this region, and in the centuries that followed, a great number of rock temples were created in a steep cliff outside the city. The murals in these temples, dating from the sixth to the twelfth centuries, have been of great importance for the study of Chinese art.

Around 1900 in one temple that had been abandoned, a man named Wang discovered a sealed-off chamber full of old writings. These texts have found their way all over the world, the most important collections of Dunhuang texts being now in London, Paris, St. Petersburg, and Peking. The cave must have been sealed soon after the year 1000, as the manuscripts date from the sixth century to that date.

The texts are of widely various kinds. The vast majority are in Chinese, but there are others in all the languages then current in Central Asia. The great bulk of the Chinese items are Buddhist texts already well known at the time of the Dunhuang discovery: copies of favorite sutras. There are also, however, many other texts, ranging from poems to contracts to penmanship exercises. The collection as a whole must probably be regarded as a kind of reverential dumping-ground for old, no longer usable paper—a fact which probably also explains why so many of the manuscripts are incomplete.

The Dunhuang manuscripts have far more than just literary-historical importance. They represent a unique source of information on various aspects of the cultural and social-economic history of the Tang period. Their importance for literary studies is of three kinds. First, they include the actual texts of certain works in *wenyan* that were previously known only by title and regarded as lost, such as Wei Zhuang's poem "Qinfu yin" and practically the complete poetry of Wang Fanzhi. Second, they have greatly extended our knowledge of certain genres, such as the *ci* or the Tang folk song. And finally they have provided textual knowledge of genres that had previously been more or less unknown, including *bianwen*.

CI POETRY

During the Tang period, Chinese music was exposed to important new influences from Central Asia in the form of new instruments and melodies. The result was a virtual revolution in popular music. The newly popularized melodies were unsuitable as settings for the *shi* form of poetry with its lines of equal length. Accordingly, the eighth, ninth and subsequent centuries saw the creation of numerous new song forms better fitted to the new tunes. For each of these song forms, there was a prescribed number of lines (not necessarily an even number), a prescribed length for each line, a prescribed tone category for certain syllables in certain lines, and obligatory rhyme positions. Some of the forms have allowable variants.

This new genre of songs is referred to in Chinese as *ci* (song: actually an abbreviation of *quzi ci*, "song texts"). The text of a *ci* is always preceded by the name of the tune for which it is written. In a few early cases, there is still some relationship between the name of the tune and the content of the *ci* lyric: songs written to the tune *Nü guanzi* (Taoist nun) often indeed describe a Taoist nun, and songs written to *Nanxiangzi* (Southern landscape) are often about a tropical scene. In general, however, there is little discernible relationship between the name of the tune and the content of the song. Writers of later *ci* often gave the individual songs titles appropriate to the contents, sometimes adding a short explanatory preface.

It is no longer known how *ci* were meant to be sung. Only a very small number of tunes have been preserved in musical notation, and even so opinions differ as to how the notation should be read. It is possible that a few *ci* melodies have survived into modern times in the context of Taoist liturgy.

The earliest *ci* consist of a single stanza, but by far the majority are in two stanzas of identical or nearly identical form. It seems reasonable to assume that the same tune was sung twice—the second time in some cases with small variations. Starting in the eleventh century, three-stanza *ci* were also written. The possible *ci* forms are of widely varying length, the shortest comprising 14 syllables and the longest 240. Eventually huge handbooks were compiled for the aspiring *ci* poet, providing model lyrics for each tune. Such formularies are known as *cipu*.

The two stanzas of a *ci* are often so written as to present a sort of contrasting pair: scene vis-à-vis feelings, dream vs. reality, emotions felt before and after an unmentioned event. A common motif is the transience of human life in contrast with the eternally recurrent life of nature; it is often combined with the theme of the waiting woman, who grows old in vain while the flowers blossom afresh year by year.

In the period 700–1000 the subject matter of *ci* remains strictly limited. In view of the fact that the *ci* originated in popular music such as was performed by courtesans, it is not surprising that love is the favorite subject. The songs most frequently describe the sorrow of the woman awaiting the return of her lover, who has left her. This subject, of course, was not unknown in the *shi* tradition, especially in the palace-style poetry collected in the *Yutai xinyong*. But in the *ci* the subject was revived with a new vigor, owing to the novel form and the use of poetic idiom enriched with vernacular elements.

Ci *Poets of the Ninth and Tenth Centuries*

The Dunhuang texts include a considerable number of anonymous *ci* songs dating from the late eighth through the tenth century. The first important identifiable *ci* poets are Wen Tingyun (812–870) and Wei Zhuang (836–910). Both were also famous as writers of *shi*. In Wen Tingyun's *ci*, the ennui of neglected palace ladies or courtesans is suggestively evoked by contrast with symbolically meaningful details of their luxurious boudoirs. Wei Zhuang's *ci*, characterized by straightforward expression of feeling (whether by the woman or by her lover), make an impression of simplicity and sincerity.

During the period of the Five Dynasties, *ci* poetry was written at the courts of the state of Shu (in Chengdu) and the Southern Tang (in Nanjing). *Ci* by Wen Tingyun, Wei Zhuang, and the Shu poets are contained in the oldest *ci* collection still in use, the *Huajian ji* (Collection [of songs to be sung] between flowers). A small earlier collection of *ci*, entitled *Yunyao ji* (Collection of ditties [that stop] the clouds) was discovered among the Dunhuang manuscripts.

The most important tenth-century *ci* poet was Li Yu (937–978), the last ruler of the Southern Tang dynasty. After being deposed, he spent his last years under house arrest in Kaifeng and is said ultimately to have been poisoned. Forty-five of his *ci* have been preserved; in subject and style, most are closely akin to the songs in the *Huajian ji*. A number of his *ci* are supposed to be expressions of pain over the death of his wife and the loss of his kingdom.

Vernacular Narratives from Dunhuang

Historians of Chinese literature use the term *bianwen* in two senses: first, as a name for all texts found at Dunhuang, written in the spoken language of their own day and intended for oral presentation, and second, as a specific designation for a particular genre of these texts: narrative texts in the spoken language of the period. We shall use *bianwen* in the second, more restricted sense only. (Some scholars, it should be noted, wish to limit the term strictly to prosimetric narratives, which were performed together with the showing of pictures.)

Buddhist monasteries and monks, showing as they did a strong interest in proselytizing, played an important role in the development and production of vernacular prose forms. Tang dynasty monks preaching for a lay audience made frequent use of the *sujiang* and *bianwen* forms.

In the case of *sujiang* (explanations for the laity), two monks sat on high seats facing each other. The first read aloud successive passages from a given sutra, after which the second provided extensive explanations and commentaries for each passage. A third monk then read a verse-form version of the same commentaries. These verses all ended with the same last line, which served as a cue for the first monk to commence reading a new passage from the sutra. This procedure probably had its origin in methods used by Confucian scholars to explicate the Classics.

The *bianwen* (transformation texts) are narrative texts on Buddhist and secular subjects. The texts are in prose, in verse, or in a mixture of the two. While the large number of Buddhist texts strongly suggests that the *bianwen* were performed by monks and nuns for the edification of the laity, contemporary descriptions of *bianwen* performances refer only to persons other than monks, probably professional performers or entertainers, and it is unclear who first borrowed the form from whom. The narration of *bianwen* could be accompanied by the display of pictures showing high points from the story, and one such picture scroll has been preserved. Scholars have pointed out that the alternation of prose and verse in some *bianwen* is reminiscent of a similar alternation of prose and *gatha* in the Buddhist sutras, and it has been argued that these prosimetric *bianwen* originated under Indian influence.

The Dunhuang find includes both *sujiang* and *bianwen* texts. Of the *sujiang* items, the most important are the extensive fragments of an explanation for the laity of the Vimalakirti Sutra. Vimalakirti was a highly popular figure in China, especially among literati interested in Buddhism. An enlightened rich layman, Vimalakirti, is described as having attained a higher plane than all other disciples of the Buddha, including the arhats. During the Tang, even Buddhists attached high importance to filial piety (*xiao*), and the Dunhuang find includes the *Fumu enzhong jing sujiang* (Explanation for the laity of the sutra on the importance of favors shown to us by our parents. The *Fumu enzhong jing* is a fake sutra, one that was actually written in China).

The *bianwen* texts can be subdivided into strictly Buddhist texts and others. In the purely Buddhist category, many items are concerned with an episode or segment of the Buddha's biography. There are a number of *bianwen* texts on the story of Mulian, a devout disciple of the Buddha who searched through the Hells for his mother, who had been condemned to suffer for her former sinful life. He eventually succeeded in freeing her from the deepest Hell. This story forms the basis of the Buddhist equivalent of All Souls' Day. In later centuries the legend of Mulian provided the plot for huge ritual plays.

Other texts deal with more or less legendary episodes from Chinese history. Favorite subjects include the wars involved in the founding of the Han dynasty; the saga of Wu Zixu (an important figure in the wars of Chu, Wu, and Yue in the sixth and fifth centuries B.C.); the story of Wang Zhaojun, the favorite concubine of a Chinese emperor, whom he is forced to give in marriage to the khan of the Xiongnu; edifying tales of the filial piety shown by Emperor Shun in his youth when his stepmother tried to kill him but he escaped miraculously on several occasions; and stories of the filial piety of Dong Yong, who, having sold himself for a period of three years in order to give his father a proper burial, was helped by a fairy from heaven to repay his debt.

The Dunhuang material also includes a few examples of lesser genres. Deserving mention here are the "Yanzi fu" (The swallow) and the *Chajiu lun* (Debate between tea and wine). The "Yanzi fu" tells of a court case involving a swallow and a sparrow (during the swallow's absence, the sparrow has taken over his nest). It has survived in two versions, one of which is a rare example of a vernacular narrative *fu* poem; the other version is in five-syllable verse throughout. The *Chajiu lun*, in which the two beverages argue over which is better, may well be the oldest extant Chinese play.

Part IV.
From the Spread of Book Printing
to the Introduction of
Western Printing Methods

CHINESE POLITICAL HISTORY, 1000–1450

During the first half of the eleventh century Song internal politics remained remarkably stable. For the first time in Chinese history the state examination system became the most important channel of entrance to a career in the bureaucracy. During the second half of the century, however, the bureaucracy was increasingly riddled with factionalism. Wang Anshi and his followers proposed far-reaching reforms in the areas of taxation and bureaucratic recruitment; they succeeded in implementing their policies when in power, but their more conservative opponents eagerly awaited their chances.

In foreign affairs the Song now had to contend not only with the Liao dynasty's continuing threat to the northeastern frontier, but also with the Xi Xia (i.e. Western Xia) kingdom (in modern Gansu and Ningxia) in the Northwest. Peace settlements with both countries, under which the Song was obligated to make yearly payments in silk and other goods, were felt by the Chinese to be extremely humiliating. In the early twelfth century, when the Jürchen to the north of the Liao founded the Jin dynasty, the Song court eagerly joined forces with them against the Liao.

However, once the Jin had succeeded in destroying the Liao, they turned against their former ally the Song, and in 1125 they suddenly appeared before the walls of Kaifeng. They were induced to leave; the Song emperor Huizong (r. 1101–1125) ceded the throne to his son, known to history as Qinzong. The next year the Jin troops came back, this time occupying the land. Both Huizong and Qinzong were taken captive and transported to Manchuria. The Jin quickly conquered all of North China.

One of the younger sons of Huizong, Gaozong, fled to the South and ascended the throne at Jiankang (now Nanjing). Pursued by Jin troops, his court moved around southeastern China before settling down at Hangzhou. After about a decade of warfare, a settlement was reached by which the Song emperor recognized the ritual suzerainty of his "elder brother" the Jin emperor. The Huai River formed the border between the two empires. One of the strongest supporters of the peace settlement was the chancellor Qin Kui, who went so far as to have the war-minded general Yue Fei (1103–1141) killed in prison to silence the opposition. Policy under the Southern Song continued to be a matter of heated debates between supporters of the prosperous status quo and those who demanded recovery of the northern territories and the return of the captive emperors Huizong and Qinzong. War frequently flared up between the Song and the Jin, but the border remained relatively stable.

In the early thirteenth century a mighty new element appeared on the East Asian scene: the Mongols, united under the leadership of Genghis Khan. After demolishing the Western Xia kingdom in 1227, they attacked the Jin and succeeded in destroying it as a dynasty in 1234. During the first decades of their rule the Mongols managed northern China rather loosely with the aid of Chinese commanders who had gone over to their side. During the second half of the thirteenth century, during the reign of Kublai Khan, they established a Chinese-style administration throughout their conquered territories, making much use of Central Asians and other foreigners to ensure their control. In 1260 Kublai Khan adopted a Chinese dynastic appellation: the Yuan. The capital of the new dynasty was at Dadu (now Peking).

Originally the Southern Song dynasty had collaborated with the Mongols in the destruction of the Jin, but once the Mongols had established themselves securely in Northern China, they turned on their former ally. The conquest of the Southern Song was a long, drawn-out process, finally completed in 1279. Meanwhile the Mongols had already occupied the area of modern Yunnan. Korea, too, accepted Mongol leadership, but Mongol campaigns against Japan and Java were unsuccessful.

The period of Mongol rule was an era of lively international contacts. But while the Mongols endorsed Zhu Xi's Neo-Confucianism, they were reluctant to reinstate the examination system. When they did so in the early fourteenth century, it was on a considerably reduced scale. By the mid-fourteenth century rebellions were sweeping China. After long and complex civil wars, the final victor was Zhu Yuanzhang, who had started out in life as an orphaned peasant boy and an itinerant monk. Establishing his capital at Nanjing, he adopted the dynastic title of Ming. In 1368 his troops drove the Mongols out of Dadu. The Mongols retreated to the steppe country, from which they continued to menace the Ming's northern border.

Zhu Yuanzhang is known to history as the Hongwu Emperor (r. 1368–1398). His government set out to re-Sinify China after the long period of Mongol rule. Zhu Xi's brand of Neo-Confucianism became state orthodoxy, and the examination system came to dominate the life of the literati. The Hongwu Emperor, though highly capable and effective, was also a suspicious and ruthless ruler: in two extensive purges he did away with many of the same generals who had brought him to power, and he placed his own sons in command of important military garrisons all over the empire.

Upon his death the Hongwu Emperor was succeeded by his grandson, the Jianwen Emperor (r. 1399–1402). On the advice of his ministers this young man set out to curb the independent military power of his uncles. One of these, Zhu Di, the prince of Yan, who was stationed at the former Dadu, rebelled and marched south. After a short but devastating civil war, he entered Nanjing. The imperial palace went up in flames and his nephew perished in the fire, though later legends would insist he had escaped and become a monk. The new emperor, the Yongle Emperor (r. 1403–1424), brutally exterminated his nephew's partisans in the bureaucracy. He returned to the North, and eventually the capital was formally transferred to what would henceforth be known as Peking (northern capital); Nanjing (southern capital) retained special status as a secondary capital.

The Yongle Emperor pursued an aggressive policy along the northern frontier. He also dispatched huge fleets, commanded by the eunuch admiral Zheng He, to South and Southeast Asia. Elements of these fleets reached Aden and the coast of East Africa. Under succeeding emperors, however, expansionist policies were discontinued, and China withdrew from active involvement on the world stage.

Chapter 15.
POETRY: *SHI, SHIHUA,* and *CI*

SHI POETRY

The *shi* was destined to remain the most widely written type of poetry in traditional China. Thanks to the invention of printing, a huge corpus of poetry has been preserved from the Song and later dynasties. The number of known poets in the Song period is roughly twice that in the Tang, and the preserved work of many Song poets is incomparably more voluminous than what was typical of Tang. For example, more than 9,200 *shi* by Lu You (1125–1200) are still extant, and this poet is known to have destroyed all the poems he wrote before the age of forty.

After the Tang, no new forms of *shi* were developed, but the *shi* of the Song (960–1279) do differ in content and style. Whereas Tang *shi* were limited to a relatively narrow range of subjects, Song *shi* are concerned with all aspects of life. Song *shi* poets did not limit themselves to presenting a lyrical formulation of a single moment of unusually intense emotion. They often described both feelings and thoughts engendered by everyday, even casual settings. The poetry of some of the more productive writers amounts to a diary in verse. Most of these poets also gave evidence of strong social concern. Nature poetry, on the other hand, played a lesser role in this period.

The tone of Song *shi* is typically one of serenity and acceptance, in contrast to the pain and plaint so characteristic of the Tang. (When Song poets wrote expressions of sorrow, they tended to do so in the *ci* form.)

Many Song *shi* are in the nature of a train of thought, a meditation on a particular subject, and the poems of such famous philosophers as Shao Yong (1011–1077) and Zhu Xi (1130–1200) are little more than philosophical tracts in verse form. The diction of Song poets went beyond the standard Tang poetic idiom to include vocabulary and constructions that would previously have been regarded as suitable only for prose. Some poets adopted elements of the spoken language of their day. Toward the end of the Southern Song there was a reaction against this trend, and poets showed renewed interest in the examples set by Tang writers.

Shi *Poetry of the Northern Song Dynasty*

For the most part, the poetry of the first years of the Song period can be described as a continuation of late Tang poetry. A sudden break with this style appears in the *shi* of Mei Yaochen (1002–1060) and Ouyang Xiu (1007–1072). Mei is famous exclusively as a *shi* writer; Ouyang is also renowned as a writer of *ci* and prose. He was, moreover, a historian and a collector of antiques. Of the two poets, Mei is surely the more original, but he owes much of his influence to the abundant praise he received from Ouyang Xiu, who enjoyed a prominent position in the intellectual and political life of the eleventh century.

Ouyang Xiu was born at Mianzhou in Sichuan. After the death of his father, he was brought up by his mother and an uncle. In 1030 he took his *jinshi* degree. Stationed first at Luoyang, he met Mei Yaochen, who remained a lifelong friend, and a number of other colleagues who shared his interest in *guwen*. Once back in the capital, he became associated with a group of reform-minded officials centering around Fan Zhongyan (989–1052), who was also a noted writer of prose and *shi*. With Fan, Ouyang was demoted and sent to a provincial post in 1035. In 1043 he returned with Fan to the capital, only to be demoted again in 1045. In 1054 he was recalled to the capital, where he eventually attained the highest political posts. He was opposed to the reform proposals of Wang Anshi (1021–1086)—a fact which once again led to his removal from the capital in 1067. In his final years he occupied a number of provincial posts. Ouyang Xiu's *shi*, full of meditative and narrative passages, are characterized by a tone of calm acceptance.

Though Mei Yaochen was admired by a number of leading persons, he had no more than a mediocre career, both in the provinces and in the capital. His personal life was not fortunate. Mei Yaochen tried deliberately to extend the range of subjects for *shi* by writing poems on themes that had never before been treated in poetry. He wrote many poems of social criticism, poems lamenting the loss of his first wife, and verses on other aspects of his private life. In all of his work Mei strove for *pingdan* (simplicity, understatement), and his poems often have a quality of spoken language. Critics have called his poems flat and lacking in spirit.

The statesman Wang Anshi (1021–1086) is famous not only for his far-reaching reforms but also for his writings in prose and *shi*. His *gutishi* of the period before 1067 are full of social criticism. His *jintishi*, written after his retirement to Nanjing in 1076, often sing the pleasures of a carefree life; some are strongly Buddhist. Wang Anshi was a great admirer of Du Fu's poetry.

Unquestionably the most famous Song poet is Su Shi (1037–1101; better known as Su Dongpo). He is famous as a *shi* and *ci* poet, a prose writer, a calligrapher, and a painter. Su Shi was born in 1037 at Meishan in Sichuan. In

1056 he went with his father and brother to the capital, where they enjoyed the patronage of Ouyang Xiu. Su Shi passed the examinations and took his *jinshi* degree in 1057. His first official post was as assistant prefect of Fengxiang, in western Shaanxi. In 1069 he was called to the capital, where he strongly criticized Wang Anshi's proposals for reform. Starting in 1071 he occupied various government posts in the provinces. In 1079, accused of *lèse-majesté* for certain satirical passages in his poetry, he was arrested and brought to the capital. He was not sentenced to death but was banned to Huangzhou, on the Yangzi, where he was forced to remain until 1084. It was here that he adopted the name by which he was later so widely known. After the death of Emperor Shenzong in 1085, Su was again summoned to the capital. Exasperated at the continuing factional struggles, he requested transfer to a provincial post, and in 1089 he was named governor of Zhejiang. When the pro-Wang Anshi faction again came to power, Su was banned in 1094 to Huizhou in Guangdong, and in 1097 to the island of Hainan. When Huizong ascended the throne in 1100, Su was allowed to return to Changzhou, where he died the following year.

Su Dongpo's poems seem to be the spontaneous expression of a boundless interest in the world around him. His diction is sometimes bright and playful, sometimes erudite. His poems breathe the spirit of an awareness of the relativity of all things and all emotions, including the writer's own pain. Some of the poems are humorous.

Su Shi's most important pupil was Huang Tingjian (1045–1105), who is also famous for his calligraphy. Like Su, Huang had a very uneven career in the bureaucracy. He is famous for his worship of Du Fu. In his own poetry Huang strove for originality of observation and phrasing, seeking especially to find novel applications for expressions and lines taken from existing poetry. Not surprisingly perhaps, his poems often make an impression of coolness and artificiality. His style was much imitated in the twelfth century; poets showing his influence are often referred to collectively as the Jiangxi School.

Another pupil of Su Shi's was the poet Chen Shidao (1053–1101), who was also a great admirer of Du Fu. Many of his poems are on everyday subjects.

Shi *Poetry of the Southern Song Dynasty*

The most important poets of the Southern Song period were Lu You (1125–1200) and Yang Wanli (1127–1206). Both belonged to the faction favoring an aggressive policy toward the Jin dynasty, and both retired to farms after unremarkable careers in officialdom. Both wrote at first in the style of the Jiangxi School but later, in a moment of insight, totally repudiated it and burned their earlier poems. Turning their backs on the artificiality of the Jiangxi School, they strove for the direct expression of spontaneous feelings. Even by Song standards, both were extraordinarily productive: Lu is the author of more than 9,000 poems, and though much of Yang's work has been lost, the preserved items still amount to about 4,000 poems. Of Lu You's poems, the most famous are his patriotic poems, written in middle age when from 1170 to 1177 he served in various positions in Sichuan. The poems of his old age give detailed descriptions of rural life in Zhejiang. Yang Wanli wrote on a wide variety of subjects, and he frequently used expressions taken from the spoken language.

Fan Chengda (1126–1193), a friend and patron of Lu You, enjoyed a successful career and spent his last years in a villa on the outskirts of Suzhou. His poems are on a variety of subjects but are stylistically more conventional than those of Lu You. Among Fan's best-known poems are a series of 72 *jueju* written during his mission to the Jin court at present-day Peking in 1170 and another series of *jueju*, written in 1186, treating rural life in each of the four seasons.

The most important Southern Song poet of the thirteenth century is Liu Kezhuang (1187–1269), who has left us several thousand *shi*, in style and subject comparable to those of Lu You. The works of Wen Tianxiang (1236–1283), the last chancellor of the Song dynasty, owe their lasting readership mainly to the unshakable patriotism of the author. His most famous poem is the "Zhengqi ge" (Song of the proper *qi*), written in praise of the patriotism of certain historical figures. Wen wrote this poem while imprisoned by the Mongols in Dadu, shortly before his death.

One of the few women poets of the Song dynasty to have left a sizeable corpus of *shi* poetry is Zhu Shuzhen, who lived in Hangzhou sometime during the twelfth century (the dates of her short life are disputed). An interesting feature of her substantial oeuvre is that it is organized according to the four seasons. Most of her poems are boudoir laments; on rare occasions she explicitly protests against the confines imposed upon her by her gender.

Shi *Poetry of the Jin and Yuan Dynasties*

The most important *shi* poet of the Jin dynasty was Yuan Haowen (1190–1257). His most noted poems describe the horrors of the Mongol invasion. After the fall of the Jin in 1234, he refused to serve under the Mongols, devoting his time instead to the compilation of an extensive anthology of the work of Jin *shi* poets, the *Zhongzhou ji* (Poems from the Central Plain).

The outstanding Yuan dynasty *shi* poet is Yang Weizhen (1296-1370), who is especially admired for his *yuefu*.

Gao Qi (1336–1374) is usually regarded as the most important *shi* poet during the first years of the Ming dynasty (1368–1644). Gao lived near Suzhou, and in the troubled years toward the end of the Yuan, he enjoyed the patronage of the local warlord Zhang Shicheng. After the founding of the Ming dynasty, he worked for a while in Nanjing on the compilation of the official history of the Yuan dynasty. Soon after his return to Suzhou, he was executed on the orders of the suspicious first Ming emperor, Zhu Yuanzhang. As a poet, Gao is praised for his *yuefu* and his keen powers of observation. A central theme in his work is the question: how can a gentleman, living in a chaotic period, manage to make a contribution to the sacred work of ordering society? Especially enjoyable are his poems of homesickness written during his stay in Nanjing.

Poetry Criticism

Unlike the Tang, the Song period saw the growth of a considerable body of poetry criticism, which was published in the form of *shihua*. *Shihua* usually consist of a collection of brief appreciative remarks on individual poems or couplets. This kind of criticism is often described as impressionistic, but a fairer term might be essentialist, as the authors of *shihua* try to pinpoint the most important features of the poet under discussion. *Shihua* may also contain anecdotes about the circumstances under which poems were written and on the life of poets. The oldest exemplar of this genre is the *Liuyi shihua* (Liuyi's remarks on poems) by Ouyang Xiu (Liuyi being one of Ouyang's names). The example of this work was widely imitated. The *shihua* of individual authors were sometimes combined to form *shihua* collections.

One of the few systematically arranged *shihua* is the *Canglang shihua* (Canglang's remarks on poems) by Yan Yu (ca. 1200). The first chapter, concerned with general theory, includes Yan Yu's famous comparison between the practice of poetry writing and the practice of Zen: in both cases, he says, a long period of preparation is followed by an unpredictable moment of enlightenment. As models for those practicing the art, Yan Yu particularly recommends the High Tang poets, especially Du Fu; he vehemently condemns the superficial verbal tricks of the Jiangxi School. Yan Yu was one of the founders of a trend in criticism which rejected the poetry of the Southern Dynasties and the Song, preferring an "orthodox" poetic tradition represented especially by the third century and the Tang. This critical trend was at its height in the early years of the Ming dynasty.

CI POETRY

During the Song dynasty the *ci* became established as a type of poetry written by the literati, though it never displaced the *shi* as the most important form, and far fewer *ci* than *shi* have been preserved.

The first significant *ci* poets of the Song were Yan Shu (991–1055) and the somewhat younger Ouyang Xiu (1007–1072). Both held, at one time or another, very high posts in the bureaucracy. Both wrote mainly *xiaoling* (short *ci* lyrics, usually in two stanzas, of no more than 58 characters in length). The style and themes of their *xiaoling* are reminiscent of southern Tang *ci*: recurrent topics include the pleasures of an untrammeled life, concern over the transitoriness of human existence, and complaints over the absence of a lover. In one particular Song edition Ouyang Xiu is also credited with the authorship of some seventy songs which quite freely use spoken-language elements and treat the theme of love with unusual boldness.

This is also the period in which Liu Yong (987?–1053?) became the first important writer of *manci* (long *ci* in two or three stanzas and from 60 to 240 characters). After a period of indulgence in the pleasure precincts, he went on to a modest career in the bureaucracy. His *ci* songs are remarkable not only for their length but for their free use of vernacular language. The songs are on rather conventional subjects: life and love among the pleasure girls and their patrons, sorrow and loneliness after the inevitable farewells. Liu's *ci* enjoyed great popularity in the eleventh century.

The first poet to achieve a real extension of the thematic range of the *ci* was Su Shi (1037–1101). He wrote *ci* on subjects which had previously been treated only in *shi*, adopting in the process vocabulary taken from the idiom of the *shi* poets. Su's critics accused him of failing to recognize the musical character of the *ci*. Su is regarded as the creator of the *haofang pai* (heroic, unbound style) in *ci* poetry, a style which aims at direct expression of the author's own feelings—sometimes, indeed, at the cost of the more musical qualities. In this it differs from more conventional *ci*, in which the poet usually assumes the persona of an abandoned woman or a lonely traveler.

Su's pupil Qin Guan (1049–1100), by contrast, is regarded as a typical exponent of the *wanyue pai* (graceful, suggestive style)—i.e., the conventional *ci* poetry with its staple subjects of transitoriness and disappointed love. These are also the main themes of the songs of Zhou Bangyan (1057–1121).

Li Qingzhao (1084–ca. 1151) is China's outstanding woman poet. Before the fall of the Northern Song, she lived in luxury with her husband. In 1126 she fled to the South, where she spent the rest of her life as a widow in pitiable circumstances. In her *xiaoling* she gives free expression to her feelings; in style and themes, her work clearly owes more to the early *ci* poets than to more recent predecessors. The preserved body of her writings is regrettably very small. Apart from some fifty *ci* and a handful of *shi*, it also comprises a moving autobiographical document in the form of a postscript written for her late husband's collection of epigraphical materials, in which she recalls their happy marriage.

Xin Qiji (1140–1207) is, after Su Shi, the most important representative of the *haofang pai*. A native of Shandong, Xin went south to seek support for a rebellion against the Jin. When the movement was suppressed, he had no choice but to remain in the South. He filled various military posts under the Southern Song. His best-known songs praise the greatness of China or express his fiery longing for the reunion of the empire.

Jiang Kui (ca. 1155–ca. 1221) wrote *ci* famous for their meticulous choice of words. He paid close attention to the musical aspects of his songs, and he was also a composer. The music of a number of his melodies has been preserved.

The *ci* of Wu Wenying (ca. 1200–ca. 1260) are noted for their mannered diction; quotes and allusions abound. Zhou Mi (1232–1298), himself a well-known *ci* poet, compiled an anthology of Southern Song *ci* entitled *Juemiao haoci* (Most remarkably good songs).

In the northern Chinese territory governed by the Jin dynasty, the patriarchs of the Quanzhen sect of Taoism often used the *ci* form to propagate their ideas. These *ci* are remarkable for their forceful use of the vernacular.

After the rise of the *qu* in the thirteenth century, the *ci* form fell into disuse; it was no longer widely practiced in the Yuan and Ming periods.

Chapter 16
PROSE: *GUWEN, BIJI, CHUANQI, PINGHUA*

During the Tang dynasty the *guwen yundong* did not lead to a lasting change in prose style, but in the eleventh century, interest in *guwen* revived. As had been the case in the Tang, the Song *guwen yundong* was not a purely literary affair; the emphasis on simple and clear prose, and on the primacy of correct content over form, was part and parcel of a Song trend toward the reevaluation and reformulation of Confucianism. This movement, known as Neo-Confucianism, must be seen as closely related to the far-reaching changes in the nature of the gentry and of the government apparatus that occurred during this period. Whereas the gentry had previously been a select hereditary group dominated by the leading families of North China, it now became a class of much wider and more fluid proportions. Membership was theoretically open to all who could demonstrate their qualification, and in practice it came to include increasing numbers of individuals of Central and South Chinese origin.

Ouyang Xiu

The leading Song exponent of the *guwen yundong* was Ouyang Xiu, who greatly admired the work of Han Yu and Liu Zongyuan. Acting in the official capacity of Examiner during the examinations at the capital in 1057, he gave ample sway to his own preferences, failing certain widely favored candidates in the process. Outrage resulted—but those granted degrees included Su Shi. From then on *guwen* became the required style for examination essays.

Ouyang Xiu saw in the simplicity and naturalness of *Dao* (the Way) the highest truth and the model for both writing and behavior. Accordingly, he demanded of prose the qualities of *xin* (truthfulness), *chang* (general validity), and *jian* (simplicity, lack of spurious ornament). His best-known prose works include various *lun* (treatises), such as the *Pengdang lun* (Treatise on cliques of friends), in which he defends the formation of factions by officials desirous of reforms; various *xu* (prefaces), such as his *Mei Shengyu shiji xu* (Preface to the collected poems of Mei Shengyu, i.e., Mei Yaochen), in which he argues that deprivation can make a man a better poet; a number of *ji* (reports, descriptions) including *Zuiweng ting ji* (Description of the pavilion of the old drunkard), which presents a self-portrait; and various *wenfu* (prose fu), e.g., the "Qiusheng fu" (The sound of autumn). His *Xin Wudai shi* (New history of the Five Dynasties) is much praised for its style.

Other Eleventh-Century Prose Writers

Historians of *guwen* often refer to the *Tang Song ba dajia* (eight great masters of the Tang and Song): Han Yu, Liu Zongyuan, Ouyang Xiu, Su Xun (1009–1066) and his sons Su Shi and Su Che (1039–1112), Zeng Gong (1019–1083), and Wang Anshi. Of the last five, Su Shi is considered the greatest.

Su Xun did not take up studying until after the birth of his sons. In 1056 he went with them to the capital, where all three enjoyed Ouyang Xiu's patronage. Su Xun refused to take part in the regular examinations, and he attained to no more than minor bureaucratic posts. As a prose writer he is remembered primarily for his undogmatic treatises (*lun*) on historical topics.

His eldest son, Su Shi, is also famous for such treatises. Also renowned are his memorials, his *ji*, such as the "Xiyu ting ji" (Description of the Pavilion for Enjoying the Rain), and especially two of his *wenfu*: the "Qian Chibi fu" (First visit to the Red Cliff) and the "Hou Chibi fu" (Second visit to the Red Cliff), both written after he was banned to Huangzhou in 1079. In these Red Cliff poems, Su Shi expresses glad acceptance of a relativistic attitude toward life, seeing himself as a participant in the eternal process of change.

Su Shi's younger brother Su Che had a checkered official career that ran in rough parallel to the ups and downs in his famous elder brother's career. Su Che wrote a number of *lun* and *ji* of lasting popularity.

Unlike Ouyang Xiu and the Su brothers, Zeng Gong owes his name entirely to his prose writings. It is difficult, however, to identify any of his individual works as especially famous. As for Wang Anshi, his role as prose writer has been completely overshadowed by his importance as a statesman.

Ancient-Style Prose in Later Centuries

The Southern Song, the Jin, and the Yuan did not produce writers specifically famous for their non-fictional prose. The most remarkable development during the twelfth century was the popularity of the travel book. Lu You wrote a lively record, *Ru Shu ji* (Journey to Shu), of his trip up the Yangzi in 1170 when he was appointed to an official post in Sichuan. The poet Fan Chengda, after serving in Chengdu, made the same trip downstream in 1177 and wrote an account of that experience entitled *Wuchuan lu* (Record of a boat trip to Wu). Fan's *Lanpei lu* (Record of holding the reins) is an account of his mission in 1170 to the capital of the Jin dynasty. His *Canluan lu* (Record of riding the simurgh) describes his trip to the southwestern city of Guilin in 1173. In the early thirteenth century one of the patriarchs of the Quanzhen sect, Qiu Chuji, was summoned to Central Asia by Genghis Khan; he wrote a record of his journey and of his conversations with the Mongol ruler entitled *Xiyou ji* (Journey to the west).

The most highly regarded prose writers of the first century of the Ming are Song Lian (1310–1381), Liu Ji (1311–1375), and Fang Xiaoru (1357–1402). Among other things, Song Lian was commissioned to compile the official *Yuan shi* (History of the Yuan). Liu Ji was important as an advisor to Zhu Yuanzhang. Fang Xiaoru is famous not least of all for his loyalty to Zhu Yuanzhang's unfortunate grandson and successor, the Jianwen Emperor.

Once *guwen* became the required style for examination essays, it was not long before a rigid new form developed for these essays. This form was subject to rules no less detailed than those of the old parallel prose. Starting in Ming times the examination essay was referred to as the *baguwen* (composition in eight parts; the expression is often translated as "eight-legged essay"). This form had found its typical shape by the late fifteenth century and remained obligatory for examination purposes until the end of the Qing.

Anthologies of *guwen* prose, suitable for study by examination candidates, soon appeared. Some of these consisted entirely of works by the "eight great masters"; others contained, in addition, selections from later writers and from the works which the *guwen* "masters" had taken as their models, especially the *Zuo zhuan*, the *Zhanguo ce*, and the *Shiji*. One of the most popular of these more comprehensive anthologies was the *Guwen guanzhi* (Perfect survey of ancient-style prose), compiled in 1692 on the basis of earlier anthologies.

THE SHORT STORY AND *BIJI*

In sharp contrast to *guwen* with its remarkable revival during the Song, the *chuanqi* faded into the background during this period, at least in qualitative terms. The only author worth mentioning is Yue Shi (930–1007), who wrote a number of *waizhuan* (unofficial traditions, i.e., collected anecdotes on a given character). He is the author, for example, of *Yang Taizhen waizhuan* (Unofficial traditions concerning Yang Taizhen, i.e., High Consort Yang: Yang Guifei).

Probably also dating from this period are a number of compilations of gossip, scandal tales, and anecdotal histories, for example, on Emperor Yang of the Sui and on the building of the Grand Canal. In northern Song *chuanqi* of this kind there is no idealizing of the past. On the contrary, negative aspects often receive special prominence. Another novel feature is that in many of these *chuanqi*, ghosts of departed persons appear for the specific purpose of correcting or adding factual details to the current versions of their life stories.

The *Taiping guangji*, completed in 978, has already been mentioned. In the course of the Song dynasty several smaller story collections were also compiled, usually consisting of concisely retold *chuanqi* together with more recent anecdotes. A noted work along these lines is the *Qingsuo gaoyi* (Elevated conversations by the green lattice), comprising 145 stories, compiled by a certain Liu Fu (eleventh century). A comparable work from the Southern Song is the *Lüchuang xinhua* (New stories by the green window), which contains 154 stories. A thirteenth-century work is the *Zuiweng tanlu* (Excerpts from the conversations of the old drunkard), compiled by one Luo Ye, concerning whom no biographical facts have been recorded. This work is important for the history of storytelling as it contains lists of subjects that were popular with storytellers.

The Song saw a tremendous flourishing of *biji* literature, and the volume of *biji* literature increased steadily after the Song. *Biji* is a general term for collections of short notes by individual authors on various subjects. *Biji* can deal with a tremendous variety of topics, depending on the author's personal interests. Some are concerned with philological observations; others are reflections on history, political anecdotes, or fragments of literary criticism.

Some *biji* consist almost entirely of supernatural stories. An example is the massive, but incompletely preserved, compilation of then-recent stories of the supernatural, *Yi Jian zhi* (Notes by Yi Jian); Yi Jian is named in the *Liezi* as a contemporary of the mythical ancient emperor Yu; he is there said to have written down records of strange happenings. The compiler of the *Yi Jian zhi* was Hong Mai (1123–1202), who also produced numerous other still-extant works. The stories in the *Yi Jian zhi* are mostly short and succinct; they show less concern with structure and composition than many of the Tang *chuanqi*.

Quite an exceptional work is "Jiaohong ji" (The story of Wang Jiaoniang and Feihong), by Song Yuan (late thirteenth century), which tells the story of the unhappy love affair between Wang Jiaoniang and her cousin Shen Chun. This work is remarkable for its length—about five times that of "Yingying zhuan"—and for the great number of *ci* which it includes. Though the "Jiaohong ji" story was repeatedly adapted for the stage in Yuan and early Ming times, the actual *chuanqi* came to be largely ignored.

Not until the first century of the Ming did the *chuanqi* once again come to the fore, albeit briefly. In Ming *chuanqi* the action is often set in the restless period of the late Yuan, and the text usually contains a great number of poems, songs, letters, etc. The best-known collections of this period are the *Jiandeng xinhua* (New stories to trim the lamp by), containing twenty-one stories, compiled by Qu You (1341–1427; also a noted poet), and the *Jiandeng yuhua* (Additional stories to trim the lamp by), containing twenty-two stories, compiled by the high bureaucrat Li Changqi (1376–1452).

PINGHUA

Dating from the second half of the thirteenth and the fourteenth century are a number of texts called *pinghua* (simple story). These present familiar legends or historical stories in a very simple style clearly influenced by the contemporary spoken language. The *pinghua* is the forerunner of the later traditional Chinese novel, and the subjects of certain *pinghua* reappeared later in novel form.

Twelfth- to fourteenth-century descriptions of Kaifeng and Hangzhou have come down to us that describe the amusement districts, the various entertainments including storytellers, and the best-known artists. It has often been suggested that *pinghua* were used as "cribs" by these professional storytellers, and alternatively, that *pinghua* were later reworkings of such cribs.

In the light of our present knowledge it seems premature to posit such an exclusive relationship between *pinghua* and the professional storytellers. To be sure, the description of historical occurrences in *pinghua* clearly owes much to sources other than the orthodox written ones. Oral tradition is also evident, as are the mannerisms employed by storytellers, actors, and other performers. For the time being, it seems safest to regard *pinghua* primarily as a form of amusement reading specially written for, and mainly read by, an audience of limited literacy.

The texts designated as *pinghua* include the following. The *Xuanhe yishi* (Anecdotes on the Xuanhe period) describes events around the fall of the Northern Song dynasty. The *Wudaishi pinghua* (Simple story of the History of the Five Dynasties) is concerned with the wars from the fall of the Tang to the founding of the Song. Its text is largely derived, directly or indirectly, from the *Tongjian gangmu*. *Quanxiang pinghua wuzhong* (Five fully illustrated simple stories) is the twentieth-century collective title of five different *pinghua*, published by the same firm, describing various periods of ancient Chinese history, such as the founding of the Zhou dynasty, the founding of the Han dynasty, and the civil wars toward the end of the Han which led to the division of the empire into three parts. The modern collective title refers to the fact that in their original edition these narratives are accompanied by illustrations at the top of each page. The *Xue Rengui zheng Liao shilue* (A brief account of the subjugation of Liao by Xue Rengui) describes the career of Xue Rengui during the campaigns mounted by Tang Taizong (Li Shimin) against what is now Korea. This text owes its preservation to the fact that it occurs in one of the extant fragments of the *Yongle dadian*, a supremely ambitious compilation intended to include all literature and reading matter then in existence, which was completed in 1408.

The *Da Tang Sanzang qu jing shihua* (The story, with poems, of how Tripitaka of the Great Tang went to obtain sutras in the Western Paradise) may well be the oldest preserved *pinghua*. It differs in several respects from the works described above. The subject is not a period in military history but a Buddhist legend, and the text is divided into numerous episodes, each ending with one or more poems spoken by characters in the stories.

Chapter 17.
QU: ZHUGONGDIAO, ZAJU AND SANQU, AND XIWEN

QU

By a process of development culminating in the twelfth century, the art of the Chinese song underwent changes that led to the rise of a new genre referred to in Chinese as *qu*—and to the rapid demise of the *ci* as sung music. The geographical center of these new developments was the North China Plain, and reference is often made to *beiqu*, "northern songs," as distinct from the new songs which were concurrently developing in China south of the Yangzi, the so-called *nanqu* or "southern songs." In what follows, unless otherwise specified, the term *qu* will be used to mean *beiqu*.

Qu differ from *ci* in a number of ways. *Qu* tended increasingly to be no longer than one stanza, and from the mid-thirteenth century on, two-stanza *qu* have disappeared. *Qu* make free use of the contemporary spoken language, especially of the North Chinese dialect that is the direct ancestor of modern standard Chinese. There were, to be sure, plenty of *qu* which fell back on conventional poetic idiom (especially that of the *ci*), but unlike *ci*, *qu* often consciously exploit the specific features of the contemporary vernacular, such as polysyllabicity.

The use of spoken-language elements was facilitated by the use of *chenzi* (filler words)—this being a third major difference between *qu* and *ci*. *Chenzi* are words that are spoken in rapid tempo rather than being sung. They can occur at the beginning of a line (often in the form of a group of three syllables) or within the line (often as a one-syllable element). *Chenzi* are often used to make clear the syntax of a line or to indicate the relationship between one line and another. Some *chenzi* are so-called "impressives," e.g., onomatopoeic words borrowed from the language of everyday speech. While some *qu* only allow a limited use of *chenzi*, others are extremely hospitable to them.

Yet another difference is that although *qu*, like *ci*, are written in prescribed forms associated with specific melodies, the forms of *qu* allow more variation than those of *ci*.

165

Qu and *ci* also differed fundamentally as regards their use as musical songs that could be put together to form suites. *Ci* were sometimes combined into song suites by repeating the same melody a number of times. Sometimes the successive reprises of the melody showed no variation, as in the *zhuanta*, which comprised several rounds of alternate *ci* and *lüshi*, the last two syllables of the *lüshi* being repeated as the first two of the following *ci*. In the *guzici* or "drum song," the same melody was repeated ten or more times, also without variation. In some types of *ci* suites, such as the *daqu* or "great songs," the reprises were subject to standard types of variation applied in a prescribed order.

In the case of *qu*, suites (*taoshu*) were formed by combining different melodies. The melodies did have to be in the same mode. Rules governed such combinations, and the suite might or might not conclude with a coda appropriate to the given mode. Within one and the same *taoshu*, regardless of its length, all the songs had to be written to the same rhyme!

The *qu* form lent itself to a number of different applications. It was used, of course, for the writing of poems. In this use, whether the poems consist of individual *qu* or of suites, they are referred to as *sanqu* (independent songs). The *sanqu* reached its pinnacle in the period 1250–1350.

Longer or shorter *qu* suites were also used in a genre of storytelling, the *zhugongdiao* or "in all keys and modes," in which the story was alternately told in prose and sung in *qu* lyrics. This genre took its name from the fact that two successive suites are almost never in the same key. The *zhugongdiao* was popular in the twelfth and thirteenth centuries.

Long *qu* suites were also used in a form of drama called *zaju* (comedy). In a *zaju*, one actor sang four long suites. The songs within each suite were not sung in unbroken succession; monologs, dialogs, and action were inserted at frequent intervals.

THE "IN ALL KEYS AND MODES"

The *zhugongdiao* tells a story alternately in prose and in verse. The verse passages show no fixed line length but are written to suites of *qu* melodies. These verse passages make up by far the greater portion of the text; with few exceptions the prose passages merely serve as connecting links or as brief summaries of material needed by listeners to understand the following *qu*.

The typical subject of *zhugongdiao* is a love story presented in an ironic light: love makes the man foolish and helpless, while the woman plays the decisive role with a sure hand. The text of a *zhugongdiao* is divided over a number of chapters, each of which ends on a high point of suspense. Each chapter contains at least one additional high point. It seems probable that a chapter was the portion of the text covered by the performer(s) during a single day, ending at an intriguing point of irresolution. The earlier climax within the chapter could have been the point at which the performer(s) paused to take up a collection.

The individual suites can be as short as a single *qu* in two stanzas followed by the coda; in some keys even the coda is absent. Over time the suites became longer. The songs within a given suite (and the suite as a whole) often build up to a clear "punch line." The language of the lyrics, depending on their function in the story, can vary from almost pure vernacular to conventional poetic idiom, mostly taken from the *ci* tradition.

The *zhugongdiao* arose shortly before the fall of the Northern Song, reached its apogee under the Jin around the year 1200, and was replaced by the *zaju* in the course of the thirteenth century. Only one *zhugongdiao* has been preserved fully intact. This is the *Xixiang ji zhugongdiao* (The story of the Western Chambers "in all keys and modes") by Dong Jieyuan, who was active in the period 1190–1208. This work in eight chapters is a detailed elaboration of Yuan Zhen's "Yingying zhuan." In preparing his version, Dong clearly drew inspiration from the story of Sima Xiangru and Zhuo Wenjun. His main additions to the story are the more detailed descriptions of the main characters; the heightened prominence of figures who are barely mentioned in "Yingying zhuan," such as Yingying's maidservant Hongniang; the creation of numerous new characters not in the original; new episodes; and a completely revised ending in which Zhang, after passing his examinations, returns to the monastery and Yingying elopes with him.

The anonymous *Liu Zhiyuan zhugongdiao* (The "in all keys and modes" on Liu Zhiyuan), thought to be a mid-twelfth-century work, has been preserved only in fragments. This *zhugongdiao* tells the story of Liu Zhiyuan, the founder of the Later Han dynasty (one of the Five Dynasties). While still a poor farm hand, he marries Li Sanniang, daughter of a well-to-do farmer; they are later separated but are reunited in the end after Liu becomes governor. The *Liu Zhiyuan zhugongdiao* is in all respects a much more modest work than the *Xixiang ji zhugongdiao*.

Of the *Tianbao yishi zhugongdiao* (Anecdotes of the Tianbao period "in all keys and modes"), written by Wang Bocheng in the second half of the thirteenth century, some fifty individual suites are extant, but nothing remains of the connecting prose passages, and the order in which the suites were originally arranged can be reconstructed no more than approximately. The subject of this *zhugongdiao* is the famous love story of Xuanzong and High Consort Yang.

THE NORTHERN DRAMA

General Characteristics of Traditional Chinese Theater

The great cities of the Song dynasty had extensive amusement districts. Here were acrobats, pole-climbers, tightrope walkers, escape artists, and sword swallowers. There were bear-baiters, flea circuses, and magicians. Puppet shows, marionette plays and shadow plays were available. Professional wrestlers vied for attention with experts in archery or other military skills.

Another major entertainment was the professional storyteller, who might specialize in historical tales, lives of Buddhist saints and Taoist immortals, love stories, or crime stories. There were performers who could improvise a poem on the spot on any given subject. There were a wide range of musical amusements including, of course, dance. Finally, there was the most direct ancestor of the theater: the farce.

Originally, the farce seems not to have amounted to much more than a comic dialog between two men, but gradually the number of players increased while the performances were made more complex by the addition of elements drawn from other genres. It seems probable that the performers of the various genres appeared one after another in a sort of variety show.

From these origins Chinese theater developed into an integrated dramatic whole in which all the various elements continued to play vital roles: text, music, song, acting, acrobatics (especially in martial-arts scenes), dance, story line, costuming, and make-up. Hardly a single form of amusement was irrelevant (save, possibly, the flea circus). As for the amusement genres, they all continued to exist in their own right apart from the drama, in many cases up to the present.

The fact that Chinese drama originated in commercial variety shows goes far toward explaining the absence of a distinction between tragedy and comedy. Such a distinction did exist in ancient Greece and in the Japanese No theater, in which serious edifying pieces alternated with farces. In the Chinese theater, as in Shakespeare's plays, there is a constant interweaving of both elements. The young hero is constantly accompanied by the clown; every chaste young lady has a servant girl who puts into bold prose the feelings her mistress hides in poetry. Even in pieces on dramatic themes of loyalty or self-sacrifice, the author frequently opens with a series of bawdy jokes to get the audience's attention. The theater often did double duty as a restaurant, and audiences were, to put it mildly, not inclined to observe strict silence.

It is not true that Chinese drama consists of nothing but comedies and trivia with happy endings. But what is indeed absent from the Chinese theater is the typical seventeenth-century Western tragedy, written after the example of Seneca's closet drama, in which a number of noble heroes express their lofty feelings in elegant language prior to their glorious demise.

Nor does the Chinese theater know rigid distinctions as to drama, opera, operetta, and musical. In traditional China a dramatic performance without musical accompaniment was unthinkable, but music was never allowed to dominate the whole. Attempts were never made to set entire texts to music. The music was not specially composed for a given play; the author chose existing melodies that seemed to him most suitable, writing his arias to known tunes. There was nothing against the introduction of new melodies, but generally speaking, each genre of drama had its own group of melodies and other characteristic musical features. The music is, in fact, the basis of the classification into various forms.

The close relationship between drama and music has produced terminological confusion in the Western languages, which can refer to Yuan "comedy," Ming "drama," and the modern Peking "opera," which all have the same relationship between text and music. But the Western terminology is no problem to the Chinese. Their problem was what to call drama that was not sung, and they had to create a new Chinese word, *huaju*, for the spoken drama which was introduced under Western influence in the early twentieth century.

For Chinese drama buffs the crux of the musical performance lies in the actor-singer's personal manner of interpretation. As the Chinese performer need not be concerned with the supposed intentions of a composer, he enjoys much greater freedom than his Western counterpart—the more so as the Chinese drama troupe did not have a director or conductor who might have wanted to impose a personal vision on all aspects of the show. Traditionally a troupe had an overall leader, who managed its affairs very much in the sense of a business manager. The modest orchestra was directed, under his supervision, by one of the older musicians, and the older actors and actresses coached their younger colleagues. All in all, there was considerable room for the leading players to indulge what they felt to be their own fortes.

The function of the theater in society had important consequences for the physical aspects of dramatic art. Theater troupes performed not only in regular theaters but also, by invitation, in private homes on festive occasions. Some troupes traveled from city to city, from town to town, performing at temple festivals. Performance had to be possible under any conditions, without a regular decor, extensive props, or complicated stage machines. The actor himself had to be able to evoke any necessary illusion. Accordingly, over the centuries, not out of philosophical conviction but from sheer necessity, the Chinese drama developed an all-inclusive language of symbolic forms. To the uninitiated, this language seems at times as esoteric and incomprehensible as the finger gestures of a Thai dancer. In Peking opera, when the commander, recognizable by the two pheasant feathers in his helmet, stands on a chair, it means that he is standing atop a hill looking out over the battlefield. If he then brandishes his whip, it means he is riding his horse.

Consequently, the actor is not much concerned with developing empathy or rapport with the character he is to portray, so as to imitate authentically the behavior characteristic of that person. The Chinese actor displays symbolic behavior in a standardized language of forms. Daily life is not imitated but presented to the audience in conventionally codified form.

But whatever was saved on stage decoration was more than lavished on costumes. These were of dazzling beauty and probably accounted for the greater part of a troupe's initial capital outlay. Even the oldest preserved pictures of actors and actresses on stage, dating from the twelfth century, depict gaudy, if simple costumes. The facial make-up (now an inseparable feature of Peking opera) is modest, but the make-up of the clown stands out with its heavy black and white stripes. Masks were not much used in China, except in simple exorcist dramas or for portraying ghosts. Face-painting, however, evolved into a full symbolic system in its own right: for those who understand it, the combination of colors and forms is often enough to identify the type and sometimes even the specific identity of a character from the first moment the actor appears on stage. Such elaborate make-up took hours to apply.

The roles in the piece were cast according to a scheme of types, and a troupe's actors and actresses were assigned specific role types. The script did not read "enter Zhang Gong, a handsome young student," but "enter the male lead as Zhang Gong." The role types were divided into male and female, civil and military, positive and negative. In earlier centuries it was not unusual for a woman to play the roles that fell under a particular male role type, such as the young hero. In recent centuries, however, in such a form as the Peking opera, it has been normal for men—and not just young boys!—to play female roles.

An actor specializing in a civilian role type was expected to be an outstanding singer; the specialist in military roles had to be a skilled acrobat who could perform spectacular martial-arts feats. Negative role types included comic and unsympathetic characters. Such clowns often appeared in duos as servants, traitors, robbers, and other unattractive types. And usually they were not only nasty but superlatively stupid, so that their dastardly plans failed through their own ignorance and clumsiness. They often played a sort of parody on the main plot: for example, while the abbot is engaged in trying to convert a brilliant young student, the acolyte seeks to seduce his servant boy. In the West, such subplots are associated with the plays of Shakespeare and his contemporaries—perhaps the closest of all Western dramatic forms to the Chinese theater.

Though professional actors and actresses sometimes earned a considerable income, their social status was low. They constituted one of the very few groups that were barred from taking the state examinations. The word "actress" was always synonymous with courtesan: girls and women skilled in the use of dance, song, music, and witty conversation to amuse well-to-do gentlemen, alone or in company, in return for suitable fees. And every courtesan, whether or not she was specifically an actress, was expected to be able to sing at least the best-loved arias from the most famous dramas.

Many an actress had a patron who was especially enamored of her and with whom she might have a more intimate relationship. The situation suggests parallels, for example, with that of the actress in eighteenth-century France. In China it was possible for an actress to become a concubine of her older, rich patron, but an even more common theme of Chinese love comedies was the courtesan-actress who falls in love with a poor student, supports him until he passes the state examinations, and subsequently becomes his legal wife.

The text of a play is but one component entering into the finished performance. In the Western dramatic tradition, the text is central; in China it plays a more modest role. It is impossible to do justice to the Chinese drama by studying texts apart from the actual performance. This is amply demonstrated by the Peking opera, which for centuries has been fascinating audiences with performances based, in all too many cases, on texts distinctly lacking intrinsic interest.

Though the oldest preserved texts of Chinese plays date only from the thirteenth century, the history of Chinese drama goes back to much earlier times, and scholars have identified a wide variety of cultural elements and art forms that can be regarded as more or less direct ancestors of the dramatic genres known to us from the thirteenth century onward. These elements include, for example, shaman seances and other religious rituals of antiquity in which priests or priestesses played the role of gods or demons. Another example is the *baixi* (hundred games), exhibitions of acrobatics and martial arts, extensive descriptions of which go back as far as Han times. It goes without saying that the arts of song and dance have contributed to the Chinese drama. Even in the days of the Zhou dynasty rulers, *you* (entertainers) were employed at court, their function resembling medieval European court jesters.

In Tang times there were various kinds of performances collectively known as *gewuju* (singing and dancing plays); others were designated as *canjunxi* (adjutant plays). *Gewuju* refers to a sort of narrative ballet in which the dancers sometimes spoke simple dialog; more often, the action being depicted was the subject of songs sung by a separate choir.

Canjunxi in their simplest form are comic dialogs between two men, somewhat comparable to the modern *xiangsheng*. According to ancient anecdotes, *canjunxi* performances at court included political satire. In some cases, apparently, the term *canjunxi* was also applied to longer plays with more than two actors. During the Northern Song, both genres existed side by side. In the twelfth century, the *canjunxi* evolved into the farce, which was referred to in the North, under the Jin, as *yuanben*, and in the South, under the Southern Song, as *zaju*.

The general category of farce actually includes a wide variety of dramatic forms, from comic dialogs for two or four voices to sketches to longish melodramatic plays, from texts exclusively in prose to texts wholly or partly in verse, with or without musical accompaniment and song. In a farce, as in later dramatic genres, the roles were divided among a number of fixed role types. The most important sources of our present-day knowledge of the farce are two preserved lists of titles, one of *yuanben* and one of *zaju*. In the North, in the thirteenth century, the farce, together with singing and dancing plays (*gewuju*) and other elements, evolved into the comedy (*zaju*), which utilized *qu* music. At the same time, in the South, especially at Wenzhou, there developed another form of drama, referred to as *xiwen* (play text).

The Musical Organization of Zaju

All known forms of traditional Chinese drama make use of music and song. In the comedy (*zaju*), the singing is limited to four long suites of *qu* (from eight to twenty melodies in all) in various modes; all four are to be sung by one and the same role type, and thus by the same actor or actress. To these four suites, one or two "wedges" could be added. A wedge (*xiezi*) consists of only one or two songs, and only certain melodies could serve as wedges. A wedge could precede the first suite or occur between two suites. The major *zaju* roles were divided into *mo* (man), *dan* (woman), *jing* (rogue, rascal), *gu* (government official), *wai* (extra), and *lai* (child). Only *mo* or *dan* were allowed to sing, but if necessary for the purposes of the play, the singing player could change character in between two suites. Men or women could play any role type. Besides these role types, there were a number of fixed types of minor roles.

Starting in the sixteenth century, text editions of comedies were divided, on the basis of the suites, into four acts with or without one or two wedges.

The songs belonging to the same suite often show a close mutual relationship, but time, place, and action often change within a given suite or act. Since convention required that only one player be allowed to sing, the character played by this person was much better able to express feeling than the other characters. Not surprisingly, this character tended to emerge in far more memorable detail and roundness than the others.

Zaju: *Texts and Themes*

The comedy (*zaju*) suddenly appeared on the scene in the mid-thirteenth century, its creation traditionally attributed to Guan Hanqing (ca. 1220–ca. 1300). The most important late-thirteenth-century authors were active in North China, especially in Dadu (the present-day Peking), while the best-known authors of the first half of the fourteenth century were those in and around Hangzhou. Only thirty comedies have been preserved in contemporary (Yuan) printed editions, and these versions provide only the text of the arias or the text of the songs together with stage directions and the essential spoken lines for the leading role type. This latter text format probably originated in the role text of the leading role type. After the founding of the Ming dynasty, the comedy enjoyed special imperial favor. The most important early-fifteenth-century author was Zhu Youdun (1379–1439), a grandson of Zhu Yuanzhang. He wrote thirty-one plays and was the first to have his works printed "with complete dialog."

The oldest available texts of most *zaju* are late sixteenth- or early seventeenth-century editions; practically all are directly or indirectly based on the texts used for performances at the imperial court. It is not clear to what degree these texts remain faithful to the originals; they were subject to court censorship, and after several centuries of continued adaptation for purposes of performance, they were edited and "polished" by literary publishers to make them more enjoyable as reading matter.

The best-known of these later anthologies is the *Yuanqu xuan* (Selected Yuan plays), published in 1616–17, which contains a hundred comedies of the Yuan and the early Ming. Of the comedies still in existence, modern scholars attribute to Yuan authors a total of 160 to 170; the number of extant pieces dating from 1250–1450 is probably fewer than 250.

Comedies enjoy practically unlimited subject matter. A tremendous variety of events, whether recent or from the hoariest antiquity, could be adapted for the stage. There are, however, certain general thematic categories.

First are the historical plays treating key moments in Chinese history. These can be subdivided into two groups emphasizing either intrigues at court or battlefield events. Battlefield plays include works dealing with the war between Xiang Yu and Liu Bang, with the wars leading to the tripartition of 220, or with the wars in which various members of the Yang family led the Northern Song in combat against the Liao. Another group of military plays takes its material from the activities of a band of noble robbers led by Song Jiang in the area of the Liangshan Marshes in the early years of the twelfth century.

Another large group of comedies focuses on the theme of a love affair between a young student and a courtesan or the daughter of a prominent family; the stories are often taken from Tang *chuanqi*. Another group tells the story of a crime and its ultimate punishment. In these works the incorruptible judge passing impeccable sentence is often Judge Bao, based on the real Bao Zheng who lived in the first half of the eleventh century.

Finally, there is a group of Taoist or Buddhist tales of salvation in which the main character, having suffered the blows of fate until he realizes the vanity of worldly existence, says farewell to the world and becomes the disciple of a master, ultimately attaining immortality (or, in the Buddhist plays, entering into Nirvana). Taoist plays of this type often feature the Eight Immortals (*ba xian*).

The Most Important Zaju Authors

The most important comedy writers lived in the second half of the thirteenth century. Guan Hanqing is credited (not altogether firmly) with the authorship of sixty-three plays, of which seventeen have been preserved. In his plays the *dan* usually has the singing role, and he is much praised for his descriptions of women's feelings. His most famous play is *Dou E yuan* (The injustice done to Dou E). The young widow Dou E, unjustly accused of murder, confesses in order to save her elderly mother-in-law from torture; she is executed, but is posthumously rehabilitated. In modern China this play has often been read as an expression of anti-Mongol sentiments.

Other famous plays by Guan Hanqing include *Jiu fengchen* (The courtesan saved), in which a shrewd courtesan succeeds in rescuing a former colleague from the hands of her dastardly husband so that she can marry a decent scholar. In *Hudie meng* (The butterfly dream), a mother shows that she would rather see her own child punished than let her stepchildren undergo punishment, whereupon Judge Bao, impressed by her virtue, has someone else executed in her son's place. *Dandao hui* (The one-sword meeting) describes an episode from the civil war at the end of the Han dynasty, with Guan Yu in the main role: his indomitable presence alone is enough to scare his opponents.

Seventeen plays can be attributed with certainty to Ma Zhiyuan (ca. 1250–between 1321 and 1324); of these, six have been preserved. His masterpiece is *Hangong qiu* (Autumn in the palace of Han). It describes the love of Emperor Yuan (r. 48–33 B.C.) for the palace lady Wang Zhaojun, whose beauty he does not discover until she has already been promised in marriage to the khan of the Xiongnu, and whose departure even he is unable to prevent. Ma Zhiyuan also wrote a number of salvation plays, including one, *Huangliang meng* (Yellow millet dream), in collaboration with professional actors. He is also one of the most important *sanqu* writers.

Bai Pu (1226–after 1306) was raised as a foster son by the poet Yuan Haowen. Of the fifteen plays attributed to him, no more than two have been preserved. He is famous mainly for the *Wutong yu* (Rain on the plane tree), which depicts the love felt by Xuanzong in his old age for High Consort Yang: even after her death, during the revolt of An Lushan which she had helped to bring about, Xuanzong's feeling for her remains.

Wang Shifu (late thirteenth century) is famous as the author of *Xixiang ji* (The story of the western chamber), the drama version of Dong Jieyuan's *Xixiang ji zhugongdiao*, which, as we saw, was derived from Yuan Zhen's classical tale "Yingying zhuan." *Xixiang ji*, probably the most famous and most widely read traditional Chinese play, is five times as long as a normal comedy; it consists of five plays of four acts each (except the second, which has five). The earliest completely preserved edition dates from 1498, and from the remainder of the Ming dynasty alone no less than sixty editions are known!

The story of the *Xixiang ji* is set in the Tang dynasty in a monastery, which also has lodgings for guests. The visitors are a poor student (Zhang Gong), a chancellor's widow, her daughter Yingying, and Yingying's servant girl Hongniang. Zhang Gong sees Yingying and falls in love. When local mutinous troops lay siege to the monastery, her mother promises to let her marry Zhang Gong if he writes a letter that will persuade a local commander, a friend of his, to take action to protect the monastery. Later, however, she tries to go back on her word. Hongniang conveys to Zhang Gong an invitation from Yingying to visit her in her room by night. When he arrives, however, Yingying lectures him for his dishonorable intentions. He retreats in despair. Fortunately Hongniang manages to change her mistress's attitude, and eventually the once-prudish Yingying nightly visits Zhang Gong in his room. Their relationship becomes known to Yingying's mother, who consents to a marriage if Zhang Gong can pass the examinations. He does so, and after a few more complications—Yingying's former fiancé suddenly turns up at the monastery—Zhang Gong and Yingying are married.

The main source of information on *zaju* authors is the *Lugui bu* (Ledger for the registration of ghosts) by Zhong Sicheng (1279–1360). This work, published in 1330, provides lists of plays written by various authors and very brief biographical summaries. Zhong Sicheng himself wrote *zaju*, though none have survived, and he has a modest name as a *sanqu* writer. A sequel to the *Lugui bu*, the *Lugui bu xubian* (Continuation of the Ledger for the registration of ghosts), is sometimes attributed to the *zaju* writer Jia Zhongming (1343–after 1422).

The Performance of Zaju

Little is known with certainty about how *zaju* were performed; our knowledge is based mainly on a few *sanqu* which describe performances and on plays set in the theater world. The *Qinglou ji* (Notes on the green houses), by Xia Tingzhi (ca. 1316–after 1368), consists of extremely brief biographical notes on Yuan courtesans, some of whom were actresses or *zhugongdiao* performers.

Somewhat more information is provided by the *Taihe zhengyin pu* (Tables of correct tones for a period of Great Peace). This is the oldest preserved *qupu* (table of songs), that is, a book listing in tabular form the various *qu* melodies with their prescribed song forms, showing the number of lines, length of the lines, prescribed tone of individual syllables, and rhyme placements—after the analogy of the *cipu*. The *Taihe zhengyin pu* was compiled by Zhu Quan (1378–1448), himself a *zaju* writer, who was a son of the Hongwu Emperor.

SANQU

The oldest preserved *sanqu* date back to the Jin, but the apogee of the genre coincides with the Yuan dynasty. *Sanqu* can take the form of single songs (in which case, as with the *ci*, the term *xiaoling* is applicable), of short suites of two to five songs, or of longer suites containing six or more songs. The rules for the composition of suites are roughly the same for *sanqu* and *zaju*, but there are slight differences. Though *sanqu* originated in the same milieu that had earlier given birth to the *ci*—that is, among courtesans and their literati patrons—there are clear differences in the character and subject matter of the two genres. The *sanqu*, which allows freer use of language and greater length (especially in *sanqu* suites), makes more detailed description possible—where *ci* are characterized by suggestiveness, *qu* are often realistic.

As in *ci*, love is a favorite subject. Many *qu* treat the familiar subject of unfulfilled longing, but many deal with other aspects of love: its pleasures, the charms of the courtesan, the stinginess of the procuress. Many *sanqu* detail the joys of living in retirement, in contrast with the perils of the office-holder's life, a theme which did not enjoy comparable prominence in *ci* poetry. There are also many descriptive *sanqu* on the subject of a specific plant, person, event, etc. Some of these are unbroken streams of praise; others are bitterly satirical.

The Most Important Sanqu *Authors*

Not surprisingly, many *zaju* authors also wrote *sanqu*. Guan Hanqing, for example, is said to be the author of the famous suite *Bu fu lao* (A refusal to grow old). The most famous of these *zaju* and *sanqu* writers is Ma Zhiyuan, who wrote many *sanqu* on the joys of living in retirement. Qiao Ji (?–1345) wrote, among other things, famous songs extolling courtesans.

A number of poets are famous exclusively for their *qu*. Zhang Kejiu (ca. 1280–after 1348) was the most productive *sanqu* writer; more than 700 of his poems have been preserved. His descriptions of nature scenes such as West Lake at Hangzhou have remained favorites. Guan Yunshi (1286–1324) abandoned a promising official career to devote himself to *sanqu*; his songs testify to his unrestrained character. The most important *sanqu* poet of the early Ming was Tang Shi, a protégé of the Yongle emperor.

Some *sanqu* writers owe their lasting fame to one or two memorable suites. *Gaozu huan xiang* (Emperor Gaozu returns to his native village), by Sui Jingchen (ca. 1300), tells how Liu Bang, founder of the Han dynasty, returns as emperor to honor his native village with a visit. Everything is seen through the eyes of one of his old fellow villagers, who is bewildered by the pomp and ceremony but remembers all the more clearly how humble Liu's origins were. The adoption by an author of an unusual persona through which to view the events described was not uncommon. Du Renjie (ca. 1201–after 1283) had already written his *Zhuangjia bu shi goulan* (A peasant knows nothing of the theater), in which he describes a drama performance in a commercial urban theater as seen through the eyes of a simple peasant. Gao Andao (second half of the thirteenth century?) described the same thing as seen from the viewpoint of blasé aficionados; in one suite the slaughtering of an ox is described in great detail as seen through the eyes of the animal.

Liu Zhi (?–between 1335 and 1338) wrote two suites both entitled *Shang Gao jiansi* (To the Censor Gao); they are remarkable within the *sanqu* tradition for their detailed description of a rural famine.

THE SOUTHERN DRAMA

Xiwen *and* Chuanqi

The new melodies that evolved in central China during the twelfth century are often referred to as *nanqu*, as distinguished from *beiqu*. The songs written to these melodies are, of course, in a southern dialect. *Chenzi* were seldom used, and the composition of suites was less common than in the North. *Nanqu* were used in a type of drama that developed in Wenzhou in the twelfth and thirteenth centuries and became popular throughout much of southern China. In the twelfth and thirteenth centuries this genre was known as *xiwen* (play text); starting in the fourteenth century, plays in this genre were called *chuanqi*. The term "southern drama" is also commonly used.

Southern drama plays are longer than *zaju*, often comprising 30 to 50 scenes. Whatever the exact theme or subject of the play, the plot ordinarily centers on a melodramatic love story: the lovers meet in one of the early scenes, are pulled apart by circumstances, undergo various adventures, and are finally reunited. The characters were played by a limited number of role types, of which some are known by other names than in *zaju*. In southern drama, unlike the *zaju*, the sung passages are performed by all the various role types in the same play rather than being restricted to one player. There were also several forms of choral singing. The number of sung lyrics per scene could range from one or two (occasionally, none at all) to several dozen, and the length of the individual scenes varied considerably. Again by contrast with the *zaju*, the *xiwen* or *chuanqi* begins with a stereotyped opening scene which provides a sort of summary of the play to follow.

The Three *Xiwen* in the *Yongle dadian*

The three oldest preserved *xiwen* make up the last *juan* or "book" of the *xiwen* section of the *Yongle dadian*; this is the only still-extant *juan* in that section. (The *zaju* section has been lost in its entirety.) These three *xiwen* date from the first half of the fourteenth century. They are probably not typical of the genre in all respects. Two of them are remarkably short and seem to be based on *zaju*; the third, *Zhang Xie zhuangyuan* (The examination top-scorer

Zhang Xie), describing its hero's shameful lack of gratitude toward his former benefactors once he has passed the examinations, may well be a parody of the stock melodramatic plot typical of the *xiwen*. Of other thirteenth- or early-fourteenth-century *xiwen*, nothing remains but a few songs.

Gao Ming's Pipa ji *and Other Early* Chuanqi

The most important early *chuanqi* is the *Pipa ji* (The story of the lute), by Gao Ming (ca. 1307-ca. 1371). *Pipa ji* tells of a young man, just married, whose father forces him to go to the capital to take part in the examinations while his bride devotes herself to caring for her parents-in-law. The young man succeeds in the examinations, whereupon a powerful minister forces him to marry his daughter and take up residence in his house. Meanwhile, the hero's native region is struck by disasters and his parents are killed; their daughter-in-law has to sell her hair to raise money for their funeral. Afterward, begging and accompanying herself on the lute, she takes up the long journey to the capital—where she is eventually aided by the minister's daughter. Reunion and reconciliation follow.

Gao Ming's *Pipa ji* goes back to an earlier version in which the hero is killed by lightning as a punishment for his unfaithfulness. The hero's name is Cai Yong; the real Cai Yong was a famous Han scholar, but the story has nothing to do with his life. In Gao Ming's version, the hero and his two wives all emerge as paragons of virtue. The songs in *Pipa ji* are praised for their simplicity.

Also dating from the second half of the fourteenth century are four other plays. Though not all are of equal value from a literary point of view, all have enjoyed great popularity on the stage down through the centuries. *Baitu ji* (The story of the white hare) is a reworking of the story of Liu Zhiyuan and Li Sanniang, which we have already encountered in the discussion of the twelfth-century *Liu Zhiyuan zhugongdiao*. *Sha gou ji* (The story of the dead dog) is an adaptation of an anonymous comedy called *Sha gou quan fu* (Warning by a dead dog), in which the elder of two brothers is finally willing to be reconciled with his younger brother after the latter turns out to be the only one willing to dispose of a corpse (the dead dog) dumped on the steps of his house. *Yougui ji* (The story of the women's quarters), also known as *Baiyue ting* (The pavilion where they pray to the moon), is a reworking of a comedy by Guan Hanqing entitled *Baiyue ting*; it is set in the turbulent last years of the Jin dynasty. The plot of *Jingchai ji* (The story of the thorn hairpin), sometimes attributed to Zhu Quan, seems at times a mirror image of *Pipa ji*: the successful young man refuses to marry the minister's daughter; his bride tries to commit suicide when her parents-in-law attempt to force her to remarry. All of these plays are very didactic in tone; the heroines, especially, are exemplars of morality in their single-minded devotion to their husbands or fiancés.

CHINESE POLITICAL HISTORY, 1450–1915

The fifteenth century witnessed an extended slump in the Chinese economy. By the sixteenth century, however, things were booming again, and the center of prosperity was in the Kiangnan area, with its many prominent cities including Nanjing, Yangzhou, Hangzhou, and, especially, Suzhou. At the same time the Chinese population began its relentless growth, reaching 150,000,000 by the end of the Ming. Despite heavy losses in the mid-seventeenth century, the population was to reach 300,000,000 by the end of the eighteenth century and 400,000,000 by the end of the nineteenth. The growing population was fed both by intensive use of existing acreage and by opening up more and more marginal land. The latter process brought with it such problems as conflicts with indigenous populations, frequent natural disasters, and extreme erosion. New food crops, including maize and potatoes, were imported from the Americas by the late sixteenth century.

The internal political scene was thick with factional disputes. The quirky personalities of the Jiajing Emperor (r. 1522–1566) and the Wanli Emperor (r. 1573–1619) exacerbated problems at court, where eunuchs once again came to wield considerable power. The eunuch Wei Zhongxian actually ruled China from 1621 to 1627 as the real power behind the throne during the reign of the weak-willed Tianqi Emperor.

The Ming government had adopted a policy of strict regulation and limitation in matters of maritime trade. Private traders and smugglers with Japanese connections troubled the southeastern coastal regions for many decades in the sixteenth century. The "Japanese pirates" were forcibly suppressed, and the regulations governing trade were made somewhat more liberal. The Portuguese, who had entered the East Asian sea lanes in the early sixteenth century, were even allowed to establish Macao as a trading post, though under strict Chinese supervision. The importation of silver from the Americas, by way of the Spanish settlement at Manila, added another stimulus to the Chinese economy.

The continuing tense situation along the northern border gave rise to a policy of extensive fortification which continued for more than a century and resulted, among other things, in what is still known as the Great Wall of China. The greatest threat to the Ming, however, eventually came not from the Mongolian steppes but from Manchuria. The Manchus, who claimed to be the descendants of the Jürchen, developed into a formidable military power during the last years of the sixteenth century. In the early decades of the seventeenth century they pushed the Ming out of southern Manchuria and repeatedly carried out raids deep into China proper.

But the Ming dynasty was ultimately finished off by rebellions originating in the poverty-stricken Northwest. Li Zicheng, one of the rebel leaders, entered Peking with his troops in the spring of 1644, just after the Chongzhen Emperor (r. 1628–1644) had committed suicide by hanging himself on Coal Hill behind the Forbidden City. When Li Zicheng unleashed a reign of terror, Wu Sangui, the commander of the huge Ming garrisons guarding the Manchurian border, invited the Manchus to enter China and subdue the rebels. As soon as the Manchus entered Peking, they declared themselves the successors of the Ming—the Qing dynasty (1644–1911).

The Qing took decades to complete their conquest of the rest of China. Rebels continued to ravage large areas for many years. Officials loyal to the Ming organized a government at Nanjing, but Manchu troops entered that city in 1645. The southern Ming court put up tenacious resistance as it slowly retreated to the southwest under the pressure of the pursuing Qing troops. When the last Ming emperor fled to Burma, the Burmese king handed him over to Wu Sangui, who had him executed. Along the southeastern coast the seaborne troops of Zheng Chenggong ("the pirate Coxinga") continued to harass the Qing. In 1662 they retreated to Taiwan, where they ousted the Dutch. When the pacification of China appeared complete, Wu Sangui and other Chinese generals rebelled against the Manchus; it took eight years of fighting (1663–1681) to suppress them. Subsequently, in 1682, Taiwan was also incorporated into the empire.

The Qing stationed Manchu garrisons throughout China. On the whole they adopted the Ming bureaucratic structure, but were careful to ensure that in the higher echelons a good balance obtained between Manchu and Chinese officials. They imposed the Manchu queue on the entire Chinese male population as a symbol of submission. Lingering anti-Manchu sentiments among the literati were weeded out in various purges and in a large-scale literary inquisition in the 1770s. In a series of military campaigns the vigorous early Qing rulers Kangxi (r. 1661–1722), Yongzheng (r. 1723–1736) and Qianlong (r. 1736–1795) extended the domain of the empire farther than it had ever reached, and by the end of the eighteenth century most of Central Asia, including the Mongol lands and Tibet, had accepted Manchu suzerainty.

From the late eighteenth century on, however, when serious rebellions broke out in the interior regions of China, the Manchu troops proved less effective. The most devastating of these rebellions was the Taiping (Taiping Tianguo or "Heavenly Kingdom of Great Peace") movement, which started out in 1849 in the province of Guangxi. The Taiping troops, inspired by the visionary teachings of their leader Hong Xiuquan, who believed himself to be the younger brother of Jesus Christ, then marched north, establishing their capital at Nanjing. The rebellion and its ultimate suppression (1849–1864) reduced vast areas of China's richest provinces to wasteland; the death toll ran to the tens of millions. For the suppression of rebellions like these, the Manchu government increasingly had to rely on newly recruited armies trained and led by Chinese officials.

In the mid-nineteenth century, though the Qing government was still strong enough to subdue internal rebellions, it found itself powerless against the Western nations. Until the first decades of the nineteenth century the Qing court had been able to conduct relations with foreign countries exclusively on its own terms. The Catholic missionaries who had been admitted to China toward the end of the Ming had been strictly regulated as regards both their number and their activities. Border disputes with Russia had been satisfactorily resolved in the seventeenth century, and attempts by the Dutch to gain a foothold on the Chinese coast had been foiled. In the eighteenth century seaborne trade with Western nations had been concentrated at Canton, where Westerners were denied permanent residence. In the Opium War (1839–1842), which broke out when China tried to stop the illegal importation of opium which was an important source of revenue for the British, the Qing government discovered that its army could not stand up to the modern weaponry of the industrialized Western countries. The Opium War resulted in the opening of five so-called treaty ports to Western trade, and in the cession of Hong Kong to Great Britain. In the treaty ports certain areas were designated "concessions"; these were administered by the foreigners themselves. Of the treaty ports, Shanghai quickly emerged as the most important, and from the second half of the nineteenth century its population grew explosively. Its concessions, with the exception of the French concession, were jointly administered as the international concession, which provided a haven for many dissident Chinese intellectuals up to the eve of World War II.

Continuing military and diplomatic conflicts between China and "the powers" resulted in further concessions to the Western nations and, starting in the late nineteenth century, Japan. China's humiliating defeat in the Sino-Japanese War of 1894–1895 brought home to Chinese intellectuals how ineffective China's attempts at modernization had been compared to those of Japan. Japan annexed Taiwan as a colony and further strengthened its position in China by its victory in the Russo-Japanese War (1904–1905), which resulted in a strong permanent Japanese military presence in Manchuria.

At court during the last quarter of the nineteenth century real power was in the hands of the conservative Empress Dowager Cixi. In 1898 her son, the

Guangxu Emperor (r. 1875–1908), sided with reform-minded intellectuals like Kang Youwei, who briefly instituted far-reaching reforms. The Empress Dowager subsequently had the emperor placed under house arrest; the reforms were rescinded, and Kang Youwei and his friends had to flee or face execution. In 1900 the Empress Dowager tried to make use of the Boxer movement to drive the hated foreigners from the capital. The attempt backfired; foreign troops entered Peking, and the Chinese government had to pay a huge indemnity. A number of reforms were now gradually introduced; the metropolitan state examinations were held for the last time in 1905.

Many students now went to Japan to study, and revolutionary organizations proliferated. One of the most active revolutionary organizers was Sun Yat-sen, the leader of the Nationalist movement. Rebellions and killings now followed in quick succession. In 1911 unrest triggered by the government's plan to nationalize the railways spread from Sichuan down the Yangzi to Wuhan. When the leader of the modernized armies in the North, Yuan Shikai, refused to support the Manchu regime, the regents for the child emperor Puyi (r. 1909–1911) decided to abdicate. The year 1912 saw the birth of the Chinese republic, of which Sun Yat-sen became the first president. It was not long, however, before Sun had to cede the presidency to Yuan Shikai, who died a few years later just as he planned to declare himself emperor.

Chapter 18.
CLASSICAL-LANGUAGE POETRY AND PROSE

SHI AND *CI* POETRY

Shi remained the most important poetic genre during this period. No new formal variants were developed, and the Song poets of the eleventh and twelfth centuries had already tried out all possible subjects and all possible registers of the classical language. Though the volume of preserved *shi* from the Ming and Qing dynasties is overwhelmingly great, including work by numerous fine poets, few authors of this period are remembered as outstandingly original. It must be borne in mind, however, that this impression is based on the present state of scholarship; so far, remarkably little research has been done on this period. It should also be pointed out that the writings of a sizeable number of women poets have been preserved from this period. None, however, achieved a reputation comparable to that of Li Qingzhao or Zhu Shuzhen. Again it should be stressed that the serious study of the women poets of the Ming and Qing is still in its infancy.

The poetry of the first centuries of the Ming was strongly influenced by the demand, voiced by many critics and put into practice by leading writers, for imitation of the great Tang poets, especially Du Fu. Especially vociferous proponents of the imitation of the High Tang were the so-called *Qian qizi* (The earlier seven gentlemen), who opposed the "beauty without content" which they saw in the the poetry of Li Dongyang (1447-1516). The most prominent representative of the *Qian qizi* was Li Mengyang (1473-1530). The others included Kang Hai (1475-1540) and Wang Jiusi (1468-1551), both also famous as authors of *zaju*.

The efforts of the *Qian qizi* were continued by the *Hou qizi* (The later seven gentlemen). The best-known authors in this group were Li Panlong (1514-1570) and Wang Shizhen (1526-1590). The latter is also credited with the authorship of the play *Mingfeng ji* (The crying phoenix; a *chuanqi*); even the novel *Jin Ping Mei* has sometimes been thought to be his.

A poet who deserves separate mention is Yang Shen (1488-1559). From Chengdu, he achieved the highest rank in the metropolitan examination of 1512. His career at court was cut short in 1524 when he was caught up in factional struggles and banished to Yunnan, where he lived for the rest of his life. He left a voluminous oeuvre, in both prose and poetry. He was not only one of the finest *shi* poets of the age, but an outstanding practitioner of *sanqu*. He is also credited with the authorship of the *Ershiyi shi tanci* (Rhymes-for-picking on the Twenty-One Histories), a rhymed summary of Chinese history in prosimetric form and the earliest text to call itself a *tanci*.

Other authors, among them Tang Yin and Xu Wei, owe much of their fame to their eccentric way of life, the resulting scandals, and the legends that arose concerning their amatory adventures. Tang Yin (1470–1523) is also famous as a painter; Xu Wei (1521–1593), also a noted painter, wrote *zaju* as well. Tang Yin became the hero of a popular romance in which he disguised himself as a slave in order to befriend a slave girl he had fallen in love with. Xu Wei became the main character in many popular jokes, in which his role is that of a trickster or practical joker.

Reacting against the mechanical imitation by many Ming poets of their admired models, Yuan Hongdao (1568–1610) proclaimed the spontaneous expression of feeling, regardless of form or style, to be the essence of poetry. He and his circle are referred to as the *Gong'an pai*; this school found a later continuation in the *Jingling pai*.

In the seventeenth century the scene was less dominated by definite schools, and poets were more inclined to seek their way individually. Qian Qianyi (1582–1664), in addition to creating a voluminous oeuvre, compiled an extensive and important anthology of Ming *shi*: the *Liechao shiji* (Poems from the successive reign periods). Poems of social criticism are prominent in the work of Wu Weiye (1609–1672); his "Yuanyuan qu" (Song of Yuanyuan) is a long narrative poem about the courtesan Yuanyuan, who was the lover of the general Wu Sangui—rumor had it that he had turned to the Manchus for help in order to avenge her death at the hands of Li Zicheng. The poet Zhu Yizun (1629–1709) also compiled an anthology of Ming *shi*: the *Ming shi zong* (Compendium of Ming *shi*).

Undoubtedly the most influential *shi* poet of the second half of the seventeenth century was Wang Shizhen (1634–1711); he is especially famous for his seven-syllable *jueju*. Wang Shizhen was also a leading critic and patron.

Of eighteenth-century poets, the most famous is Yuan Mei (1716–1797). As a critic, in his *shihua* he stressed the importance for poetry of the spontaneous expression of feelings; among his own poems, the *gushi* are most attractive. Yuan Mei was also an outstanding prose writer who produced, among other things, a cookbook and a collection of supernatural stories entitled *Zibuyu* (What the Master—i.e., Confucius—didn't talk about). Yuan Mei encouraged women to write poetry and even accepted female disciples. The best-known of the women poets associated with Yuan Mei are Xi Peilan and Luo Qilan.

Zhao Yi (1728–1814) enjoyed during his lifetime a reputation that almost equalled that of Yuan Mei. His voluminous poems are distinguished by satiric wit, which is often directed against himself. Nowadays he is best remembered as a critical historian.

The poetry of Gong Zizhen (1792–1841) is often highly obscure. His fame as prophet of the downfall of the Qing is traceable mainly to his sharp criticisms of contemporary situations and his concern for problems involving the empire's territorial integrity. There is not much of all this, however, in his *shi* and *ci*, which are far more concerned with his feelings of despair over what he felt to be the meaninglessness of his life. His bureaucratic career was cut short when he had to leave Peking abruptly, according to some because he had had an affair with the poetess Gu Taiqing, the wife of a Manchu prince.

Jin He (1818–1885) wrote poems, among other things, on the destruction caused by the Taiping Rebellion (1849–1864). Many of the regularly anthologized poets of the nineteenth century seem to have merited their inclusion more for the nobility of their patriotic sentiment than for the quality of their literary expression.

After a long period of abeyance, the *ci* enjoyed a certain revival during the final decades of the Ming. The most important representative of this renewed interest in the form was Chen Zilong (1608–1647). Many of his *ci* were written for his one-time courtesan lover Liu Rushi, who later became the concubine of Wu Weiye. Chen Zilong took an active part in the anti-Manchu struggle in the Kiangnan area, eventually committing suicide. The most important Qing writer of *ci* was a Manchu, Nalan Xingde (1655–1685), whose father was one of the highest Manchu officials of the time. Nalan Xingde's *xiaoling*, clearly influenced by Li Yu and Li Qingzhao, are remarkable for their sincere tone and straightforward diction.

Many Qing writers also wrote *cihua* (Remarks on songs), after the analogy of *shihua*. Many of these stress the serious nature of the genre and subject earlier lyrics to an allegorical interpretation which reads the songs as topical commentaries on politics. The most famous work in this genre, however, is the *Renjian cihua* (Remarks on songs from the world of men) by Wang Guowei (1877–1927), who was one of the first scholars to apply Western concepts to the study of Chinese literature.

ESSAYS IN THE CLASSICAL WRITTEN LANGUAGE

During the first centuries of the Ming, *guwen* prevailed as the dominant style for literary prose. The examination essay remained ossified in the form of the *baguwen* (eight-part essay), which was governed by strict and numerous rules. Though many literati spent their lives preparing for the examinations (and practicing *baguwen*), this in itself need not have been a reason why no new first-rank *guwen* masters appeared. There was no lack of competent practitioners. Finally, in the last years of the Ming, prose writers, influenced by the attitudes expressed by the *Gong'an pai* and *Jingling pai* poets, began to abandon the well-worn paths, and there arose a real vogue for short, informal sketches on unpretentious subjects. These are referred to as *xiaopin* (small pieces). One of the first practitioners of the genre was Yuan Hongdao. Another significant contribution to the prose of this period was the work of Xu Xiake (1568–1641), whose travel writings, full of graphic descriptions of nature, have remained popular down through the centuries. It could also be said that the autobiographical prose of the last century of the Ming achieved a degree of detail and openness that is quite remarkable within the Chinese tradition.

While the Qing saw a certain resuscitation of parallel prose, the leading position of *guwen* remained unchallenged. The most influential school of *guwen* was the *Tongcheng pai*, whose originator was Fang Bao (1668–1749). The *Tongcheng pai* emphasized the study of great examples from the past (*Zuo zhuan*, *Shiji*, the Eight Great Masters of the Tang and Song) and the didactic function of literature; ideologically this school was in favor of Zhu Xi's Neo-Confucianism. One of the most important *Tongcheng pai* writers was Yao Nai (1732–1815), who compiled a voluminous and authoritative *guwen* anthology entitled *Guwen ci leizuan* (Classified compilation of ancient-style texts).

Another writer from the same period, but of an almost opposite nature, was Shen Fu (1763–after 1809), the author of the famous *Fusheng liuji* (Six chapters of my floating life). This work, now consisting of four chapters (two others had been lost by the time the work was printed in the late nineteenth century), amounts to a systematically arranged autobiographical review of the author's life; within the Chinese tradition it is unusual for its detail and candor. Shen Fu came from an impoverished gentry family; the *Fusheng liuji* includes successive descriptions of his youth, his happy marriage, his various hobbies, his poverty, the death of his wife, and his business trips to Canton and other places.

THE *LIAOZHAI ZHIYI* AND OTHER COLLECTIONS OF SUPERNATURAL STORIES

An immense volume of *biji* has been preserved from the Ming and Qing. Some of this material is mainly of historical or philological interest; some is notable in the context of literary history; but there is little of literary value per se.

The short story in the classical language (*chuanqi*), after remaining in a fallow state through much of the fifteenth century, came back into prominence around 1600. In the century that followed, the name that stands out above all others is that of Pu Songling (1640-1715). After taking his *xiucai* degree at an early age, Pu Songling failed to pass a higher examination, much as his literary gifts were admired by such famous contemporaries as Wang Shizhen, and he ended up spending much of his life as private secretary to a noted Shandong family. His masterpiece, the *Liaozhai zhiyi* (Notes on strange matters from the Studio of Idleness), contains nearly 500 *chuanqi* and brief notes on unusual matters. Many of Pu's *chuanqi* describe contacts between this world and that of fox spirits, ghosts, flower fairies, monsters, and demons. Many are love stories; some are plainly satirical.

Pu Songling also wrote many other works. Ten performance texts are attributed to him (with varying degrees of plausibility); he was also regarded (though, as is now known, incorrectly) as the author of a bulky 100-chapter novel, *Xingshi yinyuan zhuan* (A marriage to shock the world awake).

The eighteenth century saw the writing of a number of famous collections of ghost and supernatural stories; these sometimes surpass the *Liaozhai zhiyi* in volume, but never in quality. Yuan Mei's *Zibuyu* has already been mentioned; also noteworthy is the *Yuewei caotang biji* (Notes from the Shack for the Perusal of the Insignificant), by Ji Yun (1724–1805). Ji Yun's simply told stories, collected in order to prove the factual existence of ghosts and other supernatural phenomena such as divine retribution, often have a satirical or moralistic slant. Ji Yun was also a leading scholar and played a major role in the compilation of the *Siku quanshu* and its catalog.

MAJOR COMPILATIONS

During the Qing, especially in the eighteenth century, a number of compendious works were produced which have remained vitally important for the study of traditional Chinese literature. Many were government projects. The *Kangxi zidian* (Canon of written characters of the Kangxi period), published in 1716, lists nearly 50,000 individual characters with pronunciation and meanings. The *Peiwen yunfu* (Treasury, arranged according to rhymes, of polysyllabic phrases from the Peiwen Studio), is a huge thesaurus of two- and three-character expressions. The combinations are not defined, but the oldest examples of usage are quoted. Also from the Kangxi period (1662–1722) is the *Quan Tang shi* (Complete poems of the Tang), completed in 1707, which includes nearly 50,000 poems (*shi* and *ci*) by approximately 2,200 Tang authors.

The (*Gujin*) *Tushu jicheng* (Complete collection of writings from past and present) is a gigantic encyclopedia of the traditional Chinese kind, i.e., a systematically arranged collection of excerpts. The *Tushu jicheng* covers practically all imaginable aspects of traditional Chinese society, and it was much used by nineteenth-century Western Sinologists. The compilation, begun by Chen Menglei (1651–1723 or later), was taken over by the government in the last years of the Kangxi period, and the finished work was first printed (by movable type) in 1728.

The largest compilation project was the *Siku quanshu* (The complete writings from the four storehouses), produced between 1772 and 1782 under the Qianlong Emperor (1736–1795). The *Siku quanshu* was intended as a collection of the best preserved Chinese literature. From an original list of about 16,000 possible titles, about 3,000 items were finally selected for inclusion. (Unlike the *Yongle dadian*, the *Siku quanshu* excluded novels and plays). The *Siku quanshu* was never printed during the Qing, but a complete manuscript has survived. The catalog of this project, entitled *Siku quanshu zongmu tiyao* (Main points concerning the collected titles of the complete writings from the four storehouses) contains not only the titles of items included in the main work but also many more titles which, though not included, were thought worthy of being mentioned for posterity. Each title is followed by a short bibliographic essay. Invaluable though the *Siku quanshu* has been for later scholars, the story of its compilation is marred by the fact that in its own time it served as an inquisition against all authors and works thought to represent anti-Manchu sentiments; many works were destroyed and many authors executed.

In the Jiaqing period (1796–1820), following the example of the *Quan Tang shi*, there was compiled a *Quan Tang wen* (Complete prose of the Tang). The scholar Yan Kejun (1762-1843) followed this with the compilation of *Quan shanggu Sandai Qin Han Sanguo Liuchao wen* (Complete prose of High Antiquity, the Three Dynasties, the Qin and Han, the Three Kingdoms, and the Six Dynasties), which was eventually followed in its turn by Ding Fubao's (1874-1952) *Quan Han Sanguo Jin Nanbei Chao shi* (Complete poems of the Han, the Three Kingdoms, the Jin, and the Northern and Southern dynasties).

Chapter 19.
DRAMA: *ZAJU*, *CHUANQI*, AND
REGIONAL DRAMA

In the history of Chinese drama, the second half of the fifteenth century is a blank for there is very little documentation. Not until the sixteenth and later centuries does extensive information on authors, performances, and text editions become available. Drama criticism also begins to arise in the sixteenth century. The first critics are mainly concerned with the songs, but during the seventeenth century Li Yu (1611–ca. 1679) develops a well-rounded dramaturgy.

ZAJU

The *zaju* lost more and more ground as compared with other dramatic forms. In the sixteenth century, *zaju* were still performed at Nanjing, Kaifeng, and Peking, but by the last years of the Ming they were being performed nowhere except at court. After the fall of the Ming, they disappeared entirely. Not surprisingly, over the sixteenth century, fewer *zaju* were written with an eye to actual performance, but the genre began a new career as closet drama. The plays in this category no longer adhere strictly to all conventions of the *zaju*, though the characteristic diction and phrasing are maintained. The length of these pieces could vary from one to seven suites. Songs written to southern *qu* were sometimes inserted in northern suites; some suites consisted entirely of *nanqu*; and occasionally the songs were divided among various singing roles.

Famous Zaju *Authors*

Of sixteenth-century *zaju* authors, Wang Jiusi and Xu Wei deserve mention. Wang Jiusi's (1468–1551) best-known work in this genre is *Zhongshan lang yuanben* (The farce on the Wolf of Zhongshan; in this title, *yuanben* is used in the meaning of "short play" and has nothing to do with the Jin dynasty *yuanben*). This play is an allegorical presentation of the theme

191

that "man is a wolf to man." (Wang's friend Kang Hai wrote a full-length *zaju* on the same theme.)

Xu Wei (1521–1593) wrote four *zaju*, of one, two, two, and five suites respectively; they are referred to collectively as *Si sheng yuan* (Four cries of the gibbon). The best-known is also the shortest, *Kuang gulong* (The mad drummer), in which the usurper Cao Cao gets a sound dressing down from the talented and righteous Mi Heng (173–198). Xu Wei is also taken to be the author of the oldest book on the southern drama, the *Nanci xulu* (Catalog, with introduction, of southern songs).

In the eighteenth century Yang Chaoguan (1710–1788), a friend of Yuan Mei, wrote a collection of thirty short *zaju*, mostly dealing with famous incidents from Chinese history and legend; they were published under the title *Yingfengge zaju* (*Zaju* from the Studio for Writing Poems on the Wind).

Li Kaixian

From the sixteenth century on, the growing interest in *zaju* as reading matter encouraged the publication of new editions of old plays. The first anthology of older *zaju*, mainly by Yuan authors, was prepared by Li Kaixian (1502–1568), but this collection has been lost. Li Kaixian also wrote plays of his own. His *Yuanlin wumeng* (An afternoon nap in the orchard), in which Li Wa, Cui Yingying, and their respective servant girls bawl each other out, is a sort of late imitation of a farce. His *Baojian ji* (The precious sword) is a *chuanqi* on the story of Lin Chong, one of the heroes of Liangshan Marsh, whose exploits were later to be told in the novel *Shuihu zhuan*.

CHUANQI

Beginning in the mid-sixteenth century, marked growth in the Chinese economy, especially in the Kiangnan area, went hand in hand with the flourishing of the southern drama (*chuanqi*). Almost all surviving editions of *chuanqi* date from the second half of the sixteenth century or later. Some preserved texts were clearly intended for a reading public of literati; they are often quite luxurious examples of the book producer's art. Others are much simpler, even shabby, and may well have been intended for the actors. Very few fifteenth-century *chuanqi* authors are known by name; most works thought to date from that period are anonymous, and some may be the work of *shuhui* (writing societies). In the sixteenth century, however, increasing numbers of prominent literati wrote in the *chuanqi* form, including Li

Kaixian, with his *Baojian ji*, and Wang Shizhen, generally regarded as the author of the *Mingfeng ji*.

Tang Xianzu

The most famous Ming dynasty author of *chuanqi* was Tang Xianzu (1550–1616). He wrote four *chuanqi* collectively named, after his birthplace, *Linchuan simeng* (The four "dreams" from Linchuan—in each play, a dream plays a key role). Of these four, the most renowned is *Mudanting Huanhun ji* (The Peony Pavilion: the return of the soul). This long play in fifty-five scenes tells the story of a girl who falls in love with a young man in a dream and subsequently dies of longing. The young man later happens to see her portrait and falls in love with her. She appears to him in a dream and instructs him to open her grave. He does so, whereupon she returns from the dead, and the new couple are reunited with her parents. This play is admired for the lyrical intensity of its songs, especially those in which the heroine sings first of her ennui and later of her longing. The other plays in the *Linchuan simeng* are adaptations of literary tales of the Tang dynasty, such as "Zhenzhong ji" and "Nanke taishou zhuan."

Li Yu

Li Yu (1611–ca. 1679) was an outstanding and in many ways unique figure in the world of seventeenth-century Chinese drama. For years he toured all of China as owner and manager of his own theater group, giving performances in the houses of top-ranking officials. He later settled in Nanjing, where he was very active as a writer and publisher, using the company name of *Jiezi yuan* (The Mustard-Seed Garden). In several chapters of his famous prose miscellany *Xianqing ouji* (Random notes on leisurely enjoyments), he develops a theory of theater which emphasizes the playability of the texts and their attractiveness for a mixed but largely illiterate audience. These ideas contrasted sharply with those of earlier critics, who gave most of their attention to the poetic qualities of the songs. (The other chapters of *Xianqing ouji* are devoted to a wide variety of subjects, which Li discusses in a fresh, light prose style).

Li Yu wrote sixteen plays of his own, ten of which were printed together under the title *Li Liweng shizhong* (Ten pieces by Li Liweng). A common feature of these plays is their complex but well-worked-out plots. Li also published two collections of novellas in the spoken language (*huaben*):

Wusheng xi (Silent plays) and *Shi er lou* (The twelve "towers": the word
"tower" occurs in the title of each of the stories). The stories in *Shi er lou* are
somewhat unusual in that unlike earlier works in the *huaben* genre, they are
subdivided into *hui* (chapters). The plots of Li Yu's novellas are often bizarre
and rather far-fetched, but the style is witty and engaging. He is also often
considered to be the author of the pornographic novel *Rou putuan* (The
prayer-mat of flesh).

Hong Sheng and Kong Shangren

The most famous *chuanqi* authors of the early Qing are Hong Sheng
(1645–1704) and Kong Shangren (1648–1718). Hong Sheng's masterpiece is a
chuanqi entitled *Changsheng dian* (The Palace of Eternal Life), which tells in
great detail the story of Xuanzong and High Consort Yang. Unlike Bai Pu in
the *Wutong yu*, Hong Sheng depicts their love as mutual, and at the end of his
play, after their tragic separation on earth, the lovers are joyfully reunited in
heaven.

Kong Shangren's fame rests on the *Taohua shan* (The peach blossom fan).
This *chuanqi* is about the love of Hou Fangyu (1618–1654, a noted *guwen*
writer), for the young courtesan Li Xiangjun. The action is mainly set in and
around Nanjing in 1644 and 1645: Hou Fangyu and others are desperately
trying to organize anti-Manchu resistance. All these attempts fail, owing
mainly to the corruption of the Chinese officials, including Ruan Dacheng
(1587?–1646?, a *chuanqi* writer of some repute). Within the Chinese tradition,
Taohua shan is remarkable not only for the main characters' choice of an
unhappy ending to their love affair (both ultimately enter monasteries), but
also and especially for the accuracy and boldness with which it dramatizes
recent and still extremely sensitive historical events.

The seventeenth century also saw the publication of a number of *chuanqi*
collections. Of these, the best known is *Liushi zhong qu* (Sixty plays),
published by Mao Jin (1599–1659), a famous bibliophile and publisher.

After the seventeenth century, the great period of the *chuanqi* was over.
The most famous eighteenth-century author in this genre was Jiang Shiquan
(1725–1785), a friend of the poet Yuan Mei.

REGIONAL DRAMA

From the sixteenth century on, *nanqu* appear in a great number of
regional variants. These specific forms of performance are often associated

with a very specific place of origin, and there is often a close relationship between a certain variant and a particular dialect. The forms take their name from their region of origin, but they sometimes became popular in other places as well. There was a constantly shifting process of mutual influence among local variants, variants from other regions, and local folk music, leading to the frequent development of identifiable new forms. This process has continued into the twentieth century.

In the course of the eighteenth century a new type of operatic music came to the fore which had much more popular origins. Whereas both northern and southern *qu* music distinguished a great number of different melodies, each with its accompanying verse pattern, this new type of operatic music was based on the endless repetition of a single melodic matrix, which was used to sing couplets of verse of uniform seven- or ten-syllable length. In Chinese, this type of operatic music is called *bangzi qiang* (matrix tunes). On the basis of a number of basic rhythmic variations, individual performers over the centuries added their own interpretations, eventually resulting in such wide-ranging and bewildering musical variations that thoroughgoing analysis is needed to identify the structural elements of the original matrix. From western China this type of music spread to other areas, in the process incorporating elements from other traditions. The most famous representative of this type of drama is Peking opera.

Kunqu

One variant highly popular in the sixteenth century, especially among the literati, was the *kunqu*, which takes its name from Kunshan, to the northeast of Suzhou. This style of performance is said to have become suddenly popular in Suzhou, one of the greatest economic and cultural centers of the empire, thanks to the music master Wei Liangfu. Wei revised and enriched the *kunqu* with new elements taken, among other things, from *beiqu*. The first play written specifically for *kunqu* performance was *Huansha ji* (The washing of silk thread), by Liang Chenyu (ca. 1521–ca. 1594). This play, which concerns the legend of Wu Zixu, was an immediate success, and in its wake many other pieces were written or adapted for *kunqu*. A very productive playwright in this genre, from seventeenth-century Suzhou, was Li Yu (1591?-1671?).

The *kunqu* spread from Suzhou to other regions, including Peking. In this genre, song as such played a greater role than was customary in many regional variants. This may be one reason why *kunqu*, as a more refined form of theater, was mainly loved by the more well-educated. The genre flourished in the seventeenth century but was already diminishing in popularity in the eighteenth century, and in the nineteenth it was all but wiped out by the long period of disaster associated with the Taiping Rebellion, which especially affected the region of its greatest popularity. Following the establishment of the People's Republic of China, efforts were made to revive this tradition; a revised version of *Shiwu guan* (Fifteen strings of cash), one of the plays of Zhu Hu (fl. 17th century), enjoyed considerable success in the 1950s.

Peking Opera

Between 1770 and 1870, a new drama variant evolved in Peking. Its development can be traced to a number of sources. The backbone of the music of Peking opera is provided by two types of *bangzi qiang*, respectively known as *xipi* and *erhuang*, that were brought to Peking by actors from Sichuan and Anhui. Other musical influences were the older regional style of performance and the *kunqu* melodies. The resulting variant is referred to in Chinese as *jingxi* (drama of the capital) and in English, traditionally, as Peking opera. From Peking, this form of theater spread to other places.

In Peking opera there is considerable emphasis not only on singing but also on acting, especially on fighting scenes featuring spectacular acrobatics. Another trademark is the use of elaborate and highly symbolic face-painting. The texts used in Peking opera are often individual scenes taken from older *chuanqi* or shorter whole plays deriving from oral tradition. In Peking opera it is unusual for *chuanqi* plays to be performed as a whole, and an evening's program is often made up of a series of scenes taken from various stories, selected so as to allow a particular actor to show off specific skills. (This tradition of performing individual scenes adapted and rewritten for the purpose can be traced back at least to the sixteenth century; such scenes are referred to in Chinese as *zhezixi* or "independent scenes.")

Many other forms of regional drama all over China rely for their basic music on some combination of *xipi* and *erhuang* melody patterns.

PUPPET SHOWS AND SHADOW PLAYS

China has a long tradition of puppet shows and shadow plays. Recorded from an early date, both forms were certainly flourishing at least as early as the Tang. The oldest descriptions providing some detail, however, go back no further than to Song times. Puppet shows used both hand puppets and marionettes. Shadow plays were first played with paper figures, and later with leather scraped so thin as to be translucent. No texts of Song puppet plays have survived, and in later centuries information remains scarce.

In the nineteenth and twentieth centuries puppet and shadow plays have continued to enjoy wide popularity. In these forms, too, a given region often has an identifiable prevalent variant. Not until the twentieth century were texts for these forms—mainly the shadow drama—collected and translated. Most are short; in subject and form they tend to resemble closely the repertory of the local variants of regional drama.

Chapter 20.
THE NOVEL (1450–1650)

THE EARLIEST NOVELS

China's earliest novels—in the sense of long stories, at least partly fictional, written in the contemporary vernacular and divided into chapters—are the *Sanguo zhi yanyi* (The novel of the history of the Three Kingdoms) and the *Shuihu zhuan* (The story of the water margin). Both are generally thought to date from the second half of the fourteenth century. No information on these works appears in surviving fifteenth-century sources, and the oldest printed editions we have are from the sixteenth century. It is, in other words, questionable whether these two novels are actually as old as generally believed, and even if they are indeed of fourteenth-century origin, they may well owe much to fifteenth-century revisions. What is demonstrably clear in any case is that the sixteenth-century editions vary considerably. Not until the seventeenth century do both novels become established in a form that would remain definitive at least for the next couple of centuries. The subject matter of these novels is traceable to popular story cycles known to have been used by professional storytellers at least as early as the Song. These same cycles were often tapped by authors of *zaju*, *xiwen*, and *pinghua*.

The Novel in China and in Europe

The reader who expects the Chinese novel to resemble its Western counterpart is in for a surprise. Though translators and Sinologists have traditionally used the word "novel" for the Chinese genre of *xiaoshuo*, this is as much for want of a better word as anything else. To understand the Chinese novel, it is best is to review, by way of contrast, the traditional features of the Western novel.

The simplest definition of the Western novel might be that it is a long story, divided into chapters, written in more or less vernacular prose. On these points the Chinese genre is not much different. But the Western reader does not regard just any long prose tale as a novel; a novel is expected to be a particular kind of story. From about the middle of the eighteenth century, most Western novels have centered on the story of a single main character, whose name is often the title of the book. The main character, though he or she may be a recognizable representative of a particular social group or type, is described as an individual, a unique personality, whose value lies mainly in his or her uniqueness. The individual is different from other individuals, but the differences are not absolute. The distinctions are subtle, gradual. The individual is somewhat better or worse than others—just a bit better or worse looking, moderately more intelligent. The milieu within which the main character lives, however, tends to be but weakly differentiated. This relationship between an individual and his or her environment, in which the individual is distinct by virtue of identifiable but gradual differences, has long been fundamental to the structure of the Western novel.

This characteristic relationship between the elements of the story has, in turn, determined other features of the Western novel. The Western novel must describe events in some detail because the individuality of the main figure must emerge from an accumulation of such details. Since the main character is usually distinct from his or her environment by virtue of a specific, individual manner of thinking and feeling, psychological processes and events in individual consciousness are given prominent description. The unfolding of the story, the action, is described as more or less a consequence of the person's character, typically as a consequence of one or another form of unsatisfactory adjustment to the environment. Older Western novels explicitly relate the cause of the inadequate adjustment, its consequences, and the manner of ultimate reconciliation. In more modern literary novels, the lack of integration, the alienation, is described, but no solution is offered. In some cases this leads to more or less complete paralysis of action, so that very little story line remains.

One great problem faces the Western novelist. The individual is supposed to be not only unique, more or less without exact parallel among other individuals, but also ultimately unknowable to others in the deep roots of his or her consciousness and motivation. Ultimately, this means that the best description of the character's life is liable to be that which comes out of the character's own mouth. Not surprisingly, the most natural form of the Western novel is the epistolary novel, the diary, or the autobiography. The fictional autobiography—the first-person novel—is a perennial favorite.

If the Chinese novel differs radically on a number of these points, it is certainly not because it lacks artistic depth or versatility. Nor can the features of the Chinese novel be derived from the tradition of professional storytellers with their cheap moralism and hypocritical sensationalism. The Chinese novel is simply based on types of contrast and opposition fundamentally different from those of its Western counterpart, and this fact has consequences in the areas of plot, description, characterization, and presentation.

Finally, it would be incorrect to approach the Chinese novel as a monolithic entity opposed to the Western genre. In the long history of the traditional Chinese novel, we can distinguish at least three main periods. The novels belonging to each period show certain common structural features, but the differences among the three periods are at least as great as those between "Western" and "Chinese" novels. Moreover, we have to take into account wide variations in sophistication. While some novels were written by authors familiar with high literature and read mainly by literati, others make far less demands on their readership and may well have been composed by authors of limited literacy. This contrast became more dramatic as time went by.

The Chinese Novel Before 1550

The first period in the development of the traditional Chinese novel extends until about 1550. The structure of the earliest novels is determined by an absolute conflict: the two conflicting elements, whether they are persons, states, ideals or values, are diametrically opposed, and the conflict is only ended when one party definitively triumphs over the other. The simplest story on this pattern is that of conflict between two persons, preferably heroes, each superlatively strong, one of whom ultimately defeats the other. Normally the loser is depicted as evil and the winner as good. Sometimes, however, the narrator shows sympathy for the hero who goes down fighting. A conflict-of-heroes story of this kind easily expands into the tale of a military campaign mounted by one state against another.

Matters become more complex when the main conflict is between self-interest and social obligations. Both the self-interest and the social obligations are presented as in themselves normal. The authors show their characters suppressing their own desires, even sacrificing their own lives, in order to fulfill their obligations. Frequent themes include suicide in the interest of loyalty to a friend and the undertaking of impossible missions, with fatal consequences, by generals who value loyalty more than personal safety. Often their families are sacrificed into the bargain.

Contrasting with stories of absolute loyalty and self-abnegation are those of total rebellion. Here, the hero chooses to fulfill his own desires at any cost, defying all social, legal, and religious conventions. The authors are just as capable of respecting the mettle of the lover or brigand who risks all for his heart's desire as they are of admiring the ethical courage of the self-sacrificing man.

The story is still more complex in cases of conflict between two different social obligations both of which are valid: between the claims of friendship and of loyalty to the ruler, between friendship and filial piety, or between the emperor's own obligations and his personal relationships. In these stories one of the values is preserved while the other, by definition, is betrayed.

The development of the story always proceeds toward a clear climax. The simplest type of development is what we may call linear: the hero (or heroes) is confronted with a series of trials or opponents, usually in increasing order of danger and difficulty, but wins definitive victory in a spectacular and decisive final encounter in which both sides make full use of all available means including weapons, monsters, magical abilities, and so on.

The other type is more in the nature of a spiral tracing an ever narrower circuit: as the story progresses, the conflict increases not only in physical but in emotional intensity. For example, the heroes join hands in rebellion against a tyrannical regime, but once they are successful, they fall into dispute. The leader of the victorious faction, now emperor, must consolidate his position by liquidating his former friends, who are now dangerous rivals. The new emperor may even have to have his own close relatives assassinated; the same "virtue" that made him emperor may also compel him to the heinous sin of patricide. In a story of this kind, there is no longer a clear-cut opposition of good and evil, but rather a transposition of the conflict to within the "good" side, leading to a rich array of ethical complications.

Characterization is of the simplest kind—not surprisingly, since conflicts are not perceived to have their origins in any supposedly unique individual personality of the main character. Hence there is little need to seek to penetrate into the murky depths of his soul. The character in a Chinese novel derives his salient personal attributes from the nature of his role in the conflict, and not the other way around. In most novels of this first period, the characters are well-known types—the wise ruler, the loyal general, the honest judge, the noble robber, and the chaste woman—or their opposites—the tyrant, the ambitious officer, the corrupt judge, the bandit, the femme fatale. In the interest of dramatic tension, the counterpoised opponents must be nearly equal in stature: the hero is confronted with enemies who are as intelligent and inventive, as generous and magnanimous as himself, and whom he excels in but a single decisive trait.

In the oldest novels, the story tells itself. It is written in the third person, and the author is not much in evidence. The novel's chief merit is its ability to amuse. If it succeeds in entertaining it is unimportant whether the events it narrates are based on fact. The story is often embellished with various stylistic devices: poems, passages in parallel prose, etc.

The Sanguo zhi yanyi

The oldest surviving printed version of the *Sanguo zhi yanyi* is a magnificent edition produced in 1522. The authorship of the *Sanguo zhi yanyi* is attributed to Luo Guanzhong (ca. 1330–1400), who is mentioned in the *Luguibu xubian* as the author of three *zaju*. (In the sixteenth century and later, many other novels were also attributed to him on no plausible grounds whatsoever).

Sanguo zhi yanyi tells the history of the Chinese civil wars in the period from 180 to 280. After the Yellow Turban Uprising and many other disturbances, the empire is finally divided into three regions, each with its military leader: Cao Cao in the North, Sun Quan in the Southeast, and Liu Bei in Sichuan. In 220–221, these leaders and their various sons and successors set themselves up as emperor; the Han is followed by the Three Kingdoms of Wei, Wu, and Shu-Han. Unity is not restored until 280, when the Jin, the successor to the Wei, which had annexed Shu-Han in 263, succeeds in conquering Wu.

Despite the title, the emphasis in the *Sanguo zhi yanyi* is not on the Three Kingdoms period (220–280) but on the era that led up to the tripartition. In contrast to the official histories, which regard the Wei as the legitimate successor to the Han, the novel, following the lead of the *Tongjian gangmu*, presents Shu-Han as the true lawful heir on the grounds that Liu Bei was, supposedly, a member of the imperial family of the Han. Accordingly, the main characters of the novel are, in the first place, Liu Bei and his sworn brothers: the chivalrous but overly proud Guan Yu and the heroic but impulsive and heavy-drinking Zhang Fei. Later, Liu Bei also is much aided by the wise counselor Zhuge Liang. Joining forces, Liu Bei and Sun Quan manage to turn back Cao Cao in the battle at Red Cliff, where Cao Cao's armada sailing down the Yangzi is devastated by fire. Subsequently, Guan Yu, overconfident and careless, is killed by Sun Quan's men, whereupon Liu Bei, disregarding Zhuge Liang's warnings, decides to go to war against Wu. The campaign ends in a fiasco, and Liu Bei loses his life. Zhuge Liang stays on as chancellor to Liu Bei's son, but despite his efforts to bring about the defeat of Wei, his loyalty is in vain.

Though the *Sanguo zhi yanyi* is a very long novel featuring a tremendous variety of events and a huge cast of characters, a unifying motif is that of lasting conflict: conflict between Liu Bei (Shu-Han) and Cao Cao (Wei), and also the moral conflict between *yi* (the code of honor governing the behavior of sworn brothers) and *zhong* (loyalty between ruler and minister). The heroes and heroines are kings, generals, chancellors, and concubines; their great deeds are described in epic terms. The language of the *Sanguo zhi yanyi* is a simple classical style that includes a few elements of the spoken language; the dialog ranges from purely literary to unadulterated vernacular.

The novel originally consisted of 240 *ze* (sections), which were later combined into 120 *hui* (chapters). The standard version of the novel was edited by Mao Zonggang (1632–after 1709), who also added an extensive critical commentary after the example of Jin Shengtan's edition of the *Shuihu zhuan*. The first edition of Mao Zonggang's version came out in 1680.

The Shuihu zhuan

The oldest fully preserved versions of the *Shuihu zhuan* date from the early years of the Wanli period (1573–1620), although a few chapters still survive from an earlier edition (ca. 1550). The *Shuihu zhuan* is attributed to Shi Nai'an, of whose life nothing is reliably known. The novel is said to have been revised later by Luo Guanzhong, but it has also been claimed that Luo collaborated with Shi during the original writing.

The novel centers around the tales of the noble robbers of the Liangshan Marshes under Song Jiang's leadership. There is a kernel of historical truth in this material. In the early years of the twelfth century a gang led by a certain Song Jiang is known to have operated in districts near Kaifeng. Later, however, numerous tales of different origin came to be associated with the exploits of this gang. The increasing accretions to the cycle can be clearly seen in the *Xuanhe yishi* (Anecdotes from the Xuanhe period, 1119–1125), a *pinghua* dating perhaps from the thirteenth century, and in various *zaju* of the Yuan and early Ming. Eventually the band comes to comprise, aside from the rank and file, thirty-six main and seventy-two secondary heroes and heroines, each with his or her unique background.

The first half of the novel tells the stories of the various individual heroes. In one case after another, the hero, having rebelled against iniquity and injustice, finds himself beyond the pale of the corrupt established society and is forced into a life of banditry. The second half concerns the activities of the gang as a whole. As the imperial troops are unable to subdue the bandits, they are eventually granted official pardon. Subsequently joining the regular army, they take part in various campaigns against rebels, and a number of the gang's leaders are killed. Ultimately, in order to ensure that the survivors will never again revolt, Song Jiang poisons his companion Li Kui during a final banquet: *zhong* triumphs over *yi*. The first part of the novel is undoubtedly the more attractive, including as it does a great number of more or less independent episodes and stories of great variety. These stories provide many fascinating and unretouched glimpses of premodern Chinese society.

The heroes of the *Shuihu zhuan* are bandits who were originally *yamen* runners, gentlemen farmers, monks, schoolteachers, military instructors, peasants, fishermen, and laborers. Their deeds are described minutely, often in gruesome detail. Both the dialog and the narrative are written in the spoken language of the day. Much use is made of storytellers' phrases, stereotyped ways of beginning and ending a chapter, of signaling a change of subject within a chapter, etc. Couplets, poems, songs, and rhymed passages in the parallel style are often used to voice the author's judgment of a person or situation, or to add emphasis to a description.

The earliest preserved editions fall into two groups. The first, originating mostly in Fujian, tends to include a greater number of incidents, but they are told in more summary style. The second group, mostly from Kiangnan (the area including Yangzhou, Nanjing, Suzhou, and Hangzhou), treats fewer incidents but in more detail. This second group includes some versions in 100 *hui* and other, later versions in 120; in the longer versions, the second part of the novel is expanded with a number of extra campaigns.

The standard version of the novel is the edition prepared by Jin Shengtan (1608–1661). Jin Shengtan was an original and opinionated critic. Influenced by the *Jingling pai*, he attached great importance to the novel and the drama. After his version of the *Shuihu zhuan*, he also prepared an edition of Wang Shifu's *Xixiang ji* with an extensive critical commentary. Throughout the Qing dynasty, this was destined to remain the standard version of the play.

Jin Shengtan's version of the *Shuihu zhuan* differs markedly from previous editions. He reduced the novel to seventy chapters by having it end at the moment when all 108 leaders are united. He also wrote a new finale, in which one of the heroes, Lu Junyi, witnesses in a dream the execution of all the other leaders. Jin also added his critical commentary in the form of a general introduction, introductions to the individual chapters, and interlinear comments (in which he often praises his own alterations of the text).

In the 1920s and 1930s Jin Shengtan was unanimously praised as a great early champion of *baihua* literature, but in the People's Republic of China he was long condemned; it was claimed that his edition of the *Shuihu zhuan* casts a negative light on what was actually a peasant rebellion. Since the 1980s he has again been regarded more favorably.

HISTORICAL NOVELS OF THE MID-SIXTEENTH CENTURY

The novels written around the mid-sixteenth century (before the Wanli period) are mostly historical romances—episodes from Chinese history presented in a simplified, attractive guise. Practically all of these novels are written in simple *wenyan* with the addition of certain vernacular elements; little use is made of storytellers' phrases, poems, or other inserted features. These novels often borrow their chronological framework (and, not infrequently, text passages) from the *Tongjian gangmu* or one of its sequels; at appropriate points in the framework, passages from *pinghua* or *chuanqi*, remarks from *biji*, and summaries of plays are tacked on. Eventually, virtually all of Chinese history was treated in this fashion, up through the Ming. The compilers of these novels paid most of their attention to military action and intrigues at court, treating other aspects of life but scantly. Despite their heterogenous character a few novels from this period have enjoyed lasting popularity, presumably because they were the first books in which various stories from certain periods were combined into coherent wholes.

The most famous historical romances of this period include the *Bei Song zhizhuan* and the *Yinglie zhuan*. *Bei Song zhizhuan* (History of the Northern Song) is one of at least four novels compiled by a certain Xiong Damu. It relates the history of the wars in the later tenth and earlier eleventh centuries between the Northern Song and her northern neighbors, the Liao. A central place is occupied by the legendary deeds of the generals of the Yang family, and nowadays the novel is generally known as the *Yangjia jiang yanyi* (Novel on the generals of the Yang family).

The *Yinglie zhuan* (A story of heroes) deals with the career of Zhu Yuanzhang and the founding of the Ming dynasty. It is sometimes attributed to Guo Xun (1475–1542), who enjoyed considerable power and influence in his day. Guo is, in any case, known definitely to have sponsored the printing of other works in *baihua* (an anthology of *sanqu* and suites from *zaju*; the *Shuihu zhuan*).

Some of the novels of this period were eventually superseded by later novels in which the same period was treated at more length, more systematically, or in ways more closely resembling the treatment of the same subjects in popular story cycles.

NOVELS FROM THE LAST CENTURY OF THE MING

The Wanli period (1573–1620) saw a marked upsurge in the activities of commercial publishers in Fujian and especially the Kiangnan area. Old novels were repeatedly reprinted, and many new novels were published. The longer new novels often borrow their main plot lines from older works, but show much greater freedom in their treatment of the material as compared with the older novels, which had really been more in the nature of compilations. The most important and representative works of this second period in the development of the traditional novel are the *Xiyou ji* (Journey to the West) and the *Jin Ping Mei* (an untranslatable title, based on the names of characters).

The second period runs from about 1550 to 1650. The original novel of this period is characterized by the element of reversal. In the long run everything changes into its own opposite. Unity is followed by division, prosperity by ruin, or vice versa. The reversal of fortunes can usually be explained by the process of retribution which operates in all that exists. Retribution is an old Buddhist concept: every act performed by a human being carries a certain moral valence and sooner or later is rewarded or punished accordingly. Typical popular presentations emphasize the power of supernatural beings, such as the King of Hell, to dispense these rewards and punishments. The punishment of one's sins and the rewards for one's virtues are supposed to follow in the next incarnation. But during the period from 1550 to 1650, retribution is seen more as an automatic process, inherent in life and in the ethical quality of actions, requiring for its effects no intervention by gods or demons. The emphasis shifts from retribution in some future existence to retribution in the course of one's present life. Concretely, this means that every good deed involving sacrifice of one's self-interest will eventually be rewarded; self-seeking at others' expense will be punished. A person is never confronted with a choice between two evils or two positive values. The choice is always a straightforward one between good and evil, and the person's future well-being is determined by his own choice.

The retribution process applies even to the most apparently trivial actions, and the Chinese novelist of this period pays detailed attention to everyday life and the multitude of petty sins it involves. Greed and lust are featured prominently. The ethical aspects of individuals' behavior are described in much more detail than the actual physical environment or setting. It is entirely clear *what* is done, but not necessarily *where* or *how*. The author presents the events not as unique happenings but as noteworthy, unexpected variations on general patterns. The concrete descriptions are often followed by poems or couplets that give a sort of summing-up, often by means of a familiar proverb or saying. The effect is to bring the initially unexpected back within the context of what is familiar and general.

At times there is a certain interest in personal mental processes. The authors are sometimes concerned with why some people yield to temptation while others cleave to the good in the face of all difficulties. But the action remains the thing, and the authors show nothing but contempt for those who are so weak, for whatever reason, as to make the wrong ethical choice. Man is regarded as personally responsible for the course of his life, although certainly not in any modern existential sense. The norms of good and evil are regarded as clearly drawn, and actions have inevitable consequences which emerge visibly in the course of the novel.

Usually the process of retribution runs through to its consequences within the space of a single lifetime. But a single lifetime seldom provides enough material for a novel of a hundred chapters; more often it is sufficient only to fill a novella. And toward the end of this second period—in the early seventeenth century—there was a real boom in the production of *baihua* novellas having a distinctive form of their own. These novellas typically consist of two stories—a short opening story and a longer main story—both of which illustrate the workings of one and the same explicitly formulated moral law. The opening story is usually one familiar to readers, while the main story deals with a more detailed, more recent example of the same moral. (The novella will be discussed in the next chapter).

Hardly a single novel or story from this period represents a product of its author's imagination. The author's intention is not to write fiction but to present the truth so that his fellow citizens will awaken from their benighted state of folly and better their ways. The truth means the historical truth; what is narrated must really have happened, and the author often explicitly names his sources, claiming only to have tried to make their truths more generally available. The author does not seek to add personal comments of his own; such commentary as he gives must be authentic and objective. To achieve a successful combination of these two elements, the author assumes the persona of a professional storyteller, full of folksy innocence and homespun virtue, who punctuates the story with his commonplaces.

In comparison to the novels of the first period, those of the second show a much wider range of characters from a broader scale of social backgrounds. They also give more attention to the problems of ordinary folk. But their strong concern with moral issues, together with their black-and-white characterization and mechanically simplistic ethics, has earned them a reputation for facile moralism. Though the accusation is not just in all cases, it is true that the novels and novellas of this second period lack the concept of the tragic. There is no place in them for fate or for the dilemma. Though the presence of the storyteller lends a certain liveliness to these texts, its effect is limited by the authors' determination to stick to true, or at any rate well-known, stories. Anything else, it seems, was rejected as being an insufficiently reliable basis for the didactic function of the written word.

The Xiyou ji *and Other Fantastic Novels*

The *Xiyou ji* (The Journey to the West) is supposed to have been written by Wu Cheng'en (ca. 1500–ca. 1582), probably between 1570 and 1580. The oldest surviving edition dates from 1592. Wu Cheng'en was a member of the literati who never passed higher-level examinations and held but modest office in his later years.

This novel takes its material from a very old popular story cycle. During the years 629–645 the Chinese monk Xuanzang (600–664) undertook a pilgrimage to India for the purpose of collecting sutras. Upon his return he was given the honorific name Sanzang (Tripitaka). His journey made a tremendous impression on his contemporaries and soon became a fertile source of legends, in which Xuanzang's journey reemerged as a peril-fraught pilgrimage to the Western Paradise. To aid him in overcoming the attendant dangers, such as repeated attacks by supernatural monsters, he was provided with supernatural helpers in the form of a horse, a monk, a pig, and a monkey. Various early written versions of this story cycle have survived. One example, the *Da Tang Sanzang qujing shihua* (The story, with poems, of how Tripitaka of the Great Tang fetched the sutras), may be the oldest known *pinghua*; it dates from the second half of the thirteenth century. The *Yongle dadian* also contains fragments of another *pinghua* version.

Whereas earlier versions of the legend featured the wise monk Xuanzang as their hero and started their narrative with his departure from China for faraway lands, Wu Cheng'en's 100-chapter novel has as its main character the monkey, Sun Wukong. The novel starts out with the birth of Sun Wukong. Chapters 1 to 7 describe his quest for longevity and magic powers and his rebellion against the reigning authorities in heaven, for which he is eventually imprisoned under a mountain. Chapters 9 to 100 deal with Xuanzang's birth and his pilgrimage. Soon after his departure from China, he loses his original retinue; instead, he is accompanied by Sun Wukong, who is allowed to undertake this task as penance for his rebellion. Other traveling companions are the pig Zhu Bajie and the monk Sandy. Xuanzang also gets a new horse. Together, the new company goes through eighty-one perils of all sorts, most of them involving encounters with monsters seeking to eat Xuanzang. Eighty of the perils are met with on the journey to the Western Paradise and one on the way home. In his descriptions of the perils and monsters, the author gives free reign to his humor and fantasy.

The *Xiyou ji* is, among other things, an allegorical tale. Xuanzang can be seen as man in search of Enlightenment; the horse that carries him, as his will; the monkey, as his heart (and mind); and the pig, as his physical powers and inclinations. The characterization follows the same lines: Zhu Bajie is an unintelligent and lusty glutton; Sun Wukong is ingenious but overconfident. In the allegorical interpretation, the various dangers and monsters are the illusions that stand between man and Enlightenment, though it is usually difficult to specify which illusion is associated with which monster. Not surprisingly allegory goes hand in hand with satire. The foibles of human nature, social ills in Chinese society, absurd features of the Chinese pantheon—all are subjected to scrutiny, giving rise to numerous comic passages.

Various sequels and additions have been written to the *Xiyou ji*. The most important is the *Xiyou bu* (Supplement to the Journey to the West), by Dong Yue (1620–1686), which dates from 1641. It is a relatively short novel (sixteen chapters) of strictly allegorical design: the heart is imprisoned by feelings (*qing*); Sun Wukong is the victim of Mackerel (*qing*). The *Xiyou bu* also contains many satirical passages.

Other long novels from the Wanli period, memorable for their fantastic descriptions of the supernatural, are the *Fengshen yanyi* and the *Xiyang ji*. The *Fengshen yanyi* (Novel of the enfeoffment of the gods) is also known as *Fengshen bang* (The proclamation of the enfeoffment of the gods). It is attributed usually to Xu Zhonglin (early seventeenth century), but occasionally to Lu Xixing (1520–ca. 1601). Its subject is the misconduct of King Zhou of the Yin dynasty and his overthrow at the hands of King Wu, the founder of the following Zhou dynasty. In Yuan times this historical episode had already been treated in the *Wuwang fa Zhou pinghua* (Simple story of the campaign of King Wu against the Zhou), one of the *Quanxiang pinghua wuzhong*. Of the *Fengshen yanyi*'s 100 chapters, the last 70, devoted to King Wu's final campaign, amount to a long sequence of battle descriptions. During the war both parties make use of more and more powerful magicians, who have stronger and stronger magical weapons at their disposal. After King Wu's victory, not only are the survivors enfeoffed as vassals, but the ghosts of both sides' casualties are enfeoffed as gods. The novel represents an attempt to contain the many disparate gods of the Chinese folk pantheon within a coherent myth of origins.

The full title of the *Xiyang ji* (Record of the Western Ocean, i.e., the Indian Ocean) is *Sanbao taijian (xia) Xiyang ji* (Record of the conquest of the Western Ocean by the Grand Eunuch Sanbao); it centers on the expeditions to Southeast Asia, India, and Arabia led by the eunuch Zheng He in the early fifteenth century.

The Jin Ping Mei *and Other Social Novels*

The title of the *Jin Ping Mei* (Plum blossom in golden vase) is actually untranslatable; it is composed of characters taken from the names of the three main female characters. It is an anonymous novel in 100 chapters, thought to have been written in the 1580s, but first printed in the last years of the Wanli period under the title *Jin Ping Mei cihua.*

The idea for the novel is taken from the story of Wu Song in the *Shuihu zhuan.* The *Jin Ping Mei* describes in great detail the life of the apothecary Ximen Qing and his household in a provincial town in Shandong. The novel is supposedly set in the early twelfth century, but the social setting as described is clearly that of the sixteenth century. The story is about Ximen Qing's economic and political machinations, his relationships with his various wives (eventually six), the women's mutual relationships, and Ximen Qing's amatory affairs and shady business dealings. Ximen Qing's ethical misconduct results in his early and horrible death, after which his household is broken up. The subsequent life of the other characters is in keeping with their former behavior: earlier good and evil meet with later reward and punishment. In other words a prominent theme in this novel is the working of retribution within a single lifetime.

In this novel, we also see the increased importance attributed to the life of ordinary people as examples of the process of retribution. But these ordinary characters are important not so much for their unique individuality as for their aptness in embodying certain types. Accordingly, the author is not interested in describing individual psychological processes as such, but in questioning how it came about that certain persons, under certain circumstances in a morally unambiguous world, allowed themselves to be enticed into doing evil. Sex being one of the most obvious of human inclinations, the author gives much attention to failings and misdeeds in this area, and there are a number of very explicit erotic passages.

Another anonymous early seventeenth-century novel showing great thematic similarity to the *Jin Ping Mei* is the *Sui Yangdi yanshi* (The voluptuous history of Emperor Yang of the Sui dynasty). Its subject is a great name in history, and much of the novel's treatment of him is traceable to late *chuanqi* tales. Like the *Jin Ping Mei*, it is the story of a man who destroys himself by the unbridled indulgence of his passions.

Another important novel from the last years of the Ming dynasty (or the earliest years of the Qing) is the anonymous *Xingshi yinyuan zhuan* (A marriage to awaken the world), which has been wrongly attributed to Pu Songling. Like the *Jin Ping Mei*, it is set in Shandong; it provides a detailed, lively picture of the life of the lower gentry. Events in the *Xingshi yinyuan zhuan* are also tied together by threads of retribution, but in this novel the results are sometimes not evident until a following incarnation.

CHAPBOOKS

The final decades of the Ming also saw the publication of a number of short novels, typically comprising but a few brief chapters dealing with the life stories of important figures in popular legend or belief, such as Mazu, Guanyin, and Zhong Kui. Usually they are written in very simple language. In view of their contents, style, and execution they may be called chapbooks.

Of the chapbooks of this period, the *Siyou ji* (A record of four journeys) deserves mention. *Siyou ji* is actually the collective title of four short novels, one of which is a very brief version of the *Xiyou ji*. Some scholars believe this to be copied from Wu Cheng'en's work; others think it to be, on the contrary, the source on which he based his novel.

Chapter 21.
THE NOVELLA (*HUABEN*)

In the major collections from the final decades of the Ming, the novella is a short or medium-length story in the contemporary spoken language which, in contrast to the novel, is not divided into chapters and depicts only a limited number of characters and events. No hard-and-fast distinction can be drawn between the long novella and the short novel. On occasion short novels have in fact been republished as novellas, and some novellas have been published separately as novels by inserting chapter divisions. The earliest novellas probably were written and published as independent works, but by the middle of the sixteenth century, they were usually being printed in collections. Some of the earliest collections containing novellas are not limited to this genre but also contain miscellaneous other materials. From the mid-seventeenth century on, collections also appear in which the novellas are subdivided into a limited number of chapters. As long as these novellas are published as parts of collections, they are classified as novellas. The language, as in all forms of *baihua* literature, varies from simple, almost pure *wenyan* to a racy colloquial language.

The Chinese term for the novella is *huaben*. The *huaben* may have arisen as early as the second half of the thirteenth century, but the genre did not really come into its own until the period after about 1620, especially around the middle of the seventeenth century. Thereafter, few new works of the same quality were written in this genre.

Practically all Chinese scholars are of the opinion that the oldest *huaben* originated during the Song in the stories told by professional storytellers who operated in the great capitals of Kaifeng and Hangzhou. The presence of such storytellers is well attested in contemporary descriptions of the cities. A question that immediately arises is whether the surviving printed books are more or less literal or "stenographic" reproductions of the stories as told or whether they are elaborated versions of more rudimentary cribs used by the performers. In any case, the supposition that the word *huaben* might mean something like "story-basis" or "summary" has been shown to be insupportable. It is also questionable whether the professional tellers of *xiaoshuo*, whose stories are said to have been the main source of the *huaben*, did in fact tell short stories, as has usually been assumed. It is actually more probable that these artists, like the tellers of *jiangshi* (explications of history), needed several days for the performance of a single story. The distinction between the terms *xiaoshuo* and *jiangshi* probably refers to a difference not in form but in content.

THE EARLIEST EDITIONS

From the fourteenth and fifteenth centuries the known relevant material amounts to one questionable bibliographical reference to one *huaben* and a few surviving pages from another. The earliest completely preserved printed edition dates from 1498: a short *huaben* that is included in the prefatory matter of the 1498 printing of the *Xixiang ji*. The earliest known collection of *huaben* was not published until the mid-sixteenth century, by a certain Hong Bian. This collection was originally entitled *Liushi jia xiaoshuo* (Sixty stories), but is nowadays better known as the *Qingping shantang huaben* (Novellas printed by the Qingping mountain pavilion). The collection seems originally to have contained sixty items, but slightly fewer than half of these have been preserved. Based on the surviving stories, it can be safely concluded that these *huaben* were of varied origin. Some texts are *chuanqi* tales in virtually unaltered form; some are short performance texts; some are summaries of *zaju* and perhaps occasionally of *xiwen*. Still others were obviously written shortly before the publication of the collection, but the book also includes older texts which do not fit into these categories. Barring the discovery of strikingly new evidence, this heterogeneity pleads strongly against the idea of a direct and exclusive relationship between *huaben* and the Song storytellers. What is true, however, is that later *huaben* authors had an increasing tendency to cast their narrator in the role of a professional storyteller. Unfortunately, it must be said that the quality of the *huaben* in the *Qingping shantang huaben* is very mediocre in general, though there are a few refreshing exceptions.

Research on the early history of the *huaben* was gratuitously confused by the publication, early in the twentieth century, of a collection of eight excellent novellas. According to the editor, the well-known bibliophile Miao Quansun, it was based on a late Song or early Yuan manuscript. This collection bears the title *Jingben tongsu xiaoshuo* (Capital editions of popular stories). For a long time many scholars saw in this book irrefutable evidence that the *huaben* must already have been in existence as a fully developed genre in the twelfth and thirteenth centuries. It is now clear, however, that this collection is a fake based on certain collections of *huaben*, published by Feng Menglong (1574–1646), which were not generally available at the beginning of this century—even the editions on which the stories were based have been identified.

THE *SAN YAN* AND THE PERIODIZATION OF *HUABEN*

No more than a few scattered published editions of *huaben* have been preserved from the Wanli period. The first significant collection of some length is the *San yan* (Three "words"), published by Feng Menglong. *San yan* is actually the collective title of three collections of forty novellas each. The first, *Gujin xiaoshuo* (Stories of past and present), appeared in 1620 or 1621; it was referred to in later reprintings as *Yushi mingyan* (Enlightened words to instruct the world). The second, *Jingshi tongyan* (Universal words to alarm the world), was published in 1624, and the third, *Xingshi hengyan* (Lasting words to awaken the world), in 1627. In addition to older *huaben* from the preceding centuries, the three collections include novellas written especially for inclusion in the *San yan*.

Many scholars have been occupied with the problem of the correct dating of the extant *huaben*. The most systematic effort along these lines was made by Patrick Hanan. Taking as his starting point the novellas whose date can be established with confidence on the basis of external evidence, Hanan studied the stylistic features characteristic of various periods. Following these stylistic criteria, he then divided the other *huaben* into three groups according to their presumable period of origin: (1) 1250–1450, (2) 1400–1575, and (3) 1550–1627. The year mentioned as the beginning of each period is the earliest possible date of publication of at least a few of the *huaben* within that group, but Hanan believes most of the stories to have been written within the last few years of each period.

According to Hanan, of the *huaben* preserved in the *San yan* or earlier publications, thirty-four can be assigned to the first period (1250–1450). Some of these are scarcely distinguishable from *chuanqi* (classical-language short stories); others are derived from popular materials. Of the latter, many are tales of heroes or ghosts in which the denouement is saved for the end rather than being, as in some Chinese tales, divulged at the outset. One remarkable stylistic feature of the stories in this latter group is that they often begin with a string of poems and songs having little bearing on the story which follows; in other cases the story is introduced by an account of happenings only indirectly related to the story's main action.

Hanan assigns thirty-one *huaben* to the second period (1400–1575). Many of these are based on plays (*zaju* and *xiwen*), on *wenyan* short stories, or on performance texts, though original novellas are also included. Apparently, many *huaben* from this period originated in Hangzhou. Prominent in this period are the moralistic Buddhist stories and others which embody, in one form or another, a theme that might be phrased "small misdeed, heavy consequences." These are characterized by strikingly realistic descriptions of the life of merchants and other ordinary individuals in society.

The remaining novellas, nearly eighty, belong to the third period. Most may be presumed to have been written specifically for the *San yan*. Of the original novellas in the first two collections (*Yushi mingyan* and *Jingshi tongyan*), Feng Menglong himself is probably the author of the great majority. By contrast, most of the new novellas in *Xingshi hengyan* are likely to have been written by an anonymous collaborator, who may also be the author of *Shi dian tou* (The rock nods), a collection of *huaben* that appeared soon after the *San yan*.

These new novellas usually consist of two stories: a concise introductory story that is often a well-known tale, and a main story, less well known, often of more recent setting, which is told in much more detail. The authors seldom invent their own stories, but use existing stories from *biji* or *chuanqi*. The introductory story and the main story usually both concern the same theme, illustrating a principle the validity of which is seemingly confirmed by the recurrence of tellable examples. This principle is almost invariably that of retribution within one lifetime. Those who deceive others are themselves deceived, and good and evil are requited accordingly. The element of the supernatural does occur in these stories, but it is usually no more than an agency through which the process of retribution is enabled or helped to occur. Gods and demons are incapable of arbitrarily determining the fate of humans; it is humans who construct, through their deeds, their own future. In this perspective the behavior of ordinary people takes on exemplary value. The authors are not much interested in the psychology of individual characters: what is individual, hence unique, is not of much value as an illustration of a type. Rather, they focus on how presumably normal individuals, living in a morally unambiguous world, are brought to do evil. We have already encountered this concern in the novel of the last century of the Ming, and it appears that the novella was an especially suitable format for the description of a single lifetime.

In the new novellas the narrator is nearly always cast in the role of a professional storyteller, who frequently interrupts the story to add his own "objective" comments, often in the form of couplets or poems, and who states explicitly the moral of the story. The subject matter of the new novellas is extremely varied, and some of them have remained among the most famous *huaben* because of their vivid vignettes of daily life.

Feng Menglong

Feng Menglong came from a rich Suzhou family. He spent much of his adult life working as editor for various publishers in Suzhou and Nanjing. In addition to the *San yan*, he produced collections of *min'ge* (folk songs), including the "naughty" *Shan'ge* (Popular songs), a collection of jokes entitled *Xiaofu* (The storehouse of laughs), a collection of twelve *chuanqi* plays, a popular biography of Wang Yangming, some voluminous collections of tales in the classical language, and other publications.

Feng Menglong also reworked the *Pingyao zhuan* (The subduing of the monsters), originally a twenty-chapter novel, into a new version of twice that length. In Feng's forty-chapter version, this tale of the uprising of Wang Ze in Beizhou in 1047–1048 reemerges as the miraculous history of a family of foxes, who undergo countless adventures before their daughter marries Wang Ze and uses her magical abilities to ensure the initial success of the rebellion. The fox family is assisted by Pellet, a monk. In addition to its many fairy-tale elements, the story includes satirical passages, in which religious credulity is a favorite target. Feng's version of the novel has remained popular down through the centuries.

Under the title *Xin Lieguo zhi* (New history of the various states), Feng Menglong also produced a new edition of the historical-romance version of Chinese history for the periods covered by the *Chunqiu* and the *Zhanguo ce*. Later (in the eighteenth century) this novel was revised and republished as *Dong Zhou Lieguo zhi* (History of the various states under the Eastern Zhou Dynasty). It deals with Chinese history from the fall of the Western Zhou and the transfer of the capital to Luoyang to the unification of China under the Qin. Unlike many other historical romances, it adheres closely to the orthodox historiography of the given period.

LING MENGCHU AND THE *LIANG PAI*

Probably at least partly inspired by the commercial success of the *San yan*, in 1628 and 1633 Ling Mengchu (1580–1644) published two novella collections: *Chuke Pai'an jingqi* ([Stories] at which to pound the table in amazement, Volume one), containing forty novellas, and *Erke Pai'an jingqi* (idem, Volume two), which comprises thirty-nine *huaben* and one *zaju*. The two collections are referred to jointly as the *Liang pai*. Practically all the *huaben* in the *Liang pai* were written by Ling Mengchu himself. The plots are almost always taken from existing fictional texts in *wenyan*. Most of Ling's novellas are constructed along the same lines as the new novellas in the *San yan*, that is, they consist of a concise introductory story followed by an elaborate main tale, both dealing with the same theme and illustrating the same moral. Practically all of his *huaben* show the workings of retribution in the lives of ordinary people. The long-term results of human misbehavior being inevitable and in a sense predictable, evil is not so much a sin as an indication of stupidity, and the author often describes his sinners with undisguised sarcasm. Though the *Liang pai* contains a number of excellent novellas, as a whole the collection lacks the diversity of the *San yan*, and many novellas in the *Liang pai* give the impression of having been written hastily according to formula in order to fill out bulk for the published collections.

Ling Mengchu came from a family of literati-publishers who were famous for the quality of their printing. Ling compiled and wrote many works for the family business, but most of these have been lost. He also has a certain reputation as a *zaju* author. During the last years of his life he held a low-level bureaucratic job and he died fighting insurgents.

LATER *HUABEN* COLLECTIONS

In 1640 or thereabouts, an anthology of forty *huaben* from the *San yan* and the *Liang pai* was compiled under the title *Jingu qiguan* (Strange scenes from past and present). Of the included novellas, twenty-nine are from the *San yan* and eleven from the *Liang pai*; those taken from the *San yan* are mostly of the newer category. The *Jingu qiguan* was very popular under the Qing, so much so that the *San yan* and *Liang pai* were practically forgotten. Almost all nineteenth- and early twentieth-century Western translations of *huaben* are based on the *Jingu qiguan*.

The last years of the Ming period saw the publication of a number of noteworthy *huaben* collections. *Shi dian tou* (The rock nods) is a collection of fourteen *huaben* probably written by Feng Menglong's anonymous collaborator, who also wrote the new novellas in the *Xingshi hengyan*. In style and structure these stories are comparable to those in the *Xingshi hengyan*. Occasionally *Shi dian tou* deals with more daring subject matter, such as cannibalism and homosexual love.

Zui xing shi (The rock on which a drunkard sobers up) contains fifteen *huaben*. It was written by an anonymous author, possibly from Shandong, shortly before the fall of the Ming. These stories are full of the social ills that prevailed in late Ming times. A technical feature of this collection is that the stories usually contain not just one but two or more short introductory tales before the main story.

Xihu erji (On West Lake, Second collection) consists of thirty-four *huaben* in which the main story is set in the vicinity of West Lake at Hangzhou. The best-known stories, however, are not included in this volume, but are found in a sixteen-novella collection called *Xihu jiahua* (Beautiful stories of West Lake), of which the oldest surviving editions date from the Qing. These two collections exemplify a trend, observable during the final years of the Ming, towards thematic coherence in *huaben* collections. Of the *huaben* collections from early Qing times, Li Yu's *Wusheng xi* and *Shi er lou* have already been mentioned. The novellas in *Wusheng xi* are characterized by risqué subject matter and rather far-fetched plots. Those in *Shi er lou* are sometimes subdivided into two, three, or four chapters; the plot is often extremely far-fetched, but the stories are made readable by the author's witty style.

Zhao shi bei (A lamp to light the world) comprises four humorous novellas dating from the first years of the Qing. The collection *Doupeng xianhua* (Gossip under the bean trellis) is probably from the same period. It contains twelve *huaben* connected by a framing story. In recent years a number of hitherto inaccessible collections of *huaben* have been reprinted. These show that the genre retained its vitality well into the eighteenth century, albeit rarely resulting in works of the same high quality as the seventeenth-century collections.

CRIME STORIES

In the Wanli period, a number of collections of *gong'an* (legal cases) appeared. A *gong'an* is the story of a crime, often murder, and of the eventual sentencing of the criminal by a judge of unquestionable integrity. *Gong'an* are usually written in simple *wenyan* with certain vernacular traits; storyteller's phrases are seldom used. In some collections the same judge appears in nearly all the stories. The only collection to remain popular in later centuries was that in which Judge Bao solved all the cases. The book originally contained 100 stories, but in later editions, bearing the title *Longtu gong'an* (Cases of Judge Bao), the number is considerably reduced.

Chapter 22.
THE NOVEL (1650–1875)

Between 1650 and 1875 the novel falls into two overall categories that were already evident in the later years of the period from 1450 to 1650. There were the novels written for literati by literati who were thoroughly familiar with the traditional gentry culture, and there were novels written for an audience of limited literacy, probably by authors who were themselves not highly schooled. Novels in the first category often have original plots, and the authors are often known by name. In the second category, the stories are often traceable to popular story cycles and are almost always of unknown authorship. The first category includes, in addition to long novels of 50 to 100 chapters, two important subgenres of short novels—"talent and beauty" novels and those that can be called "reductionistic." The second category is represented most notably by the so-called military romances.

LITERATI FICTION FROM 1650 TO 1875

The structure of the novel in this period is characterized by the parity of contrasted elements, what Andrew Plaks has called "complementary bipolarity." Reality is presented as a compound of contrasting elements which are simultaneously present. For example, at one and the same moment, beauty and ugliness both exist, as do the sublime and the ridiculous, success through flattery and through honest achievement, failure with and without reason. There are good people and bad people, honest citizens and liars. It is as possible to strive for worldly success as it is to seek escape from the world. The primary subject is the contrast between appearance and truth, pretense and ability, dream and reality, play-acting and fact, and, of course, male and female, feminine and masculine.

The panoramic presentation of these contrasting features and developments within a single character, a single household, or any other single social unit proved at times a most difficult but challenging technical problem for Chinese novelists. Often the authors tried their hand, with varying degrees of success, at combining two, four, or eight threads of narrative into a single story. Sometimes a novel comprises two parts which seem virtually unrelated or even mutually contradictory. But it is exactly in this element of contrast that the unity of the novel resides.

By comparison with the novels of the first and second periods, these have less dynamic and free-flowing action. There are constant shifts between various strands of the narrative, and purely descriptive passages, employed in pairs for contrast, are often prominent. There are more characters, and contrasting qualities are often assigned to pairs of brothers or sisters. Occasionally the novelist tries to build up complex characters by giving contradictory features to one and the same person. In other cases, he attempts a satiric effect by endowing men and women with attributes of the opposite sex or by generally creating an upside-down world—for example, a world in which women rule and men must undergo the agonies of footbinding, as in the *Jinghua yuan* (Flowers in the mirror) by Li Ruzhen (1763? –1830?).

The novel in this period is presented as a mixture of truth and fantasy— half autobiography or history and half dream or ideal. The author presents himself as the man who may manipulate the course of the story at will, meanwhile commenting ironically on his own role.

NOVELS OF SOME LENGTH

Sui Tang yanyi *and* Nüxian waishi

The first long novels of the period from 1650 to 1875 that can be regarded as examples of this complementary bipolarity and panoramic structure are the *Sui Tang yanyi* and the *Nüxian waishi*. The *Sui Tang yanyi* (History of the Sui and Tang), in 100 chapters, was written by Chu Renhuo; the author's preface dates from 1695. *Sui Tang yanyi* deals with the history of China from the ascension of Emperor Yang of the Sui until the suppression of the An Lushan rebellion. Xuanzong and High Consort Yang are regarded as reincarnations of Emperor Yang and one of his favorite concubines. Much of the text is originally from two older novels, the *Sui Yangdi yanshi* and the *Suishi yiwen* (Anecdotes from Sui history), both dating from the last years of the Ming. *Sui Yangdi yanshi* describes the luxurious life of Emperor Yang in his palace; *Suishi yiwen* is mainly concerned with the life history of Qin Qiong, one of the heroes who helped Li Shimin to establish the Tang and become emperor. Chu Renhuo took passages from both these novels and wove them into a new mosaic in which luxury and deprivation are shown in continual contrast. Besides these two novels, Chu made at least incidental use of numerous other sources.

The *Nüxian waishi* (Unofficial history of the female immortal), in 100 chapters, was written by Lü Xiong toward the end of the seventeenth century. Mixing historical facts with bizarre fantasy, it describes the usurpation of the throne by the Yongle Emperor and the rebellion of Tang Sai'er (1420) as parts of one and the same story, in which Tang Sai'er appears as the guardian angel of the Jianwen Emperor. The scene jumps abruptly from the activities of the Yongle Emperor and his cronies to those of Tang Sai'er and her party, from battlefield action to festive banquets, and so on. Tang Sai'er is presented as a reincarnation of the Goddess of the Moon; the Yongle Emperor is a reincarnation of the Wolf Star (Sirius), which causes eclipses of the moon. Their earthly struggle ends in the same stalemate as their heavenly conflict. The *Nüxian waishi* attracted comments and notes by many leading intellectuals of the day, but it has not had the lasting popularity of the *Sui Tang yanyi*.

The Rulin waishi

The most famous long novels of the period 1650–1875 are unquestionably the *Rulin waishi* and the *Honglou meng*. The *Rulin waishi* (Unofficial history of the literati) was written by Wu Jingzi (1701–1754). Wu's family had once enjoyed high standing, but his father's career was mediocre, and Wu himself only succeeded in the lowest examinations, those at the prefectural level. Wu lived for a while on his inheritance, but when his means were almost exhausted he moved in 1733 to Nanjing, where he was to spend the rest of his life. Though recommended as a candidate for the special examinations held at the capital in 1736, he did not participate. He probably wrote his novel between 1740 and 1750, and it is generally thought that one of the main characters, Du Shanqing, is a self-portrait of the author, idealized but not without self-criticism and irony.

The novel was never printed during Wu's lifetime. The earliest edition of the *Rulin waishi* is in fifty-six chapters. In structure and style, *Rulin waishi* differs markedly from earlier novels. Storyteller's phrases are seldom used, and there are no inserted couplets, poems, or descriptions in verse form. There are, however, many prose descriptions of nature scenes. There is no single overall plot; rather, the novel consists of numerous independent episodes of varying length. The episodes are usually connected by having a main character in one episode reappear as a less central figure in the following one. The resulting effect is that of a series of snapshots of eighteenth-century gentry life in China (the novel claims to be set in the Ming dynasty). The various gentry types are presented in contrasting pairs; the author returns again and again to the ever-shifting balance between appearance and reality, reputation and achievement, pretension and ability, behavior and intention. Most of the characters sooner or later prove unable to realize their ideals in this world; willingly or unwillingly, they strike compromises. In the first and penultimate chapters, however, the author presents a few individuals who do succeed in living up to their ideals, and whose words are not incompatible with their deeds. The final chapter is devoted to the description of posthumous imperial honors for deserving literati. Notwithstanding Wu's satirical treatment of numerous social ills, especially the rampant abuses of the examination system and the pedantry and hypocrisy of many scholars, his own ideal is and remains a purified version of Confucianism.

The Honglou Meng

The *Honglou meng* (Red chamber dream), in 120 chapters, was written by Cao Xueqin (1715–1764). Cao's grandfather was Cao Yin (1658–1712), a protégé of the Kangxi Emperor; as director of the Imperial Textile Factory in Nanjing, he was an extremely rich man. Cao Yin had a strong interest in literature; he supervised the publication of the *Quan Tang shi* and wrote *chuanqi* plays. In 1735 the Yongzheng Emperor dismissed Cao Xueqin's father from the post of Textile Commissioner. The family returned to Peking, where Cao Xueqin spent the rest of his life in more and more modest circumstances. Jia Baoyu, the main character of the *Honglou meng*, undoubtedly embodies numerous autobiographical elements. (The exact dates of Cao Xueqin's life and his exact relationship to Cao Yin are matters of heated debate among scholars.)

Honglou meng describes in great detail the life of the eminently rich family Jia and their many servants and employees. One of the main contrasts in the novel is that between the happy life led by the young Jia Baoyu and twelve half-sisters and cousins of his own age in the Daguanyuan (Garden of Great Contemplation) and the ugly intrigues and machinations going on elsewhere in the huge compound. One of the main plot lines traces Jia Baoyu's contrasting relationships with two female cousins who are diametrically opposed: the sickly, complaining Lin Daiyu and the healthy, extroverted Xue Baochai. After a long series of adventurous complications, Jia Baoyu is finally ready to marry Lin Daiyu—or so he thinks. Once in the bridal chamber, he discovers his bride to be Xue Baochai instead. Lin Daiyu dies soon afterward. After begetting a son and succeeding in the examinations, Jia Baoyu says farewell to the world, becoming the disciple of a Taoist master and a Buddhist monk.

Another major plot line concerns the activities of Wang Xifeng, one of the daughters-in-law of the family Jia, who gradually becomes more and more involved in the management of the family finances, with disastrous consequences. If Jia Baoyu is an overly feminine boy, Wang Xifeng is an overly masculine woman.

The main theme of the novel is the relation between appearance and reality. "Appearance" (*se*) is the world as it seems to be; man maintains attachments to appearance through the agency of "feeling" (*qing*). Appearance is, in other words, phenomenal reality in its seductive aspect: the word *se* also refers to sex, and *qing* also means "feelings for the other sex; love; desire." The highest truth is the insight that phenomenal reality is ultimately empty (*kong*) and that whatever exists is impermanent, so that attachment must inevitably result in suffering. Those who are attached to appearances regard this highest truth as nonsense; those who recognize the true nature of reality reject the world as false—in Chinese, *jia*, undoubtedly intentionally homophonous with Jia Baoyu's family name.

The *Honglou meng* follows Jia Baoyu from the first arousal of his feelings (during the dream in the red chamber) through all the consequent troubles and complications, until the point at which he finally liberates himself from feelings by abandoning the world. Jia Baoyu is an exemplar of the stubborn, foolish human individual (a "stone") who cannot attain purification and insight except through suffering. (Another title of the novel is *Shitou ji*, the "Story of a Stone.")

Honglou meng is written in a lively style. The descriptive passages and dialogs are based on eighteenth-century Peking usage and quite closely resemble the modern spoken language. The novel touches on practically all aspects of traditional Chinese culture and includes countless poems, letters, riddles, etc. in various registers of *wenyan*.

During the author's lifetime the novel circulated only in manuscript form. The first printed editions date from 1792 in a text prepared by a certain Gao E. The majority of known manuscripts, whatever their differences in detail, contain no more than eighty chapters, so many scholars have assumed that the last forty chapters were written by Gao E on the basis of indications and elements present in the first eighty and an outline by Cao himself. Long and bitter arguments rage to this day over the question of how great Gao E's own contribution was, and whether or not he diverted the novel from its original course.

Ever since 1792 the *Honglou meng* has been immensely popular in China. It has been subjected to amazingly different interpretations, some of them quite bizarre. In the People's Republic of China it has usually been read as a plea for young people's right to choose their own marriage partners and as a sharp condemnation of the corruption prevalent in traditional ("feudal") society.

Other Eighteenth-Century Novels

The *Lüye xianzong* (Tracks of Immortals on the green field), by Li Baichuan (ca. 1750), shows a certain thematic resemblance to the *Honglou meng*. This eighty-chapter novel (there is also a manuscript version in 100 chapters) tells of the social decline of Leng Yubing, the descendant of a prominent gentry family, who eventually says goodbye to this world in order to become an Immortal. Though somewhat uneven in quality, the novel contains numerous fascinating scenes from the life of the rural gentry.

The *Yesou puyan* (Unvarnished words of a simple old man), in 154 chapters, was written by Xia Jingqu (1705–1787) but only appeared in print a century after his death. Its main character, Wen Suchen, is presented as the perfect human being—master of all the arts of peace and war, he is proof in word and deed against all the perils posed by his civil and bureaucratic life. Virtually all aspects of traditional Chinese culture are described in this veritably encyclopedic novel. Though it has been suggested that the character of Wen Suchen may have been based at least partly on the statesman and philosopher Wang Yangming, the author himself adheres strictly to the orthodox Neo-Confucianism of Zhu Xi. The *Yesou puyan* can perhaps best be described as a fantasy expressing the unbridled wishes of a cramped spirit.

The *Wu Zetian si da qi'an* (Four big remarkable legal cases in the days of Wu Zetian), which probably dates from the last years of the eighteenth century, is set in the reign of Empress Wu (684–705). The main character in this anonymous sixty-four-chapter novel is Di Renjie (607–700). In this work, too, an attempt is made to show the main character as a complex but perfect official. The first thirty chapters present Di as district magistrate and defender of his people; he clears up crimes by refusing to be deceived by initial appearances. The last thirty-four chapters show the erstwhile impeccable judge in a new role at the imperial court as defender of the dynasty. Having cleverly enticed various henchmen of the empress to sign false confessions, to go disguised as a eunuch, etc., he then sees that they are treated accordingly (for example, the well-endowed lover of the empress, who had disguised himself as a eunuch in order to be able to visit her more easily in her private apartments, is castrated). The result is that the empress abdicates in favor of the legal heir to the throne. The first half of *Wu Zetian si da qi'an* was translated by Robert Van Gulik and served as the model for his own Judge Dee mystery novels.

The sixty-chapter *Feilong zhuan* (Story of the flying dragons), by Wu Xuan, is a new reworking of the history of the founding of the Song; the material had already been treated in historical-romance form by Xiong Damu in his sixteenth-century *Nan Song zhuan* (History of the [prince of] Nan Song, i.e., Zhao Kuangyin). The *Feilong zhuan* centers on the contrast between two bosom friends who both later become real emperors: the timid umbrella-seller Chai Rong, who reigned as Shizong of the later Zhou from 954 to 960, and the dauntless fist-fighter Zhao Kuangyin, who later became the founder of the Song when his troops placed him on the throne.

Nineteenth-Century Novels

The most important long novels of the first seventy-five years of the nineteenth century are the *Jinghua yuan*, *Pinhua baojian*, *Hua yue hen* and *Ernü yingxiong zhuan*.

The *Jinghua yuan* (Flowers in the mirror), in 100 chapters, was written by Li Ruzhen (1763?–1830?), who also gained lasting recognition for his work in the field of phonology. The *Jinghua yuan* is set in the reign of empress Wu Zetian. The novel opens with a short fairy-tale-like introduction, in which the empress in her arrogance orders all the hundred flowers to blossom on New Year's Day. When the flower-Immortals obey her, they are punished for their irresponsible behavior by being sent down to earth, where they will be reborn as girls. The main body of the novel consists of two parts, which can be seen more or less as mirror images of each other. In the first part a certain Tang Ao journeys to the capital, competes in the examinations, succeeds, but is soon dismissed, whereupon he returns home and, taking his daughter Tang Guichen with him, embarks on a ship owned by his brother-in-law, Lin Zhiyang. During their trip across the oceans, they visit many strange countries; the local society is often organized so as to present a striking contrast with some aspect of traditional China. They encounter, for example, a country in which sellers ask low prices and buyers make high bids, another in which people's moral standing is immediately visible from the color of the clouds on which they ride, another in which all teachers are stupid and pedantic, another in which even the humblest girls are extremely well-educated, and yet another in which women hold all power while men wear earrings and have bound feet. In the course of his journey Tang Guichen picks up various female traveling companions, all reincarnated flower-Immortals.

In the second part of the main body of the novel Tang Guichen makes another long sea voyage, this one much more briefly narrated, after which she accompanies numerous female friends to the capital, where they are to take part in a special examination for girls. Both during the journey to the capital and after their subsequent success in the examination, the girls amuse themselves with all kinds of games. The novel concludes with the description of a number of allegorical battles between the partisans of the empress and those who support the rightful heir to the throne. Following the defeat of her party, the empress abdicates, and the world returns to order.

It is especially the first part of this novel that has been perennially popular, and it has sometimes been compared to *Gulliver's Travels*. The episode of the Kingdom of Women has often been cited as a protest against the subordinate role of women in traditional Chinese society. The *Jinghua yuan* is often mentioned together with the *Yesou puyan*, another example of a novel in which many rather erudite subjects are discussed. But whereas the style of the *Yesou puyan* is grave and heavy throughout, the *Jinghua yuan* is one of the wittiest books in all of Chinese literature.

The *Pinhua baojian* (The precious mirror for judging flowers), a novel in sixty chapters by Chen Sen (after 1797–before 1870), provides a panoramic view of the life led by the various types of boy actors and their patrons in early-nineteenth-century Peking. The action is divided over a great number of simultaneous story lines, which interact at certain points. This work gives an intriguing picture of the attractive and not-so-attractive features of life in fashionable circles at the capital, and it was very popular in the nineteenth century. In the prudish twentieth century, however, its existence has been largely ignored.

The *Hua yue hen* (Regrets over flowers and moonlight), in fifty-two chapters by Wei Xiuren (1819–1874), describes the amorous relations of two *muke* (members of the private staff of a high official) with two courtesans. For no evident reason, one of the couples is plagued with misfortune, while the other enjoys continual good luck. The novel contains poems which are valued in their own right.

The *Ernü yingxiong zhuan* (A tale of love and courage), in forty chapters and a prologue, was written by the Manchu Wen Kang (ca. 1850), who is much admired for his skillful use of the language of Peking. The story is about an effeminate young man and a tomboy who eventually develop into "normal" adults and marry. The book is full of humorous passages, especially in the first few chapters, in which the thoroughly impractical young man undertakes a journey to help his father. The father, an official, has gotten himself into trouble thanks to his integrity. In the inns of North China our hero is repeatedly swindled, robbed, and threatened. At the last moment he is rescued by the girl, who has become expert in the use of arms through her efforts to avenge her father. The second half of *Ernü yingxiong zhuan* also contains many amusing episodes from Chinese family life as our tomboy is transformed into a modest wife and her husband learns to assert his place in society.

SHORT NOVELS

"Talent and Beauty" Novels

"Talent and beauty novels" (*caizi jiaren xiaoshuo*) is the modern term for a large group of novels, mostly short (twelve to twenty-six chapters), in which the intrigue revolves around a more or less standard story: a handsome young man of great literary gifts loves a beautiful and intelligent girl; the young man eventually succeeds in the metropolitan examinations with highest honors, and the ending is invariably happy. This subgenre first came to prominence in the second half of the seventeenth century, but it continued to be written throughout the eighteenth and nineteenth centuries. At their best these novels, with their frequent disguises and misunderstandings, are reminiscent of eighteenth-century French comedies. At their worst, however, they are pedantic and soporific Chinese equivalents of the dime novel.

A good example of the subgenre is the *Ping Shan Leng Yan* (The title is made up of four characters taken from the names of the four main "good" characters), a late-seventeenth-century novel in twenty chapters by Zhang Shao or Zhang Jun. The first five chapters are about the talents of Shan Dai, daughter of a minister, who passes with flying colors the intelligence tests devised by the pedantic *muke* Song Xin. The following five tell how a poor but intelligent girl, Leng Jiangxue, is sent to be Shan Dai's servant girl. On the way, she is deeply impressed by a poem written by the poor student Ping Ruheng. Ping himself is on his way to Songjiang, where he will become friends with the rich Yan Baihan. Full of admiration for the widely renowned Shan Dai, Ping and Yan subsequently travel incognito to Peking; meanwhile, their works are plagiarized by other suitors (chapters 11-15). In the last five chapters all impostors are unmasked and all misunderstandings cleared up; Ping and Yan demonstrate their true gifts and marry Leng Jiangxue and Shan Dai, respectively.

The most famous exemplar of the subgenre is probably the anonymous eighteen-chapter *Haoqiu zhuan* (The fortunate union). In this work the young man is, in addition to being a skilled writer, an accomplished fighter. On his travels he happens to arrive in the town where the heroine lives just at the moment when her uncle is attempting to force a marriage upon her. He liberates her, and during his subsequent illness she nurses him in her own home. Despite all rumors, they turn out to have kept their chastity, whereupon they are allowed to marry happily.

A number of these "talent and beauty novels" were translated into European languages in the late eighteenth and early nineteenth centuries; they were among the first examples of Chinese literature to be brought to the attention of a Western audience.

Reductionistic Novels

The term "reductionistic novels" will be used here to refer to a small group of short novels in which the author limits himself to describing a single aspect of reality, or to using a single register of the language. In some cases this limitation seems to have been chosen as a means of attracting special attention to a given area of literary virtuosity, but often the one-sidedness is clearly a device for satire and caricature.

Dong Yue's *Xiyou bu* and the *Rou putuan*, both already mentioned above, could be regarded as the oldest examples of this subgenre. In the *Xiyou bu* the whole world has degenerated into one multi-faceted manifestation of *qing* (passion); in the *Rou putuan* the world is reduced to sex. The latter, with its highly artificial plot, must be seen as a parody of the many "retribution-within-one-lifetime" stories of the period 1550–1650.

In the ten-chapter *Zhangui zhuan* (The story of the beheading of the ghosts), by Liu Zhang of the early Qing, the world is described as inhabited only by ghosts (*gui*), including the Liquor Ghost, the Sex Ghost, the Dirt Ghost, the Money Ghost, etc., with whom Zhong Kui, the demon-exterminator, does battle. This same subject is treated in an independent sixteen-chapter version.

In the *Caomu chunqiu* (Annals of herbs and trees), all the characters are named after medicines; in the *Baiguo zhuan* (Story of the various fruits), a late imitation of the *Caomu chunqiu*, disunity has arisen among the various types of fruit. The late eighteenth-century *Yanshan waishi* (Story of [a young man whose family originally came from] Yanshan), by Chen Qiu, is famous for being written entirely in parallel prose. The *Hedian* (Which source?), by Zhang Nanzhuang, is an eighteenth-century collage of standard sayings and clichés.

MILITARY ROMANCES AND OTHER CHAPBOOK FICTION

The novels described above were written by literati for literati. The period from 1650 to 1875 also saw the production of numerous novels apparently intended for a less-well-educated audience. For the most part these are written in very simple *wenyan,* with elements taken from the spoken language. The style and phrasing show little originality, and not much use is made of inserted poems, etc. However, on the positive side it should be noted that many tell a brisk, lively story. Practically all these works are of unknown authorship, and the published editions were often of modest quality.

This group is represented most importantly by the so-called military romances, in which a central role is played by the battlefield feats of famous generals. These novels take much of their material from popular story cycles in which, as time went by, more and more spectacular exploits were attributed to the heroes, the stories were extended to include the heroes' children and grandchildren (who, in turn, distinguished themselves in combat), etc. In contrast to the older historical romances, each of which describes a specific period of Chinese history, a military romance is concerned with the life of one particular hero, starting with his birth and youth and proceeding to his first feats of prowess, subsequent recognition, and glorious career. After the hero's death, typically, the story goes on—whether in the same book or in a separate sequel—to tell of the adventures of his sons and grandsons.

A good example of this process of literary description-and-embellishment is the figure of Yue Fei as treated in an historical romance and, on the other hand, a military romance. In the historical romance *Da Song zhongxing tongsu yanyi* (Popular novel of the restoration of the Great Song), written by Xiong Damu in the mid-sixteenth century, Yue Fei is no more than one of the many important generals fighting on the side of the Southern Song. But in the eighty-chapter military romance *Shuo Yue quanzhuan* (Complete story of Yue Fei), by a certain Qian Cai (mid-eighteenth century), Yue Fei's life story is overgrown with countless legendary episodes, and his ultimate failure to reconquer North China is avenged by a preposterously implausible campaign undertaken by his (mainly fictitious) sons.

A number of important military romances focus on the founding of the Tang and the prominent role played by various members of the Xue family. The *Shuo Tang* (Story of the Tang) is about Qin Qiong, Yuchi Gong, and others, but in the sequel, *Xue Rengui zheng Dong* (Xue Rengui subjugates the East, i.e., Korea), as its title suggests, Xue Rengui is the main hero. His son, Xue Dingshan, becomes the main character in a following book, *Xue Dingshan zheng Xi* (Xue Dingshan subjugates the West, i.e., Central Asia), and in *Xue Gang fan Tang* (Xue Gang restores the Tang), yet another descendant contributes to the overthrow of empress Wu Zetian's regime.

Another important name in connection with this subgenre is that of the eleventh-century general Di Qing, whose youth and early exploits are described in the *Wanhua lou* (Tower of ten thousand flowers). His subsequent adventures with his comrades-in-arms are related in the *Wuhu ping Xi* (Five tigers pacify the West) and the *Wuhu ping Nan* (Five tigers pacify the South, i.e., Vietnam).

In some of these novels, such as *Xue Dingshan zheng Xi*, an important role is played by women swordfighters. They are usually barbarian women; at first their prowess poses a formidable obstacle to the Chinese troops, but once conquered, they marry Chinese commanders and become allies.

In many respects, the military romances can be seen as forerunners of the later *wuxia xiaoshuo* (novels of knights-errant).

Another important subgroup in this class of fiction comprises tales of emperors traveling through the realm in disguise, righting wrongs to the innocent and punishing the wicked. As an example we may mention the *Qianlong you Jiangnan* (The travels of the Qianlong Emperor through the Kiangnan area). In the case of the *Zhengde you Jiangnan* (The travels of the Zhengde Emperor through the Kiangnan area), the alienation of the emperor from the realities of his subjects' everyday life becomes a source of fun. Some novels deal with the merry adventures of figures from the popular pantheon.

Chapter 23.
PERFORMANCE TEXTS AND ORAL LITERATURE

PERFORMANCE TEXTS

Except for the sections on drama, in the preceding chapters we have been mainly concerned with genres and texts meant to be read. In view of the high percentage of illiteracy in traditional Chinese society, these texts were intended for a definite minority. The vast bulk of the population knew literature at first hand only in the form of texts that were sung, read aloud, or performed on stage. Certain genres were meant to be performed for a wide and varied audience; this is true, for example, of the various genres of drama and of *shuochang wenxue* (tell-and-sing literature). The dramatic forms have been described above, but *shuochang wenxue* has so far been discussed only in the context of *bianwen* and *zhugongdiao*. *Shuochang wenxue* is the overall term for the various genres of narrative or descriptive texts that were intended to be recited or performed for a general audience by one artist (sometimes two or three); the performer or performers do not represent or play any one specific role in the text. The term *shuochang wenxue* is also used for prosimetric texts which adopt the format of these genres but were written from the beginning for reading purposes only.

Professional Storytellers

Shuochang wenxue texts were performed by storytellers, who have probably constituted a recognized element in Chinese society from very early times. They are known, in any case, to have been active in the capital city of Chang'an during the Tang Dynasty (618–906). They are first mentioned in some detail in descriptions of the Song capitals of Kaifeng and Hangzhou in the twelfth and thirteenth centuries. These descriptions name storytellers, their performances, and their specialties. The storytellers include both men and women; many had memorable nicknames, referring in some cases to their appearance and in others to peculiarities of their education, knowledge, or performance.

In the subsequent dynasties, both male and female storytellers are known to have been active. There is, however, little surviving reliable information about them—even less, in fact, than in the case of actors and actresses. The reason for this may be that the social status of storytellers was even lower than that of actors and actresses for their one-man or one-woman performances were much cheaper. A professional storyteller could operate at a fixed location (e.g., a teahouse) or could travel from place to place giving performances at definite times and places. Storytellers could also be invited to perform in private homes. Depending on the genre, a storyteller might use musical accompaniment, either performed by the teller or by a separate musician or musicians. People usually became storytellers by a kind of apprenticeship to a master, whose stories and style they adopted. Certain families maintained the profession of storyteller as a family business from generation to generation. There were also, however, some storytellers who had had no formal training.

Possibly China's most famous storyteller is Liu Jingting, who played a role in China's anti-Manchu resistance in 1645, thereby earning himself a place in Kong Shangren's play *Taohua shan*.

In addition to the professional storytellers, there were others who made use of performance texts in the wider context of their activities. The performance of *bianwen* by Tang dynasty Buddhist monks has already been mentioned; in later centuries nuns gave edifying performances for women in the houses of their patrons, using *baojuan* (precious rolls), i.e., performance texts on Buddhist subjects. There were, of course, also amateurs, their social standing varying from gentry to peasant, who presented performance texts. No really strict line can be drawn between amateur and professional performers, and some of the amateurs were actually semi-professional, giving their performances only at certain times of year or in certain circumstances.

Forms of Shuochang wenxue

The storytellers performed a number of distinct genres. The first distinction that can be made is that between genres in which the story is told wholly or mostly in prose and those in which there is prominent alternation of prose and verse. The genres in the first category went by different names in different places—*shuoshu, pingshu, pinghua*, etc.—and were performed mostly by men. There was no accompaniment, and the storyteller had no props other than the "waking block," with which he made rapping or clapping sounds to mark certain high points in the story, and a fan that was put to the most ingenious uses in depicting various characters and situations. The professional storyteller did not use a fully written-out text, and an important aspect of his art was the facility with which he could improvise in accordance with the audience or the mood of the moment. He did sometimes have a crib (*diben*, "peeking book") that might contain summaries of one or more long stories, verbatim texts of recurrent key passages, etc. It was not until the 1950s that performances of these first-category performers were recorded (mostly in the People's Republic) and the texts—in a few cases—transcribed, edited, and published.

The second category consists of the genres in which the story is told in alternating prose and verse. In most of these texts the verse passages are in the form referred to as *ci*. *Ci* means, in this case, verses with a fixed line length of seven or ten syllables, the even lines rhyming. Seven-syllable lines have a caesura after the third or fourth syllable. Ten-syllable lines are subdivided into syllable groups in several different possible ways, the most common patterns being 3-3-4 and 3-4-3. The prose passages were spoken; the verse parts were recited with musical accompaniment. The various genres in which *ci* were used as the verse form are distinguished not on the basis of textual form but according to the style of recitation, the instruments used for the musical accompaniment, and the dialect spoken.

In this second category, full written texts were used, and they could be really voluminous. These texts were used during performance but also as reading matter; in later periods some of them were written primarily to be read. A number of texts in these genres were eventually rewritten as novels, the verse passages being summarized in prose, modified, or simply deleted.

Until the sixteenth century, texts written alternately in prose and *ci* were called by the general name of *cihua* (story with verse passages). Very few *shuochang wenxue* texts have survived from the years preceding the Wanli period (1573–1620). Scholarship in this field has been aided by the recent discovery of a collection of sixteen rather short *cihua* printed in the Chenghua period (1465–1487). The subjects of these stories include episodes from Chinese history, tales of Judge Bao, and an animal fable (the tale of a filial parrot).

A *cihua* dating from the late sixteenth century is the *Da Tang Qinwang cihua* (The story with verse passages of the prince of Qin of the Great Tang), by Zhu Shenglin. It tells the story of Li Shimin's forcing his father to rebel against the Sui and become the first Tang Emperor; Li Shimin is subsequently rewarded and named prince of Qin. In his new capacity he plays a major role in wiping out the other claimants to the throne, but his growing power arouses the jealousy of his older brothers, who seek to kill him. Li Shimin's stalwarts finally force him to eliminate his brothers, whereupon his father abdicates in his favor.

(The term *cihua* also occurs in the sixteenth century in the title of the novel *Jin Ping Mei cihua*, but in that case it means no more than "long story in the contemporary spoken language"; the same term, *cihua*, is also the name of a genre of poetry criticism: remarks on *ci* songs.)

From the sixteenth century on, the texts written in alternate prose and *ci* are divided into distinct genres, the most important of which are the *guci*, the *tanci*, the *muyushu* and the *baojuan*. *Gu(zi)ci* (Drum verses) is the term for a North Chinese genre of long narrative texts divided into numerous chapters and written in alternate prose and verse. The genre gets its name from the fact that originally the drum was the instrument chiefly used to accompany the recitation of the *ci*. As regards content, *guci* relate (and elaborate upon) elements from the popular story cycles, including love stories and heroic sagas. But it is the combat scenes that are most famous, possibly because this genre was performed most commonly by men.

Within the genre of *guci* a great number of performance styles are distinguished; these are named after a particular region, a specific musical instrument, or a particular artist who first made the style famous. In North China there existed, besides the long *guci*, various shorter forms which allowed the artist to finish an episode in one or just a few sittings, or which were mainly descriptive. *Dagu(shu)* (Big drum [texts]) , for example, were popular from the eighteenth century on. *Zidishu* (Texts of the young rich) were performed especially by amateurs belonging to Manchu families in Peking. *Zhuizishu* (Fanhandle texts) were famous in Henan; *kuaiban* (fast-beat) in Shandong.

Tanci (Verses for picking) is the term for long narrative texts, divided into chapters and written in alternate prose and verse, as these were known in the Yangzi area. The name of the genre refers to the fact that the *ci* were often recited to the accompaniment of string instruments. There are many distinct styles of *tanci* performance, the Suzhou *tanci* being the most renowned. An unusual feature of the *tanci* was that the text was sometimes performed by more than one person, the same artists representing the same characters throughout. The subject matter of *tanci* included all possible elements of the traditional repertory, but the best-known *tanci* are long and highly complicated love stories. This may be related to the fact that *tanci* were often performed by women.

Many of the *tanci* written to be read were authored by women. One of the earliest examples may be the *Tian yu hua* (Heaven rains flowers), dating from the middle of the seventeenth century and attributed to a certain Tao Zhenhuai. This *tanci* is set during the Wanli (1573–1620) and Tianqi (1621–

1627) periods; its main heroes are the upright official Zuo Weiming and his daughter Zuo Yizhen, who are caught up in the political struggles at court. One of the villains of the piece is the infamous eunuch Wei Zhongxian. So far as is known, the *Tian yu hua* was never adapted for performance. Another example is the *Zaisheng yuan* (A marriage extending over two lifetimes) by Chen Duansheng (1751–1790) et al. This work, which comprises no less than 600,000 lines, has as its heroine a certain Meng Lijun, who, disguised as a man, succeeds with high honors in the metropolitan examinations and is quickly promoted to the post of prime minister. Eventually the emperor discovers her true sex, but she successfully fends off his advances and is happily reunited with her fiancé. This text has been praised as one long *pailü* poem. Following its publication it was quickly adapted for performance. The theme of the woman in male disguise who succeeds in the examinations also occurs in the *Bi sheng hua* (Flowers from a brush) by Qiu Xinru (ca. 1805–ca. 1873), another extremely voluminous work.

Whether or not they originated in the *tanci*, shorter forms of *shuochang wenxue* also developed. *Muyushu* (Wooden-fish texts) are scarcely distinguishable in form or content from *guci* and *tanci*; their special feature is that, originating in Guangdong and Guangxi, they are written in Cantonese.

Baojuan (precious rolls) is the genre name for long narrative texts, divided into chapters and written in prose and *ci*, of Buddhist content. Their content is often taken from Buddhist legends. *Baojuan* were often performed by nuns, though in the nineteenth century they were also performed by lay persons (courtesans). Some Buddhist and syncretist sects made use of *baojuan* as a device for disseminating their teachings. Clearly Taoist *shuochang wenxue* texts are called *daoqing*. *Baojuan* and *daoqing* were known throughout China.

Besides the texts which made use of *ci*, and which we have referred to in this section as the "second category," there were also genres in which the verse passages took the form of songs written to existing melodies. There are examples of such texts from Shandong; the songs are written to tunes taken from the musical repertoire of the regional drama. These texts, together with a few other *shuochang wenxue* texts dating from the eighteenth and nineteenth centuries in the same region, are attributed to Pu Songling; they are collectively known as the *Liaozhai liqu* (Rustic songs from the Studio of Idleness).

ORAL LITERATURE

Shuochang wenxue must not be confused with oral literature. For the most part the performers of *shuochang wenxue* were professionals who made direct or indirect use of texts of some kind, whether written by themselves or by others. The term oral literature, on the other hand, refers to the vast corpus of stories, myths, legends, jokes, riddles, ditties, and so on that were orally transmitted among the illiterate or semi-literate segments of the population. To be sure, it is not always possible to draw a clear line between oral literature and *shuochang wenxue*. Oral literature has undoubtedly existed in China from the very earliest times, but our knowledge of it prior to the twentieth century is limited to texts that were prepared or edited by the literati. Such texts can be regarded as no more than indirect sources; in the process of being transcribed and published, the texts were inevitably adapted to the norms prevalent in the literary tradition. This process can be clearly seen in the case of the early *yuefu*, the early *ci* (songs) and *qu*, the *min'ge* of the later dynasties, and the *huaben* that derive from popular stories. Also, it is often difficult to draw a clear line between materials of purely oral origin and those which derive, wholly or in part, directly or indirectly, from written sources. Reliable information concerning Chinese oral literature has only gradually begun to emerge, thanks to research done by folklorists and anthropologists in the twentieth century. One thing has become clear. If oral literature was a strong influence on the forms and themes of the literary tradition, whether high or low, the reverse is no less true. That is, oral literature was much influenced by such literary forms as the drama and *shuochang wenxue*.

Fairy Tales

Belonging to the realm of oral literature are folk tales which clearly represent the original versions of stories later made famous in novels or plays. There are also many popular fairy tales—a genre of great regional diversity. Some areas, especially South China, seem much more productive of such tales than others. Certain fairy tales are specifically Chinese, while others belong to recognizable types which occur in many other lands as well; the latter are often of Indian origin. Chinese popular fairy tales are often short and are told in a rather matter-of-fact fashion. Fairy-tale material was occasionally adopted by writers of *biji* and *chuanqi*. But stories of ghosts and fox-spirits, such as those in Pu Songling's *Liaozhai zhiyi*, are very seldom found in the fairy-tale tradition.

Jokes

It is difficult to draw sharp distinctions between popular fairy tales and other folk tales. One important group is concerned with the humorous recounting of practical jokes attributed to specific persons, such as Lü Dongbin, one of the Eight Immortals, and Xu Wenchang, also known as Xu Wei, an eccentric Ming dynasty painter and poet who appears in popular stories in a Don Juan-like role.

It is but a short step from the humorous folk tale to the joke. At first sight, the joke might seem to belong exclusively to the category of oral literature. But the earliest known written collection of Chinese jokes, Handan Chun's *Xiaolin* (Forest of laughs), dates from about A.D. 200. Some collections of anecdotes have been preserved from the following few centuries, but from Southern Song times on, there are many known collections of jokes in the ordinary sense, and there is considerable overlapping of content among these books.

An important late Ming collection is the *Xiaofu* (Storehouse of laughs), published by Feng Menglong, which later was the basis of the best-known Qing collection, *Xiaolin guangji* (Wide-ranging notes from the forest of laughs). In form, these jokes are scarcely distinguishable from the traditional European variety. The subject matter includes practically all imaginable human foibles, as well as certain social ills characteristic of traditional Chinese society. Favorite subjects include greedy mandarins, stupid schoolteachers, and the equivalents of our familiar four-letter words. Quintessentially Chinese jokes include those based on Chinese words and their written forms and those dealing with the relationship of father-in-law and daughter-in-law.

Proverbs and Sayings

Spoken Chinese is rich in proverbs and more or less standardized phrases. Their origin varies. Some were originally quotes from the Classics or other widely read books; others are anonymous. Many proverbs and sayings belong to more or less recognizable formal types. Set phrases, for example, are very often in the form of four-character expressions. Many proverbs have a five- or seven-syllable line reminiscent of traditional poetry; others are rhymed or unrhymed couplets.

A special category of set phrases is that of the *xiehouyu*: the first clause strongly suggests a particular follow-up, but the latter is homophonous with a third element, left unstated, which is actually the punch line.

Needless to say, there is also a long tradition of Chinese riddles.

Folk Songs

In the preceding chapters we have seen how new forms of poetry, such as the *yuefu*, *ci*, and *qu*, often developed out of folk songs and popular music. Numerous collections of so-called *min'ge* (folk songs) survive from Ming and Qing times, but it is questionable whether many are strictly authentic folk songs. Originally they were undoubtedly sung to contemporary tunes, many of which enjoyed no more than local and ephemeral popularity. The heavy use of risqué puns and double-entendre often suggests that these songs originated in the world of courtesans and their rich young patrons. A good example is the collection entitled *Shan'ge* (Popular songs), published by Feng Menglong.

In the twentieth century various authentic collections of folk songs and children's rhymes have been published. In the People's Republic of China the folk song has often been seen as a native Chinese (hence desirable) alternative to modern Western poetic modes. During the Great Leap Forward, for example, a mass campaign encouraged the writing of "new folk songs" in praise of current social developments.

Part V.
The Transition to Modern Literature
(1875–1915)

Chapter 24.
THE TRANSITIONAL PERIOD

Beginning with the Opium War (1839–1842) and the subsequent opening of China to foreign contacts, the great empire was increasingly exposed to Western ideas and technology. In the nineteenth century, Catholic and Protestant missionaries played a major role in this process. To the extent (never quantitatively great) that the missionaries were successful, their appeal was mainly to the illiterate populace, though they made every effort to reach the literati as well. The missionaries were surprised and appalled by the part Christian concepts played in the rise of the Taiping ideology. It was not until China's defeat in the Sino-Japanese War (1894–1895) that large numbers of Chinese literati, suddenly conscious of China's relative backwardness, began to take an interest in Western thought. Western technology, by contrast, was accepted much earlier and more easily. In the beginning the Chinese were interested chiefly in military technology, but starting in the 1870s, Western printing techniques—lithography and machine printing—were also introduced. The consequences for Chinese literature were enormous.

The transitional period from 1875 to 1915 can be divided in two. From 1875 to 1895 the main new factor was technical—the presence and utilization of modern printing techniques—while in the period from 1895 to 1915, Western culture and ideas, and the Chinese reactions to these strikingly new elements, came increasingly to the forefront of the literary scene.

LITHOGRAPHY AND *WUXIA XIAOSHUO*

Lithography, used in Europe mainly for the printing of illustrations, was widely employed for book production in China because the lithograph process was cheaper than the traditional block-print method. The slow and expensive carving of printing blocks could now be dispensed with, and it became possible to reproduce very small characters legibly, so that the paper cost per book was sharply reduced. Naturally enough, countless existing Chinese books began to appear in inexpensive lithographic reprints, but the marked drop in book prices also encouraged the development of new genres.

The sudden popularity of *wuxia xiaoshuo* (novels of knights-errant) is undoubtedly related to the introduction of lithography. As the name suggests, *wuxia xiaoshuo* are primarily concerned with the heroic deeds of fighters skilled in the use of sword, lance, stick, and fists. These novels are packed with violent action; the characters are drawn in strict black and white, and the hero triumphs in the end against huge odds. The *wuxia xiaoshuo* can be seen as the Chinese equivalent of Western action fiction.

Generally regarded as the first important example of *wuxia xiaoshuo* is the 120-chapter *Sanxia wuyi* (The three valiant and five righteous men). This anonymous novel has its origins in more or less stenographic transcriptions of the story of Judge Bao as told by the *shuochang wenxue* performer Shi Yukun (mid-nineteenth century). Shi Yukun developed a unique personal style of *guci* performance: *Shi pai shu*. In Shi's version of Judge Bao's adventures, as the story progresses Judge Bao recedes more and more into the background while his subordinates, the martial-arts experts to whom the title refers, become more prominent. From its first appearance the *Sanxia wuyi* was a great success. The famous scholar Yu Yue (1821–1906) prepared an "improved" edition entitled *Qixia wuyi* (Seven valiants and five righteous), and many other sequels appeared, including the *Xiao wuyi* (The younger five righteous men) and the *Xu Xiao wuyi* (Sequel to the younger five righteous), each of 124 chapters.

Other *wuxia xiaoshuo* stemming from popular story cycles include *Shi gong an* and *Peng gong an*. The main character in *Shi gong an* (Legal cases of Mr. Shi) is the mandarin Shi Shilun (d. 1722); in *Peng gong an* it is the mandarin Peng Peng (1637–1704). These are lengthy books: 528 and 431 chapters, respectively!

Unusual as regards its main character, but otherwise similar to *wuxia xiaoshuo*, is *Ji gong zhuan* (The story of Mr. Ji), in which Jidian, an insane monk, comes to the help of the disadvantaged while teaching the high and mighty of this world a lesson. Jidian really existed; he lived during the Southern Song dynasty, and by Ming and Qing times the legends involving his name had provided material for a number of short novels. *Ji gong zhuan* includes many supernatural episodes, but this is also typical of *wuxia xiaoshuo*.

Before long, the authors of *wuxia xiaoshuo* ceased relying on popular stories for their subject matter. Countless novels were written, still having their starting point in some historical incident but soon expanding into pure fiction and fantasy. Throughout the twentieth century *wuxia xiaoshuo* have remained very popular, though the People's Republic of China suppressed this type of writing for many years.

Lithography was also used to print China's first illustrated magazine, the *Dianshi zhai huabao* (Illustrated magazine from the Lithographic Studio), which appeared from 1884 to 1898.

MACHINE PRINTING AND THE MODERN PRESS

The introduction of machine printing was of decisive importance for the rise of the modern Chinese press. In traditional China there were certain identifiable forerunners of the modern media, including the *Jing bao* and *xinwen zhi*, but newspapers, weeklies and other magazines did not appear until the nineteenth century. The *Jing bao* (capital news; in the Qing period often referred to as *Peking Gazette*) was a summary of the most important court edicts. Its production was fast and inexpensive: the text was cut in wax.

The *xinwen zhi* (news sheets) were one-page reports, sometimes illustrated, of noteworthy happenings; they were sold by hawkers.

Even before the Opium War, Protestant missionaries outside China published magazines in Chinese. The first Chinese newspapers appeared in Hong Kong in the 1860s. Soon afterward the first papers in China proper were published in Shanghai, which had become an important economic and cultural center since its designation as a treaty port (1842) and especially after the Taiping Rebellion. One of the most important Shanghai newspapers was the *Shenbao*, which was first published in April 1872. An important competitor of the *Shenbao* was the *Hubao*, which first appeared in April 1882.

The First Journalists

With the rise of the modern press a new figure appeared on the Chinese literary scene—the journalist. The first journalists all received a traditional education and most of them were literati hailing from the major cities of the Kiangnan area. For some, the newspaper was little more than a means of gaining a wide readership for their traditional-style literary productions; others, however, depended on the new journalism for their livelihood.

One of the outstanding nineteenth-century journalists was Wang Tao (1828–1897). After failing in the examinations, he did editorial work for such famous missionaries as W. H. Medhurst and A. Wylie, and for a long time he was James Legge's collaborator in translating the Chinese Classics. He accompanied Legge back to Europe. Upon his return to China he worked as a publisher and editor in Hong Kong and Shanghai; his name is associated with the *Shenbao*, among other things. He was also an accomplished essayist.

Novels on Modern Life in Shanghai

Soon after the *Hubao* had published in serial form the eighteenth-century novel *Yesou puyan*, in 1892 the *Shenbao* began issuing China's first literary magazine, the *Haishang qishu* (Remarkable writings from Shanghai). This publication—first a fortnightly, later a monthly—ran to fifteen issues. The *Haishang qishu* was filled almost entirely with the writings of Han Bangqing (1856–1894): each issue included two chapters of his novel *Haishang hua liezhuan* (Exemplary biographies of flowers of Shanghai). Han Bangqing came from a family of literati and mandarins. He had been unsuccessful in the examinations, and he spent the last years of his life in Shanghai, where he worked on the *Shenbao*. His sixty-four-chapter *Haishang hua liezhuan*, which appeared in book form in 1894, describes in detail the life led by courtesans and their patrons in contemporary Shanghai. The author was undoubtedly influenced by such forerunners as the *Pinhua baojian*, for in Han's novel definite types of courtesans and patrons are described in pairs. Unlike the *Pinhua baojian*, however, Han's work has a main character, Zhao Puzhai. Zhao, a young man of rural origins, comes to Shanghai, where he cannot resist the allurements of the big city with its glitter of sin. But the problems of adjustment to his new environment are too much for him, and he comes to a bad end, ultimately dragging his mother and sister down with him. In Zhao Puzhai, Han Bangqing succeeded in creating a memorably "modern" fictional hero.

The *Haishang hua liezhuan* is notable for its well-structured narrative. The story is told in numerous episodes, the transition from one to another being arranged so that a character in the preceding episode becomes involved with the characters and adventures in the following one. Han Bangqing claimed to have learned this method from the *Rulin waishi*, but in his own novel, unlike the *Rulin waishi*, the same characters eventually return to focus. The story actually consists of a number of definite strands unwinding concurrently. The narrator strictly abstains from describing the inner life of the characters; only their words and actions are given. Another noteworthy feature are the shifts in linguistic register: the descriptive passages are always in vernacular Mandarin, but the dialogs are written, wherever the context allows, in the local Wu dialect.

In the 1920s the *Haishang hua liezhuan* was highly praised by such proponents of modern literature as Lu Xun and Hu Shi. Since then it has been largely ignored; the reasons are probably to be sought in its subject matter and in its frequent use of regional dialect.

The early years of the twentieth century saw the publication of several other novels on life in Shanghai; the most famous of these is undoubtedly *Jiu wei gui* (The nine-tailed tortoise).

INTELLECTUAL DEVELOPMENTS AFTER 1895

Kang Youwei and Liang Qichao

For many Chinese intellectuals China's defeat in the Sino-Japanese War was the signal to begin studying the ideas on which Western (and Japanese) strength was based. Reflection on China's situation and her apparently disadvantaged position led many to believe in the necessity of reform. Kang Youwei (1858–1927) is associated with the attempts at quick and far-reaching institutional reform favored by the young Guangxu Emperor which culminated in the so-called "hundred days of 1898"—and in the bloody thwarting of those developments after the intervention of the Dowager Empress Cixi. After the Boxer fiasco of 1900, the dynasty began to admit reforms, but too late and too grudgingly to avert its eventual downfall.

One of the most influential spokesmen for reform was Kang Youwei's younger associate Liang Qichao (1873–1929). Starting in 1898 Liang spent fourteen years in Japan, where he founded several Chinese periodicals in which he published essays expounding his ideas. These magazines enjoyed a wide readership in China. His essays, in *wenyan*, were characterized by a fluent but highly emotional style; his vocabulary included many neologisms, often borrowed from Japanese, used to translate Western terms. Liang Qichao saw the novel and the theater as important factors contributing to the political education of the populace, and he favored novels with a clear political message. His own works in these genres, which were never completed, are practically unreadable. Following the fall of the Qing dynasty, Liang Qichao filled several ministerial posts in the increasingly powerless cabinets in Peking. After World War I he journeyed through Europe and was thoroughly disappointed by what he saw.

Yan Fu and Lin Shu

A vital role in the introduction of Western ideas was played by two translators who are often mentioned together: Yan Fu (1853–1921) and Lin Shu (1852–1924). They were the last great representatives of the Qing dynasty *Tongcheng pai* school of prose with its didactic ideals. The striking excellence of their translations into *wenyan* helped to make the new ideas more attractive to Chinese literati.

Yan Fu was a naval officer who had spent several years studying in England. Having come out in favor of reform between 1895 and 1898, he subsequently translated into Chinese a number of classical eighteenth- and nineteenth-century Western works on political and social subjects, such as Huxley's *On Evolution*, Adam Smith's *An Inquiry into the Wealth of Nations*, and Montesquieu's *L'Esprit des lois*.

Lin Shu, who was especially productive in the period from 1900 to 1910, translated more than a hundred novels and stories. Having no personal knowledge of even the rudiments of any foreign language, Lin Shu worked with informants who translated the works orally. Lin Shu transformed their oral versions into written *wenyan*, often severely editing the resulting text in accordance with his own stylistic taste. Lin's informants were mostly students who had spent time abroad; their knowledge of the languages often left much to be desired. He depended on them not only linguistically, but also for the selection of the works to be translated. As a consequence he not only translated works by Scott, Dickens, Balzac, and Tolstoy, but also by Conan Doyle and various now-forgotten writers of detective and adventure stories.

Both Yan Fu and Lin Shu were disappointed by the consequences of the Revolution of 1911, and Lin Shu was one of the few who protested publicly against the Literary Revolution of 1917 with its demand for the abolishment of *wenyan* and the general adoption of *baihua*.

Huang Zunxian

At the same time that *wenyan* prose was serving as a vehicle of important new developments, poetry showed few signs of being affected by social and intellectual ferment. One exception was the work of Huang Zunxian (1848–1905). Huang Zunxian occupied various posts in China's new diplomatic service, spending time in Japan, England, and the United States. A known advocate of reform, he was dismissed from office after the events of 1898. In his poems, mostly in *gushi* form, he described life and landscape as he had seen them in foreign countries, commented on contemporary events (including the Sino-Japanese War), and gave voice to his concern for China's fate.

NOVELS OF THE PERIOD 1900–1920

One of the most remarkable features of literary development in the period from 1895 to 1915 was the flourishing of the novel in the last decade of the Qing dynasty. This trend must be attributed at least in part to the stimulating influence of Liang Qichao. Liang was convinced that in eighteenth- and nineteenth-century Europe the novel, with its broad readership, had been a vital instrument in the dissemination of new ideas that eventually led to social change. He hoped that the novel could have a comparable function in China. In his own magazines he serialized various novels which criticized contemporary Chinese social ills, and in which reform-minded or even revolutionary characters played prominent roles. Other periodicals also featured novels in serial form. The four most significant novels of the late Qing (1901–1911) are generally considered to be the *Ershi nian mudu zhi guai xianzhuang* by Wu Woyao, the *Guanchang xianxing ji* by Li Baojia, the *Lao Can youji* by Liu E, and Zeng Pu's *Nie hai hua*.

Wu Woyao

Wu Woyao (1866–1910) worked as a journalist from his twentieth year on, and his collected works are voluminous. His best-known novel is the *Ershi nian mudu zhi guai xianzhuang* (Strange phenomena, seen with one's own eyes, of the past twenty years). This 100-chapter novel, told in the first person, is a chain of episodes in which the protagonist describes the adventures and events he has undergone, witnessed, or heard of in the course of his extensive travels about Shanghai. The book catalogs the social ills of contemporary China. The bureaucracy, in particular, is mercilessly exposed in all its incompetence, corruption, and cowardice. The Manchus are portrayed as unskilled and immoral, though it is also made plain that the whole bureaucracy from top to bottom is hopelessly sick.

Other novels by Wu Woyao are *Tong shi*, *Hen hai*, and *Jiu ming qi'an*. *Tong shi* (A painful story), an unfinished novel in twenty-seven chapters, is concerned with the events surrounding the fall of the Southern Song; it is full of praise for the unyielding Wen Tianxiang. *Hen hai* (A sea of sorrow), in ten chapters, is a highly sentimental love story set against the background of the Boxer Rebellion. *Jiu ming qi'an* (An extraordinary crime that cost nine lives) is a revamping of an older novel on a bloody feud between two Guangdong families over a disputed gravesite; it is an outspoken attack on the widespread practice of geomancy. The novel starts with a vivid description of the fire that is responsible for the death of the victims and then traces out the origins of the feud.

Li Baojia

Li Baojia (1867–1906) established himself as a journalist when success in the examinations eluded him. He too produced an impressive body of work. His most famous novel is the *Guanchang xianxing ji* (The present-day situation in the bureaucratic world). Li managed to complete 60 of a planned 120 chapters. In a succession of episodes the novel documents nearly every conceivable defect of the bureaucracy. There is no single main character.

Li's *Wenming xiaoshi* (A brief history of modern culture), in sixty chapters, satirizes various half-hearted and ill-considered reform measures. His *Huo diyu* (Living hell) attacks Chinese jurisprudence and the contemporary prison system.

In addition to his novels, Li Baojia made use of the *tanci* form to express his ideas.

Liu E's Lao Can youji

Lao Can youji (The travels of Lao Can), in twenty chapters, is the only novel by Liu E (1857–1909). Liu E was descended from a family of literati, but he himself refused to take part in the examinations. In 1888 he became well known for the role he played in the repair of collapsed dikes along the Yellow River. In subsequent years he was involved in various business ventures. Interested in the construction of railroads and mines, he was in favor of attracting foreign capital. After the Boxer Rebellion he was accused of embezzling state-owned grain during the foreign military occupation of Peking. Banished to Urumchi in 1908, he died soon thereafter. Liu E had strong archaeological interests; he was one of the first to recognize the importance of the oracle bones that had only recently been discovered, and he published some writings on the subject.

Lao Can youji describes the adventures of the physician-literatus Lao Can (Old Derelict) in Shandong. Lao Can solves all manner of problems but manages to disappear whenever officials try to recommend him for a bureaucratic appointment. The extremely varied episodes are held together only by the unifying figure of Lao Can. In one episode Lao Can appears as a detective, "the Chinese Sherlock Holmes." The novel is especially praised for its descriptive passages, including a memorable description of a *dagushu* performance. Liu E started a sequel to the novel but completed only a number of chapters.

Zeng Pu's Nie hai hua

The writer and translator Zeng Pu (1872–1935) owes his lasting fame to his thirty-chapter novel *Nie hai hua* (Flowers in a sea of sin). After passing the provincial examinations Zeng Pu tried unsuccessfully to prepare himself for a diplomatic career. He knew French and published translations from that language, including works by Victor Hugo. After the establishment of the Republic he occupied various government posts, and in the last years of his life he was active as a publisher.

Nie hai hua is obviously a roman-à-clef. It is built on two main story lines, one concerning the activities of Chinese revolutionaries, the other being the love affair between the bureaucrat and diplomat Jin Wenqing and the courtesan Fu Caiyun. (Jin is modelled upon Hong Jun, 1840–1893, a successful diplomat and noted scholar; Fu Caiyun is based on the real-life Saijinhua, 1874–1936, who for a while was Hong's concubine.) Posing as his wife, Fu Caiyun accompanies Jin Wenqing on his foreign travels, but in the end she turns out to have betrayed him.

Other Works

The late Qing saw publication of many other novels which attacked social ills. Sometimes the authors even addressed problems beyond the boundaries of China proper, such as the conditions faced by Chinese coolies abroad. Before long, however, most of the novels serialized in the Chinese press were sentimental love stories. The most prominent development in the field of the novel between 1910 and 1920 was the so-called *Yuanyang hudie pai* (School of mandarin ducks and butterflies). An early bestseller of this type was *Yuli hun* (Jade pear soul) by Xu Zhenya (ca. 1876–?), the tragic tale of a doomed romance between a young widow and her son's private tutor. Through its ample use of letters and poems, the focus of this novel shifts from fact to sentiment. The final chapter, describing the young widow's altruistic suicide, shows the influence of Lin Shu's translation of *La dame aux camélias*. This type of partly modernized traditional fiction had great commercial success in the twenties and thirties. An outstanding proponent of this school was Zhang Henshui (1895–1967); some of his action-packed novels, set in warlord-wracked China, were adapted for the screen at an early date.

Some late Qing writers used various forms of *shuochang wenxue*, especially the *tanci*, for the expression of their political ideas. Li Baojia, for example, wrote the *Gengzi guobian tanci* (*Tanci* on the turmoils in the state in the year *gengzi*) in response to the Boxer Rebellion.

Qiu Jin (1875–1907) wrote, but was unable to complete, a *tanci* entitled *Jingwei shi* (Indelible hate) on the oppressed position of women in traditional Chinese society. After a period of study in Japan, Qiu Jin devoted her life to revolutionary activities, for which she was eventually executed. A significant part of her efforts involved the liberation of women. Her own life is the subject of the novel *Liuyue shuang* (Frost in midsummer), whose true author is unknown.

SOME MEMORABLE FIGURES

Su Manshu

One of the most colorful literary figures of the late Qing and the early Republic was Su Manshu (1884–1918). Born in Yokohama, the son of a Chinese merchant and his Japanese concubine, he spent his youth alternately in China and in Japan. He worked as a journalist, became a Buddhist monk for a short period, visited Thailand and Ceylon intending to learn Sanskrit, and eventually earned his living as a teacher in various places including Surabaya. His last years, like his youth, were spent alternately in Japan and China.

Su Manshu knew French and English; his publications include translations from Hugo's *Les misérables* and a collection of poems by Byron. His own poetry, though frequently marred by heavy self-pity, has a certain charm because of its unusual setting. His stories, written in clear and simple *wenyan*, are highly sentimental love tales. The most famous is his novella *Duanhong lingyan ji* (The lone swan), in which the main character is thrown back and forth between worldly love and his monastic calling.

Wang Guowei

One of the first literary critics to employ Western ideas, Wang Guowei (1877–1927) was strongly influenced by Schopenhauer and other nineteenth-century German philosophers. He was the first to write a history of the Chinese theater, the groundbreaking *Song Yuan xiqu kao* (A study of the dramatic literature of the Song and Yuan). His *Renjian cihua* has already been mentioned. In his *Honglou meng pinglun* (A critical discussion of the Red Chamber Dream), he compared Cao Xueqin's novel with Goethe's *Faust*. After the fall of the Qing, Wang Guowei devoted himself exclusively to philological and historical research.

Part VI.
Modern Literature
(1915–1990)

CHINESE POLITICAL HISTORY, 1915–1990

China's lack of international standing was glaringly revealed in early 1919 at the Versailles peace conference, when China's demand for the restitution of former German concessions on Chinese soil was ignored. In Peking, outraged students took to the streets on May 4, 1919, igniting protests and demonstrations all over China. While the so-called May Fourth Movement did result in some changes in the central government, they made little difference for by this time the government in Peking had already lost most of its control over the provinces. With the death of Yuan Shikai, China had entered the warlord era. Provincial governors and commanders acted autonomously and warred against each other. Some of these campaigns were extremely destructive, for the troops lived off the land.

The Nationalist movement, now organized as the Guomindang party, established a territorial base in Canton in the early 1920s. At an early stage it chose to cooperate with the fledgling Chinese Communist Party. In 1925 the Guomindang troops, headed by Chiang Kai-shek, embarked on their Northern Expedition for the reunification of China, and revolutionary fervor spread through large areas of the country. However, upon reaching Shanghai in the spring of 1927, Chiang suddenly turned on the Communists and their sympathizers. Communists went underground or retreated to outlying areas.

In 1928, Chiang Kai-shek's Northern Expedition produced the nominal reunification of China under Guomindang rule. The central government was moved to Nanjing, and Peking was renamed Beiping (northern peace). The Nanjing decade (1927–1937) witnessed remarkable economic development and considerable progress in the modernization of the country. On the military side, however, repeated campaigns failed to eradicate the Jiangxi Soviet established by Mao Zedong and Zhu De. Mao and Zhu were eventually forced to evacuate their original territory; of the 100,000 that initially broke through the Guomindang encirclement, 10,000 survivors arrived in northern Shaanxi in 1935. They established their base at Yan'an.

Meanwhile, the Japanese army had tightened its hold on Manchuria. In 1933 the Japanese established the "independent" state of Manchukuo, appointing Puyi as its "emperor." They went on to expand their influence in northeastern China. In 1936 the Nationalists and Communists agreed to form a united front to resist Japanese aggression. The Japanese army replied by launching all-out war against China. Peking and Shanghai were occupied; Nanjing was taken and its civilian population subjected to appalling atrocities. The Guomindang moved its capital first to Wuhan and later to Chongqing in the southwestern province of Sichuan.

Effective collaboration between the Guomindang and the Communists came to an end in 1941. During the war years the Communists greatly expanded the area under their control in northern China as they conducted effective guerrilla warfare. At the same time the Guomindang increasingly alienated large sectors of the population with its widespread corruption and political oppression. When Japan surrendered in 1945, the Guomindang moved to occupy the major cities, while the Communists strengthened their position in the countryside. The ensuing civil war (1946–1949) resulted in the defeat of the Guomindang armies. The Nationalist government fled to Taiwan, which had been restored to China in 1945. In October 1949 the People's Republic of China was proclaimed, with Peking as its capital.

The People's Republic was closely allied with the Soviet Union. The disruption of relations with the West became still more dramatic during the Korean War (1950–1953), in which a Chinese "volunteer" army fought against American troops. The United States continued to support the Guomindang government on Taiwan. On the Chinese mainland the Communist Party set out to reorganize society in such a way that every unit and every individual would be completely under its control. All independent organizations were effectively suppressed.

The internal politics of the People's Republic featured an almost uninterrupted series of mass campaigns which entailed persecution of selected target groups and persons: landowners, rich farmers, "reactionary elements"— and those with whom the leaders of the campaigns had personal scores to settle. Physical violence was commonplace. In the countryside, landholdings were first distributed to tenants and poor farmers; in subsequent campaigns, cooperative farming was organized on an ever larger scale. In the cities, industrial and commercial enterprises were nationalized. Intellectuals were required to study Marxism and the writings of Mao Zedong. In 1956 they were invited, during the Hundred Flowers campaign, to voice criticism of the regime. When the criticism turned out to be far more acute than the Party had anticipated, it was countered by the Anti-Rightist campaign, which for many intellectuals meant the beginning of decades-long imprisonment. In 1958 Mao launched the Great Leap Forward, a millenarian attempt to overtake the Western nations in productivity within a few years. In the countryside, the Great Leap entailed large-scale collectivization of agriculture and a revolutionary new concept of social organization: the People's Communes. Utterly unrealistic policy directives and drastic mismanagement combined with natural disasters to produce a national catastrophe in which millions starved. The regime was forced to adjust its policies.

The failure of the Great Leap Forward resulted not only in a dramatic break with the Soviet Union—in 1960 all Soviet advisors in China were recalled—but also in intensified dissension within the highest ranks of the Chinese Communist Party. Mao Zedong had to yield some of his power to Liu Shaoqi and others, who implemented a more sober set of policies in the early 1960s. Eventually, however, Mao and his partisans struck back by launching the Cultural Revolution (1966-1969). Mao Zedong's most important supporter at this time was Marshal Lin Biao, commander of the army, who led a campaign for Maoist indoctrination of the armed forces. Mao's wife, Jiang Qing, also started to play an active role in culture and politics. A former actress, she took special interest in the theater world, effectively demanding the suppression of all forms but the "revolutionary model opera."

Mao called upon students and school pupils to rebel; they became the notorious Red Guards. The period of the Cultural Revolution was a nightmare in which China went through utter chaos and extreme violence. Many Party leaders, artists and intellectuals, professors and teachers were subjected to every imaginable form of psychological and physical maltreatment. Many died, committed suicide, or were crippled for life.

Eventually, when armed Red Guard factions took to warring with each other, the army stepped in to impose peace and order. But the more moderate elements in the Party had been removed from the stage, and power remained in the hands of the narrow-minded radical faction. Lin Biao fell out with Mao and died attempting to fly to Russia in 1971, but Jiang Qing and her accomplices, later commonly called the Gang of Four, remained in power until Mao's death. Upon his demise in 1976 they were imprisoned and a new leadership evolved; Deng Xiaoping emerged as the most powerful figure.

Starting in 1978 the radical economic policies of the preceding decades were gradually abolished. Contacts with the outside world, including the United States, were resumed. Foreign investment was welcomed. The collective system of agriculture was dismantled, and private enterprise was encouraged. During the 1980s mainland China showed remarkable, though uneven, economic growth. At the same time, though criticism of the abuses of the Anti-Rightist campaign and the Cultural Revolution was welcomed, the Party made it clear that it would brook no fundamental questioning of its dominant position in society: examples were the handling of the Peking Democracy movement of 1978–1980 and the brutal suppression of the student protests in June 1989.

On Taiwan during the fifties and sixties the Guomindang government maintained strict ideological control. All contacts with the mainland were outlawed, and opinions even vaguely smacking of leftist or pro-Communist sympathy were systematically suppressed. Economic policies stressed export and were impressively successful. During the seventies and eighties the standard of living in Taiwan steadily rose. After the death of Chiang Kai-shek ideological control was relaxed somewhat; at the same time tensions between the native Taiwanese Chinese and the immigrants from the mainland, who had originally arrived in the period from 1945 to 1949, became more open and pronounced.

The population of Hong Kong increased explosively after World War II, mainly owing to the influx of political and economic refugees from the People's Republic. Effective government, highly skilled labor, and low labor costs all contributed to spectacular economic development, which could not help but affect the neighboring province of Guangdong.

Chapter 25
MODERN LITERATURE: AN INTRODUCTION

THE LITERARY REVOLUTION AND
THE MAY FOURTH MOVEMENT

Modern Chinese literature is often said to have begun in 1917, the year in which Hu Shi and Chen Duxiu published, in the columns of the magazine *Xin qingnian* (New youth), their articles calling for the creation of a "new literature." The term Literary Revolution of 1917 refers to these articles and their aftermath. Hu Shi and Chen Duxiu demanded that literature should be written not in the classical written language but in the contemporary vernacular (*baihua*), regardless of subject or genre. *Xin qingnian*'s discussions of the suitability of *baihua* as a vehicle for literature continued into 1918, and in the spring of that year the same magazine published the first important creative work along the new lines: Lu Xun's short story "Kuangren riji" (Diary of a madman). This story, written in *baihua*, took its form from Western models; its content amounted to a frontal assault on traditional Confucian society, which was characterized as cannibalistic.

Other scholars see modern Chinese literature as beginning in 1919, the year of the May Fourth Movement (*wusi yundong*). The May Fourth Movement was the first great nationwide protest. It was staged by Chinese university and secondary-school students against the concessions in China awarded by the Treaty of Versailles to foreign powers, especially Japan. After an initial demonstration held in Peking on May 4, 1919, a wave of protests rapidly swept through China's major cities. Countless new periodicals were hastily published, and since the students hoped to arouse support among the broad masses of the population, their publications were practically all in *baihua*. Within a short time *baihua* came into general use for purposes which had traditionally been reserved for *wenyan*. There was little opposition to the abandonment of *wenyan*; even the protest of such an eminent translator as Lin Shu went largely unheard. In the early 1920s the Ministry of Education passed successive decisions leading to the general replacement of *wenyan* by *baihua* as the language of primary- and secondary-school instruction, even in the field of Chinese language and literature.

Important though it was, the switch from classical to modern Chinese was only one aspect of the Literary Revolution. No less fundamental was the new literature's fundamental opposition to Confucian morality and the traditional social order. From the start the new literature reflected its authors' fervent desire to hasten the coming of a new, modern, powerful China. Not surprisingly, these writers looked to Western literature as a source of relevant themes, ideas, and artistic techniques.

Chen Duxiu

Chen Duxiu and Hu Shi were among the most influential Chinese intellectuals of the first half of the twentieth century. Chen Duxiu (1879–1942) came from a rich family and was educated in the traditional manner. After taking his *xiucai* degree in 1896, he came under the influence of Kang Youwei, Liang Qichao, and other advocates of intellectual and ideological modernization. From 1901 to 1903 he studied in Japan. After returning to China he published and contributed to various *baihua* newspapers. He is supposed to have studied for a while in Paris between 1907 and 1910. After the 1911 Revolution, he served briefly in the government. In 1915 in Shanghai he founded the magazine *Qingnian zazhi* (Youth), in which he published articles strongly supporting such Western values as individualism, democracy, science, and the equality of the sexes.

At the invitation of the head of Peking University, Cai Yuanpei (1868–1940), Chen Duxiu became dean of the Faculty of Letters. His magazine, under the new title *Xin qingnian* (New youth), became a forum for reform-minded young staff members of the university. After coming out in support of the student protesters and the May Fourth Movement, Chen Duxiu was arrested and briefly imprisoned. Resigning his post as dean, he was more than ever attracted to Marxism, and in 1921 he became the first secretary-general of the Chinese Communist Party. He was ousted from this position in 1927 and ejected from the Party in 1930. In 1932 he was again imprisoned; the Guomindang government did not release him until the formation of the Second United Front (1936).

Chen Duxiu is a central figure in the intellectual development of modern China; his specific role in the rise of the new literature was the limited but crucial one of publishing and lending his authoritative support to Hu Shi's proposals.

Hu Shi

Hu Shi (1891–1962), who came from an impoverished family of officials, spent the years from 1906 to 1910 in Shanghai, attending a school in that increasingly cosmopolitan city until 1908. From 1910 to 1917 he studied in the United States on a scholarship, first at Cornell University and later at Columbia. At Columbia he attended John Dewey's (1859–1952) classes in philosophy, subsequently adopting Dewey's pragmatism as his own philosophy of life. He wrote his first articles for *Xin qingnian* while he was still in America. After returning to China, he became professor of philosophy at Peking University. He pursued an active and varied career in education while continuing to publish widely read books and articles. His writings reflected his frank admiration of Western values. Though strongly critical of the Guomindang, he continued to advocate gradual and peaceful change rather than radical overthrow of the existing system; accordingly he opposed the Communist Party.

From 1938 to 1942 Hu Shi was China's ambassador to the United States. From 1946 to 1949, he served briefly as chancellor of Peking University. In the early 1950s he again went to live in America, but his last years were spent in Taiwan, where he had been named head of the Academia Sinica in 1958. In the People's Republic of China, Hu Shi was subjected to intense criticism in the early 1950s as the type of the overly Westernized, pro-American intellectual who insists on remaining politically independent.

Hu Shi's importance for the development of modern Chinese literature goes far beyond his 1917 articles in *Xin qingnian*. He was one of the first authors to attempt poetry in *baihua*; his collection *Changshi ji* (Experiments) was published in 1919. Hu Shi emphasized that even in traditional China, *baihua* literature had existed side by side with the classical genres, and that *baihua* literature had been the source of all the important renovations in *wenyan* literature. His *Baihua wenxue shi* (History of spoken-language literature) was never completed; the first volume, which appeared in 1928, goes no further than the tenth century.

In the 1920s Hu Shi also devoted much time to research on the great traditional novels and to their republication in editions that could satisfy the demands of critical scholarship. His own publications in this field include important studies of various novels from the *Shuihu zhuan* to the *Haishang hua liezhuan*. He was especially interested in the *Honglou meng*; Hu Shi and his follower Yu Pingbo (1899–1982) emphasized its autobiographical character. In 1954 they were both attacked in the People's Republic for taking this position, their critics claiming that their view did no justice to the novel's importance as an exposé of feudal society and the traditional family system.

LITERATURE AND POLITICS

Modern literature's break with tradition was, of course, much less sudden and absolute than a term like Literary Revolution would seem to imply. Actually the modernization had already begun before 1917, and the old tradition continued to survive in many ways.

Long before 1917 the traditional Confucian culture had begun abandoning its claim to be the sole guide to life in an obviously changing society. The most dramatic example was the abolishment of the old-style state examinations, which were held nationwide for the last time in 1905. From then on, literary studies as traditionally conceived—that is, as a preparation for office-holding—seemed to have lost their meaning. Starting around the turn of the century traditional education was increasingly replaced by modern forms of primary, secondary, and university education. Japan, the first model for educational reforms, was eventually displaced by America. From the turn of the century on a steady stream of translations made a wide range of Western literature available in Chinese. Some of these translations were made via existing Japanese versions; others, such as Lin Shu's translations of Western novels and Su Manshu's renderings of Western poetry, were based on the originals. The first performance of a Western play in Chinese translation was staged by students in Tokyo in 1905. If anything, it is surprising in retrospect that the Literary Revolution did not emerge in full force until 1917. In any case by 1917 social and cultural conditions were ripe for the change. Chinese intellectuals had had ample contacts with certain facets of Western culture; a growing number of Chinese had had at least some experience of living abroad; and at the same time traditional Chinese culture had declared its own bankruptcy by the abolishment of the examinations and the government's inability to defend and strengthen China.

The great majority of young intellectuals came to reject the traditional cultural forms associated with Confucianism, and few of them sought, or received, bureaucratic appointments along the old lines. In this period writers became not so much an elite as an intelligentsia, and many found employment in the new educational system. Nevertheless most writers remained loyal to what had been the most fundamental ideal in the Confucian polity—concern for the welfare of society. No more than a tiny minority of writers regarded literature as a goal in itself. For most it was a vehicle, a weapon with which to speed the transition from an old and ailing society to a powerful new nation. Practically all modern writers blamed traditional Confucianism for China's backwardness in the twentieth century. Their opposition was directed not only at traditional statecraft but also, in particular, at all aspects of the traditional family system.

Writers revealed their antipathy to traditional culture in their writings and also in their personal lives. Where Confucianism had made the individual subordinate to the group, modern writers stressed the freedom of the individual. For most of them, however, individualism was not an absolute value; it was of social importance as a factor in the dismantling of Confucianism and the building of a new China. Just as many Chinese writers of the 1920s adopted a more politicized stance after the events of 1925–1928, many 1930s writers who originally sought their highest ideal in individual happiness, or in art, became more socially concerned as the political situation deteriorated, especially after the outbreak of the Sino-Japanese War in 1937.

So even after the Literary Revolution, literature remained for most writers subordinate to politics. The question in their minds was not *whether* literature could serve political ends, but *how*, and especially *who*—the writers themselves or the political authorities—was to determine the norms and applications. As far as this dimension is concerned, modern Chinese literature can be divided into two periods: 1917–1942 and post-1942.

In the 1917–1942 period, writers had substantial freedom to choose the ways and means of advancing their political ideals. Government censorship was omnipresent and, in certain periods, strongly repressive. But the conflicts between the successive governments and various writers were typically caused by the latter's own political choices and initiatives. Moreover, after 1917 there were a few short periods of voluntary and relatively enthusiastic cooperation between writers and the government. Such interludes occurred between 1925 and 1927 (the first period of cooperation between the Guomindang and the Chinese Communist Party) and between 1937 and 1941 (the initial phase of the Sino-Japanese war and the second period of Nationalist-Communist collaboration). The Guomindang's flagrant corruption and apparent inability to bring about improvements eventually led many intellectuals, and especially writers, to shift their political loyalties to the Communist side. (This transfer was often a matter of desperation rather than of true conviction—a fact which, as we will see below, eventually led to conflicts under the post-1949 regime.)

In 1942 Mao Zedong delivered the famous Yan'an talks in which he bluntly stated that it was the responsibility of political authorities to dictate how writers were to do their jobs in society. After that, the main line of literary development was determined by political directives. The government sought to regulate both the form and the content of literary works, and the conflicts between government and writers were mainly a matter of certain writers' efforts to preserve for literature at least a marginal independence.

The first few years of the People's Republic were another period in which the majority of writers spontaneously supported government policies.

REFORM AND TRADITION

Marxism enjoyed increasing popularity among Chinese intellectuals from the 1920s on, and in the 1950s it was very widely accepted. The obvious reasons for its success in China are to be sought, of course, in the impressive victory of the Russian Revolution in 1917 and in the relative effectiveness of the Communist Party on the Chinese political scene. But deeper factors were also involved. Of Western philosophies and ideologies, there is probably none which resembles Confucianism on as many points as does Marxism. Both Confucianism and Marxism are *total* ideologies, which seek to provide solutions for all issues of ultimate concern. In both, the ultimate truth is seen as an underlying law or regularity which is immanent in the historical process; in both, political activity is supremely important. In both, a leading political role is assigned to a small group of people who have become, through study, experts in the truth. Finally both Confucianism and Marxism assign to this group both the right and the responsibility to educate the rest of society.

In this sense Marxism made it possible for twentieth-century Chinese intellectuals to assume their traditional political role in a modernized form. Rather than defending the status quo, they could now be revolutionaries in the service of a new China. But this transformation did not require fundamental rethinking of the basic interrelationships of truth, elite, state, and society. Drastic though the social consequences of Marxism were, psychologically it was probably easier for many Chinese to embrace Marxism than a religion of the revealed type, such as Christianity, or a political liberalism along Western lines, which would have been based on a principle of pluralistic egalitarianism.

The more strictly literary facets of the Literary Revolution included the introduction into China of Western theories of literature, wide-ranging experiments with Western forms of prose and poetry, and the extensive use of *baihua*. The champions of the new literature made heavy use of Western theories in formulating their proposals; these theories were later to be more systematically publicized in China. One curious feature of this process was that conceptions of literature that had been current in widely separated periods of Western history were more or less simultaneously presented to the Chinese public. In the 1920s, for example, Chinese critics introduced Romanticism, but also Realism, Marxist literary theory, and many hybrids and later forms. The twenties and thirties saw frequent and colorful debates among the proponents of the various schools.

Another important effect was the adoption of the Western evaluation of individual genres. In addition to poetry and the essay, fiction and drama were now regarded as serious literature; in quantitative terms at least, they actually became the predominant forms. The models for these genres were taken not from the traditional Chinese equivalents but from Western works, which modern Chinese writers could read in translation if not in the original. Though the 1920s and 1930s also witnessed a strong and positive reevaluation of traditional Chinese *baihua* literature, the forms of modern Chinese literature were basically rooted in the nineteenth-century European novel (Dickens, Zola, and others), the nineteenth-century European theater (e.g., Ibsen, Shaw) and nineteenth-century Western poetry (Byron, Whitman). Other significant influences came to include nineteenth-century East European literature as well as twentieth-century developments in Western literature. Practically all work in these new genres was in *baihua*, but it should not be thought that *wenyan* died out entirely. Writers who had begun their careers before the Literary Revolution (for example, the poet Liu Yazi, 1887–1958) were often entirely untrained in *baihua* writing, and they continued to use *wenyan*. Especially in the 1920s and 1930s, but on a lesser scale even up to the present, certain magazines and newspapers have continued to use a more or less conventionalized mixture of *baihua* and *wenyan*. Prominent political figures such as Wang Jingwei and Mao Zedong paid tribute to their traditional education by publishing *wenyan* poetry in the traditional forms; this practice has continued under the People's Republic. Even such conspicuously "modern" authors as Lu Xun, Yu Dafu, and Guo Moruo did not shrink from publishing, later in their lives, traditional-style poetry.

The new literature's audience, at least in the twenties and thirties, was limited to modern intellectuals. The hub of modern literary life in these years was and remained Shanghai. Shanghai had become one of China's very largest cities. It enjoyed thriving commercial relations with foreign countries and played a leading role in the educational and publishing worlds. Another reason for its literary prominence was that the foreign concessions in Shanghai allowed a measure of freedom from Chinese government censorship. Peking, mainly because of its universities, was another important center of literary life. But the popularity of modern literature was negligible compared to that of the various traditional Chinese genres, which now enjoyed a vastly increased readership thanks to widespread public education and inexpensive modern printing techniques. Modern novels could seldom match the circulation of *wuxia xiaoshuo* or of works in the *yuanyang hudie pai* vein, and modern drama could not hope to compete with the traditional theater in its various regional forms.

Starting approximately in the late 1920s the failure of modern literature to reach the masses became a topic of spirited discussion, especially among leftist writers. The situation was often blamed on the difficulty of modern *baihua*, which was often disproportionately full of neologisms and syntactically cluttered with dubious new constructions obviously borrowed from Western languages. Starting in the 1940s the Communist Party strove to bring about an integration of sorts between the new literature and the perennially popular traditional genres. In his famous *Talks at the Yan'an Forum*, held in 1942, Mao Zedong stipulated that writers were to aim their works at an audience consisting primarily of workers, peasants, and soldiers. Just as the Communist Party made use for propaganda purposes of the various regional forms of drama and performative art, writers were to study and apply the forms and diction characteristic of popular traditional genres. After 1949 literary works meant for mass readership were often printed in hundreds of thousands of copies. At the same time there was a distinct channel of "internal" (*neibu*) publications—that is, works not authorized for general sale and distribution. Throughout the period of the People's Republic, *neibu* publications, including books thought to be politically or morally controversial, have continued to be made available to a highly select readership.

Perhaps the extreme examples of the joining of old forms to new content were the five model operas (revolutionary Peking operas) which, during the Cultural Revolution of 1966 to 1969, were virtually the only literary works tolerated by the Party. Though these cannot be said to be typical of the post-1949 period as a whole, it is true that the influence of Western literature declined sharply after the 1940's, not only in drama but in fiction and poetry as well. If the period from 1917 to 1942 had been one of variety and experiment, the decades thereafter, extending at least into the late 1970s, were marked by organized conformity.

The downfall of the Gang of Four and the subsequent "liberalization" were followed by a remarkable flowering of literature as many young writers boldly experimented with new themes, forms, and styles. Within a few years, however, the Party apparatus started to reassert its ideological control.

Chapter 26.
MODERN LITERATURE 1917–1942:
THE SHORT STORY AND THE NOVEL

THE SHORT STORY

After the 1917 Literary Revolution the first modern genre to achieve convincing successes was the short story: Lu Xun's story *Kuangren riji* was published in April 1918 in the magazine *Xin qingnian*. The early 1920s witnessed a real flourishing of the short story, and many of the most famous modern Chinese authors first made their names in that genre. The first significant modern novels appeared in the second half of the decade, partially displacing the short story as the main focus of interest, but the short story has continued to be immensely popular to the present time. Much of the early work of the 1920s authors was autobiographical, with easy parallels between the main characters and the real-life authors. Moreover, many famous autobiographies were written in this period—by Hu Shi and Guo Moruo, among others.

Needless to say, we cannot do justice here to the many writers of lasting importance. The following sections will merely introduce a few outstanding authors and their works. As short story writers we shall mention Lu Xun, Yu Dafu, Ye Shengtao and Shen Congwen. Famous women writers included Bing Xin and Ding Ling. Of novelists in this period, Mao Dun, Ba Jin and Lao She have remained among the most famous.

Lu Xun

Lu Xun is the best-known pseudonym of Zhou Shuren (1881–1936), who hailed from Shaoxing in the province of Zhejiang. His grandfather had been the first in his family to earn the *jinshi* degree, but he later became involved in a bribery scandal and spent years in prison. Lu Xun's father was plagued by ill health, and the family suffered from increasing poverty. Lu Xun's childhood experiences in this milieu provided the material for many of his stories. After several years of study in Nanjing, he stayed in Japan on a government scholarship from 1902 to 1909. After preparatory studies in Tokyo, he studied medicine at Sendai for almost two years, only to conclude that it was more important to heal the minds than the bodies of his fellow Chinese. Returning to Tokyo, he joined his brother Zhou Zuoren (1885–1966, later one of China's most prominent essayists) in literary activities. Besides essays, the first results included a collection of East European short stories which the brothers translated from German into *wenyan*.

After returning to China, Lu Xun, at the recommendation of the dynamic minister of education Cai Yuanpei, was employed by the Ministry of Education, with which he continued to be associated until 1925. His job in Peking soon proved to be a sinecure, and he eventually combined his bureaucratic work with teaching at Peking University and elsewhere. One of the lasting results was his book *Zhongguo xiaoshuo shilue* (A concise history of Chinese fiction).

Lu Xun wrote his first *baihua* short story at the request of several writers on *Xin qingnian*; it was published in April 1918 as "Kuangren riji" (Diary of a madman). Though both the title and the form of the story were borrowed from Gogol, the content was original: the diarist is the only character in the story who consciously realizes he is living in a society in which people are trying to kill, even to eat each other. In this society ethics is no more than a facade maintained to justify the existing situation. "Kuangren riji" is a merciless exposé of the lovelessness and injustice in Chinese society. The story was an immediate success.

Lu Xun published two collections of short stories. *Nahan* (Battle cries, 1923) contains stories written from 1918 to 1922; those written in 1924 and 1925 are collected in *Panghuang* (Wanderings, 1926). Most of these stories are rather short and are based on the author's personal experiences during his childhood in Shaoxing and in the first few years after the 1911 Revolution. Not surprisingly, many are written in the first person. Lu Xun's style is remarkably concise and shows the strong influence of *wenyan*. The characters in his stories are often no more than summarily described. They are often types: the traditional-style intellectual as hypocritical defender of the status quo or as victim of the examination system, the half-baked modern intellectual, the woman as a victim of traditional morality, etc.

A special place in Lu Xun's oeuvre is occupied by the long, episodic novella *A Gui zhengzhuan* (The true story of Ah Q), which dates from 1922. Ah Q is a poor, unattached laborer from a small village. His outstanding trait is his ability to interpret every defeat, every humiliation, as a psychological victory while in fact failing utterly as a fighter, lover, thief, and revolutionary. Eventually, Ah Q is unjustly condemned and executed. The story represents Lu Xun's contempt for the widespread attitude of refusing to realize the seriousness of China's situation and escaping into hollow dreams of past and future glory.

In 1926 Lu Xun, being involved in political troubles, left Peking. After short sojourns in Amoy and Canton, he settled in 1928 in Shanghai, where he was to remain until his death, supporting himself by translations and journalism. He was a productive translator, and as an essayist he won respect and fear for his short, caustic essays on a wide variety of subjects (*zawen*), which were collected in many volumes. It was only his enormous personal prestige that saved him from falling victim to political persecution. His other significant works include *Yecao* (Weeds, 1927), a short collection of prose poems; *Zhaohua xishi* (Morning flowers picked in the evening, 1928), containing childhood reminiscences; and *Gushi xinbian* (Old happenings newly told, 1935), a collection of satirical retellings of old Chinese myths and legends.

During his years in Shanghai Lu Xun was active in various organizations including, from 1930 to 1935, the League of Leftist Writers. Despite his growing sympathy for the Communist Party, he never became a member. After his death he was canonized by the Party.

Yu Dafu

Yu Dafu (1896–1945) was, like Lu Xun, a native of Zhejiang. From 1911 to 1922 he studied economics in Tokyo. After his return to China he worked, among other things, as a journalist and a college teacher. He and Guo Moruo became two of the most prominent figures in the *Chuangzao she* (Creation Society). This organization, originally founded by Chinese students in Japan in 1921, was especially active in Shanghai. The Creation Society emphasized both the expression of individual feelings and the exposure and criticism of social ills.

It is the element of individual expression that is most prominent in Yu Dafu's work, and his work as a whole is strongly autobiographical. In addition to stories, he was noted for his essays and diaries. Characteristically, he made his literary debut with a novella describing the sexual frustrations, increasing loneliness, and ultimate suicide of a Chinese student in Japan. In this work, *Chenlun* (Sinking, 1921), the emphasis is on the inner experiences of the main character—who, in many respects, resembles Yu Dafu himself. Many of Yu's later stories are about the gradual personal degeneration of intellectuals. In the 1930s Yu Dafu published two novels. After the outbreak of war in 1937 he lived first in Hong Kong, then in Singapore, and eventually on the island of Sumatra. Shortly after the Japanese surrender, he was shot by the Japanese military police.

Ye Shengtao

Ye Shengtao (1894-1988), who originally published under the name Ye Shaojun, was born in Suzhou. After a traditional-style primary education, he attended a modern secondary school. Starting in 1911 he worked as a schoolteacher, first in Suzhou and later in Shanghai. Like Lu Xun, Ye wrote his first short story before the Literary Revolution, in *wenyan*. After the Literary Revolution he became a member of the *Wenxue yanjiu hui* (Society for the Study of Literature). Other members of this organization, founded in 1920, included Zhou Zuoren and Mao Dun.

By 1937, Ye Shengtao had published six collections of short stories. One recurrent theme is the oppression of children under the strongly authoritarian educational system; another is the powerlessness of reform-minded intellectuals, often of very modest social status, in a provincial town. Ye Shengtao was, of course, eminently equipped by his personal experiences to write on these subjects. The same themes are again in the foreground in his 1930 novel *Ni Huanzhi*. Ye held teaching jobs in various cities from 1921 until 1923, when he returned to Shanghai to pursue, in addition to his creative writing, an active career as an editor of magazines and textbooks. In 1937 he fled to Sichuan, where he worked as editor for the Kaiming Press. After 1945 he continued to work in this capacity in Shanghai. Even before the proclamation of the People's Republic of China in 1949 he had accepted a post in the new government, and in 1954 he became vice-minister of education. He wrote few stories after 1949.

Shen Congwen

Shen Congwen's (1903–1988) family had a long military tradition but had become impoverished during the Boxer Rebellion. Starting when he was fifteen, Shen Congwen served in the army for three years in western Hunan, where banditry was endemic and there were frequent conflicts between the Chinese and the Miao. This period remained a prime source of material for Shen Congwen's stories. In 1922 he went to Peking. Partly because he needed money, but also owing to the personal encouragement of Ding Ling and others, he began to write stories and novellas. In 1927 he went with Ding Ling and her husband to Shanghai, where he worked as writer, teacher, and editor. His productivity throughout these years was phenomenal: in 1935 his collected works were published in 35 volumes!

Shen Congwen is first and foremost an enthusiastic storyteller although technically his stories often seem carelessly written. Of the leading modern writers he was probably the one who kept closest to the traditional Chinese novel in his style, subject matter, and conception of the writer's role.

In 1937 he fled to Kunming, where he became a professor at the Southwestern United University. In 1945 he became professor of Chinese literature at Peking University. In 1946 he completed his autobiography, *Congwen zizhuan*. Soon after the founding of the People's Republic he was heavily criticized as a "rightist element"—in his writings he had maintained a remarkably apolitical stance as compared with most of his fellow writers. After an unsuccessful attempt at suicide, he took a job at the Palace Museum, where he devoted his time to research in archaeology and art history.

Bing Xin

Bing Xin (pseudonym of Xie Wanying, 1900–) was one of the first women authors to achieve prominence in the new literature. Her father, a naval officer, was stationed at various places along the Chinese coast. Bing Xin enrolled at Yanjing University in Peking in 1918; the following year she was an enthusiastic participant in the May Fourth Movement. She won initial fame with *Chaoren* (*Superman*, 1923), a collection of short stories that might better be described as lyrical sketches, and two collections of short free-verse lyric poems, *Fanxing* (The stars, 1923) and *Chunshui* (Waters of spring, 1923). In 1923 she went to America, where she attended Wellesley College, taking an MA degree in 1926. While in America she wrote *Ji xiao duzhe* (Letters to young readers), which established her as a leading writer of children's literature.

After returning to China she taught at Yanjing University. In 1929 she married a colleague, Wu Wenzao. In 1937 they went to Kunming and in 1941 to Chongqing. In 1946 Bing Xin went with her husband to Tokyo, where he had been appointed to the Chinese legation, but in 1951 the couple returned to the Chinese mainland. Bing Xin's publications of the 1930s and 1940s, revealing her explicit Christian beliefs and mystical tendencies, were received less enthusiastically than her earlier works. In the People's Republic, in addition to her writing, she has served on various governmental and cultural organizations including the National People's Congress.

Ding Ling

Ding Ling (pseudonym of Jiang Weiwen, 1904–1986) was born at Changde, Hunan. Her father, a *xiucai* degree holder who had studied in Japan, died shortly after her birth. Remarkably for those days, her mother went to Changsha to be trained at a teachers' training college, and she subsequently worked as a teacher in Changde. Ding Ling first studied at the normal school in Taoyuan. After the May Fourth Movement she went to Changsha and then, in 1921, to Shanghai where she met the Marxist theoretician Qu Qiubai (1899–1935), who was to serve as secretary-general of the Chinese Communist Party in 1927–1928. Two years later Ding Ling went on to Peking, where in 1925 she married the unsuccessful poet Hu Yepin (1903–1931).

With the encouragement of Ye Shengtao and others, Ding Ling published her first stories in 1927. Especially well received was her novella *Shafei nüshi de riji* (Sophie's diary), which was remarkable for its frank description of the physical desires of a tubercular girl. In her other stories, too, Ding Ling often focused on the position of the modern woman in contemporary China.

Meanwhile Ding Ling and Hu Yepin had gone to Shanghai with Shen Congwen. Their efforts to establish various magazines were unsuccessful. Eventually Hu Yepin, as a member of the Communist Party, became involved in underground activities. After his execution by the Guomindang in 1931, Ding Ling herself joined the Communist Party. Kidnapped by the Guomindang in 1933, she was eventually released and stayed in Nanjing until 1936, when she slipped away to Yan'an. Her criticism of the differences in status which continued to exist within the Party in supposedly egalitarian Yan'an, and of the inferior position of women, was one of the main subjects of the famous 1942 Yan'an Forum on Literature and Art.

In 1949 Ding Ling published a long novel dealing with land reform in North China. For this work, *Taiyang zhao zai Sangganhe shang* (The sun shines over the Sanggan River), she received the Stalin Prize for Literature in 1951. In 1955 conflicts developed in her relationship with the Party, and after pleading for the independence of literature during the Hundred Flowers campaign in 1956, she was expelled from the Party as a "rightist element" in 1957. In 1978 she was rehabilitated, having first been put to work for eight years in a land reclamation area in North China, subsequently maltreated by Red Guards during the Cultural Revolution, held prisoner in Peking from 1970 to 1975, and finally banned to a commune in Shanxi for three years.

THE NOVEL

The three foremost novelists of the period from 1917 to 1942—Mao Dun, Ba Jin, and Lao She—shared the critical attitude of the short-story writers toward traditional and contemporary Chinese society. Their individual approaches, however, were very different. Mao Dun was a realist, Ba Jin a sentimentalist and Lao She a humorist, though these are rough classifications which apply mostly to their early works. With regard to the solutions they sought for China, these writers also differed. Mao Dun was an early convert to communism, Ba Jin was an anarchist, and Lao She tended to avoid taking a definite stance in party politics.

Mao Dun

Mao Dun (pseudonym of Shen Yanbing, 1896–1981) was born in Zhejiang. After studying in Peking, he worked in various capacities from 1916 to 1923 for the Commercial Press in Shanghai, eventually serving as editor of the influential monthly *Xiaoshuo yuebao* (The short story). In the early twenties Mao Dun was especially eminent as a critic who strongly supported Zola's naturalism. After leaving the Commercial Press, he took part in the Northern Expedition (1926–1927), for a while doing editorial work for the Guomindang and the national government. When the anti-leftist purge began, in April 1927 he fled Shanghai, secretly returning in August of the same year.

In 1927 and 1928 Mao Dun wrote three novellas that were published together in 1930 under the title *Zhi* (Eclipse). All three concerned the experiences of young intellectuals during the Northern Expedition; their initial high hopes stand in stark contrast to their ultimate disappointment. After producing several other works in great haste, Mao Dun published his novel *Ziye* (Midnight, 1933), a panoramic story of Shanghai in 1930, which describes the lives and interaction of capitalists, managers, intellectuals, laborers, and other modern types. In addition to his novels, Mao Dun wrote short stories, including the famous "Chuncan" (Spring silkworms). Unlike most of the rest of his works, which are situated in large modern cities, this story is set in the countryside; it depicts the helplessness of the peasants in the face of new economic developments at the national and global level.

After the outbreak of the Sino-Japanese war in 1937, Mao Dun was forced to shift his locale frequently, living in Hong Kong, Wuhan, Urumchi, Yan'an, and Guilin before arriving in Chongqing in 1942. His best-known work of this period is the unfinished novel *Fushi* (Corruption), an exposé of abuses under the Guomindang regime. During the remaining years of the war he wrote, among other things, a collection of short stories. After a visit to the Soviet Union (1946–1947), he went to live in Hong Kong, returning to Peking in 1949. From 1949 to 1964 he was minister of culture in the government of the People's Republic. He published little new work after 1945, and died in 1981.

Ba Jin

Ba Jin (pseudonym of Li Feigan, 1904–?) was born in 1904 in Chengdu, where he spent most of his childhood in the home of his grandfather after the decease of his parents. While still in Chengdu, Ba Jin became attracted to anarchism. In 1923 he went to Shanghai for further studies; he was active in Shanghai as an anarchist writer from 1925 to 1927. From 1927 to 1929 he lived in Paris, devoting his time to studies, translation, and original writing.

It was in Paris that Ba Jin wrote his first novel, *Miewang* (Destruction), which was based on his own experiences in the years preceding his departure from China. *Miewang* appeared in 1929 in *Xiaoshuo yuebao* and was a major success, so when Ba Jin returned to China he was a famous man. Throughout the period before 1949 he remained an exceptionally prolific author, producing numerous short stories in addition to novels. Many of his works show signs of having been written in great haste, and the political moral is often presented without subtlety. His frequently avowed anarchism drew attacks from Communist writers, though he was also an outspoken critic of the Guomindang regime. From 1932 on he was engaged in anti-Japanese activities, and as early as 1935 he was one of the first to urge the formation of a new United Front against Japan.

Unquestionably the most famous of Ba Jin's novels is *Jia* (Family), which appeared in 1931 as the first part of what became the autobiographical trilogy *Jiliu* (The torrent); the second and third volumes were *Chun* (Spring, 1938) and *Qiu* (Autumn, 1940). *Jia* depicts life in a large traditional gentry household; the younger generation's chances at happiness are ruined by the marriages their elders arrange for them against their will. A heavily sentimental novel, it has been read with a strong sense of identification by generations of modern Chinese readers.

Though the main characters in most of Ba Jin's novels are modern intellectuals, he also wrote works dealing with the life of mine workers. In these the influence of Zola is clearly present.

After 1949 Ba Jin filled various posts in the Chinese Writers' Union. His later writings included a collection of short stories written after a visit to the front during the Korean War.

Lao She

Lao She (pseudonym of Shu Qingchun, 1899–1966) was born in Peking, the son of a Manchu who died at the time of the Boxer Uprising. After primary school he attended normal school and became a schoolteacher at the age of seventeen. He later held various other jobs in education. From 1924 to 1929 he lived in London and taught Chinese at the School of Oriental Studies; among other activities he assisted Clement Egerton with his translation of the sixteenth-century novel *Jin Ping Mei*.

Inspired by the novels of Dickens, which he read to improve his English, Lao She wrote his first three novels while still living in London. The first, *Lao Zhang de zhexue* (Zhang's philosophy, 1926), deals with the conflicts between two honest youths and a mean schoolmaster. *Zhao Ziye* (1927) describes the life of Zhao Ziyue, a modern student in Peking, who appears in heavy caricature as stupid, lecherous, and easily bribable. In *Er Ma* (The two Mas, 1929), two Chinese, father and son Ma, operate an arts-and-curiosities shop in London.

In 1930 Lao She returned via Singapore to China. He tried to devote himself entirely to writing, but from time to time he also taught at various universities. In the early thirties he published, among other things, several volumes of short stories and the novels *Maocheng ji* (City of cats, 1933) and *Lihun* (Divorce, 1933). *Maocheng ji* is satirical science fiction: Cat City, where the pilot finds himself after an emergency landing, is inhabited by lazy cats who believe that slogans will solve their problems. In *Lihun*, the main character makes every effort to change his wife from a simple country girl into a modern big-city woman.

These early novels by Lao She emphasize the failure of individuals to realize their ideals. In the works he wrote from the middle thirties on, however, the focus shifts to the powerlessness of the individual in the face of social upheaval. His most famous book along these lines is the novel *Luotuo Xiangzi* (Camel Xiangzi), which dates from 1937 but was not published until 1939. It describes the life of a Peking rickshaw puller, whose efforts to attain a decent standard of living all fail, leaving him a physical and mental wreck.

In 1938, after the outbreak of war with Japan, Lao She was chosen as head of the Anti-Japanese Writers' League; he continued in this capacity until 1945. During the war years he wrote a number of propaganda plays, as well as various short performance texts (*quyi*). Partly owing to the success of *Luotuo Xiangzi* in America (under the title *Rickshaw Boy*, 1945), he went to live in the United States from 1946 to 1949. During this period he wrote his last novel, *The Drum Singers*. After returning to the People's Republic of China, he mainly wrote plays, in both *huaju* and Peking-opera forms. His most famous *huaju* is *Chaguan* (Teahouse), which depicts the changing lives of various strata of Peking's population in the first half of the twentieth century. In October 1966 Lao She committed suicide after suffering ill-treatment at the hands of the Red Guards. In the following years he was often criticized in the media; among other things, *Maocheng ji* was said to have been an attack on the Communist Party. In the late seventies he was posthumously rehabilitated.

OTHER WRITERS OF THE THIRTIES AND FORTIES

In the 1930s a number of younger writers created memorable works in which they experimented with more intense psychological descriptions. Their work reveals the authors' awareness of Freud as well as of stream-of-consciousness techniques. These experiments, centered in Shanghai, were short-lived owing to political developments, but in recent years there has been renewed interest in the work of Shi Zhecun (1905-), Liu Na'ou (1900-1939), and Mu Shiying (1912-1940). Another writer who won a lasting place for himself in this period was Zhang Tianyi (1906-1985); he published a number of satirical novels in the early 1930s, and some of his short stories have continued to be anthology favorites.

After the Japanese occupation of Manchuria, novels appeared depicting the anti-Japanese guerrilla war. Famous authors included Xiao Hong (pseudonym of Zhang Naiying, 1911-1942) and Xiao Jun (1907-1988; also wrote as Tian Jun). Among the most famous of Xiao Hong's works are her novel *Shengsi chang* (The field of life and death, 1935), a description of primitive rural conditions in northern China during the anti-Japanese struggle, and the autobiographical *Hulanhe zhuan* (Tales of the Hulan River, 1942). Xiao Jun made his name with the novel *Bayuede xiangcun* (Village in August, 1935).

One of the most famous books to appear in the forties was *Weicheng* (Fortress beseiged, 1946), the only novel by Qian Zhongshu (1910-). As a specialist in comparative literature, Qian was intimately familiar with the wartime academic milieu which the novel satirizes.

Chapter 27.
MODERN LITERATURE 1917–1942: POETRY, DRAMA, AND ESSAY

MODERN POETRY

After the Literary Revolution, the possibility of writing novels and short stories in *baihua* was readily accepted. But for many readers it seemed less obvious that the new medium was suited for the production of poetry that would bear serious comparison with the classical tradition. To demonstrate the possibility of writing poems in the modern spoken language, Hu Shi wrote his collection *Changshi ji* (Experiments), which we have already mentioned. It was followed by numerous collections by other authors.

Free verse figures prominently in the poetry of the early 1920s, many writers abandoning traditional formal concepts entirely. One logical consequence was the appearance of prose poems, such as those in Lu Xun's 1926 collection *Yecao*. In the late twenties a certain following was won by poets who tried to adapt Western verse forms to the linguistic features of Chinese or to develop new forms based on the specific characteristics of *baihua*.

As regards content, in the twenties Romanticism remained the main influence: Byron was widely studied, as were Keats and Shelley. Free-verse poets were often inspired by Walt Whitman. In the 1930s a wider palette of colors appeared in modern Chinese poetry as younger poets, better aware than their elders of the most recent developments in Western poetry, began to write verse influenced by such modern movements as Imagism and Symbolism. With the coming of the war with Japan, these new trends fell into relative abeyance as the simpler forms of folk poetry enjoyed a temporary vogue.

Guo Moruo

Poets who came to prominence in the early twenties included Zhu Ziqing (1898–1948), Yu Pingbo, Bing Xin, and Guo Moruo (1892–1978). Of these,

Guo Moruo became the most renowned specifically for his poetry; Bing Xin became famous for her "feminine" prose, Yu Pingbo for his scholarly and critical writings, and Zhu Ziqing for the *baihua* essay.

Guo Moruo's lasting fame was due not least to the leading administrative role he played in China's cultural life for many years. A native of Sichuan, he went to study in Japan in 1914, taking his medical degree from Kyushu University in 1921. Guo Moruo is one of the few modern Chinese writers who were influenced not only by literature in English (Whitman, Shelley, Tagore) but by German writers as well. His translations include Goethe's *Faust* and *The Sorrows of Young Werther*.

Guo Moruo made his name as poet with the publication of his collection *Nüshen* (The goddesses) in 1921. These poems, in free form, expressed the author's feelings of cosmic union with all that exists; the imagery was often bathetic and the tone was heavily rhetorical. Whitman's influence is obvious in the long, prose-like lines and the catalogs of people, places, and natural and geographic features.

After returning to Shanghai, Guo plunged into the activities of the Creation Society. Full of revolutionary ideals, he joined the Communist Party in 1925. He took part in the Northern Expedition, but after Chiang Kai-shek's 1927 coup he fled to Japan, where he devoted much time to archaeological and paleological research, eventually becoming an authority on ancient China's history. He did not return to China until 1937. He held a number of posts in Chongqing. During the war years he wrote his most famous play, *Qu Yuan* (1942), on the tragic life of a patriotic poet. After 1949 Guo Moruo filled various high-ranking posts in the People's Republic; he was, among other things, president of the Academy of Sciences until his death.

After *Nüshen*, Guo Moruo published eight more collections of poetry, none equalling the success of *Nüshen*. His later poems show him returning to traditional forms. Besides poetry, Guo published translations, plays, historical studies, essays, and short stories. His autobiography, which covers his life from early childhood until after 1945, fills nine volumes. When the Cultural Revolution began in 1966, Guo Moruo dramatically stated that he rejected everything he had thus far written.

Wen Yiduo

After the early experiments with free verse, some poets made systematic efforts to develop new poetic forms based on the aural and prosodic features of *baihua*. Two of the most famous pioneers were Wen Yiduo and Xu Zhimo. Wen Yiduo (1899–1946) received a traditional education and subsequently attended Tsinghua University. From 1922 to 1925 he lived in the United States, where he studied painting. In Chicago he met several outstanding modern American poets, but his taste in poetry leaned more toward Keats and Li Shangyin. He won fame as a modern Chinese poet with two collections: *Hongzhu* (The red candle, 1923) and *Sishui* (Dead water, 1927). Wen Yiduo rejected Hu Shi's plea for the use of natural rhythms in poetry. Instead, he wrote poems with prominent rhyme and metrical structure which have been admired by generations of Chinese readers. The poems in *Sishui* reflect the author's public and private sorrow, sorrow over China's economic and political weakness and sorrow over the death of his young daughter. The author is clearly tormented by the clash between his romantic sensibility and his Confucian sense of duty.

After 1927 Wen Yiduo devoted much time to the study of classical Chinese literature, becoming a recognized authority on the *Chuci*, among other things. He taught at a number of universities; during the Sino-Japanese war he was professor of Chinese literature at Southwestern United University in Kunming. His political activities brought him into conflict with the Guomindang regime, and he was assassinated in 1946.

Xu Zhimo

Xu Zhimo (1897–1931) has sometimes been called the greatest modern Chinese poet. Born into a family of bankers, he was spared the financial problems that beset most modern Chinese writers. He was a favorite pupil of Liang Qichao, who inspired him to strive to play a prominent role in the building of a strong modern China. In 1918 he went to America; at first he planned to study economics, but he soon discovered a much stronger interest in literature. In 1920 he went to Cambridge, England, returning to China in 1922.

Xu Zhimo was a great admirer of the nineteenth-century Romantic poets, and in 1924 he accompanied Tagore on a tour of China. From 1924 to 1931 he taught at several universities, visiting Europe again in 1925 and 1928. From 1925 to 1927, while living in Peking, he worked together with Wen Yiduo on various literary projects including the monthly *Xinyue yuekan* (Crescent monthly).

Xu Zhimo's romanticism was not limited to his writings. In his personal life, too, he tried to live by his ideals. Divorcing the wife his family had selected for him, he continued to maintain friendly relations with her—a highly unconventional situation in those days. A stormy affair with the wife of a highly placed army officer was followed by her divorce and remarriage to Xu Zhimo. Xu's diary of their sensational affair was published in 1937. Xu

Zhimo's penchant for flying proved fatal: he died in an airplane crash. Xu Zhimo's most lastingly famous verses are short love poems. Like Wen Yiduo, he experimented with new strophic forms. His poems were published in four volumes between 1925 and 1932.

Feng Zhi

While some poets worked at developing new forms for *baihua* poetry, others adapted Western verse forms. The most famous modern Chinese practitioner of the sonnet is Feng Zhi (1906-1993). In the late twenties Feng Zhi published two volumes featuring, like the works of Wen Yiduo and Xu Zhimo, much use of strophic forms. Besides the short verses which gave voice to his despair and loneliness, he wrote long narrative poems based on traditional legends. His experiences in Harbin in 1927 inspired him to write the long sequence *Beiyou* (The journey to the North).

From 1930 to 1935 Feng Zhi studied German literature at Berlin and Heidelberg. He translated various works, including Rilke's sonnets. His own famous cycle of twenty-seven sonnets dates from 1941, when he was teaching at Southwestern United University in Kunming. Feng's sonnets show subtle variation as to line length and rhyme schemes. Owing to their contemplative tone, Feng has sometimes been called a "metaphysical" poet. After 1949 Feng Zhi wrote short patriotic poems.

As we have seen, the 1920s produced wide-ranging experiments in poetry varying from the total abandonment of forms to the invention of new forms suitable for use in *baihua*. These efforts were followed by a period of increased interest in the highly personal use of imagery, but the technical accomplishments of the early experimenters, and the respect accorded to poetic form, remained important influences. Other new influences came from French Symbolism and Anglo-American Imagism, though many poets' experiments were guided not so much by any particular school as by a natural tendency to rebel against the failure of their predecessors to break convincingly with traditional Chinese imagery. Their unusual images and often illogical associations earned for some of the newer poets the reputation of being obscure. This was true, for example, of Li Jinfa (1900–1976), the first Chinese Symbolist, who published three collections of poetry in the mid-twenties; at the time they were virtually ignored.

Poets of the Thirties and Forties

The most famous Symbolist of the pre-World War II period is undoubtedly Dai Wangshu (1905-1950). Dai had already written some Symbolist poems—more melodious and accessible than those of Li Jinfa—before he went to Europe in 1932. After a stay in France and Spain he returned to China. In 1938 he fled to Hong Kong to evade the Japanese. When Hong Kong fell, Dai Wangshu was imprisoned for a number of months. This experience broke his health, and he died young of a lung ailment. His poetry continues to be admired for the elusive quality which Kai-yu Hsu once described as the "finesse of his thought and sentiment."

Zang Kejia (1905-) published his first collection in 1934. As befitted a former pupil of Wen Yiduo, he paid much attention to the formal qualities of his poems, which were built on an unusually successful combination of social concern and technical virtuosity. From the first, patriotism was prominent in his poems; memorable verses record his indignation over the Japanese occupation of Manchuria and his sympathy for the countless dispossessed Chinese.

Bian Zhilin (1910-) published his first volume in 1933, but he became truly famous after the appearance of the collections *Yumu ji* (Fish eyes, 1935) and *Hanyuan ji* (The Han garden, 1936); the latter was a collaboration with He Qifang (1912-1977) and Li Guangtian (1906-1968). Bian's poems on Peking street scenes, like much of the rest of his pre-World War II poetry, are characterized by a subtle, technically refined synthesis of Chinese and Western (especially Symbolist) elements. Like Feng Zhi's, his poetry has a meditative quality. During World War II he wrote patriotic poems; since 1949 his most important new works have been translations, including a very successful verse translation of *Hamlet* (1957).

In the 1930s He Qifang wrote refined and intimate lyrics as well as prose poems which were very well received. During the war years he went to Yan'an, where he found it difficult to combine his earlier attitude toward writing with the new demands of living in a Communist society. In Yan'an he taught at the Lu Xun Academy, and after 1942 he emerged as a staunch defender of Mao Zedong's notions of the social role of literature.

Ai Qing (pseud. of Jiang Haicheng, 1910-1996) was a leading exponent of the free-verse form. Upon his return from France in 1932 he was immediately imprisoned for three years for his "dangerous ideas." His first book of poetry, *Dayanhe*, which appeared in 1936, was full of memories of his youth. The gulf between rich and poor served as a dramatic backdrop to the fate of his nurse, Dayanhe. Ai Qing went to Yan'an at an early date. His descriptions of the North Chinese countryside have remained famous. Together with Ding Ling's, his criticisms of the Party occasioned the convocation of the famous

Yan'an Forum on Literature and Art in 1942. The many poems he wrote after that event (and after 1949) have not, on the whole, been as well received as his earlier work. After being made a prime target of criticism in 1957, he spent many years in prison camps. He was rehabilitated in 1978 and has often been called the greatest poet of the People's Republic of China.

The poet Tian Jian (pseud. of Tong Tianjian, 1916–1985) started publishing in 1932. His long patriotic poems with extremely short lines, meant to be read "on the streetcorners," made quite a stir in the late 1930s. Tian Jian's work was clearly influenced by the Russian poet Mayakovsky.

THE "TALKING DRAMA"

Any discussion of the modern Chinese theater in the twentieth century should begin with a reminder of the continuing popularity and vitality of traditional-style Chinese drama in its various forms. These traditional forms have not been averse to adopting technical devices from the modern drama, such as sets, lighting, and the use of a curtain. Some traditional drama forms even adopted Western musical instruments and melodies. Traditional-style regional drama forms have continued to develop in the twentieth century. The specifically modern drama is called in Chinese *huaju* (talking drama) because the text is spoken, not sung, and there is no musical accompaniment.

The modern Chinese drama was originally modeled on late nineteenth-century European theater. This period occupies an extreme position within the Western tradition on account of its pronounced realism: the effort to reproduce on stage the exact details of language, gesture, costume, and decor as they would be found in real life. The playwrights most influential on the early Chinese modern drama were Ibsen and Shaw. The late nineteenth-century social problems with which these authors were concerned were easily recognizable to modern Chinese audiences.

The first experiments with *huaju* antedate the Literary Revolution by some ten years: in 1905 a group of Chinese students in Tokyo performed a translation of a stage adaptation of the novel *La dame aux camélias* by A. Dumas *fils*. It was followed in 1907 by a stage version of *Uncle Tom's Cabin*. After the revolution of 1911, *huaju* on revolutionary subjects, called *wenmingxi* (enlightenment theater), were briefly popular in the larger cities. The same period saw short-lived attempts to introduce far-reaching changes in the Peking opera.

Tian Han and Ouyang Yuqian

The May Fourth Movement was followed by a new wave of interest in *huaju*. Its leading exponents were Tian Han and Ouyang Yuqian, both of whom were directors and actors as well as playwrights. Tian Han (1898–1968) came from Changsha. He studied in Japan, where he became friends with Guo Moruo and Yu Dafu. After his return to China in 1921, he worked in Shanghai, where he became a versatile champion of modern literature, especially the theater. He wrote many plays; the earliest may be described as romantically pessimist, while his works of the 1930s show a stronger interest in patriotism and the necessity of social change. Tian Han also taught at various institutions, led his own theater troupe, and collaborated on various films; at one time he was head of a cinema company.

Tian Han was frequently at loggerheads with the political authorities, and in the spring of 1932 he was briefly imprisoned. He spent most of World War II in Guilin, where he worked on modifications to the traditional Peking opera; his version of the story of the White Snake (*Baishe zhuan*) was especially popular. After the war he returned to Shanghai. He filled various important posts in the People's Republic. He continued to write plays, including *Guan Hanqing* (1960), which tells the story of how that famous *zaju* author came to write his *Dou E yuan*. During the Cultural Revolution Tian Han was sharply attacked, and he died in prison in 1968. In the late 1970s, however, his *Baishe zhuan* was once again performed in Peking.

Ouyang Yuqian (1889–1962) was born to a prominent family of officials. He studied in Tokyo from 1901 to 1911 and was one of the Chinese students who staged *Uncle Tom's Cabin* in 1907. After his return to China, he played female roles in *wenmingxi* and later also in the Peking opera. In the 1920s he was also active in the *huaju* field, and for a while he collaborated with Tian Han. He spent the war years in Guilin. Ouyang Yuqian wrote various *huaju* and a screenplay (the latter based on the legend of Mulan, the girl who dresses as a man and goes in her father's place when he is called up for military service), but he was more important as an actor, director and teacher.

The same can probably be said of Hong Shen (1894–1955), who published the first of his own *huaju* in the 1930s, and of Xia Yan (pseud. of Shen Duanxian, 1900–1995). The physicist Ding Xilin (1893–1974) became famous for the humorous one-acters which he wrote between 1923 and 1939.

Cao Yu

Undoubtedly the most important *huaju* writer of this period is Cao Yu (pseudonym of Wan Jiabao, 1910–). Cao Yu was born to a well-to-do family and studied at Tsinghua University. His first play, *Leiyu* (Thunderstorm), was performed in 1935 under the direction of Ouyang Yuqian and Hong Shen; it was a great success throughout China.

Leiyu has an extremely involved plot: a rich young man tries to put an end to his clandestine love affair with his stepmother, since he has meanwhile embarked on a relationship with a servant girl who will eventually turn out to be his half-sister. The ending is tragic; the girl and a younger brother both die, the young man himself commits suicide, and the stepmother goes insane. The play takes its name from the thunderstorm that comes up during the denouement. *Leiyu* embodies two themes which often recur in Cao Yu's later works: the power that money confers and the suffocating effects of traditional morality.

The dehumanizing tendency of money is one of the themes of Cao Yu's second play, *Richu* (Sunrise, 1935), which is set mainly in a luxurious hotel/bordello in Tianjin. The main character is an expensive prostitute; in the end, having realized to the full what miserable circles she moves in, she commits suicide. The 1940 *Beijing ren* (Peking man) shows how an arranged marriage has ruined the life of the main character, a member of an impoverished gentry family in Peking. In 1941 Cao Yu also adapted Ba Jin's novel *Jia* for the stage. His later plays lack the psychological depth of his early works.

While the *huaju*, thanks partly to the success of Cao Yu's works, was gaining some popularity among modern intellectuals in the larger cities, various political movements, including the Communist Party, experimented for propaganda purposes with such simple theater forms as "live newspapers." The traditional theater forms, which were sure to succeed with rural audiences, were also much used for propaganda ends.

THE ESSAY

Zhou Zuoren

In addition to their stories, novels, poems, and plays, nearly all modern Chinese writers have written essays in which they elaborate upon their literary work or present their views on contemporary problems. In the case of Lu Xun, to name one, the essays actually make up the main bulk of the oeuvre. Lu Xun's *zawen* (short, often satirical essays on current subjects) were read by a vast audience and were often imitated by other writers.

One writer whose fame rests primarily on his essays is Lu Xun's younger brother Zhou Zuoren (1885–1966). Like Lu Xun, Zhou Zuoren studied in Japan (from 1906 to 1911), where he devoted his time to literary pursuits almost from the beginning. In 1917 he followed Lu Xun to Peking, where he was to teach at a number of institutions of higher education. At first he shared Lu Xun's attitudes; in the early 1920s he was one of the most vocal spokesmen for modern literature and enjoyed special distinction for his exceptional knowledge of foreign literatures, ranging from modern Japanese to ancient Greek. Later, in sharp contrast to Lu Xun, he came around to an apolitical stance, favoring a sort of enlightened Confucianism. In 1937 he remained in Peking, eventually accepting a post in the regime installed by the Japanese. After World War II he was sentenced to fifteen years in prison (of which he actually served four) for collaboration. After 1949 he published memoirs on Lu Xun. His essays are admired for their clear, uncomplicated style.

Other Essayists

In the 1920s Lin Yutang (1895–1976) wrote numerous articles in the magazine *Yu si* (Threads of talk), with which the names of Lu Xun and Zhou Zuoren were prominently associated. From 1932 to 1935 he edited his own magazine, *Lunyu banyuekan* (Analects fortnightly), which featured, among other things, familiar essays. The lively and often humorous essays of Lin and his colleagues in this period were partly inspired by the great English essayists; at the same time there was a certain conscious throwback to the traditional *xiaopin* of Ming times. Lin Yutang wrote in a sophisticated prose style and enjoyed considerable success for a while. In the long run, however, his approach proved to be at variance with the times. Often sarcastically critical of traditional Chinese ways, he was no less averse to the modern Left with its demand for *engagement.* After the encouraging success of his English-language *My Country and My People* (1935), he went to live in America and published numerous books in English, including translations from the Chinese classics. His publications continued to appear in Chinese as well, but his foreign residence contributed to his image as a rather marginal figure in the ongoing developments. In recent years there has been a revival of interest in this important twentieth-century writer.

Zhu Ziqing (1898–1948), who was also a noted poet in the early May Fourth period, was a member of the Society for the Study of Literature in the 1920s. Besides essays in literary criticism, he wrote numerous personal essays and travel sketches. At a time when the new vernacular prose was plagued with growing pains, Zhu Ziqing was praised for his smooth, expressive style. Some of his essays were generally recognized as models of good *baihua* prose and have continued to be studied by generations of high-school students.

Though most famous as a poet, Xu Zhimo also wrote essays that have remained popular. He Qifang, too, achieved real fame as a writer of poetic prose. His collection *Huamenglu* (Sketches of dreams) was warmly welcomed on its appearance in 1936; some of the pieces became anthology favorites.

In the 1920s the literary critic, translator, and familiar essayist Liang Shiqiu (1902–1987) was one of the leading opponents of leftist views on literature, but he was also a spokesman for a frankly individualist and romantic approach. Like Hu Shi and Xu Zhimo, Liang belonged to the Crescent Moon Society. He translated and introduced numerous works of English literature; partly under the influence of the American scholar and critic Irving Babbitt, he concentrated on recognized masterpieces rather than on ephemeral present-day movements. After 1949 Liang Shiqiu went to Taiwan, where he continued to be productive as a teacher, translator, and essayist.

Aside from essayistic prose in a narrow sense, the 1930s saw the rise of the reportage as a distinct prose genre, though it was often difficult to distinguish formally from the essay (which often deals with subjects just as factual) or the short story (which sometimes amounts to a thinly fictionalized presentation of real events). The liveliness and everyday relevance of these "reports" gave them a wide readership. Many famous writers have contributed to the genre. After the founding of the People's Republic, "reportage literature" (*baogao wenxue*) was at times in the foreground of literary interest.

Chapter 28.
MODERN LITERATURE: 1942–1990

LITERARY LIFE IN THE "LIBERATED AREAS"

After the Xi'an Incident of December 1936, the Nationalist Government and the Communist Party formed a new United Front, this time directed against Japanese aggression. This made it easier for many Chinese writers who had fled from the East Chinese cities to go to the Communist base area in Shaanxi with its capital at Yan'an. In their new environment many of them continued to be active writers, seeking to contribute in their own way to the war effort. Though many of the writers who went to Yan'an regarded the Guomindang regime as corrupt and ineffective, they were by no means all convinced Communists who uncritically accepted all features of what they saw happening around them in Yan'an. For example, despite the general atmosphere of shared poverty and deprivation, hierarchical differences in lifestyle continued to exist, and women were often obviously subjected to discrimination.

In spring 1942 a number of leading authors including Ding Ling and Ai Qing published articles attacking the Communist Party's policies. The Party responded by convening a Forum on Literature and Art in Yan'an in summer of the same year. Mao Zedong's opening and concluding talks at the Forum formed the basis of the Party's approach to literary and cultural matters for decades to come, though the official interpretation was not the same in all periods.

Mao based his ideas on the Party's experiences on the propaganda front. He stipulated that literary work was to be regarded as an integral component of the Party's propaganda effort. All literature was inseparably associated with the standpoint of a given class, so writers who intended to serve the proletarian cause should follow the guidelines laid down by the Communist Party, the leading organization of the proletariat. Since many writers came from petit-bourgeois backgrounds, they must be re-educated to the proletarian standpoint. And because the audience for literature consisted of workers, peasants, and soldiers, authors must write about their experiences in a way that would be recognizable and attractive to workers, peasants, and soldiers. Wherever possible, they were to clothe the revolutionary message in time-honored popular forms to which the masses could easily respond; Mao sharply condemned blind imitation of Western forms and themes. The task of literature was to make the workers, peasants, and soldiers conscious of their present situation, to point the way to a better future under Communist leadership, and to hold up positive models of desirable conduct.

Needless to say, before 1949 Mao's talks were an effective guideline only within the so-called "liberated areas," and even there the unstable situation often made full implementation difficult. Nevertheless, such writers as Ding Ling, Ai Qing and He Qifang did try to write in accordance with the guidelines. One of the first successful applications of a traditional popular genre for revolutionary purposes was the drama *Baimao nü* (The white-haired girl), originally dating from 1944 but later frequently revised, by He Jingzhi (1924–) and Ding Yi (1921–). *Baimao nü* is a modern revolutionary legend: a tenant farmer's daughter is forced into slavery to a landowner when her father can no longer pay his rent. After being raped by the landowner, she runs away to live in a cave with her child; lack of sunlight turns her hair white. For a while she lives on offerings brought to her by the terrified peasants, who take her for a ghost. In the end she is saved by the Red Army, the landowner is punished, and her hair turns black again. The play employs the traditional elements of music and song, and it enjoyed great popularity.

In poetry, attempts were made to put the performance-text tradition to new use. The most famous example is the long narrative poem *Wang Gui yu Li Xiangxiang* (Wang Gui and Li Xiangxiang) by Li Ji (1921–1980), in which the farmhand Wang Gui joins the guerrillas and succeeds in marrying Xiangxiang, a tenant's daughter, after the landowner is expelled from the village. The text is in the form of *xuntian you* (spontaneous rambling), a North Chinese folk-song form in which a story is told in rhymed couplets of varying length, the story line being interspersed with images taken from nature.

The best-known novelist to emerge in these years was Zhao Shuli (1906–1970). A native of Shanxi, he worked for a few years in Taiyuan before joining the Red Army in 1939. His stories (the first was written in 1943) were meant to be read aloud. His first novel, *Lijia zhuangde bianqian* (The transformation of Lijiazhuang Village) dates from 1946; it details the changes in a Shanxi village between 1928 and 1946. Zhao Shuli worked on his novel *Sanliwan* from 1953 to 1955; it describes the land reform and the organization of agricultural cooperatives in the village of the same name. Zhao's novels are stylistically reminiscent of the traditional Chinese novel. During the Cultural Revolution he was strongly criticized, and he died under unclear circumstances.

LITERARY LIFE IN THE PEOPLE'S REPUBLIC OF CHINA
BEFORE 1978

Official Policy

In 1949 a national writers' union was formed, and practically all important writers became members. From that moment on the Party's standards were applicable to all literary publications. Writers were required to undergo re-education in various forms—studying Marxism, actually participating in land reform, contributing labor to the mammoth construction projects. The idea was that "cultural workers" should have first-hand experience of the life led by the masses. Favorite themes in the 1950s (and later) included episodes from early Party history, guerrilla warfare during and after the Japanese occupation, land reform, and the ongoing process of "socialist construction."

From 1949 to 1966 the leading spokesman for the Party's official line was the vice director of the Propaganda Department, Zhou Yang (1908–1989). Zhou Yang had collaborated with Lu Xun in the 1930s and been active in Yan'an starting in 1937. The party line was by no means constant. In the early years, literary works were required to embody "socialist realism," but in 1958 the demand was changed to "the combination of revolutionary realism and revolutionary romanticism." There was an ongoing discussion on the portrayal of "in-between characters": those who were neither bad (reactionary) nor good (revolutionary), but vacillated before coming to a final decision. The in-between character was often a petit-bourgeois intellectual dangling somewhere between proletarian heroes and capitalist villains. In the 1960s the in-between character was banished from the scene, and discussion shifted to the proper technique of depicting heroes and villains. The critic Yao Wenyuan (1931–), who was strongly supported by Mao's wife Jiang Qing (1910–1991), took an extreme position: absolute black and white contrast was to be employed.

During the Cultural Revolution this became the official Party position, and practically all literature written in the preceding years was rejected. This extreme standpoint was not really abandoned until the fall of the Gang of Four in 1976 and the gradual rehabilitation of leaders, such as Zhou Yang, who had been deposed during the Cultural Revolution. The late 1970s saw a return to something more like the 1950s position. At times when the prevailing climate was especially "leftist" (e.g., the 1958–1959 Great Leap Forward and the Cultural Revolution), the importance of professional writers declined while amateur writers from among "the masses" were brought to the fore.

Persecution of Writers

The formulation of the Communist Party's policies on literature and the arts cannot be understood without reference to personal rivalries and power struggles within the Party leadership. In the many cases of conflict between authors and the Party, it is often misleading to conclude that no more was at stake than a simple conflict between art and propaganda. Many writers had become Party members even before the founding of the PRC, and their long-standing personal quarrels with other Party members were often decisive. Rivalry of this kind seems to have played a role in the first great clash between the Party and writers: the campaign against Hu Feng.

Hu Feng (pseudonym of Zhang Gufei, 1902–1985) had studied in Japan from 1928 to 1933. After returning to China he worked as a writer and editor in Shanghai, where he became one of Lu Xun's most important disciples. During World War II he worked for the Party in the Guomindang-ruled area. After 1949 he came into conflict with Party authorities, a basic problem being his continued championing of the importance of the individual element in literature. In 1955, after an intensive criticism campaign, he was expelled from the Party and imprisoned; he was not released until 1965.

In 1957, in the context of the Anti-Rightist campaign, Ding Ling and Ai Qing (among others) were made targets of criticism; during the Hundred Flowers campaign of the previous year they had protested against the strict control under which they were required to work.

After the outbreak of the Cultural Revolution in 1966, practically all established writers came under fire; very many were beaten, tortured, and otherwise maltreated by the Red Guards. Not a few died in prison (Tian Han, Zhao Shuli) or committed suicide (Lao She). Ironically, practically none of them had ever voiced substantial criticism of the regime, and most had made real efforts to conform to the ever-shifting dictates of official policy. After 1978 the long list of rehabilitated writers included not only Cultural Revolution victims but also those who had fallen on hard times in the 1950s, such as Ding Ling and Ai Qing.

New Novelists

Though a number of writers who had already become famous before World War II continued to publish in the late 1950s and early 1960s, the literary podium was dominated by newer writers. Prominent novelists included Zhou Libo, Yang Mo and Hao Ran. Zhou Libo (1908–1979) worked in Shanghai from 1927 on. From 1932 to 1934 he was imprisoned by the

Guomindang, and he spent the war years in Yan'an. Though Zhou Libo also wrote short stories, he became most famous as the author of three novels: *Baofeng zhouyu* (Rainstorm, 1949), which deals with land reform in North China; *Tieshui benliu* (Torrent of smolten iron, 1955), which describes the reconstruction of China's industry; and *Shanxiang jubian* (Big changes in a mountain village, 1958-1960), on the collectivization of agriculture.

Yang Mo (1914-) owed her fame to the novel *Qingchun zhi ge* (The song of youth, 1958), which describes the process by which young intellectuals developed into revolutionaries in the 1930s. The novel was heavily criticized in 1959, and a revised version appeared the following year.

Hao Ran (pseudonym of Liang Jinguang) was born in 1932 to a poor peasant family on the outskirts of Peking. From the age of sixteen he was a Party member and a soldier. In the 1950s he worked as a journalist and published several collections of short stories. His first novel, *Yanyang tian* (Sunny skies) appeared in 1964-1966; its subject is the land reform and the organization of the mutual aid teams. Hao Ran was one of the few writers who were not criticized during the Cultural Revolution. *Jinguang dadao* (The golden road, 1972-1974), his next novel, is also about land reform and collectivization.

Modern and Traditional Drama

In the 1950s, the main accent in drama was on the reform of traditional theater, which continued to attract a much wider audience than the *huaju*. The classical repertoire was subjected to a rigorous process of selection, and the surviving plays were often rewritten to rid them of "feudal dregs." New plays were also written in traditional genres. Efforts were made to promote *huaju*, sometimes by writing plays on historical subjects (so that colorful traditional costumes could be used) and by injecting songs. An example of these newer *huaju* is Tian Han's *Guan Hanqing* (1960), on the great thirteenth-century dramatist of the same name. The same approach was used in Wu Han's (1909-1969) *Hai Rui ba guan* (Hai Rui dismissed from office, 1961), in which the main character, the able official Hai Rui of Ming times, calls the emperor's attention to current social ills. Yao Wenyuan and his associates took this play to be a thinly veiled defense of Marshal Peng Dehuai, who had been dismissed in 1959, and hence as an attack on Mao Zedong.

The publication of Yao's criticism of Wu Han unleashed a storm of controversy that became a precipitating factor in the Cultural Revolution. Since 1964 Jiang Qing and Yao Wenyuan had fervently promoted "modern revolutionary Peking opera"—that is, plays which made use of the traditional music and acting techniques of Peking opera, but which dealt with more recent subjects (such as episodes from the Sino-Japanese war or the civil war of 1946–1949), and in which the costumes and decor were contemporary and realistic. A small number of these plays (the so-called model operas, which were repeatedly rewritten to make the heroes still more positive and the villains still more dastardly) were the only plays tolerated during the Cultural Revolution.

LITERARY LIFE IN THE PEOPLE'S REPUBLIC OF CHINA SINCE 1978

In literature, as in so many other areas of Chinese life, the thirteen-year span from the death of Mao Zedong in 1976 to the June Fourth Incident of 1989 was a period of bewildering innovation, experiment, adventure—and ambivalence. In contrast to the preceding Cultural Revolution or "ten years of calamity," this seemed to many observers, both within and outside China, to be the long-awaited turning point at which political policies and social structures originating in the Mao era would finally cease to determine the face of Chinese life. In the cultural sphere, throughout most of this period indications seemed overwhelming that a new scene for Chinese literature and art was in the making, one which would be vastly more liberal, modern, and cosmopolitan than anything previously seen in the PRC, yet by that very fact also more amenable to rapprochement with traditional Chinese culture.

Just how naive those expectations were became evident in the summer of 1989. In retrospect it was clear that the voices of repression and reaction never ceased to speak out strongly. Hopeful as the new cosmopolitan cultural developments seemed to foreign observers, and to the very small minority of People's Republic citizens who were in a position to appreciate them, they were marginal in comparison to what remained the primary governing factor in Chinese life—namely, the enforcement of political and social complaisance.

As this volume is intended to be a general overview of Chinese literature from its earliest beginnings, the authors feel it would be disproportionate to discuss this newest period in much detail. In any case, too little time has elapsed for the most recent writers and trends to prove their lasting importance. Classification and evaluation are hazardous at best, and we will attempt no more than to indicate what seem from this vantage point—1994—to have been some of the most significant developments.

One of the salient features of this period is the almost unimaginable haste with which the modern, modernist, and post-modern culture of Europe and the Americas was introduced to, and to some extent assimilated by, Chinese writers and readers. As recently as the late 1970s, virtually all of post-World War I Western culture was still considered unsuitable for the Chinese public. Even university textbooks of Western literature did not venture much beyond the nineteenth century. And even without reference to foreign culture, prevailing levels of general education were breathtakingly poor. The disruptions of the Cultural Revolution period had made it impossible for many Chinese citizens even to receive an adequate school education, let alone to attend a university. To this fact should be added the ubiquitous influence of an officially favored style of written Chinese, heavily influenced by literal translations of Marxist classics, which deviated on innumerable points from what would traditionally have been considered correct or attractive modern Chinese. This idiom, the so-called *Mao wen ti* (Mao style), has been experienced by numerous Chinese writers as a formidable obstacle to their own development of an expressive, authentic style. These two factors— inadequate schooling and the dearth of acceptable stylistic models—have weighed so heavily that many present-day Chinese writers have been, of necessity, virtually self-taught in all matters linguistic and artistic.

These were hardly optimal conditions in which to take on the works of Kafka, Sartre, Beckett, Borges, Marquez, and Vargas Llosa. Still another complicating factor is that "Western" or "modernist" literature itself is not at all the homogenous, neatly classifiable entity Chinese critics often seemed to want to make of it. The steadily advancing cultural diversification of the non-Chinese world, in which the boundaries between more and less significant art forms seemed increasingly elusive, was difficult enough even for well-educated post-modern readers to understand. For Chinese writers and intellectuals in the PRC, it has often been next to impossible to go beyond a mere name-dropping level of acquaintance with these new cultural factors.

As if all these difficulties were not enough, proper appreciation of the emerging new Chinese literature was made still more difficult by the continuing tendency of Chinese critics to evaluate literary works on the basis of their "national" importance. At the same time that Chinese writers were struggling to assimilate cosmopolitan features that were by definition incompatible with traditional ideas of nationality, they often had to justify themselves by claiming that their work embodied a supposed "Chinese" essence whose nature was not easily defined. Even very sophisticated Chinese readers who had not grown up under the Mao regime were unfortunately prone to demand of the new literature an identifiable "Chineseness," apparently forgetting that any such parochial focus was, by international standards, blatantly incompatible with the whole tenor of the "modern."

Inside the PRC, the climate of discussion was such that many terms were used (or bandied about) in senses different from their meaning in ordinary international usage. Chinese critics often seemed to use the word "modernist" to refer almost to the entire body of twentieth-century world literature, whereas scholars in the West typically confined its application to a much narrower corpus. What was referred to in the PRC as "stream of consciousness" often lacked the elements of irrationality and preverbal associativeness with which Western readers had been familiar since the days of such writers as Joyce and Woolf. "Surrealism," too, often seemed to be used in slapdash fashion to condemn whatever the particular critic felt to be disconcertingly complex.

Allegations of "influence" were often made for the wrong reasons: to say that a given writer was "influenced by Latin American Magical Realism" was often no more than a cheap and defensive way of playing down what might really have been a significant new development in the Chinese context. On the other hand, it was undeniably true that many Chinese writers were disproportionately obsessed with technical experiment, and their work often showed signs of overly hasty study of and borrowing from famous world writers or the works of currently popular theoreticians. The assessment of the literary merit of their efforts remains difficult at this short distance in time.

The first clearly "new" literature to emerge after the Cultural Revolution was the so-called "scars literature" of 1977–1978. These stories were about the personal suffering of individuals who had been persecuted, physically or psychically maltreated, or deprived of their rights during the Cultural Revolution. Starting in about 1979, a second wave of new fiction appeared. Called by such various names as "literature of disclosure," "the New Realism," etc., it went beyond the 1966–1976 period to deal with sociopolitical excesses, corruption within Party ranks, glaring inequalities, and other social problems in both earlier and later periods of PRC history. A prominent and controversial theme in this newer literature was individual love—an area in which individuals' personal and emotional priorities could easily clash with collective norms and responsibilities.

This period witnessed the rehabilitation of many writers who had been removed from the literary arena for political reasons. This was true not only of post-1949 authors but of many older writers, such as Ai Qing, Ding Ling, and Ba Jin. At the same time renewed attention was given to writers of a somewhat earlier period who had been prematurely swept to the sidelines in the turbulent intervening decades. Among these were the poets of the "Nine Leaves" group (named after a famous anthology of their poetry), who had written outstanding poetry in the 1940s. In particular, two women poets of this group won renewed recognition in the 1980s: Chen Jingrong (1917–1989) and Zheng Min (1920–). Though their intimate tone often encouraged critics to use the facile designation "feminine" for both these poets, their poetry had a sophisticated, wide-ranging, contemplative quality that was refreshing to post-Cultural Revolution readers.

Wang Meng, born in 1934, had been a promising fiction writer in the 1950s. Condemned as a "rightist element" in 1957, he had disappeared from view for many years. In 1978 he reappeared and came increasingly to be regarded as one of the foremost story writers of the day. Though he made use of fictional techniques that were said to be "advanced" (such as stream of consciousness), he took a conservative stance on many contemporary issues and for a while served as minister of culture.

In 1978–1979, a daring samizdat literature began to appear in the PRC. These publications were often associated with the Democracy Movement of those years. Writers whose work appeared in these channels included a number of young poets who would go on to national fame in the 1980s. The samizdat magazine *Jintian* (Today) published works by such poets as Mang Ke (pseudonym of Jiang Shiwei, 1950–), Bei Dao (pseudonym of Zhao Zhenkai, 1949–), and Gu Cheng (1956–1993). The experimental poetry of these writers, which attempted to break with standard themes and with the linguistic clichés of the Mao style, was quickly branded *menglong shi* ("obscure" or "misty" poetry). Their work represented an early breakthrough in the struggle for a more effective modern literary *language*—and did not fail to draw fire from establishment critics.

The search for a new language of expression quickly spread into fiction. In the mid-1980s there emerged a new type of fiction called *xungen* (roots-searching). *Xungen* writers, rather than focusing exclusively on critical-realist treatment of recent social problems, went back to explore language, settings, and perennial themes characteristic of pre-Maoist phases of Chinese culture. They seldom wrote from an ideological stance; instead, their writing was full of lively anecdotes and timeless human vignettes. Their interest in a broader, often regionally colored palette went hand in hand with renewed appreciation of Shen Congwen and his works. One of the best-received writers of this school, Han Shaogong (1953–), followed in Shen's footsteps by writing stories set in Hunan. A Cheng (pseudonym of Zhong Acheng, 1949–), though himself from Peking, also wrote stories set in the Southwest. The Tibetan Zhaxi Dawa (1959–) gave new foregrounding to traditional religious ideas and practices.

Though critics in the PRC often regarded *xungen* fiction as important primarily for its thematic extension beyond the prevailing scope of realist fiction, practicing writers were more technically impressed by the richer, livelier prose that was developing. Meanwhile, realist writing in the form of reportage literature (*baogao wenxue*) continued to compete for readers' favor. Undoubtedly the most famous reportage writer was Liu Binyan (1925–). In the 1950s, after publishing several incisive exposures of Party malpractice, he was condemned as a rightist. After long years of labor reform and enforced silence, he was finally rehabilitated in 1979. His long reportage *Renyao zhijian* (People or monsters?) became a nationwide sensation after its publication in 1979. A writer of great boldness and integrity, Liu was expelled from the Chinese Communist Party in 1987 and subsequently went to live abroad.

As the decade proceeded, still newer types of fiction emerged that were far more innovative in content, form, and language. In this experimental writing, the plot element often became disjointed or even nonexistent, while intense attention was given to exploring and exploiting the suggestive possibilities of language and of the internal rhythm and flow of the narration itself. Setting, character, and incident (to the extent they still recognizably existed) were often no longer specifically "Chinese" as writers sought to address themselves to the human condition in general. Ma Yuan (1953–) was often cited as a gifted and ground-breaking "experimental" writer. Mo Yan (pseudonym of Guan Moye, 1956–), though he is difficult to characterize, was much admired and gained international recognition when two of his stories were adapted for Zhang Yimou's film *The Red Sorghum*. Can Xue (pseudonym of Deng Xiaohua, 1953–) writes what is sometimes called *guai xiaoshuo* (fiction of the bizarre or uncanny); her evocation of dream- or nightmare-like realities has invited comparison with Kafka. Other prominent experimental writers included Yu Hua (1960–), Su Tong (pseudonym of Tong Zhonggui, 1963–) and Ge Fei (1964–). Though Western observers tended to hail the new experimental fiction as a welcome advance, in the PRC it was strongly criticized for its defiance of established conventions regarding theme, characterization, and plot.

CHINESE LITERATURE IN TAIWAN SINCE 1949

A remarkable body of modern Chinese literature has been written and published in Taiwan since 1949. Though this stream is much more thematically varied than the literature of the PRC and shows much more technical affinity with modern Western literature, until very recently it has been largely ignored in the West. The reasons for this have been largely extraliterary; some of the most obvious are:

1) the more spectacular political developments in the PRC, together with the tendency of Western countries to pay more urgent attention to their often troubled relations with the Peking regime;

2) the strong traditional identification of the Chinese language with "China" as a political and national entity, and the consequent tendency on

both sides of the Taiwan Strait to regard literary works as important to the extent that they seemed relevant to politics;

3) the reluctance of certain Sinologists to take seriously as "Chinese" the cultural products of Taiwan under Nationalist rule; and

4) the difficulty felt by even sympathetic readers in attempting to place Taiwan literature, since many of the leading authors described themselves as exiles or have actually taken up permanent residence in Western countries.

It is clear that post-1949 Taiwan literature must be included in any meaningful discussion of modern Chinese literature, not only as a curious appendage to the PRC but as a fully competent, cosmopolitan, and creative body of literature which for decades has sought, and perhaps in some cases already found, possible solutions for the difficulties faced by Chinese writers vis-à-vis world literature. Owing precisely to their isolation from the Chinese mainland, writers in Taiwan were forced to make lightning adjustments to economic and social modernization. Unlike the situation in the PRC, Western cultural influences were a prominent factor. At the same time, the traditional Chinese cultural heritage, though much more assiduously studied than in the PRC in most periods, was subjected to searching criticism in the light of an emerging new era. The styles of written Chinese practiced by Taiwan authors, though often so strongly influenced by the classical tradition as to have a distinctly quaint ring in young mainlanders' ears, have also been enriched by the influx of new international vocabulary, often via English. But the autochtonous Hokkien vernacular, too, inexorably made inroads on the accepted "standard" Mandarin. (The increasing influence, linguistic and otherwise, of the indigenous tradition has been especially marked in very recent years, and there has been an upsurge of interest in pre-1949 Taiwanese writers.)

Fictional Prose in Taiwan

The fundamental backdrop to the development of new literature on Taiwan in the 1950s was the Guomindang regime's absolute rejection of all things even indirectly suggestive of Communism. Much of the modern literature of the 1920s and 1930s, including practically all the important novels and short stories, was forbidden as politically suspect. Official doctrine was that reconquest of the mainland was imminent, so that the sojourn of writers and other intellectuals in Taiwan was a highly temporary situation justifying emergency levels of censorship and supervision. Accordingly, in the 1950s, aside from classical Chinese literary works, the publishing scene was dominated by anti-Communist novels and stories of dubious literary value.

An important exception was the work of Jiang Gui (pseudonym of Wang Lindu, 1908–1980), whose literary talent was obvious from the first appearance of his novel *Xuanfeng* (Whirlwind) in 1959. His novels are often set in the China of the 1920s and 1940s, but they are much subtler than those of many of his contemporaries. *Xuanfeng* is a panoramic novel telling the history of China from the May Fourth Movement to the Sino-Japanese war.

In these earliest years not much priority was given to the study and translation of Western literature. Toward the end of the 1950s, however, thematic and technical horizons began to widen. Unofficially the realization began to dawn that the supposedly imminent return to the mainland was an illusion, and that Taiwan, with its unique Sino-Japanese culture and Hokkien dialect background, was likely to be the permanent residence of the Mandarin-speaking immigrants.

In the 1960s a strong interest in literary modernism was evinced by many younger writers including Bai Xianyong (1937–) and Wang Wenxing (1939–). The magazine *Xiandai wenxue* (Modern literature) played a major role in introducing Western works and critical theories. Before long the new vogue for more or less experimental literature, full of non-"Chinese" themes, settings, and imagery, evoked a reaction in the form of the so-called *xiangtu wenxue* (native literature). *Xiangtu wenxue* was concerned not with technically refined depictions of the life of big-city intellectuals and cosmopolitan types, but with ordinary Taiwanese characters and scenes. The aim was not technical or psychological subtlety but recognizability, often of a bluntly moralistic kind. Prominent *xiangtu* authors included Huang Chunming (1939–), Chen Yingzhen (pseudonym of Chen Yongshan, 1936–), and Wang Zhenhe (1940–1990). *Xiangtu* authors' sympathy with underprivileged local elements sometimes brought them into sharp political and legal conflict with the authorities.

In recent years Taiwan writers have continued to explore a wide range of possible identities, both personal and national. The problems they have faced for the past decade have been comparable to those discovered by mainland Chinese writers in very recent years: simplistic approaches of a political, xenophobic, or regionalist kind are unacceptable by cosmopolitan literary standards, yet exaggeratedly cosmopolitan or would-be "modernism" continues to leave the majority of Chinese readers cold.

One of the first Taiwan writers to receive real attention in the West was Chen Ruoxi (pseudonym of Chen Xiumei, 1938–), a native of Taiwan who later moved to Canada. Though an admirer of literary modernism, Chen Ruoxi empathized so strongly with the fate of the Chinese people in her own time that she went to live in the PRC from 1966 to 1973. Her experiences as a wife and mother during the Cultural Revolution provided the material for a memorable collection of short stories, *Yin Xianzhang* (Mayor Yin, 1976), which was soon translated into many languages.

Poetry in Taiwan

Like fiction, poetry has gone through a fascinating development in Taiwan. Even in the 1950s a varied, lively, and thoroughly controversial new poetry was in evidence. The introduction of Western "modernist" themes and techniques on a significant scale began somewhat earlier than in fiction—but the new elements were far from generally accepted. In the succeeding decades a number of very different poets have produced oeuvres of admirable scale and quality. Only time will tell the lasting status of their work in the overall context of the Chinese-speaking world.

Among the many mainlanders who have been prominent in the emerging literary establishment, one of the key figures is Yu Guangzhong (1928–). As a translator, editor (of *Xiandai wenxue*, among other things), and professor of English, he has made outstanding contributions to the introduction of Western literature in Taiwan. His own poetry, which is highly regarded by contemporaries, preserves elements of the classical Chinese tradition within a cosmopolitan context.

Zheng Chouyu (pseudonym of Zheng Wentao, 1933–) is another clearly "modern" poet who shows the continuing influence of the Chinese classical tradition, especially in the use of nature imagery to evoke mood. Zhou Mengdie (pseudonym of Zhou Qishu, 1920–) combines a modern and "difficult" technique (showing influence of Western poetry in translation) with a metaphysical or meditative tone; Buddhist, Taoist, and Judeo-Christian allusions all have a place in his apparently timeless, strangely vital verse.

Luo Fu (pseudonym of Mo Luofu, 1927–), famous both as original poet and as editor of the leading poetry magazine *Chuangshiji* (Epoch), has won quite a following for his poems, in which veins of Surrealism and Existentialism can be traced. The name of Ya Xian (pseudonym of Wang Qinglin, 1932–), poet and author of valuable studies of earlier twentieth-century Chinese poetry, is also associated with the Epoch school.

Contrasting with the works of these mainlanders was the poetry of Bai Qiu (pseudonym of He Jinrong, 1937–), a native Taiwanese who emerged in the 1960s as the leading figure of the *li* (bamboo hat) school. This movement appeared as a reaction against the obscurity and "Westernization" of more cosmopolitan poets, though its own poetry was not always the mere product of regionalism and anti-intellectualism that critics made it out to be.

As in the case of fiction, some of the new poetry's proponents are no longer resident in Taiwan, though they have continued their associations with Taiwan-based academic and publishing circles. Wang Jingxian (1940–), a native of Taiwan, early took up residence in the United States, where he has had a versatile career as poet, teacher and scholar. A professor of comparative literature, he has published as C. H. Wang, while his original poetry has appeared in many collections under the noms-de-plume Ye Shan and (after 1972) Yang Mu. His many-sided poetry shows affinity with classical Chinese verse, nature poetry, and modern Western poets including Yeats, Lorca, and Stevens.

CONCLUSION

In very recent years a number of leading writers have left the PRC and taken up more or less permanent residence in Europe, North America, Australia, and New Zealand. Their newer writings reflect the experience of intense confrontation with Western cultural modes as well as the continuing effort to come to terms with recent decades in the personal and national past. The revived magazine *Jintian*, published abroad since 1990, has been an important forum for these more or less exiled writers and for concerned scholars and critics. Since 1990, prominent emigré writers from the PRC include the poets Bei Dao, Duoduo (pseudonym of Li Shizheng, 1951–), and Yang Lian (1955–) and the dramatist, novelist, and literary theorist Gao Xingjian (1940–).

A somewhat different cultural role has been played by Chinese writers who had originally become famous in Taiwan literary circles and subsequently lived for decades in the United States. These authors include the fiction writers Bai Xianyong, Yu Lihua (1931–) and Zhang Xiguo (1944–) and the poets Yang Mu, Yip Wai-lim (Ye Weilian, 1937–) and Zhang Cuo (pseudonym of Zhang Zhen'ao, 1943–). Their unusual grounding in both Chinese and Western cultures lends their works a cosmopolitan allure that is much admired by younger writers.

The increasing number of Chinese writers living abroad includes, in addition to the more or less clearly PRC- or Taiwan-affiliated authors, a number of important figures who are difficult to classify in geographic or generational terms, but who are generally recognized as major twentieth-century Chinese writers. Their status in the world of Chinese literature is difficult to determine; their residence outside China tends to exclude them from the customary framework of discussion, as does the fact that in some cases they have also become famous for works written not in Chinese but in

English. Possibly the most important of these authors until her death in 1995 was Zhang Ailing (English name: Eileen Chang). Born in Shanghai in 1920, she made her name as a short-story writer in the 1940s. Her style combines modern Western elements with a thorough background in the Chinese tradition. In 1952 she left the PRC for Hong Kong. In 1954 she published two novels, *Yangge* (The rice-sprout song) and *Chidi zhi lian* (Love in redland *or* Naked earth), both of which described in moving terms the effects on individuals' lives of the transition to Communism. After 1955 Zhang Ailing lived in the United States; her publications continued to appear in both Chinese and English.

Chinese writers whose fame rests primarily on works written in English fall outside the scope of this history, though their following in the English-speaking world has often been considerable. The same applies to authors of Chinese extraction who have grown up in a Western country and become best-selling authors in the language of that country.

It is probable that Chinese literature will continue its present trend toward diversification and that it will be increasingly difficult to draw a sharp line between "Chinese" literature and world literature in general. Many new Chinese authors will consciously seek assimilation to a modern or post-modern literary milieu in which specifically national features are of less importance. On the other hand, there is no question but that traditional Chinese forms and themes will continue to survive; affection for and loyalty to these may actually prove strongest among the most highly educated readers, those who still have some knowledge of the classical language.

Mainland China will in all likelihood continue to judge literary works by traditional standards—that is, by political and ideological criteria which are the modern variants on Confucian didacticism.

BIBLIOGRAPHY

This selective bibliography is an abridged version of that contained in the hardcover edition of this book and is arranged in the same sequence as the chapters in the text. Within each chapter, wherever possible, the bibliography is arranged according to subjects in the chapter subdivisions. Items within any section are arranged by date of publication.

In general, an item is listed only once. Accordingly, it will often be useful to refer not only to the section giving the most specific information on the given subject, but also to sections which list more general background material. For example, information on the novelist Lao She is listed in the specific section of Chapter 26 that is concerned with him, but useful sources may also be found under the general sections for Chapters 26 ("Modern Literature: The Short Story and the Novel") and 25 ("Modern Literature: An Introduction").

Chapter 1. The concept of literature

Introductions to traditional Chinese literature
Watson, Burton. *Early Chinese Literature*. New York: Columbia University Press, 1962.

Liu, James J. Y. *The Art of Chinese Poetry*. Chicago: University of Chicago Press, 1962.

Liu Wu-chi. *An Introduction to Chinese Literature*. Bloomington: Indiana University Press, 1968.

Frankel, Hans H. *The Flowering Plum and the Palace Lady*. New Haven: Yale University Press, 1976.

The Indiana Companion to Traditional Chinese Literature. Edited by William H. Nienhauser, Jr. Bloomington: Indiana University Press, 1986.

Anthologies
Anthology of Chinese Literature. Edited by Cyril Birch. Vol. I: *From Earliest Times to the 14th Century*. New York: Grove Press, 1965; idem, Vol. II: *From the 14th Century to the Present Day*. New York: Grove Press, 1972.

The Orchid Boat: Women Poets of China. Translated by Kenneth Rexroth and Ling Chung. New York: McGraw-Hill, 1972. (A brief anthology including both modern and traditional poems.)

Sunflower Splendor: Three Thousand Years of Chinese Poetry. Edited by Wu-chi Liu and Irving Y. C. Lo. Bloomington: Indiana University Press, 1975. (A generous selection; translations by various sinologists.)

Traditional Chinese Stories: Themes and Variations. Edited by Y. W. Ma and Joseph Lau. New York: Columbia University Press, 1978.

Watson, Burton. *The Columbia Book of Chinese Poetry from Early Times to the Thirteenth Century*. New York: Columbia University Press, 1984.

The Columbia Book of Traditional Chinese Literature. Edited by Victor Mair. New York, Columbia University Press, 1994.
Inscribed Landscapes: Travel Writing from Imperial China. Translated by Richard E. Strassberg. Berkeley: University of California Press, 1994.
An Anthology of Chinese Literature: Beginnings to 1911. Edited and translated by Stephen Owen. New York: Norton, 1996.

Thematic studies
Liu, James. *The Chinese Knight-Errant.* London: Routledge and Kegan Paul, 1967.
Expressions of Self in Chinese Literature. Edited by Robert E. Hegel and Richard C. Hessney. New York: Columbia University Press, 1985.
Owen, Stephen. *Remembrances. The Experience of the Past in Classical Chinese Literature.* Cambridge, MA: Harvard University Press, 1986.
Yue Daiyun. *Intellectuals in Chinese Fiction.* Berkeley: Center for Chinese Studies, University of California, 1988.
Paradoxes of Traditional Chinese Literature. Edited by Eva Hung. Hong Kong: Chinese University Press, 1994.
Wu, Yenna. *The Chinese Virago: A Literary Theme.* Cambridge MA: Harvard University Press, 1995.
Wu, Qingyun. *Female Rule in Chinese and English Literary Utopias.* Liverpool: Liverpool University Press, 1995.

Chapter 2. Language and writing, paper and printing, education and literature

Tsien, Tsuen-hsuin. *Written on Bamboo and Silk: The Beginnings of Chinese Books and Inscriptions.* Chicago: Chicago University Press, 1962.
Rawski, Evelyn Sakakida. *Education and Popular Literacy in Ch'ing China.* Ann Arbor: University of Michigan Press, 1979.
Chaffee, John W. *The Thorny Gates of Learning in Song China: A Social History of Examinations.* Cambridge: Cambridge University Press, 1985.
Popular Culture in Late Imperial China. Edited by David Johnson, Andrew J. Nathan, and Evelyn S. Rawski. Berkeley: University of California Press, 1985.
Tsien, Tsuen-hsuin. *Paper and Printing.* Volume 5, Part 1 of *Science and Civilization in China.* Edited by Joseph Needham. Cambridge: Cambridge University Press, 1985.
Norman, Jerry. *Chinese.* Cambridge: Cambridge University Press, 1988.
Billeter, Jean François. *The Chinese Art of Writing.* New York: Rizzoli, 1990.
Boltz, William G. *The Origin and Early Development of the Chinese Writing System.* New Haven, CT: n.p., 1994.

Chapter 3. Traditional Chinese society

Chinese history
Reischauer, E. and J. K. Fairbank. *East Asia: The Great Tradition.* London: George Allen & Unwin, 1960.
————. *East Asia: The Modern Transformation.* London: George Allen & Unwin, 1965.
Hucker, Charles O. *China's Imperial Past: An Introduction to Chinese History and Culture.* Stanford: Stanford University Press, 1975.

The literati

Ho Ping-ti. *The Ladder of Success in Imperial China: Aspects of Social Mobility 1368–1911*. New York: Columbia University Press, 1962.

Johnson, David G. *The Medieval Chinese Oligarchy*. Boulder, CO: Westview Press, 1977.

Buckley, Patricia Ebrey. *The Aristocratic Families of Early Imperial China: A Case Study of the Po-ling Ts'ui family*. Cambridge: Cambridge University Press, 1978.

McMullen, David. *State and Scholars in T'ang China*. Cambridge: Cambridge University Press, 1988.

Chapter 4. The Central Tradition in traditional society

Introductions to Chinese thought

Waley, A. *Three Ways of Thought in Ancient China*. London: Allen & Unwin, 1939; rpt. 1953.

Mote, F. W. *Intellectual Foundations of China*. New York: Alfred A. Knopf, 1971.

Fingarette, H. *Confucius: The Secular as Sacred*. New York: Harper and Row, 1972.

Henderson, John B. *Scripture, Canon, and Commentary: A Comparison of Confucian and Western Exegeses*. Princeton: Princeton University Press, 1991.

Historical outlines of Chinese philosophy

Fung, Yu-lan. *A Short History of Chinese Philosophy*. Edited by D. Bodde. New York: MacMillan, 1948.

————. *A History of Chinese Philosophy*. Translated by D. Bodde. 2 vols. Peking, 1937. Rpt. Princeton: Princeton University Press, 1953.

de Bary, W. M. Theodore, et al. *Sources of Chinese Tradition*. New York: Columbia University Press, 1960.

Chan, Wing-tsit. *A Source Book in Chinese Philosophy*. Princeton: Princeton University Press, 1963.

Buddhist and Taoist literature

Boltz, Judith. *A Survey of Taoist Literature, Tenth to Seventeenth Centuries*. China Research monograph 32. Berkeley: Institute of Asian Studies, University of California, Berkeley, 1987.

The Lotus Sutra: Translations from the Asian Classics. Translated by Burton Watson. New York: Columbia University Press, 1993.

Women and literature

"Symposium on Poetry and Women's Culture in Late Imperial China." Edited by Charlotte Furth. *Late Imperial China* 13, no. 1 (1992).

Ko, Dorothy. *Teachers of the Inner Chambers: Women and Culture in Seventeenth-Century China*. Stanford: Stanford University Press, 1994.

Chapter 5. The Way and the government. Truth and literature.

Government and literature

Goodrich, L. C. *The Literary Inquisition of Ch'ien-lung*. Baltimore: Waverley Press, 1935.

Chan, Hok-lam. *Control of Publishing in China Past and Present*. The 44th Ernest Morrison Lecture in Ethnology, 1983. Canberra: Australian National University, 1983.

The Chinese conception of literature

Liu, James J. Y. *Chinese Theories of Literature.* Chicago: University of Chicago Press, 1975.

Chinese Approaches to Literature, from Confucius to Liang Ch'i-ch'ao. Edited by Adele Austin Rickett. Princeton: Princeton University Press, 1978.

Theories of the Arts in China. Edited by Susan Bush and Christian Murck. Princeton: Princeton University Press, 1983.

Owen, Stephen. *Traditional Chinese Poetry and Poetics: Omen of the World.* Madison: University of Wisconsin Press, 1985.

Bol, Peter K. *"This Culture of Ours": Intellectual Transitions in T'ang and Sung China.* Stanford: Stanford University Press, 1992.

Owen, Stephen. *Readings in Chinese Literary Thought.* Cambridge, MA: Harvard University Press, 1992.

Zhang, Longxi. *The Tao and the Logos: Literary Hermeneutics, East and West.* Durham: Duke University Press, 1993.

Sun, Cecile Chu-chin. *Pearl from the Dragon's Mouth: Evocation of Feeling and Scene in Chinese Poetry,* Ann Arbor: Center for Chinese Studies, University of Michigan, 1995.

Chapter 6. The study and translation of Chinese literature in the West

General

The Chinese Written Character as a Medium for Poetry. Edited by Ezra Pound and Ernest F. Fenollosa. San Francisco: City Lights Books, 1968. (Originally printed 1936. Presents the "ideogram" notion of the Chinese script, as applied by Pound in his translations.)

Yip, Wai-lim. *Ezra Pound's Cathay.* Princeton: Princeton University Press, 1969.

Madly Singing in the Mountains: An Appreciation and Anthology of Arthur Waley. Edited by Ivan Morris. London: Allen & Unwin, 1970.

Mungello, David. *Curious Land: Jesuit Accommodation and the Origin of Sinology.* Stuttgart: Steiner-Verlag-Wiesbaden GmbH, 1985.

Eoyang, Eugene Chen. *The Transparent Eye: Reflections on Translation, Chinese Literature, and Comparative Poetics.* Honolulu: University of Hawaii Press, 1993.

Yip, Wai-lim. *Diffusion of Distances: Dialogues between Chinese and Western Poetics.* Berkeley: University of California Press, 1993.

Europe Studies China: Papers from an International Conference on the History of European Sinology. Edited by Ming Wilson and John Cayley. London: Han-shan Tang Books, 1995.

Eoyang, Eugene, and Lin Yaofu. *Translating Chinese Literature.* Bloomington: Indiana University Press, 1995.

An Encyclopedia of Translation, Chinese-English, English-Chinese. Edited by Sin-wai Chan and David Pollard. Hong Kong: Chinese University Press, 1995.

Bibliographies

Lynn, Richard John. *Chinese Literature: A Draft Bibliography in Western European Languages.* Canberra: Faculty of Asian Studies in association with Australian National University Press, 1979.

Nienhauser, William H., Jr. *Bibliography of Selected Western Works on T'ang Dynasty Literature.* Taipei: Center for Chinese Studies, 1988.

Collections of comparative studies

Chinese-Western Comparative Literature: Theory and Strategy. Edited by John J. Deeny. Hong Kong: Chinese University Press, 1980.

China and the West: Comparative Literature Studies. Edited by William Tay et al. Hong Kong: Chinese University Press, 1980.

The Chinese Text: Studies in Comparative Literature. Edited by Ying-hsiung Chou. Hong Kong: Chinese University Press, 1986.

Owen, Stephen. *Mi-Lou, Poetry and the Labyrinth of Desire.* Cambridge, MA: Harvard University Press, 1989.

Studies in Chinese-Western Comparative Drama. Edited by Yun-tong Luk. Hong Kong: Chinese University Press, 1990.

Chapter 7. Historical prose

General

Gardner, Charles S. *Chinese Traditional Historiography.* Cambridge, MA: n.p., 1961. (Originally published 1938. A general introduction to traditional Chinese historiography.)

Early Chinese Texts: A Bibliographical Guide. Edited by Michael Loewe. Berkeley: Institute of Asian Studies, University of California, 1993.

Shujing

Legge, James. *The Chinese Classics.* Vol. III, Part I/II. London: Oxford University Press, 1865.

Waltham, Clae. *Shu Ching: Book of History: A modernized version of the translations of James Legge.* Chicago: Gateway, 1971.

Chunqiu, Zuo zhuan

Legge, James. *The Chinese Classics . . .* Vol. V, Part I/II. London: Oxford University Press, 1872.

Tso Ch'iu-ming. *The Tso-chuan: Selections from China's Oldest Narrative History.* Translated by Burton Watson. New York: Columbia University Press, 1989.

Zhanguo ce and other works attributed to Liu Xin

O'Hara, Albert Richard. *The Position of Woman in Early China According to the Lieh Nü Chuan.* Washington, DC: Catholic University of America Press, 1945. (Includes a translation of the *Lienü zhuan.*)

Crump, James I. *Intrigues: Studies of Chan-kuo Ts'e.* Ann Arbor: University of Michigan Press, 1964.

Chan-kuo Ts'e. Translated by James I. Crump, Jr. Oxford: Clarendon Press, 1970; rev. ed. with index, Ann Arbor: University of Michigan Center for Chinese Studies, 1996.

Shiji: Translations and Studies

Watson, Burton. *Ssu-ma Ch'ien, Grand Historian of China.* New York: Columbia University Press, 1958. (A study of the life and work of Sima Qian.)

Records of the Grand Historian of China: Translated from the Shi chi of Ssu-ma Ch'ien. Translated by Burton Watson. New York: Columbia University Press, 1961. Revised ed., 1993. (Translations of texts relating to the Han.)

Records of the Historian, Written by Szuma Ch'ien. Translated by Hsien-yi Yang and Gladys Yang. Hong Kong: Commercial Press, 1974. (An anthology from the *Shiji.*)

Sima Qian. *Historical Records.* Translated by Raymond Dawson. Oxford: Oxford University Press. (Small selection.)

Ssu-ma Ch'ien. *The Grand Scribe's Records.* Vol. I, *The Basic Annals of Pre-Han China.* Vol. VII, *The Memoirs of Pre-Han China.* Translated by Tsai-fa Cheng, Zongli Lu, William H. Nienhauser, Jr., and Robert Reynolds. Edited by William H. Nienhauser, Jr. Bloomington: Indiana University Press, 1994.

Records of the Grand Historian: Qin Dynasty. Translated by Burton Watson. New York: Columbia University Press, 1993.

Durrant, Stephen W. *The Cloudy Mirror: Tension and Conflict in the Writings of Sima Qian.* Albany: State University of New York Press, 1995.

Han shu and Hou Han shu

Swann, Nancy Lee. *Pan Chao, Foremost Woman Scholar of China, First Century A.D.: Background, Ancestry, Life, and Writings of the Most Celebrated Chinese Woman of Letters.* New York: Century Co., 1932.

Dubs, Homer H. *The History of the Former Han Dynasty by Pan Ku.* 3 volumes. Baltimore: Waverley Press, 1938-1955.

Watson, Burton. *Courtier and Commoner in Ancient China: Selections from the History of the Former Han by Pan Ku.* New York: Columbia University Press, 1974.

Chapter 8. The philosophers

Confucianism

Lunyu

The Confucian Classics . . . ; Translated by James Legge. Vol. I. London: Oxford University Press, 1861.

The Analects of Confucius. Translated by Arthur Waley. London: George Allen & Unwin, 1938.

Confucius. *The Analects.* Translated by D. C. Lau. Harmondsworth: Penguin, 1979.

Mengzi

The Confucian Classics . . . ; Translated by James Legge. Vol. 2. London: Oxford University Press, 1861.

Mencius. Translated by W. A. C. M. Dobson. Toronto: University of Toronto Press, 1963.

Mencius. Translated by D. C. Lau. Harmondsworth: Penguin, 1970.

Xunzi

Xunzi. *Hsün-Tzu: Basic Writings.* Translated by Burton Watson. New York: Columbia University Press, 1963. (An anthology.)

————. *Xunzi: A Translation and Study of the Complete Works.* Translated by John Knobloch. Stanford: Stanford University Press, 1988–.

Liji and Yili

The I-li or Book of Etiquette and Ceremonial. 2 volumes. Translated by John Steele. London: Probsthain and Co., 1917. (Full translation; extensive commentary.)

The *Sacred Books of China. The Texts of Confucianism, Part III, Part IV: The Li Ki.* Translated by James Legge. Oxford: Oxford University Press, 1885.

Xiaojing
The Sacred Books of China. The Texts of Confucianism: Part I. Translated by James Legge. Oxford: Oxford University Press, 1879. (Includes the *Xiaojing.*)

Chunqiu Fanlu
Queen, Sarah A. *From Chronicle to Canon: The Hermeneutics of the Spring and Autumn, According to Tung Chung-shu.* Cambridge: Cambridge University Press, 1996.

Taixuan jing
Yang Hsiung. *The Canon of Supreme Mystery: A Translation with Commentary of the T'ai Hsüan Ching.* Translated by Michael Nylan. Albany: State University of New York Press, 1993.

Yijing
The Sacred Books of China. The Texts of Confucianism, Part II: The Yi King. Translated by James Legge. Oxford: Oxford University Press, 1882.
The I Ching or Book of Changes: The Richard Wilhelm Translation. Rendered into English by Cary F. Baynes. Foreword by C. G. Jung. Preface to the Third Edition by Hellmut Wilhelm. Princeton: Princeton University Press, 1967.
The Classic of Changes: A New Translation of the I Ching as Interpreted by Wang Bi. Translated by Richard J. Lynn. New York: Columbia University Press, 1994.

Kongzi jiayu
Ariel, Yoav. *K'ung-ts'ung-tzu: The K'ung Family Master's Anthology; Study and Translation of Chapters 1-10, 12-14.* Princeton: Princeton University Press, 1989.
——— *K'ung-ts'ung-tzu, A Study and Translation of Chapters 15-23 with a Reconstruction of the Hsiao Erh-ya Dictionary.* Leiden: E. J. Brill, 1996.

Mohism, logicians, and legalists
Mozi
Mo Tzu: Basic Writings. Translated by Burton Watson. New York: Columbia University Press, 1963. (A brief anthology.)
Graham, A. C. *Later Mohist Logic, Ethics and Science.* London: University of London, S.O.A.S., 1978. (A translation and study of the most difficult books.)

Gongsun Longzi
Perleberg, Max. *The Works of Kung-sun Lung-tzu.* Hong Kong, 1952.

Sunzi
Sun-tzu. *The Art of Warfare: The First English Translation Incorporating the Recently Discovered Yin-ch'üeh-shan Texts.* Translated with an introduction and commentary by Roger Ames. New York: Ballantine Books, 1993.
Sun Pin. *Military Methods.* Translated with introduction and commentary by Ralph D. Sawyer, with the collaboration of Mei-chün Lee Sawyer. Boulder: Westview Press, 1995.

Legalists

The Book of Lord Shang. Translated by J. J. L. Duyvendak. London: Arthur Probsthain, 1928.

The Complete Works of Han Fei Tzu. Translated by W. K. Liao. London: Arthur Probsthain, 1939, 2 vols.

Han Fei Tzu: Basic Writings. Translated by Burton Watson. New York: Columbia University Press, 1964.

Taoism

Daode jing

Waley, Arthur. *The Way and Its Power: A Study of the Tao Te Ching and Its Place in Chinese Thought.* With Introduction, Commentaries, Full Appendices and Notes. London: George Allen & Unwin, 1934.

Lao Tzu. *A Translation of Lao Tzu's Tao Te Ching and Wang Pi's Commentary.* Translated by Paul J. Lin. Ann Arbor: Center for Chinese Studies, University of Michigan, 1977.

Lau Tzu. *Lau Tzu: Tao Te Ching.* Translated by D. C. Lau. Harmondsworth: Penguin, 1963; rev. ed. Hong Kong: Chinese University Press, 1983.

Henricks, Robert G. *Lao Tzu: Te-Tao Ching.* New York: Ballantine Books, 1990.

Lao Tzu. *Tao Te Ching: The Classic Book of Integrity and the Way.* Translated by Victor H. Mair. New York: Bantam Books, 1990.

Zhuangzi

The Complete Works of Chuang Tzu. Translated by Burton Watson. New York: Columbia University Press, 1968.

Graham, A. C. *Chuang-tzu: The Seven Inner Chapters and Other Writings from the Book Chuang-tzu.* London: George Allen & Unwin, 1981.

Liezi

The Book of Lie-tzu. Translated by A. C. Graham. London: John Murray, 1960.

Baopuzi

Alchemy, Medicine, Religion in the China of A.D. 320: The Nei P'ien of Ko Hung (Pao-p'u tzu). Translated by James Ware. Cambridge, MA: MIT Press, 1966.

Sailey, Jay. *The Master Who Embraces Simplicity: A Study of the Philosopher Ko Hung A.D. 283–343.* San Francisco: Chinese Materials Center, 1978.

Other texts

Guanzi

Kuan-Tzu: A Repository of Early Chinese Thought. Vol. I. Translated by W. Allyn Rickett. Hong Kong: Hong Kong University Press, 1965.

————. *Guanzi: Political, Economic and Philosophical Essays from Early China. A Study and Translation.* Vol. I. Princeton: Princeton University Press, 1985.

Huainanzi

Ames, Roger T. *The Art of Rulership: A Study in Ancient Chinese Thought.* Honolulu: University of Hawaii Press, 1983.

Le Blanc, Charles. *Huai-Nan Tzu: Philosophical Synthesis in Early Han Thought—the Idea of Resonance,* With a Translation and Analysis of Chapter Six. Hong Kong: Hong Kong University Press, 1985.

Yantie lun
Discourses on Salt and Iron. Translated by E. M. Gale. Leiden: E.J. Brill, 1931.

Baihu tong
Tjan Tjoe Som. *Po Hu T'ung: The Comprehensive Discussions in the White Tiger Hall.* 2 vols. Leiden: E. J. Brill, 1949.

Lunheng
Lun Heng. Part I: Philosophical Essays of Wang Ch'ung. Translated by Alfred Forke. Leipzig: Harrassowitz, 1907; idem, *Part II: Miscellaneous Essays of Wang Ch'ung.* Berlin: Harrassowitz, 1911.

Others
Shryock, J. K. *The Study of Human Abilities: The Jen wu chih of Liu Shao.* With an Introductory Study. New Haven: American Oriental Society, 1937.
Pokora, Timoteus. *Hsin-lun (New Treatise), and Other Writings by Huan T'an (43 B.C.-28 A.D.).* Ann Arbor: Center for Chinese Studies, University of Michigan, 1975.
Ch'en, Ch'i-yün. *Hsün Yüeh and the Mind of Late Han China: A Translation of the Shen-chien.* With Introduction and Annotations. Princeton: Princeton University Press, 1980.
Paper, Jordan D. *The Fu-tzu: A Post-Han Confucian Text.* Leiden: E. J. Brill, 1987.
Ku, Mei-kao. *A Chinese Mirror for Magistrates: The Hsin-yü of Lu Chia.* Canberra: Faculty of Asian Studies, Australian National University, 1988.
Kinney, Anne Behnke. *The Art of the Han Essay: Wang Fu's Ch'ien-fu lun.* Tempe: Center for Asian Studies, Arizona State University, 1992.

Chapter 9. Poetry

Shijing: Translations and Studies
The Chinese Classics. Vol. IV, Part I, II: *The She-king, Or the book of Poetry.* Translated by James Legge. London: Henry Frowde, 1871.
Granet, Marcel. *Festivals and Songs of Ancient China.* Translated by E. D. Edwards. London: Routledge, 1932.
The Book of Songs. Translated by Arthur Waley. London: Constable and Co., 1937.
Karlgren, Bernhard. *The Book of Odes.* Stockholm: Museum of Far Eastern Antiquities, 1950.
Han Shih Wai Chuan: Han Ying's Illustrations of the Didactic Application of the Classic of Songs. Translated by James R. Hightower. Cambridge, MA: Harvard University Press, 1952.
The Classic Anthology Defined by Confucius. Translated by Ezra Pound. Cambridge, MA: Harvard University Press, 1954. (The famous creative re-translation by one of the most famous American poets.)
Wang, C. H. *The Bell and the Drum: Shih Ching as Formulaic Poetry in an Oral Tradition.* Berkeley: University of California Press, 1974.
Yu, Pauline R. *The Reading of Imagery in the Chinese Poetic Tradition.* Princeton: Princeton University Press, 1987.
Saussy, Haun. *The Problem of a Chinese Aesthetic.* Stanford: Stanford University Press, 1993.

Chuci

Chu Tz'u: The Songs of the South. Translated by David Hawkes. Oxford: Oxford University Press, 1959. (Full translation of the *Chuci*, with extensive introduction.)

Schneider, Laurence A. *A Madman of Ch'u: The Chinese Myth of Loyalty and Dissent.* Berkeley: University of California Press, 1980. (A study of the myth of Qu Yuan in later ages, especially in the twentieth century.)

Waters, Geoffrey R. *Three Elegies of Ch'u: An Introduction to the Traditional Interpretation of the Ch'u-Tz'u.* Madison: University of Wisconsin Press, 1985.

Fu. **General**

The Temple and Other Poems. Translated by Arthur Waley. London: Allen & Unwin, 1923. (An anthology of *fu*, preference is given to shorter examples of the genre.)

Chinese Rhyme-Prose: Poems in the Fu Form from the Han and the Six Dynasties Period. Translated by Burton Watson. New York: Columbia University Press, 1971.

Fu: Mei Sheng and Yang Xiong

The Han Rhapsody: A Study of the Fu of Yang Hsiung (53 B.C.–A.D. 18). Cambridge: Cambridge University Press, 1976.

The Han-shu Biography of Yang Xiong. Translated by David R. Knechtges. Tempe: Center for Asian Studies, Arizona State University, 1982.

Mair, Victor H. *Mei Cherng's "Seven Stimuli" and Wang Bair's "Pavilion of King Terng": Chinese Poems for Princes.* Lewiston, ME: Edwin Mellen Press, 1988.

Chapter 10. *Fu,* **prose, and literary criticism**

Parallel prose

Hightower, James R. "Some Characteristics of Parallel Prose." In *Studia Serica Bernhard Karlgren Dedicata.* Edited by Søren Egerod and Elsa Glahn. Copenhagen, 1959. (Also included in *Studies in Chinese Literature.* Edited by J. L. Bishop. Cambridge, MA: Harvard University Press, 1965.)

Fu. **Xi Kang and contemporaries**

Hsi K'ang and his Poetical Essay on the Lute. Translated by R. H. Van Gulik. Tokyo: Sophia University, 1941. (Translation of the "Qin fu." with extensive annotation.)

Philosophy and Argumentation in Third-Century China: The Essays of Hsi K'ang. Edited and translated by Robert G. Henricks. Princeton: Princeton University Press, 1983.

Literary criticism

Yeh, Chia-ying and Jan W. Walls. "Theory, Standards and Practice of Criticizing Poetry in Chung Hung's *Shih-p'in.*" In *Studies in Chinese Poetry and Poetics.* Edited by R. C. Miao, pp. 43-80. San Francisco: Chinese Materials Center, 1978.

Early Chinese Literary Criticism. Edited and translated by Siu-kit Wong. Hong Kong: Joint Publishing Co., 1983. (A collection of early texts on literary theory, dating from early times to the sixth century.)

Shih, Vincent. *The Literary Mind and the Carving of Dragons.* New York: Columbia University Press, 1959. (Revised bilingual edition, Hong Kong: Chinese University Press, 1983.)

Anthologies

Birrell, Anne. *New Songs from a Jade Terrace*. New York: Allen & Unwin, 1982. (Translation of *Yutai xinyong*.)

Wen xuan, Or Selections of Refined Literature. Translated by David R. Knechtges. Edited by Xiao Tong. Princeton: Princeton University Press, 1982-.

Supernatural stories and anecdotes

General

The Man Who Sold a Ghost: Chinese Tales of the 3rd–6th Century. Translated by Hsien-yi Yang and Gladys Yang. Peking: Foreign Languages Press, 1958.

DeWoskin, Kenneth J. *Doctors, Diviners and Magicians of Ancient China: Biographies of Fang-shih*. New York: Columbia University Press, 1983.

Classical Chinese Tales of the Supernatural and the Fantastic: Selections from the Third to the Tenth Century. Edited by Karl S. Kao. Bloomington: Indiana University Press, 1985.

Birrell, Anne M. *Chinese Mythology: An Introduction*. Baltimore: Johns Hopkins University Press, 1993.

Yuan Ke. *Dragons and Dynasties: An Introduction to Chinese Mythology*. New York: Penguin, 1993.

Campany, Robert Ford. *Strange Writing: Anomaly Accounts in Early Medieval China*. Albany: State University of New York Press, 1996.

Shoushen ji

In Search of the Supernatural: The Written Record. Translated by Kenneth J. DeWoskin and J. I. Crump, Jr. Stanford: Stanford University Press, 1996. (Complete translation.)

Shishuo xinyu

Mather, Richard B. *Shih-shuo Hsin-yü: A New Account of Tales of the World by Liu I-ch'ing, with Commentary by Liu Chün*. Minneapolis: University of Minnesota Press, 1976.

North Chinese writers

Family Instructions for the Yen Clan (Yen-shih chia-hsun). Translated by Teng Ssu-yü. Leiden: E. J. Brill, 1968.

Jenner, William J. F. *Memories of Loyang: Yang Hsuan-chih and the Lost Capital (493–534)*. Oxford: Oxford University Press, 1981.

Yang Hsüan-chih. *A Record of Buddhist Monasteries in Lo-yang*. Translated by Yi-t'ung Wang. Princeton: Princeton University Press, 1984.

Chapter 11. Poetry: *shi* and *yuefu* (100–700)

General

Watson, Burton. *Chinese Lyricism: Shih Poetry from the Second to Twelfth Century*. New York: Columbia University Press, 1971.

The Vitality of the Lyric Voice: Shih Poetry from the Late Han to the T'ang. Edited by Shuen-fu Lin and Stephen Owen. Princeton: Princeton University Press, 1986.

Mair, Victor H. *Four Introspective Poets: A Concordance to Selected Poems by Roan Jyi, Chen Tzyy-arng, Jang Jeou-ling, and Lii Bor*. Tempe: Center for Asian Studies, Arizona State University, 1987.

Cai, Zong-qi. *The Matrix of Lyric Transformation: Poetic Modes and Self-Presentation in Early Chinese Pentasyllabic Poetry.* Ann Arbor: Center for Chinese Studies, University of Michigan, 1997.

Yuefu and early *shi*
An Anthology of Chinese Verse: Han Wei Chin and the Northern and Southern Dynasties. Translated by J. D. Frodsham and Ch'eng Hsi. Oxford: Oxford University Press, 1967.
A Cold Orchid: The Love Poems of Tzu Yeh. Translated by Lenore Mayhew and William McNaughton. Rutland, VT: Charles E. Tuttle, 1972.
Birrell, Anne. *Popular Songs and Ballads of Han China.* London: Unwin Hyman, 1988.
Allen, Joseph R. *In the Voice of Others: Chinese Music Bureau Poetry.* Ann Arbor: Center for Chinese Studies, University of Michigan, 1992.

Shi poets of the third century
Cao Zhi, Ruan Ji, and contemporaries
Kent, George W. *Worlds of Dust and Jade: 47 Poems and Ballads of the Third Century Chinese Poet Ts'ao Chih.* New York: Philosophical Library, 1969.
Dunn, Hugh. *Ts'ao Chih: The Life of a Princely Chinese Poet.* Taipei: China News 1970.
Holzman, Donald. *Poetry and Politics: The Life and Works of Juan Chi, AD 210-263.* Cambridge: Cambridge University Press, 1976.
Miao, Ronald C. *Early Medieval Chinese Poetry: The Life and Verse of Wang Ts'an (A.D. 177-217).* Wiesbaden: Franz Steiner Verlag, 1982.
Ruan Ji. *Songs of My Heart: The Chinese Lyric Poetry of Ruan Ji.* Translated by Graham Hartill and Wu Fusheng. London: Wellsweep, 1988.

Poets of the period 350-450
General
Chang, Kang-i Sun. *Six Dynasties Poetry.* Princeton: Princeton University Press, 1986.

Tao Qian
T'ao The Hermit: Sixty Poems by T'ao Ch'ien (365-427). Translated by William Acker. London: Thames and Hudson, 1952.
The Poetry of T'ao Ch'ien. Translated by James R. Hightower. Oxford: Oxford University Press, 1970.
Davis, A. R. *T'ao Yüan-ming (A.D. 365-427): His Works and Their Meaning.* 2 volumes. Cambridge: Cambridge University Press, 1983.

Xie Lingyun
Frodsham, J. D. *The Murmuring Stream: The Life and Works of the Chinese Nature Poet Hsieh Ling-yun (385-433), Duke of K'ang-Lo.* 2 volumes. Kuala Lumpur: University of Malaya Press, 1967.

Palace-style poetry and other poets of the fifth and sixth centuries
Marney, John. *Liang Chien-wen Ti.* Boston: Twayne, 1976.
———. *Chiang Yen.* Boston: Twayne, 1981.
Beyond the Mulberries: An Anthology of Palace-Style Poetry by Emperor Chien-wen of the Liang Dynasty (503–551). Translated by John Marney. San Francisco: Chinese Materials Center, 1982.

Chapter 12. Poetry: *Shi* (700–1000)

General: Anthologies
One Hundred and Seventy Chinese Poems. Translated by Arthur Waley. London: Constable and Co., 1918 (many reissues).
————. *More Translations from the Chinese.* London, 1919.
Poems of the Late T'ang. Translated by A. C. Graham. Harmondsworth: Penguin, 1965.
Wu, John C. H. *The Four Seasons of T'ang Poetry.* Rutland, VT: Charles E. Tuttle, 1972.
Stimson, Hugh M. *Fifty-Five T'ang Poems: A Text in The Reading and Understanding of T'ang Poetry.* New Haven: Yale University Press, 1976.

General: Studies
Stimson, Hugh M. *T'ang Poetic Vocabulary.* New Haven: Yale University Press, 1976.
Liu, James J. Y. *The Interlingual Critic: Interpreting Chinese Poetry.* Bloomington: Indiana University Press, 1982.

General: Thematic studies
Schafer, Edward H. *The Divine Woman: Dragon Ladies and Rain Maidens in Tang Literature.* Berkeley: University of California Press, 1973.
Cahill, Suzanne E. *Transcendence and Divine Passion: The Queen Mother of the West in Medieval China.* Stanford: Stanford University Press, 1993.
Spring, Madeline. *Animal Allegories in T'ang China.* New Haven: American Oriental Society, 1993.

Early Tang
Owen, Stephen. *Poetry of the Early T'ang.* New Haven: Yale University Press, 1977.
Ho, Richard M. W. *Ch'en Tzu-ang: Innovator in T'ang Poetry.* Hong Kong: Chinese University Press, 1993.

High Tang
Owen, Stephen. *The Great Age of Chinese Poetry: The High T'ang.* New Haven: Yale University Press, 1981.

Wang Wei
Yip, Wai-lim. *Hiding the Universe: Poems by Wang Wei.* New York: Grossmann, 1972.
Yu, Pauline. *The Poetry of Wang Wei: New Translations and Commentary.* Bloomington: Indiana University Press, 1980.
Wagner, Marsha L. *Wang Wei.* Boston: Twayne, 1981.

Li Bai
Obata, Shigeyoshi. *The Works of Li Po, The Chinese Poet.* New York: Dutton, 1922.
Waley, Arthur. *The Poetry and Career of Li Po, 701-762 A.D.* London: George Allen & Unwin, 1950. (Still the only biography available in English.)
Cooper, Arthur. *Li Po and Tu Fu.* Harmondsworth: Penguin, 1973.
Wong, Siu-Kit. *The Genius of Li Po, A.D. 701–762.* Hong Kong: Centre of Asian Studies, University of Hong Kong, 1974.

Du Fu

Hung, William. *Tu Fu: China's Greatest Poet.* 2 volumes. Cambridge, MA: Harvard University Press, 1952.

Hawkes, David. *A Little Primer of Tu Fu.* Oxford: Oxford University Press, 1967.

Davis, A. R. *Tu Fu.* New York: Twayne, 1971.

McCraw, David R. *Du Fu's Laments from the South.* Honolulu: University of Hawaii Press, 1992.

Chou, Eva Shan. *Reconsidering Tu Fu: Literary Greatness in a Cultural Context.* Cambridge: Cambridge University Press, 1995.

Others

Chan, Marie. *Kao Shih.* Boston: Twayne, 1978.

Kroll, Paul W. *Meng Hao-jan.* Boston: Twayne, 1981.

Lee, Joseph J. *Wang Ch'ang-ling.* Boston: Twayne, 1982.

The Middle Tang

General

Owen, Stephen. *The End of the Chinese 'Middle Ages': Essays in Mid-Tang Literary Culture.* Stanford: Stanford University Press, 1996.

Bai Juyi

Waley, Arthur. *The Life and Times of Po Chü-i, 772-846 A.D.* London: George Allen & Unwin, 1949. (Extensive biography; includes many translations.)

Translations from Po Chü-i's Collected Works. 6 volumes. New York: Paragon Book Reprint Co. and San Francisco: Chinese Materials Center, 1971–78.

Bai Juyi: 200 Selected Poems. Translated by Rewi Alley. Peking: New World Press, 1983.

Yuan Zhen, Han Yu, and others

Frodsham, J. D. *The Poems of Li Ho (791–817).* Oxford: Oxford University Press, 1970.

Owen, Stephen. *The Poetry of Meng Chiao and Han Yü.* New Haven: Yale University Press, 1975.

Palandri, Angela Jung. *Yüan Chen.* Boston: Twayne, 1977. (A short study of Yuan Zhen's life and work. Includes translations.)

Hanson, Kenneth O. *Growing Old Alive: Poems by Han Yü.* Port Townsend: Copper Canyon Press, 1978.

Tu, Kuo-ch'ing. *Li Ho.* Boston: Twayne, 1979.

Late Tang

Li Shangyin

Liu, James J. Y. *The Poetry of Li Shang-yin, Ninth Century Baroque Chinese Poet.* Chicago: University of Chicago Press, 1967.

Du Mu

Du Mu. *Plantains in the Rain: Selected Chinese Poems.* Translated by R. F. Burton. London: Wellsweep Press, 1990.

Kung, Wen-kai. *Tu Mu (805–852): His Life and Poetry.* San Francisco: Chinese Materials Center, 1990.

Others

Nienhauser, William H., Jr. *P'i Jih-hsiu*. Boston: Twayne, 1979.

Schafer, Edward H. *Mirages on the Sea of Time: The Taoist Poetry of Ts'ao T'ang*. Berkeley: University of California Press, 1985.

Brocade River Poems: Selected Works of the Tang Dynasty Courtesan Xue Tao. Translated by Jeanne Larsen. Princeton: Princeton University Press, 1987.

Yates, Robin D. S. *Washing Silk: The Life and Selected Poetry of Wei Chuang (834?–910)*. Cambridge, MA: Harvard University Press, 1988.

Rouzer, Paul E. *Writing Another's Dream: The Poetry of Wen Tingyun*. Stanford: Stanford University Press, 1993.

Poetry criticism

Wong Yoon Wah. *Ssu K'ung T'u: A Poet Critic of the T'ang*. Hong Kong: Chinese University of Hong Kong, 1976.

Poetry of Buddhist inspiration
General

Nielsen, Thomas. P. *The T'ang Poet-Monk Chiao-jan*. Tempe: Center for Asian Studies, Arizona State University, 1972.

Hanshan

Snyder, Gary. *Riprap & Cold Mountain Poems*. San Francisco: Four Seasons Foundation, 1958. (A popular selection by a leading American poet.)

Cold Mountain: 100 Poems by the T'ang Poet Han-shan. Translated by Burton Watson. New York: Columbia University Press, 1962.

Red Pine. *Han-shan: The Collected Songs of Cold Mountain*. Port Townsend, Wash.: Copper Canyon Press, 1983.

Chapter 13. Tang Prose: Ancient-style prose (*guwen*) and short stories (*chuanqi*) (700–1000)

General

Liu, Shih Shun. *Chinese Classical Prose: The Eight Masters of the T'ang-Sung Period*. Hong Kong: Chinese University Press, 1979.

Chen, Yu-shih. *Images and Ideas in Chinese Classical Prose: Studies of Four Masters*. Stanford: Stanford University Press, 1988.

Han Yu, Liu Zongyuan, and others

Nienhauser, William H. Jr. et al. *Liu Tsung-yüan*. New York: Twayne, 1973.

Hartman, Charles. *Han Yu and the Tang Search for Unity*. Princeton: Princeton University Press, 1986.

Barrett, T. H. *Li Ao: Buddhist, Taoist or Neo-Confucian?* Oxford: Oxford University Press, 1992.

Chen, Jo-shui. *Liu Tsung-yüan and Intellectual Change in T'ang China, 773–819*. Cambridge: Cambridge University Press, 1992.

Anthologies and studies of Tang *chuanqi*

Edwards, E. D. *Chinese Prose Literature of the T'ang Period.* 2 volumes. London: Probsthain, 1937–38.

The Dragon King's Daughter: Ten Tang Dynasty Stories. Translated by Hsien-yi Yang and Gladys Yang. Peking: Foreign Languages Press, 1954. (A brief selection.)

Bauer, Wolfgang., and Herbert Francke.. *The Golden Casket: Chinese Novellas of Two Millennia.* Translated from the German by Christopher Levenson. New York: Harcourt, Brace and World, 1964.

Levy, Howard S. *China's First Novellette: The Dwelling of Playful Goddesses by Chang Wen-ch'eng (ca. 657–730).* Tokyo: Dai Nippon Insatsu, 1965. (Translation of the *You xianku.*)

Dudbridge, Glen. *The Tale of Li Wa: Study and Critical Edition of a Chinese Story from the Ninth Century.* London: Ithaca Press, 1983.

Chang, H. C. *Chinese Literature 3: Tales of the Supernatural.* New York: Columbia University Press, 1984.

Lee, Yu-hwa. *Fantasy and Realism in Chinese fiction: T'ang Love Themes in Contrast.* San Francisco: Chinese Materials Center, 1984.

Dudbridge, Glen. *Religious Experience and Lay Society in T'ang China: A Reading of Tai Fu's Kuang-i chi.* Cambridge Studies in Chinese History, Literature, and Institutions. Cambridge: Cambridge University Press, 1995.

Chapter 14. Popular literature: *Ci* **and** *Bianwen* **(700–1000)**

Dunhuang **Manuscripts**

Gates, Lionel. *Six Centuries at Tunhuang: A Short Account of the Stein Collection of Chinese Mss. in the British Museum.* London: China Society, 1944. (Also reprinted in *Nine Dragon Screen* [London: China Society, 1965].)

Ci: **General**

Chang, Kang-i Sun. *The Evolution of Chinese Tz'u Poetry from T'ang to Northern Sung.* Princeton: Princeton University Press, 1980.

Voices of the Song Lyric in China. Edited by Pauline Yu. Berkeley: University of California Press, 1993.

Ci: **Tang-Five Dynasties**

The Song-Poetry of Wei Chuang (836–910 A.D.). Translated by John Timothy Wixted. Tempe: Center for Asian Studies, Arizona State University, 1979.

Fusek, Lois. *Among the Flowers: The Hua-chien-chi.* New York: Columbia University Press, 1982.

Bryant, Daniel. *Lyric Poets of the Southern T'ang: Feng Yen-ssu, 903–960 and Li Yü, 937–978.* Vancouver: University of British Columbia Press, 1982.

Wagner, Marsha L. *The Lotus Boat: The Origins of Chinese Tz'u Poetry in Tang Popular Culture.* New York: Columbia University Press, 1984.

Bianwen

Ballads and Stories from Tunhuang: An Anthology. Translated by Arthur Waley. London: George Allen & Unwin, 1960.

Mair, Victor H. *Tun-huang Popular Narratives.* Cambridge: Cambridge University Press, 1983.

————. *Painting and Performance: Chinese Picture Recitation and its Indian Genesis.* Honolulu: University of Hawaii Press, 1988.

————. *T'ang Transformation Texts: A Study of the Buddhist Contribution to the Rise of Vernacular Fiction and Drama in China.* Cambridge, MA: Harvard University Press, 1989.

Chapter 15. Poetry: *Shi, Shihua* and *Ci* (1000–1450)

General

Yoshikawa, Kojiro. *An Introduction to Sung Poetry.* Translated by Burton Watson. Cambridge, MA: Harvard University Press, 1976.

The Columbia Book of Later Chinese Poetry: Yüan, Ming and Ch'ing Dynasties (1279–1911). Translated by Jonathan Chaves. New York: Columbia University Press, 1986.

Yoshikawa, Kojiro. *Five Hundred Years of Chinese Poetry, 1150–1650. The Chin, Yuan and Ming Dynasties.* Translated with a Preface by John Timothy Wixted. Including an Afterword by William B. Atwell. Princeton: Princeton University Press, 1989.

Ouyang Xiu

Liu, James T. C. *Ou-yang Hsiu, An Eleventh-Century Neo-Confucianist.* Stanford: Stanford University Press, 1967.

Egan, Ronald C. *The Literary Works of Ou-yang Hsiu (1007–72).* Cambridge: Cambridge University Press, 1967.

Love and Time: The Poems of Ou-yang Hsiu. Translated and edited by Jeremy Seaton. Port Townsend, WA: Copper Canyon Press, 1989.

Mei Yaochen, Huang Tingjian, and others

Lin Yutang. *The Gay Genius: The Life and Times of Su Tungpo.* New York: John Day Co., 1947.

Mote, Frederick W. *The Poet Kao Ch'i, 1336–1374.* Princeton: Princeton University Press, 1962.

Su Tung-p'o: Selections from a Sung Dynasty Poet. Translated by Burton Watson. New York: Columbia University Press, 1965.

Chaves, Jonathan. *Mei Yao-ch'en and the Development of Early Sung Poetry.* New York: Columbia University Press, 1976.

Wixted, John Timothy. *Poems on Poetry: Literary Criticism by Yuan Hao-wen (1190–1257).* Stuttgart: Franz Steiner Wiesbaden, 1982.

Fuller, Michael. *The Road to East Slope: The Development of Su Shi's Poetic Voice.* Stanford: Stanford University Press, 1990.

Grant, Beata. *Mount Lu Revisited: Buddhism in the Life and Writings of Su Shih.* Honolulu: University of Hawaii Press, 1993.

Palumbo-Liu, David. *The Poetics of Appropriation: The Literary Theory of Huang Tingjian.* Stanford: Stanford University Press, 1993.

Egan, Ronald C. *Word, Image, and Deed in the Life of Su Shi.* Harvard-Yenching Institute Monograph Series 39. Cambridge MA: Harvard University Press, 1994.

Pease, Jonathan. *Wang An-kuo's Jade Rewards and Millet Dream.* American Oriental Series, vol. 77. New Haven: American Oriental Society, 1994.

Southern Song, Jin and Early Ming: *Shi*

Lu You

The Old Man Who Does As He Pleases: Selections from the Poetry and Prose of Lu Yu. Translated by Burton Watson. New York: Columbia University Press, 1973.

Duke, Michael S. *Lu Yu.* Boston: Twayne, 1977.

Chang, Chung-shu and Joan Smythe. *South China in the Twelfth Century: A Translation of Lu Yu's Travel Diaries, July 3–December 6, 1170.* Hong Kong: Chinese University Press, 1981.

Yang Wanli

Heaven My Blanket, Earth My Pillow: Poems by Yang Wan-li. Translated by Jonathan Chaves. New York: Weatherhill, 1975.

Schmidt, J. D. *Yang Wan-li.* Boston: Twayne, 1976.

Fan Chengda

The Golden Year of Fan Ch'eng-ta: A Chinese Rural Sequence. Translated by Gerald Bullet. Cambridge: Cambridge University Press, 1946.

Schmidt, J. D. *Stone Lake: The Poetry of Fan Chengda (1126–1193).* Cambridge: Cambridge University Press, 1992.

Southern Song, Jin and Early Ming: *Ci*

General

Liu, James J. Y. *Major Lyricists of the Northern Sung, AD 960–1126.* Princeton: Princeton University Press, 1974.

Li Qingzhao

Hu, Pin-ching. *Li Ch'ing-chao.* New York: Twayne, 1965.

Li Ch'ing-chao: Complete Poems. Translated by Kenneth Rexroth and Ling Chung. New York: New Directions, 1979.

Xin Qiji, Jiang Kui, and Wu Wenying

Lo, Irving Yucheng. *Hsin Ch'i-chi.* New York: Twayne, 1971.

Lin, Shuen-fu. *The Transformation of the Chinese Lyrical Tradition: Chiang K'uei and Southern Sung Tz'u Poetry.* Princeton: Princeton University Press, 1978.

Fong, Grace S. *Wu Wenying and the Art of Southern Song Ci.* Princeton: Princeton University Press, 1987.

Chapter 16. Prose: *guwen, biji, chuanqi, pinghua* (1000–1450)

Liu Ts'un-yan. *Buddhist and Taoist Influences on the Chinese Novel I: The Authorship of the Feng-shen yen-i.* Wiesbaden: Otto Harrassowitz, 1962.

Ito Sohei. "Formation of the *Chiao-hung chi*: Its Change and Dissemination." *Acta Asiatica* 32 (1977): 73-95.

Proclaiming Harmony. Translated by William Hennessey. Ann Arbor: University of Michigan, Center for Chinese Studies, 1981. (Translation of *Xuanhe yishi.*)

Kerr, Katherine L. "*Yijian zhi*: A Didactic Diversion." *Papers on Far Eastern History* 35 (1987): 79-88.

Wang, Richard G. "The Cult of *Qing*: Romanticism in the Late Ming Period and in the Novel *Jiao Hong Ji*." *Ming Studies* 33 (1994): 12-55.

Chapter 17. *Qu: zhugongdiao, zaju* and *sanqu,* and *xiwen* (1000–1450)

Zhugongdiao
Ballad of the Hidden Dragon (Liu Chih-yuan chu-kung-tiao). Translated by M. Dolezelová-Velingerová and James I. Crump, Jr. Oxford: Oxford University Press, 1971. (A translation of the preserved fragments of the *Liu Zhiyuan zhugongdiao*.)
Master Tung's Western Chamber Romance (Tung Hsi-hsiang chu-kung-tiao): A Chinese Chantefable. Translated by Li-li Ch'en. Cambridge, MA: Cambridge University Press, 1976. (A translation of the *Xixiangji zhugongdiao*.)
West, Stephen H. *Vaudeville and Narrative: Aspects of Chinese Theater*. Wiesbaden: Franz Steiner Verlag, 1977. (Chapters 2 and 3 concern the *zhugongdiao*.)

Plays, *yuanben* and *zaju*
General: Anthologies
Chang, H. C. *Chinese Literature. Vol. 1: Popular Fiction and Drama*. Edinburgh: Edinburgh University Press, 1973.
Dolby, William. *Eight Chinese Plays*. London: Paul Elek, 1978.

General and early history of the theater
Dolby, William. *A History of Chinese Drama*. London: Paul Elek, 1976.
Idema, Wilt L., and Stephen H. West. *Chinese Theater 1100–1450: A Source Book*. Wiesbaden: Franz Steiner Verlag, 1982.
Chinese Theater, from Its Origin to the Present Day. Edited by Colin Mackerras. Honolulu: University of Hawaii Press, 1983.
Hsu, Tau Ching. *The Chinese Conception of the Theatre*. Seattle: University of Washington Press, 1985.
Ritual Opera, Operatic Ritual: 'Mulien Rescues his Mother' in Chinese Popular Culture. Edited by David Johnson. Berkeley: Institute of East Asian Studies, 1989.
Mackerras, Colin. *Chinese Drama: A Historical Survey*. Peking: New World Press, 1990.
Lopez, Manual D. *Chinese Drama: An Annotated Bibliography of Commentary, Criticism and Plays in English Translation*. Metuchen, NJ: Scarecrow Press, 1991.

Zaju: Studies and anthologies
Six Yüan Plays. Translated by Jung-en Liu. Harmondsworth: Penguin, 1972.
Shih, Chung-wen. *The Golden Age of Chinese Drama: Yüan Tsa-chü*. Princeton: Princeton University Press, 1976. (A general introduction to the *zaju*.)
Crime and Punishment in Medieval Chinese Drama: Three Judge Pao Plays. Translated by George A. Hayden. Cambridge, MA: Harvard University Press, 1978.
Perng, Ching-hsi. *Double Jeopardy: A Critique of Seven Yüan Courtroom Dramas*. Ann Arbor: Center for Chinese Studies, University of Michigan, 1978.
Johnson, Dale R. *Yuarn Music Dramas: Studies in Prosody and Structure and a Complete Catalogue of Northern Arias in the Dramatic Style*. Ann Arbor: Center for Chinese Studies, University of Michigan, 1980.

Crump, James I. *Chinese Theater in the Days of Kublai Khan.* Tucson: University of Arizona Press, 1981; rpt. Ann Arbor: Center for Chinese Studies, University of Michigan, 1991.

Guan Hanqing
Selected Plays of Kuan Han-ch'ing. Translated by Hsien-yi Yang and Gladys Yang. Shanghai: New Art and Literature Publishing House, 1958.
Shih, Chung-wen. *Injustice to Tou O (Tou O yuan): A Study and Translation.* Cambridge: Cambridge University Press, 1972.

Xixiang ji
The Romance of the Western Chamber (Hsi Hsiang Chi). Translated by S. I. Hsiung. London: Methuen and Co., 1935 (rpt. with a foreword by C. T. Hsia. New York: Columbia University Press, 1968). (A complete and reliable translation of the Jin Shengtan edition.)
Wang Shifu. *The Moon and the Zither: The Story of the Western Wing.* Edited and translated with an introduction by Stephen H. West and Wilt L. Idema. With a Study of the Woodblock Illustrations by Yao Dajun. Berkeley: University of California Press, 1991. Reissued in paperback as Wang Shifu, *The Story of the Western Wing.*

Zhu Youdun
Idema, Wilt L. *The Dramatic Oeuvre of Chu Yu-tun, 1379–1439.* Leiden: E. J. Brill, 1985.

Sanqu
Fifty Songs from the Yuan: Poetry of 13th Century China. Translated by Richard F. S. Yang and Charles R. Metzger. London: George Allen & Unwin, 1967.
Schlepp, Wayne. *San-ch'ü: Its Technique and Imagery.* Madison: University of Wisconsin Press, 1970. (Formalistic introduction.)
The Wine of Endless Life: Taoist Drinking Songs from the Yuan Dynasty. Translated by Jerome B. Seaton. Ann Arbor: Ardis, 1978.
Lynn, Richard J. *Kuan Yun-shih.* Boston: Twayne, 1980.
Crump, James I. *Songs from Xanadu: Studies in Mongol-Dynasty Song-Poetry (San-ch'ü).* Ann Arbor: Center for Chinese Studies, University of Michigan, 1983.
Radtke, Kurt W. *Poetry of the Yuan Dynasty.* Canberra: Faculty of Asian Studies, Australian National University, 1984.
Crump, James I. *Song-Poems from Xanadu.* Ann Arbor: Center for Chinese Studies, University of Michigan, 1993.

Xiwen and *chuanqi*
Zbikowski, Tadeusz. *Early Nan-hsi Plays of the Southern Sung Period.* Warsaw: Wydawnictwa Universytetu Warszawskiego, 1974.
The Lute: Kao Ming's P'i-p'a chi. Translated by Jean Mulligen. New York: Columbia University Press, 1980.
Leung, K. C. *Hsü Wei as Drama Critic: An Annotated Translation of the Nan-tz'u hsü-lu.* Eugene: University of Oregon, 1988.

Chapter 18. Classical-language poetry and prose (1450–1875)

Poetry
Ming poets

Pilgrim of the Clouds: Poems and Essays by Yüan Hung-tao and His Brothers. Translated by Jonathan Chaves. New York, Tokyo: Weatherhill, 1978.

Chou, Chih-p'ing. *Yüan Hung-tao and the Kung-an School.* Cambridge: Cambridge University Press, 1988.

Chang, Kang-i Sun. *The Late Ming Poet Ch'en Tzu-lung: Crisis of Love and Loyalism.* New Haven: Yale University Press, 1991.

Qing poets

Waley, Arthur. *Yüan Mei, Eighteenth Century Chinese Poet.* London: George Allen & Unwin, 1956.

Wong, Shirleen S. *Kung Tzu-chen.* Boston: Twayne, 1973.

Waiting for the Unicorn: Poems and Lyrics of China's Last Dynasty, 1644–1911. Edited by Irving Yucheng Lo and William Schultz. Bloomington: Indiana University Press, 1986.

Pohl, Karl Heinz. *Cheng Pan-ch'iao, Poet, Painter and Calligrapher.* Nettetal: Steyler Verlag, 1990.

Chaves, Jonathan. *Singing of the Source: Nature and God in the Poetry of the Chinese Painter Wu Li.* Honolulu: University of Hawaii Press, 1993.

Choy, Elsie. *Leaves of Prayer: The Life and Poetry of He Shuangqing, a Farmwife in Eighteenth-Century China.* Hong Kong: Chinese University Press, 1993.

Shihua

Wong, Siu-kit. *Notes on Poetry from the Ginger Studio.* Hong Kong: Chinese University Press, 1987.

Chinese Literary Criticism of the Ch'ing Period. Edited by John Wang. Hong Kong: n.p., 1993.

Ci

McCraw, David R. *Chinese Lyricists of the Seventeenth Century.* Honolulu: University of Hawaii Press, 1990.

Wang Guowei and his *Renjian cihua*

Poetic Remarks in the Human World. Translated by Ching-i Tu. Taipei: Chung Hwa Book Co., 1970.

Wang Kuo-wei's Jen-chien Tz'u-hua: A Study in Chinese Literary Criticism. Translated by Adele Austin Rickett. Hong Kong: Hong Kong University Press, 1977.

Prose
Ming prose

The Travel Diaries of Hsu Hsia-k'o. Translated by Li Chi. Hong Kong: Chinese University of Hong Kong, 1974. (An anthology from the works of Xu Xiake.)

Plaks, Andrew H. "The Prose of Our Time." In *The Power of Culture, Studies in Chinese Cultural History.* Edited by Willard Peterson et al., pp. 206-17. Hongkong: Chinese University Press, 1994. (Translation and analysis of an examination essay.)

Qing prose

Shen Fu and his *Fusheng linji*

"Six Chapters of a Floating Life." Translated by Lin Yutang. In *The Wisdom of China and India*. Edited by Lin Yutang, pp. 964-1050. New York: Randon House, 1942.

Shen Fu: Six Records of a Floating Life. Translated by Leonard Pratt and Su-hui Chiang. Harmondsworth: Penguin, 1983.

Ji Yun

Chan, Leo Tak-hung. *The Discourse on Foxes and Ghosts: Ji Yun and Eighteenth-Century Literati Storytelling*. Hong Kong: Chinese University Press, 1997.

Pu Songling and his *Liaozhai zhiyi*: Translations and studies

Pu Songling. *Strange Tales of Liaozhai*. Translated by Lu Yunzhong et al. Hong Kong: Commercial Press, 1982.

P'u, Sung-ling. *Strange Tales from Make-Do Studio*. Beijing: Foreign Languages Press, 1989.

Zeitlin, Judith T. *Historian of the Strange: Pu Songling and the Chinese Classical Tale*. Stanford: Stanford University Press, 1993.

Compilations

Guy, R. Kent. *The Emperor's Four Treasuries: Scholars and the State in the Late Ch'ien-lung era*. Cambridge, MA: Harvard University Press, 1987.

Loewe, Michael. *The Origins and Development of Chinese Encyclopaedias*. London: China Society, 1987.

Chapter 19. Drama: *Zaju, Chuanqi,* and regional drama (1450–1875)

Chuanqi: General

Huang Hung, Josephine. *Ming Drama: Drama of the Ming Dynasty*. Taipei: Heritage Press, 1966. (Superficial introduction.)

Tang Xianzu

Tang Xianzu. *The Peony Pavilion (Mudan Ting)*. Translated by Cyril Birch. Bloomington: Indiana University Press, 1980. (Full translation; superbly readable.)

Li Yu

Mao, Nathan. *Li Yü's Twelve Towers*. Hong Kong: Chinese University of Hong Kong, 1975. (Not so much translations as rather mediocre retellings.)

———— and Liu Ts'un-yan. *Li Yu*. Boston: Twayne, 1979.

Henry, Eric P. *Chinese Amusement: The Lively Plays of Li Yu*. Hamden, CT: Archon Books, 1980.

Hanan, Patrick. *The Invention of Li Yü*. Cambridge, MA: Harvard University Press, 1988.

Li Yu. *The Carnal Prayer Mat (Rou Putuan)*. Translated by Patrick Hanan. New York: Ballantine Books, 1990.

————. *Silent Operas*. Edited by Patrick Hanan. Hong Kong: Chinese University of Hong Kong, 1990.

Chang, Chun-shu and Shelley Hsueh-lun Chang. *Crisis and Transformation in Seventeenth-Century China: Society, Culture and Modernity in Li Yü's World*. Ann Arbor: University of Michigan Press, 1992.

Li Yu. *A Tower for the Summer Heat*. Translated by Patrick Hanan. New York: Ballantine Books, 1992.

Hong Sheng's *Changsheng dian*

Hung Sheng, *The Palace of Eternal Youth*. Translated by Yang Hsien-yi and Gladys Yang. Peking: Foreign Languages Press, 1955.

Kong Shangren's *Taohua shan*

K'ung Shang-jen. *The Peach Blossom Fan*. Translated by Chen Shih-hsiang, Harold Acton, and Cyril Birch. Berkeley: University of California Press, 1976.

Strassberg, Richard E. *The World of K'ung Shang-jen: A Man of Letters in Early Ch'ing China*. New York: Columbia University Press, 1983.

Peking opera

Arlington, L. C. *The Chinese Drama from the Earliest Times until Today*. Shanghai: Kelly and Walsh, 1930.

Zung, Cecilia. *Secrets of the Chinese Drama*. London: G. G. Harrap and Co., 1937.

Scott, A. C. *The Classical Theatre of China*. London: Allen & Unwin, 1957.

———. *Traditional Chinese Plays*. 3 volumes. Madison: University of Wisconsin Press, 1967–75.

Mackerras, Colin P. *The Rise of the Peking Opera 1770–1870: Social Aspects of the Theatre in Manchu China*. Oxford: Oxford University Press, 1972.

Wu, Zuguang, Huang Zuolin, and Mei Shaowu. *Peking Opera and Mei Lanfang*. Peking: New World Press, 1984.

The Fox Cat Substituted for The Crown Prince: A Peking Opera Set in The Song Dynasty. Translated by Donald K. Chang and John D. Mitchell. Midland, MI: Northwood Institute Press, 1985.

The Phoenix Returns to its Nest: A Beijing Opera Created by Mei Lanfang. Translated by Elizabeth Wichman. Peking: New World Press, 1986.

Wichman, Elizabeth. *Listening to Theatre: The Aural Dimension of Beijing Opera*. Honolulu: University of Hawaii Press, 1991.

Pan, Xiafeng. *The Stagecraft of Peking Opera, From Its Origins to the Present Day*. Peking: New World Press, 1995.

Puppet plays

Obraztsov, Sergei. *The Chinese Puppet Theatre*. London: Faber and Faber, 1961.

Stalberg, Roberta Helmer. *China's Puppets*. San Francisco: China Books, 1984.

Shadow plays

March, Benjamin. *Chinese Shadow-Figure Plays and Their Making*. Detroit: n.p., 1938.

Broman, Sven. *Chinese Shadow Theatre*. Stockholm: Etnografiska Museet, 1981.

Liu Jilin. *Chinese Shadow Puppet Plays*. Peking: Morning Glory Publishers, 1988.

Chin, Chen-an. *The Mainstay of the Chinese Shadow Show: The Lanchou Shadow Show*. Taipei: Student Book Company, 1993.

Chapter 20. The novel (1450–1650)

General

Chinese Novels, Translated from the Originals, To Which Are Added Proverbs and Moral Maxims Collected from Their Classical Books and Other Sources. Translated by John Francis Davis. London, 1822; rpt. Delmar, NY: Scholars' Facsimiles & Reprints, 1977.

Lu Hsun. *A Brief History of Chinese Fiction.* Peking: Foreign Languages Press, 1959.

Hsia, C. T. *The Classic Chinese Novel: A Critical Introduction.* New York: Columbia University Press, 1968.

Idema, Wilt L. *Chinese Vernacular Fiction: The Formative Period.* Leiden: E. J. Brill, 1974. (Concerns the relationships between *pinghua* and the historical romances.)

Chinese Narrative: Critical and Theoretical Essays. Edited by Andrew Plaks. Princeton: Princeton University Press, 1977.

Yang, Winston et al. *Classical Chinese Fiction: A Guide to its Study and Appreciation, Essays and Bibliographies.* Boston: G. K. Hall, 1978.

Critical Essays on Chinese Fiction. Edited by Winston L. Y. Yang and Curtis P. Adkins. Hong Kong: Chinese University Press, 1980.

Hegel, Robert E. *The Novel in Seventeenth Century China.* New York: Columbia University Press, 1981.

Plaks, Andrew H. *The Four Masterworks of the Ming Novel: Ssu-ta Ch'i-shu.* Princeton: Princeton University Press, 1987. (Successive chapters—each voluminous—are devoted to *Jin Ping Mei*, *Xiyou ji*, *Shuihu zhuan* and *Sanguo zhi yanyi*. Plaks sees "self-cultivation" as the central theme; he emphasizes the ironic distance between the authors and their characters.)

Literary Migrations: Traditional Chinese Fiction in Asia (17th–20th centuries). Edited by Claudine Salmon. Peking: International Culture Publishing Corporation, 1987.

Berry, Margaret. *The Chinese Classic Novels: An Annotated Bibliography of Chiefly English-Language Studies.* New York: Garland Publishing, 1988.

How to Read the Chinese Novel. Edited by David L. Rolston. Contributors: Shuen-fu Lin, David T. Roy, Andrew D. Plaks, John Y. Wang, David L. Rolston, Anthony C. Yu. Princeton: Princeton University Press, 1990.

Chang, Shelley Hsueh-lun. *History and Legend: Ideas and Images in the Ming Historical Novel.* Ann Arbor: University of Michigan Press, 1990.

Lu, Sheldon Hsiao-peng. *From Historicity to Fictionality: The Chinese Poetics of Narrative.* Stanford: Stanford University Press, 1994.

Zhao, Henry Y. H. *The Uneasy Narrator: Chinese Fiction from the Traditional to the Modern.* Oxford: Oxford University Press, 1995.

Rolston, David L. *Traditional Chinese Fiction and Fiction Commentary.* Stanford: Stanford University Press, 1997.

Sanguo zhi yanyi: Translations

Roberts, Moss. *Three Kingdoms: China's Epic Drama* New York: Pantheon Books, 1976. (Translation of related fragments, mainly from Chapters 20-85.)

Luo Guanzhong. *Three Kingdoms: A Historical Novel, Attributed to Luo Guanzhong.* Translated by Moss Roberts. Berkeley: University of California Press, 1992.

Shuihu zhuan: Translations and studies

All Men are Brothers. Translated by Pearl S. Buck. New York: John Day, 1933. (Translation of the seventy-chapter version.)

Irwin, Richard G. *The Evolution of a Chinese Novel: Shui-hu-chuan*. Cambridge, MA: Harvard University Press, 1953.

Wang, John C. Y. *Chin Sheng-t'an*. New York: Twayne, 1972.

Outlaws of the Marsh. 3 volumes. Translated by Sidney Shapiro. Peking: Foreign Languages Press, 1980.

Widmer, Ellen. *The Margins of Utopia: Shui-hu hou-chuan and the Literature of Ming Loyalism*. Cambridge, MA: Harvard University Press, 1987.

The Broken Seals: Part One of the Marshes of Mount Liang: A New Translation of the Shihu zhuan or Water Margin of Shi Naian and Luo Guanzhong. Translated by John and Alex Dent-Young. Hong Kong: Chinese University Press, 1994.

Novels in and after the Wanli period
Xiyou ji and its sequels: Translations and studies

Monkey. Translated by Arthur Waley. London: John Day, 1942.

Dudbridge, Glen. *The Hsi-yu chi: A Study of the Antecedents to the Sixteenth-Century Chinese Novel*. Cambridge: Cambridge University Press, 1970.

Brandauer, Frederick W. *Tung Yüeh*. Boston: Twayne, 1978.

Tower of Myriad Mirrors: A Supplement of Journey to the West, by Tung Yüeh (1620–1686). Translated by Shuen-fu Lin and Larry Schulz. Berkeley: Asian Humanities Press, 1978.

Wu Cheng'en. *Journey to the West*. 3 volumes. Translated by W. J. F. Jenner. Peking: Foreign Languages Press, 1982–1986. (A complete translation in three volumes.)

The Journey to the West. 4 volumes. Translated by Anthony C. Yu. Chicago: University of Chicago Press, 1977–83. (Complete translation.)

Seaman, Gary. *Journey to the North: An Ethnohistorical Analysis and Annotated Translation of the Chinese Folk Novel Pei-yu-chi*. Berkeley: University of California Press, 1987.

Liu, Xiaolian. *The Odyssey of the Buddhist Mind, The Allegory of the Later Journey to the West*. Lanham, MD: University Press of America, 1994.

Fengshen yanyi: Translations and studies

Liu, Ts'un-yan. *Buddhist and Taoist Influences on Chinese Novels*. Vol. I: *The Authorship of the Feng-shen yen-i*. Wiesbaden: Otto Harrassowitz, 1962.

Creation of the Gods. 2 volumes. Translated by Zhizhong Gu. Peking: New World Press, 1992.

Jin Ping Mei: Translations and studies

The Golden Lotus. 4 volumes. Translated by Clement Egerton. London: Routledge, 1939. (Complete translation.)

Carlitz, Katherine. *The Rhetoric of "Chin p'ing mei."* Bloomington: Indiana University Press, 1986.

The Plum in the Golden Vase, or, Chin P'ing Mei. Vol. I: *The Gathering*. Translated by David T. Roy. Princeton: Princeton University Press, 1993.

Rushton, Peter H. *The Jin Ping Mei and the Non-Linear Dimensions of the Traditional Chinese Novel*. Lewiston: Edwin Mellen Press, 1994.

The Bonds of Matrimony: Hsing-shih yinyüan chuan (Vol. One), A Seventeenth Century Novel. Translated by
  Even Alison Nyren. Chinese Studies vol. I. Lewiston, ME: Edwin Mellen, 1995. (Translates
  chapters 1-20 of *Xingshi yinyuan zhuan.*)

Chapter 21. The novella (*huaben*) (1450–1650)

Earliest editions

Translations: General and *San yan*

The Inconstancy of Madam Chuang: and Other Stories from the Chinese. Translated by E. Howell
  Butts. London: T. W. Laurie, 1924. (Six *huaben* from the *Jingu qiguan.*)
The Restitution of the Bride; and Other Stories from the Chinese. Translated by E. Howell Butts.
  London: T. W. Laurie, 1926. (Six *huaben* from the *Jingu qiguan.*)
Four Cautionary Tales. Translated by Harold Acton and Lee Yihsieh. London: John Lehman,
  1947. (Contains four *huaben* from the *Xingshi hengyan.*)
The Courtesan's Jewel Box: Chinese Stories of the Xth-XVIIth Centuries. Translated by Hsien-yi
  Yang and Gladys Yang. Peking: Foreign Languages Press, 1957. (Contains twenty
  novellas from the *San yan* and *Liang pai.*)
*Stories from a Ming Collection: Translations of Chinese Short Stories, Published in the Seventeenth
  Century.* Translated by Cyril Birch. London: Bodley Head, 1958. (Contains six novellas
  from *Gujin xiaoshuo.*)
Eight Colloquial Tales of the Song. Translated by Richard F. S. Yang. Taipei: China Post, 1972.
  (A translation of the novellas in the *Jingben tongsu xiaoshuo.*)
The Perfect Lady by Mistake. Translated by William Dolby. London: Paul Elek, 1976.
  (Translates six *huaben* from the *San yan.*)
McLaren, Anne E. *The Chinese Femme Fatale: Stories from the Ming Period.* University of Sidney East
  Asian Series, no. 8. Broadway: Wild Peony, 1994. (Contains three short stories from *Sanyan.*)

Other texts published by Feng Menglong: Translations

Birch, Cyril. *Chinese Myths and Fantasies.* London, 1961. (Contains, on pp. 113-200, an
  abridged retelling of Feng Menglong's *Pingyao zhuan.*)
Mowry, Hua-yuan Li. *Chinese Love Stories from "Ching-shih".* Hamden: Anchor Books, 1983.

Studies: General and *San yan*

Hanan, Patrick. *The Chinese Short Story: Studies in Dating, Authorship and Composition.*
  Cambridge, MA: Harvard University Press, 1973.
Idema, Wilt L. *Chinese Vernacular Fiction: The Formative Period.* Leiden: E. J. Brill, 1974.
Hanan, Patrick. *The Chinese Vernacular Story.* Cambridge, MA: Harvard University Press,
  1981.

Liang pai: Translations

The Lecherous Academician. Translated by John Scott. London: Rapp and Whiting, 1973.

Chapter 22. The novel (1650–1875)

Novels written by literati for literati
General
Huang, Martin W. *Literati and Self-Re/Presentation, Autobiographical Sensibility in the Eighteenth-Century Chinese Novel.* Stanford: Stanford University Press, 1995.

McMahon, Keith. *Misers, Shrews, and Polygamists, Sexuality and Male-Female Relations in Eighteenth-Century Fiction.* Durham: Duke University Press, 1995.

Rulin waishi: Translations and studies
Wu Ching-tzu. *The Scholars.* Translated by Hsien-yi Yang and Gladys Yang. Peking: Foreign Languages Press, 1957.

Wong, Timothy C. *Wu Ching-tzu.* Boston: Twayne, 1978.

Ropp, Paul C. *Dissent in Early Modern China: Ju-lin wai-shih and Ch'ing Social Criticism.* Ann Arbor: University of Michigan Press, 1981.

Honglou meng: Translations
Dream of the Red Chamber. Translated by Chi-chen Wang. London: George Routledge, 1929. (Radically abridged.)

The Story of the Stone. 5 volumes. Translated by David Hawkes (volumes 1-3) and John Minford (volumes 4-5). Harmondsworth: Penguin, 1973–86.

A Dream of Red Mansions. 3 volumes. Translated by Hsien-yi Yang and Gladys Yang. Peking: Foreign Languages Press, 1978–1980. (A nearly complete translation.)

Honglou meng: Studies
Wu, Shih-Ch'ang. *On the Red Chamber Dream: A Critical Study of Two Annotated Manuscripts of the XVIIIth Century.* Oxford: Oxford University Press, 1961.

Spence, Jonathan D. *Ts'ao Yin and the K'ang-hsi Emperor: Bondservant and Master.* New Haven: Yale University Press, 1966. (Fascinating biographical study of Cao Xueqin's grandfather.)

Miller, Lucien. *Masks of Fiction in Dream of the Red Chamber: Myth, Mimesis and Persona.* Tucson: University of Arizona Press, 1975.

Plaks, Andrew. *Archetype and Allegory in the Dream of the Red Chamber.* Princeton: Princeton University Press, 1976.

Na, Tsung Shun. *Studies on the Dream of the Red Chamber: A Selected and Classified Bibliography.* Hong Kong: Lung Men, 1979.

———. *Studies on Dream of the Red Chamber: A Supplement to The Selected and Classified Bibliography.* Hong Kong: Lung Men, 1981.

Wang, Jing. *The Story of Stone: Intertextuality, Ancient Chinese Stone Lore and the Stone Symbolism of the Dream of the Red Chamber, Water Margin, and the Journey to the West.* Durham: Duke University Press, 1992.

Li, Wai-yee. *Enchantment and Disenchantment: Love and Illusion in Chinese Literature.* Princeton: Princeton University Press, 1993.

Edwards, Louise P. *Men and Women in Qing China: Gender in The Red Chamber Dream.* Leiden: E. J. Brill, 1994.

Wu Zetian si da qi'an: Translations and studies
Dee Goong An: Three Murder Cases Solved by Judge Dee. Translated by R. H. Van Gulik. Tokyo: Toppan Printing Company 1949.
Idema, Wilt L. "The Mystery of the Halved Judge Dee Novel." *Tamkang Review* 8 (1977): 155-70.

Jinghua yuan
Flowers in the Mirror. Translated by Tai-yi Lin. London: Owen, 1965. (Much abridged.)
Kao, Hsin-sheng C. *Li Ju-chen.* Boston: Twayne, 1981.

Qilu deng
Borotová, Lucie. *A Confucian Story of the Prodigal Son: Li Lüyuan's Novel Lantern at the Crossroads.* Bochum: Brockmeyer, 1991.

"Talent and Beauty" novels
The Fortunate Union: A Romance. 2 volumes. Translated by John Francis Davis. London: Oriental Translation Fund, 1829.
Cheung, Kai Chong. *The Theme of Chastity in Hau Ch'iu Chuan and Parallel Western Fiction.* Eurosinica, Vol. VI. Bern: Peter Lang, 1994.

"Military romances"
Hsia, C. T. "The Military Romance: A Genre of Chinese Fiction." In *Studies in Chinese Literary Genres.* Edited by Cyril Birch, pp. 339-90. Berkeley: University of California Press, 1974.
General Yue Fei, A Novel by Qian Cai of the Qing Dynasty. Translated by T. L. Yang. Hong Kong: JPC, 1995.

Chapbooks
Seven Taoist Masters: A Folk Novel of China. Translated by Eva Wong. Boston: Shambhala, 1990.

Chapter 23. Performance texts (*shuochang wenxue*) (1450–1875)

Professional storytellers and their stories
Hung, Chang-tai. *Going to the People: Chinese Intellectuals and Folk Literature, 1918–1937.* Cambridge, MA: Harvard University Press, 1985.
Bördahl, Vibeke. *The Oral Tradition of Yangzhou Storytelling.* NIAS Monograph Series, no. 73. Richmond: Curzon Press, 1996.

Cihua
The Story of Hua Guan Suo. Translated by Gail Oman King. Tempe: Center for Asian Studies, Arizona State University, 1989.

North China
Meng Chiang Nü (Chinese Drum Song), The Lady of the Long Wall: A Ku Shih or Drum Song of China. Translated by Genevieve Wimsatt and Geoffrey Chen. New York: Columbia University Press, 1934.

South China (Guangdong and Guangxi)

Hensman, Bertha and Mack Kwok-ping. *Hong Kong Tale Spinners: A Collection of Tales and Ballads Transcribed and Translated from Story-Tellers in Hong Kong.* Hong Kong: Chinese University of Hong Kong, 1968.

Hensman, Bertha. *More Hong Kong Tale-Spinners: Twenty-Five Traditional Chinese Tales Collected by Tape-Recorder and Translated into English.* Hong Kong: Chinese University of Hong Kong, 1971.

Baojuan

Dudbridge, Glen. *The Legend of Miao-shan.* London: Ithaca Press, 1978. (Discusses a *baojuan* on Guanyin.)

Texts in Women's Script

Chiang, William W. *"We Two Know the Script; We Have Become Good Friends": Linguistic and Social Aspects of the Women's Script Literacy in Southern Hunan, China.* Lanham, MD: University Press of America, 1995.

Oral literature

Popular fairy tales

Ting, Nai-tung. *A Type Index of Chinese Folktales In the Oral Tradition and Major Works of Non-Religious Classical Literature.* Helsinki: Suomalainen Tiedeakatemia, 1978.

Favourite Folktales of China. Translated by John Minford. Peking: New World Press, 1983.

Chin, Ming-bien, Yetta S. Center, and Mildred Ross. *Traditional Chinese Folktales.* Armonk, NY: East Gate/M. E. Sharpe, 1989.

Jokes, etc.

Chinese Wit and Humor. Edited by George Kao. New York: Coward-McCann, 1946.

Levy, Howard. *Chinese Sex Jokes in Traditional Times.* Taipei: Chinese Association for Folklore, 1974.

Proverbs, etc.

Smith, Arthur H. *Proverbs and Common Sayings from the Chinese.* Revised edition. Shanghai: American Presbyterian Mission Press, 1902.

Lai, T. C. *Selected Chinese Sayings.* Hong Kong: University Book Store, 1960.

Lai, T. C. *More Chinese Sayings.* Hong Kong, 1972.

Bueler, William M. *Chinese Sayings.* Rutland, VT: Charles E. Tuttle, 1972.

Nursery rhymes

Vitale, Guido. *Pekinese Rhymes.* Peking: Vetch and Lee, Ltd., 1896.

Johnson, Kinchen. *Peiping Rhymes.* Peiping: Commercial Printing & Co., 1932.

Chapter 24. The transitional period: 1875–1915

Wuxia xiaoshuo: Ji gong zhuan

The Drunken Buddha. Translated by Ian Fairweather. Brisbane: University of Queensland Press, 1965.

Newspapers, etc.

Britton, Roswell S. *The Chinese Periodical Press 1800–1912*. Shanghai: Kelly & Walsh, Ltd., 1933.

Lin Yutang. *A History of the Press and Public Opinion in China*. Shanghai: Kelly & Walsh, Ltd., 1936. (General introduction.)

Cohen, Paul A. *Between Tradition and Modernity: Wang T'ao and Reform in Late Ch'ing China*. Cambridge, MA: Harvard University Press, 1974.

Reformers and the introduction of Western ideas

Harrell, Paula. *Sowing the Seeds of Change: Chinese Students, Japanese Teachers, 1895–1905*. Stanford: Stanford University Press, 1992.

Yeh, Wen-hsin. *The Alienated Academy: Culture and Politics in Republican China, 1919–1937*. Cambridge, MA: Harvard University Press, 1990.

Liang Qichao

Levenson, J. *Liang Ch'i-ch'ao and the Mind of Modern China*. Cambridge, MA: Harvard University Press, 1953.

Chang, Hao. *Liang Ch'i-ch'ao and Intellectual Transition in China, 1890–1907*. Cambridge, MA: Harvard University Press, 1971.

Yan Fu and Lin Shu

Schwartz, Benjamin. *In Search of Wealth and Power: Yen Fu and the West*. Cambridge, MA: Harvard University Press, 1964.

Lee, Leo Ou-fan. *The Romantic Generation of Modern Chinese Writers*. Cambridge, MA: Harvard University Press, 1973. (Chapter 3 is devoted to Lin Shu.)

Huang Zunxian

Schmidt, J. D. *Within the Human Realm: The Poetry of Huang Zunxian, 1848–1905*. Cambridge: Cambridge University Press, 1994.

Novels: General

The Chinese Novel at the Turn of the Century. Edited by Milena Dolezelová-Velingerová. Toronto: University of Toronto Press, 1980.

Link, E. Perry, Jr. *Mandarin Ducks and Butterflies: Popular Fiction in Early Twentieth Century Chinese Cities*. Berkeley: University of California, 1981.

Chinese Middlebrow Fiction From the Ch'ing and Early Republican Eras. Edited by Ts'un-yan Liu. Hong Kong: Chinese University Press, 1984.

Kockum, Keiko. *Japanese Achievement, Chinese Aspiration: A Study of the Japanese Influence on the Modernisation of the Late Qing Novel*. Orientaliska studiers skrift serie nr. 24. Stockholm: Orientaliska Studier, University of Stockholm, 1990.

Chow, Rey. *Woman and Chinese Modernity: The Politics of Reading between West and East*. Minneapolis: University of Minnesota Press, 1991.

Wu Woyao

Vignettes from the Late Ch'ing: Bizarre Happenings Eyewitnessed over Two Decades. Translated by Shih-shun Liu. Hong Kong: Chinese University of Hong Kong, 1975. (A much abridged translation of the *Ershi nian mudu zhi guai xianzhuang*.)

Wu Jianren and Fu Lin. *Two Turn-of the-Century Chinese Romantic Novels: Stones in the Sea by Fu Lin and The Sea of Regret by Wu Jianren.* Translated by Patrick Hanan. Honolulu: University of Hawaii Press, 1995.

Li Baojia
Lancashire, Douglas. *Li Po-yuan.* Boston: Twayne, 1981.
Li, Boyuan. *Modern Times, A Brief History of Enlightenment.* Translated by Douglas Lancashire. A *Renditions* Book. Hong Kong: Research Centre for Translation, Chinese University, 1996.

Liu E
Liu E. *A Nun of Taishan (A Novelette) and Other Translations.* Translated by Lin Yutang. Shanghai: Commercial Press, 1936. (Includes a free translation of Chapters 21 to 26 of the *Lao Can youji.*)
The Travels of Lao Ts'an. Translated by Harold Shadick. Ithaca: Cornell University Press, 1952. (A translation of the *Lao Can youji*, Chapters 1-20.)

Zeng Pu
That Chinese Woman: The Life of Sai-chin-hua. Translated by H. McAleavy. London: Allen & Unwin, 1959.
Peter Li. *Tseng P'u.* Boston: Twayne, 1980.

Su Manshu
Leung, George Kin. *The Lone Swan: The Autobiography of the Great Scholar and Monk, the Reverend Mandju.* Shanghai: Commercial Press, 1924.
McAleavy, Henry. *Su-Manshu, a Sino-Japanese Genius.* London: China Society, 1960.
Liu, Wu-chi. *Su Man-shu.* New York: Twayne, 1972.

Wang Guowei
Bonner, Joey. *Wang Kuo-wei: An Intellectual Biography.* Cambridge, MA: Harvard University Press, 1986.

Chapter 25. Modern literature: an introduction

The Literary Revolution and the May Fourth Movement
General reference works and anthologies

Schijns, Jos. et al. *1500 Modern Chinese Novels and Plays: Present Day Fiction and Drama in China.* Peking: Catholic University Press, 1948.
Gibbs, Donald and Yun-chen Li. *A Bibliography of Studies and Translations of Modern Chinese Literature 1918-1942.* Cambridge, MA: Harvard University Press, 1975.
Lau, Joseph S. M. *Columbia Anthology of Modern Chinese Literature.* New York: Columbia University Press, 1995.

General surveys and collections

Hu Shih. *The Chinese Renaissance: The Haskell Lectures 1933.* Chicago: University of Chicago Press, 1934.
Chow, Tse-tsung. *The May 4th Movement: Intellectual Revolution in Modern China.* Cambridge, MA: Harvard University Press, 1960.

Scott, A. C. *Literature and the Arts in Twentieth Century China*. New York: Doubleday, 1963. (An attractive, readable introduction including film and the arts.)

Hsia, Tsi-an Hsia. *The Gate of Darkness: Studies on the Leftist Literary Movement in China*. Seattle: University of Washington Press, 1968.

Lee, Leo Ou-fan. *The Romantic Generation of Modern Chinese Writers*. Cambridge, MA: Harvard University Press, 1973.

Modern Chinese Literature in its Social Context. Edited by Göran Malmqvist. Stockholm: Nobel Symposium, 1975.

Modern Chinese Literature in the May Fourth Era. Edited by Merle Goldman. Cambridge, MA: Harvard University Press, 1977.

Lin, Yü-sheng. *The Crisis of Chinese Consciousness: Radical Antitraditionalism in the May Fourth Era*. Madison: University of Wisconsin Press, 1979.

Průšek, Jaroslav. *The Lyrical and the Epic: Studies of Modern Chinese Literature*. Edited by Leo Ou-fan Lee. Bloomington: Indiana University Press, 1980.

Gunn, Edward. *The Unwelcome Muse: Chinese Literature in Shanghai and Peking 1937–1945*. New York: Columbia University Press, 1980.

China Handbook Series: Literature and the Arts. Translated by Bonnie S. McDougall and Hu Liuyu. Peking: Foreign Languages Press, 1983.

Schwartcz, Vera. *The Chinese Enlightenment: Intellectuals and the Legacy of the May Fourth Movement of 1919*. Berkeley: University of California Press, 1986.

Eide, Elizabeth. *China's Ibsen: From Ibsen to Ibsenism*. London: Curzon Press, 1987.

Wong, Wang-chi. *Politics and Literature in Shanghai: The Chinese League of Left-Wing Writers, 1930–1936*. Manchester: Manchester University Press, 1991.

Larson, Wendy. *Literary Authority and the Modern Chinese Writer: Ambivalence and Autobiography*. Durham: Duke University Press, 1991.

Gunn, Edward. *Rewriting Chinese: Style and Innovation in Twentieth Century Chinese Prose*. Stanford: Stanford University Press, 1991.

Herdan, Innes. *The Pen and the Sword: Literature and Revolution in Modern China*. London: Red Books, 1992.

Modern Chinese Writers' Self Portrayals. Edited by Helmut Martin and Jeffrey Kinkley. Armonk, N.Y.: M. E. Sharpe, 1992.

Words from the West: Western Texts in Chinese Literary Context. Edited by Lloyd Haft. Leiden: Centre of Non-Western Studies, 1993.

Politics, Ideology and Literary Discourse in Modern China. Edited by Kang Liu and Xiaobing Tang. Durham: Duke University Press, 1993.

From May Fourth to June Fourth: Fiction and Film in Twentieth Century China. Edited by Ellen Widmer and David Der-wei Wang. Cambridge, MA: Harvard University Press, 1993.

Hung, Chang-tai. *War and Popular Culture: Resistance in Modern China, 1937-1945*. Berkeley: University of California Press, 1994.

Liu, Lydia H. *Translingual Practice, Literature, National Culture, and Translated Modernity, China, 1900-1937*. Stanford: Stanford University Press, 1995.

Zhang, Yingjin. *The City in Modern Chinese Literature and Film: Configurations of Space, Time and Gender*. Stanford: Stanford University Press, 1996.

Women in modern Chinese literature

Hsu, Vivian Ling. *Born of the Same Roots: Stories of Modern Chinese Women*. Bloomington: Indiana University Press, 1981.

Women and Literature in China. Edited by Anna Gerstlacher et al. Bochum: Brockmeyer, 1985. (Also contains some articles on traditional literature.)

Gender, Writing, Feminism, China. Edited by Tani Barlow. Theme issue, *Modern Chinese Literature* 4, nos. 1 and 2 (1988).

Chow, Rey. *Woman and Chinese Modernity: The Politics of Reading between West and East.* Minnesota: University of Minnesota Press, 1991.

Gender and Sexuality in Twentieth-Century Chinese Literature and Society. Edited by Tonglin Lu. Albany: State University of New York Press, 1993.

Gender Politics in Modern China: Writing and Feminism. Edited by Tani Barlow. 1994. (*Modern Chinese Literature* 4 [1988].)

Hu Shi and Chen Duxiu

Grieder, Jerome B. *Hu Shi and the Chinese Renaissance: Liberalism in the Chinese Revolution, 1917–1937.* Cambridge, MA: Harvard University Press, 1970.

Kuo, Thomas C. *Ch'en Tu-hsiu (1879–1942) and the Chinese Communist Movement.* South Orange, NJ: Seton Hall University Press, 1975.

Chou, Min-chih. *Hu Shih and Intellectual Choice in Modern China.* Ann Arbor: University of Michigan Press, 1984.

Literary criticism

McDougall, Bonnie S. *The Introduction of Western Literary Theories into Modern China 1919–1925.* Tokyo: Centre for East Asian Cultural Studies, 1971.

Gálik, Marián. *The Genesis of Modern Chinese Literary Criticism (1917–1930).* London: Curzon Press, 1980. (A very detailed study.)

Eber, Irene. *Voices from Afar: Modern Chinese Writers on Oppressed Peoples and their Literature.* Ann Arbor: Center for Chinese Studies, University of Michigan, 1980.

Modern Chinese Literary Thought: Writings on Literature, 1893–1945. Edited by Kirk A. Denton. Stanford: Stanford University Press, 1996.

Traditional literature after 1917: Poetry

Poems of Wang Ching-wei. Translated by Seyuan Shu. London: Allen & Unwin, 1938.

The Poems of Mao Tse-tung. Translated by Willis Barnstone. London: Barrie & Jenkins, 1972. (A free, creative translation.)

In Quest: Poems of Chou En-lai. Translated by Nancy T. Lin. Hong Kong: Joint Publications, 1979.

Soaring: Poems of Liao Chung-k'ai and Ho Hsiang-ning. Translated by Wen-yee Ma. Hong Kong. Joint Publishing, 1980.

Traditional literature after 1917; novels: Translations and studies

Rupprecht, Hsiao-wen Wang. *Departure and Return: Chang Hen-shui and the Chinese Narrative Tradition.* Hong Kong: Joint Publishing, 1987.

Huanzhulouzhu, Blades from the Willows, A Chinese Novel of Fantasy and Martial Arts Adventure. Translated by Robert Chard. London: Wellsweep, 1991.

Jin Yong. *Fox Volant of Snowy Mountain.* Translated by Olivia Mok. Hong Kong: Chinese University Press, 1993.

Traditional literature after 1917; drama: Translations and studies
Chu Su-chen. *Fifteen Strings of Cash*. Translated by Yang Hsien-yi and Gladys Yang. Peking: Foreign Languages Press, 1957.
Chinese Village Plays from the Ting Hsien Region. Edited by Sidney D. Gamble. Amsterdam: Philo Press, 1970.
Yung, Bell. *Cantonese Opera: Performance as Creative Process*. Cambridge: Cambridge University Press, 1989.

Chapter 26. Modern literature, 1917–1942: the short story and the novel

General: Studies
Hsia, C. T. *A History of Modern Chinese Fiction*. New Haven: Yale University Press, 1961; 2nd ed., 1971.
Modern Chinese Fiction: A Guide to its Study and Appreciation: Essays and Bibliographies. Edited by Winston Yang and Nathan Mao. Boston: G. K. Hall, 1981.
A Selective Guide to Chinese Literature 1900–1949. Vol. I, *The Novel*. Edited by Milena Dolezelová-Velingerová. Leiden: E. J. Brill, 1988.
A Selective Guide to Chinese Literature 1900–1949. Vol. II, *The Short Story*. Edited by Zbigniew Slupski. Leiden: E. J. Brill, 1988.
Ng, Mao-sang. *The Russian Hero in Modern Chinese Fiction*. Hong Kong: Chinese University Press; 1988.
Anderson, Marston. *The Limits of Realism: Chinese Fiction in the Revolutionary Period*. Berkeley: University of California Press, 1990.
Wang, David Der-wei. *Fictional Realism in Twentieth Century China: Mao Dun, Lao She, Shen Congwen*. New York: Columbia University Press, 1992.

The short story: General; anthologies
Twentieth Century Chinese Stories. Edited by C. T. Hsia and Joseph S. M. Lau. New York: Columbia University Press, 1971.
Straw Sandals: Chinese Short Stories 1918–1933. Edited by Harold Isaacs. Foreword by Lu Hsün. Cambridge, MA: MIT Press, 1974.
Modern Chinese Stories and Novellas 1919–1949. Edited by Joseph S. M. Lau, C. T. Hsia, and Leo Ou-fan Lee. New York: Columbia University Press, 1981.
Stories from the Thirties. 2 volumes. Peking: Panda Books 1982.

Lu Xun: Translations
Selected Works of Lu Hsun. 4 volumes. Translated by Hsien-yi Yang and Gladys Yang. Peking: Foreign Languages Press, 1956–60.
Lu Xun, Dawn Blossoms Plucked at Dusk. Translated by Hsien-yi Yang and Gladys Yang. Peking: Foreign Languages Press, 1976. (Translation of *Zhaohua xishi*.)
Lu Xun. *Complete Poems: A Translation with Introduction and Annotation*. Translated by David Y. Ch'en. Tempe: Center for Asian Studies, Arizona State University, 1988.
————. *Diary of a Madman and Other Stories*. Translated by William Lyell. Honolulu: University of Hawaii Press, 1990.

Lu Xun: Studies

Lyell, William A., Jr. *Lu Hsün's Vision of Reality*. Berkeley: University of California Press, 1976.

Hsü, Raymond S. W. *The Style of Lu Hsün: Vocabulary and Usage*. Hong Kong: Centre of Asian Studies, University of Hong Kong, 1979.

Lu Xun and His Legacy. Edited by Leo Ou-fan Lee. Berkeley: University of California Press, 1985.

Lee, Leo Ou-fan. *Voices from the Iron House: A Study of Lu Xun*. Bloomington: Indiana University Press, 1987.

Lundberg, Lennart. *Lu Xun as a Translator: Lu Xun's Translation and Introduction of Literature and Literary Theory, 1903–1936*. Stockholm: Orientaliska Studier, Stockholm University, 1989.

Kowallis, John. *The Lyrical Lu Xun: A Study of His Classical Style Verse*. Honolulu: University of Hawaii Press, 1996.

Yu Dafu: Studies

Dolezalová, Anna. *Yü Ta-fu: Specific Traits of his Literary Creation*. Bratislava: Publishing House of the Slovak Academy of Sciences, 1970.

Ye Shengtao: Translations

Schoolmaster Ni Huan-chih. Translated by A. C. Barnes. Peking: Foreign Languages Press, 1958.

Yeh Sheng-tao. *The Scarecrow: A Collection of Stories for Children*. Peking: Foreign Languages Press, 1963.

Shen Congwen: Translations and studies

The Chinese Earth: Stories by Shen Tsung-wen. Translated by Ching Ti and Robert Payne. London: Allen & Unwin, 1947.

Nieh, Hua-ling. *Shen Ts'ung-wen*. New York: Twayne, 1972.

The Border Town and Other Stories. Translated by Gladys Yang. Peking: Panda Books, 1981.

Shen Congwen. *Recollections of West Hunan*. Translated by Gladys Yang. Peking: Panda Books, 1982.

Kinkley, Jeffrey C. *The Odyssey of Shen Congwen*. Stanford: Stanford University Press, 1987.

Peng, Hsiao-yen. *Anthithesis Overcome: Shen Congwen's Avant-Gardism and Primitivism*. Taipei: Institute of Chinese Literature and Philosophy, Academia Sinica, 1994.

Shen Congwen. *Imperfect Paradise*. Edited by Jeffrey Kinkley. Translated from the Chinese by Jeffrey Kinkley et al. Honolulu: University of Hawaii Press, 1995.

Ding Ling: Translations and studies

The Sun Shines over the Sangkan River. Translated by Hsien-yi Yang and Gladys Yang. Peking: Foreign Languages Press, 1954.

Feuerwerker, Yi-tsi Mei. *Ding Ling's Fiction: Ideology and Narrative in Modern Chinese Literature*. Cambridge, MA: Harvard University Press, 1982.

Ding Ling. *Miss Sophie's Diary*. Translated by W. J. F. Jenner. Peking: Foreign Languages Press, 1985.

I Myself Am a Woman: Selected Writings of Ding Ling. Edited by Tani E. Barlow and Gary J. Bjorge. Boston: Beacon Press, 1989.

Novels

Mao Dun: Translations and studies

Mao Tun. *Spring Silkworms and Other Stories*. Translated by Sidney Shapiro. Peking: Foreign Languages Press, 1956.

Midnight. Translated by Meng-hsiung Hsu and A. C. Barnes. Peking: Foreign Languages Press, 1957. (Translation of *Ziye*.)

Gálik, Marián. *Mao Tun and Modern Chinese Literary Criticism*. Wiesbaden: Franz Steiner Verlag, 1969.

Chen, Yu-shih. *Realism and Allegory in the Early Fiction of Mao Dun*. Bloomington: Indiana University Press, 1986.

Ba Jin: Translations and studies

The Family. Translated by Sidney Shapiro. Peking: Foreign Languages Press, 1958. (A translation of *Jia*; reprinted with additions, Garden City, NY: Anchor Books, 1972.)

Lang, Olga. *Pa Chin and his Writings: Chinese Youth Between the Two Revolutions*. Cambridge, MA: Harvard University Press, 1967.

Cold Nights: A Novel by Pa Chin. Translated by Nathan K. Mao and Liu Ts'un-yan. Hong Kong: Chinese University of Hong Kong Press, 1978. (A translation of *Hanye*.)

Mao, Nathan K. *Pa Chin*. Boston: Twayne, 1978.

Ba Jin. *Autumn in Spring and Other Stories*. Peking: Panda Books, 1981.

―――. *Random Thoughts*. Translated by Geremie Barmé. Hong Kong: Joint Publishing Co., 1984.

Lao She: Translations

The Quest for Love of Lao Lee. Translated by Helen Kuo. New York: Reynal and Hitchcock, 1948. (A translation of *Lihun*.)

The Yellow Storm. Translated by Ida Pruitt. New York: Harcourt, Brace and Co., 1951. (An abridged translation of *Sishi tongtang* [Four generations under one roof], a trilogy on life in Peking during the Japanese occupation, which appeared between 1946 and 1950.)

Heavensend. Translated by Ida Pruitt. London: J. M. Dent and Sons, 1951. (A translation of the novel *Niu Tianci zhuan*, 1934.)

The Drum Singers. Translated by Helen Kuo. New York: Harcourt, Brace and Co., 1952.

Dragon Beard Ditch: A Play in Three Acts. Translated by Liao Hung-ying. Peking, Foreign Languages Press, 1956. (A translation of *Longxu gou*.)

Cat Country: A Satirical Novel of China in the 1930s. Translated by William A. Lyell. Columbus: Ohio State University Press, 1970. (A translation of *Maocheng ji*.)

Rickshaw: The Novel Lo-t'o Hsiang Tzu. Translated by Jean M. James. Honolulu: University of Hawaii Press, 1979. (A new American translation of *Luotuo Xiangzi*.)

Ma and Son: A Novel by Lao She. Translated by Jean M. James. San Francisco: Chinese Materials Center, 1980. (Translation of *Er Ma*.)

Teahouse: A Play in Three Acts. Translated by John Howard-Gibbon. Peking: Foreign Languages Press, 1980. (Translation of *Chaguan*.)

Beneath the Red Banner. Translated by Don J. Cohn. Peking: Panda Books, 1982. (A translation of Lao She's unfinished autobiographical novel *Zheng hongqi xia*.)

Lao She: Studies

Slupski, Zbigniew. *The Evolution of a Modern Chinese Writer: An Analysis of Lao She's Fiction with Biographical and Bibliographical Appendices.* Prague: Czechoslovak Academy of Science, 1966.

Vohra, Ranbir. *Lao She and the Chinese Revolution.* Cambridge, MA: Harvard University Press, 1974.

Two Writers and the Cultural Revolution: Lao She and Chen Jo-hsi. Edited by George Kao. Hong Kong: Chinese University Press, 1980.

Other novelists: Translations

Xiao Jun. *Village in August.* Translated by Evan King. New York: Smith and Durrell, 1942. (Translation of the novel *Bayue de xiangcun.*)

Qian Zhongshu. *Fortress Besieged.* Translated by Jeanne Kelly and Nathan K. Mao. Bloomington: Indiana University Press, 1979. (Translation of the novel *Weicheng.*)

Hsiao Hung. *The Field of Life and Death; and Tales of Hulan River.* Translated by Howard Goldblatt and Ellen Yeung. Bloomington: Indiana University Press, 1979. (Translation of *Shengsi chang* and *Hulan he zhuan.*)

―――. *Selected Stories of Xiao Hong.* Peking: Panda Books, 1982.

Hsiao Ch'ien. *Traveler Without a Map.* Translated by Jeffrey Kinkley. Stanford: Stanford University Press, 1993. (Autobiography of Xiao Qian, 1910–).

Other novelists: Studies

Goldblatt, Howard. *Hsiao Hung.* Boston: Twayne, 1976. (A biographical study.)

Huter, Theodore. *Qian Zhongshu.* Boston: Twayne, 1982.

Bördahl, Vibeke. *Along The Broad Road of Realism: Qin Zhaoyang's World of Fiction.* London: Curzon Press, 1990.

Williams, Philip F. *Village Echoes: The Fiction of Wu Zuxiang.* Boulder: Westview Press, 1993.

Chapter 27. Modern literature, 1917–1942: poetry, drama, and essay

Poetry: General

Translations

Modern Chinese Poetry. Translated by Harold Acton and Ch'en Shih-hsiang. London: Duckworth, 1936.

Contemporary Chinese Poetry. Edited by Robert Payne. London: Routledge and Sons, 1947.

Twentieth Century Chinese Poetry: An Anthology. Translated by Kai-yu Hsu. Garden City, NY: Doubleday, 1963. Reissued in paperback, Ithaca: Cornell University Press, 1970. (An extensive anthology; very informative introduction.)

Anthology of Modern Chinese Poetry. Edited and translated by Michelle Yeh. New Haven: Yale University Press, 1992.

Yip, Wai-lim. *Lyrics from Shelters. Modern Chinese Poetry 1930–1950.* New York: Garland Publishing, 1992.

Studies

Lin, Julia C. *Modern Chinese Poetry: An Introduction.* Seattle: University of Washington Press, 1972.

A Selective Guide to Chinese Literature 1900–1949. Vol. III, *The Poem.* Edited by Lloyd Haft. Leiden: E. J. Brill, 1989.

Yeh, Michelle. *Modern Chinese Poetry: Theory and Practice since 1917.* New Haven: Yale University Press, 1991.

Hockx, Michel. *A Snowy Morning: Eight Chinese Poets on the Road to Modernity.* Leiden: Center of Non-Western Studies, 1994.

Guo Moruo: Translations and studies

Selected Poems from The Goddesses. Translated by John Lester and A. C. Barnes. Peking: Foreign Languages Press, 1958.

Roy, David T. *Kuo Mo-jo: The Early Years.* Cambridge, MA: Harvard University Press, 1971.

Five Historical Plays. Translated by Fumin Peng, Bonnie S. McDougall, Yang Xianyi and Gladys Yang. Peking: Foreign Languages Press, 1984.

Wen Yiduo

Red Candle: Selected Poems by Wen I-to. Translated by Tao Tao Sanders. London: Cape, 1972.

Hsu Kai-yu. *Wen I-to.* Boston: Twayne, 1980. (A detailed biographical study.)

Feng Zhi

Cheung, Dominic. *Feng Chih.* Boston: Twayne, 1979.

Poets of the thirties and forties

Dai Wangshu

Lee, Gregory. *Dai Wangshu, The Life and Poetry of a Chinese Modernist.* Hong Kong: Chinese University Press, 1989.

Bian Zhilin

Haft, Lloyd. *Pien Chih-lin: A Study in Modern Chinese Poetry.* Dordrecht: Foris Publications, 1983.

He Qifang

Paths in Dreams: Selected Prose and Poetry of Ho Ch'i-fang. Translated by Bonnie S. McDougall. St. Lucia: University of Queensland Press, 1976.

Ai Qing

The Black Eel. Translated by Yang Xianyi and Robert C. Friend. Peking: Panda Books, 1982. (A translation of the long narrative poem *Heiman,* 1954.)

Selected Poems. Translated by Eugene Chen Eoyang. Peking: Foreign Languages Press, 1982.

Drama, general: Translations and studies

Mackerras, Colin P. *The Chinese Theatre in Modern Times: From 1840 to the Present Day.* London: Thames and Hudson, 1975.

Twentieth Century Chinese Drama: An Anthology. Edited by Edward M. Gunn. Bloomington: Indiana University Press, 1983.

A Selective Guide to Chinese Literature 1900–1949. Vol. IV: *The Drama.* Edited by Bernd Eberstein. Leiden: E. J. Brill, 1990.

Tian Han and contemporaries

Hsia Yen. *The Test: A Play in Five Acts.* Translated by Ying Yu. Peking: Foreign Languages Press, 1956. (A translation of *Kaoyan*, 1953.)

Tien Han. *The White Snake: A Peking Opera.* Translated by Yang Hsien-yi and Gladys Yang. Peking: Foreign Languages Press, 1957.

————. *Kuan Han-ching: A Play.* Peking: Foreign Languages Press, 1961.

Li, Jianwu. *It's Only Spring and Thirteen Years: Two early plays by Li Jianwu.* Translated by Tony Hyder. London: Bamboo Publishing, 1989.

Cao Yu: Translations and studies

Thunderstorm. Translated by Tso-liang Wang and A. C. Barnes. Peking: Foreign Languages Press, 1958. (Translation of *Leiyu.*)

Sunrise: A Play in Four Acts. Translated by A. C. Barnes. Peking: Foreign Languages Press, 1960. (Translation of *Richu.*)

Lau, Joseph S. M. *Ts'ao Yü, The Reluctant Disciple of Chekhov and O'Neill: A Study in Literary Influence.* Hong Kong: Hong Kong University Press, 1970.

Hu, John Y. H. *Ts'ao Yü.* New York: Twayne, 1972.

The Wilderness. Translated by Christopher Rand and S. M. Lau. Hong Kong: Indiana University Press, 1980. (A translation of Cao Yu's *Yuanye*, 1937.)

The Consort of Peace. Translated by Monica Lai. Hong Kong: Kelly & Walsh, 1980. (A translation of *Wang Zhaojun*, 1978.)

Peking Man. Translated by Leslie Nai-kwai Lo et al. New York, Columbia University Press, 1986.

Essays

Liang, Shih-ch'iu. *Sketches of a Cottager.* Translated by Chao-ying Shih. Taipei, 1960.

Wolff, Ernst. *Chou Tso-jen.* New York: Twayne, 1971.

Pollard, D. E. *A Chinese Look at Literature: The Literary Values of Chou Tso-jen in Relation to the Tradition.* London: C. Hurst and Co., 1973.

Li, Guangtian. *A Pitiful Plaything and Other Essays.* Translated by Gladys Yang. Peking: Panda, 1982.

Chapter 28. Modern literature, 1942–1980

1942–1949

General

Holm, David L. *Art and Ideology in Revolutionary China.* Oxford: Oxford University Press, 1991.

Mao's talks

McDougall, Bonnie S. *Mao Zedong's 'Talks at the Yan'an Conference on Literature and Art': A Translation of the 1943 Text with Commentary.* Ann Arbor: Center for Chinese Studies, University of Michigan, 1980.

Pickowicz, Paul C. *Marxist Literary Thought in China: The Influence of Ch'ü Ch'iu-pai.* Berkeley: University of California, 1981.

Dai Qing. *Wang Shiwei and "Wild Lilies": Rectification and Purges in the Chinese Communist Party 1942–1944.* Edited by David E. Apter and Timothy Cheek. Translated by Nancy Liu and Lawrence R. Sullivan. Documents compiled by Song Jinshou. Armonk, NY: M. E. Sharpe, 1994.

He Jingzhi
Ho, Ching-chih and Ting Yi. *The White-haired Girl: An Opera in Five Acts.* Translated by Yang Hsien-yi and Gladys Yang. Peking: Foreign Languages Press, 1954.

Li Ji
Wang Kuei and Li Hsiang-hsiang. Translated by Hsien-yi Yang and Gladys Yang. Peking: Foreign languages Press, 1954. (Translation of *Wang Gui yu Li Xiangxiang.*)
Songs from the Yumen Oilfield. Translated by Ko-chia Yuan. Peking: Foreign Languages Press, 1957.

Zhao Shuli
Zhao Shuli. *Rhymes of Li Yu-tsai and Other Stories.* Peking: Cultural Press, 1950.
Changes in Li Village. Translated by Gladys Yang. Peking: Foreign Languages Press, 1953. (A translation of the novel *Lijiazhuang de bianqian.*)
Sanliwan Village. Translated by Gladys Yang. Peking: Foreign languages Press, 1957.

1949–1978
Reference works
Gibbs, Donald A. *Subject and Author Index to Chinese Literature Monthly (1951–1976).* New Haven: Far Eastern Publication, 1978.
Bibliography of English Translations and Critiques of Contemporary Chinese Fiction 1945–1992. Edited by Kam Louie and Louise Edwards. Taipei: Center for Chinese Studies, 1993.

General
Chinese Communist Literature. Edited by Cyril Birch. New York: Praeger, 1963. literature in the PRC.)
Fokkema, D. W. *Literary Doctrine in China and Soviet Influence 1956–1960.* The Hague: Mouton, 1965.
Nunn, R. *Publishing in Mainland China.* Cambridge, MA: MIT Press, 1966.
Goldman, Merle. *Literary Dissent in Communist China.* Cambridge, MA: Harvard University Press, 1973.
Hsu, Kai-yu. *The Chinese Literary Scene: A Writer's Visit to the People's Republic.* New York: Vintage Books, 1975.
Chu, Godwin C. *Popular Media in China: Shaping New Cultural Patterns.* Honolulu: University of Hawaii Press, 1978.
Literature of the People's Republic of China. Edited by Kai-yu Hsu and Ting Wang. Bloomington: Indiana University Press, 1980.
Literature of the Hundred Flowers. Vol. I. *Criticism and Polemics.* Vol. II. *Poetry and Fiction.* Edited by Hualing Nieh. New York: Columbia University Press, 1981.
Essays in Modern Chinese Literature and Literary Criticism. Edited by Wolfgang Kubin and Rudolf G. Wagner. Bochum: Brockmeyer, 1982.
Popular Chinese Literature and the Performing Arts in the People's Republic of China, 1949–1979. Edited by Bonnie S. McDougall. Berkeley: University of California Press, 1984.

Clark, Paul. *Chinese Cinema, Culture and Politics since 1949.* Cambridge: Cambridge University Press, 1987.

Kaikkonen, Marja. *Laughable Propaganda: Modern Xiangsheng as Didactic Entertainment.* Stockholm: Institute of Oriental Languages, 1990.

Wagner, Rudolf. *Inside a Service Trade: Studies in Contemporary Chinese Prose.* Cambridge, MA: Harvard University Press, 1992.

Fiction: General

Huang, Joe C. *Heroes and Villains in Communist China: The Contemporary Chinese Novel as a Reflection of Life.* New York: Pica Press, 1973.

Tsai, Meishi. *Contemporary Chinese Novels and Short Stories: An Annotated Bibliography.* Cambridge, MA: Harvard University Press, 1979.

Berman, Pär. *Paragons of Virtue in Chinese Short Stories During the Cultural Revolution.* Stockholm: Förerningen för Orientaliska Studier, 1984.

Zhou Libo

The Hurricane. Translated by Meng-hsiung Hsu. Peking, Foreign Languages Press, 1955. (Translation of *Baofeng zhouyu.*)

Great Changes in a Mountain Village. Vol. I. Translated by Derek Bryan. Peking: Foreign Languages Press, 1961. (First part of a translation of *Shanxiang jubian.*)

Sowing the Clouds: A Collection of Chinese Short Stories. Peking: Foreign Languages Press, 1961. (Includes stories by Zhou Libo.)

Yang Mo

The Song of Youth. Translated by Nan Ying. Peking: Foreign Languages Press, 1964. (Translation of *Qingchun zhi ge.*)

Hao Ran

Hao Jan. *Bright Clouds.* Peking: Foreign Languages Press, 1974.

Hao Jan. *The Call of the Fledgeling and Other Children's Stories.* Peking: Foreign Languages Press, 1974.

Haoran. *The Golden Road: A Story of One Village in the Uncertain Days After Land Reform.* Translated by Carma Hinton and Chris Gilmartin. Peking, 1981.

Poetry: General

Songs of the Red Flag. Translated by A. C. Barnes. Peking: Foreign Languages Press, 1961. ("Folk Songs" of the Great Leap Forward.)

Drama: General

Modern Drama from Communist China. Edited by Walter J. Meserve and Ruth I. Meserve. New York: New York University Press, 1970.

Wu Han. *Hai Jui Dismissed from Office.* Translated by C. G. Huang. Honolulu, 1972. (A translation of *Hai Rui ba guan.*)

The Red Pear Garden: Three Great Dramas of Revolutionary China. Edited by John D. Mitchell. Boston: David R. Godine, 1973. (Three Peking operas, including *Baishe zhuan,* and a model opera.)

Mackerras, Colin P. *Amateur Theatre in China, 1949–1966.* Canberra: Australian National University Press, 1973.

Five Chinese Communist Plays. Edited by Martin Ebon. New York: John Day Company, 1973. (*Baimao nü* and four model operas.)

Howard, Roger. *Contemporary Chinese Theatre.* London: Heinemann Educational Books, 1978.

Wagner, Rudolf G. *The Contemporary Chinese Historical Drama: Four Studies.* Berkeley: University of California Press, 1990.

Literary life in the PRC since 1978

General: Translations

Prize-Winning Stories from China, 1978–79. Peking: Foreign Languages Press, 1981.

Seven Contemporary Chinese Women Writers. Peking: Panda Books, 1982.

Fragrant Weeds. Edited by W. J. F. Jenner. Translated by Geremie Barmé and Bennett Lee. Hong Kong: Joint Publishing Co., 1983. (Stories from 1956–1957 by Wang Meng and other writers who came to the fore after 1978.)

Mao's Harvest: Voices from China's New Generation. Edited by Helen Siu and Zelda Stern. New York: Oxford University Press, 1983.

The New Realism: Writings from China after the Cultural Revolution. Edited by Lee Yee. New York: Hippocrene Books, 1983.

Stubborn Weeds: Popular and Controversial Chinese Literature after the Cultural Revolution. Edited by Perry Link. Bloomington: Indiana University Press, 1983.

———. *Roses and Thorns: The Second Blooming of the Hundred Flowers in Chinese Fiction, 1979–80.* Berkeley: University of California Press, 1984.

Trees on the Mountain: An Anthology of New Chinese Writing. Edited by Stephen C. Soong and John Minford. Hong Kong: Chinese University Press, 1984.

Contemporary Chinese Literature: An Anthology of Post-Mao Fiction and Poetry. Edited by Michael S. Duke. New York: East Gate Books, 1985.

One Half of the Sky: Selections from Contemporary Women Writers of China. Translated by R. A. Robert and Angela Knox. London: Heinemann, 1987.

100 Modern Chinese Poems. Edited by Bingjun Pang and John Minford, with Seán Golden. Hong Kong: Commercial Press, 1987.

Seeds of Fire: Chinese Voices of Conscience. Edited by Geremie Barmé and John Minford. New York: Hill and Wang, 1988.

The Rose Colored Dinner: New Works by Contemporary Chinese Women Writers. Translated by Nienling Liu et al. Hong Kong: Joint Publishing, 1988.

The Red Azalea: Chinese Poetry Since The Cultural Revolution. Edited by Edward Morin. Translated by Fang Dai, Dennis Ding, and Edward Morin. Honolulu: University of Hawaii Press, 1990.

The Serenity of Whiteness: Stories by and about Women in Contemporary China. Translated by Hong Zhu. New York: Ballantine Books, 1991.

Worlds of Modern Chinese Fiction. Edited by Michael S. Duke. Armonk: M.E. Sharpe, 1991.

Women of the Red Plain: An Anthology of Contemporary Chinese Women's Poetry. Translated by Julia Lin. Peking: Chinese Literature Press and Penguin, 1992.

Out of the Howling Storm: The New Chinese Poetry. Edited by Tony Barnstone. Hanover: University Press of New England, 1993.

Nativism Overseas: Contemporary Chinese Women Writers. Edited by C. Hsin-sheng Kao. Albany: State University of New York Press, 1993.

Running Wild: New Chinese Writers. Edited by David Der-wei Wang and Jeanne Tai. New York: Columbia University Press, 1994.

Chairman Mao Would Not Be Amused: Fiction from Today's China. Edited by Howard Goldblatt. New York: Grove Press, 1995.

General: Studies
Mackerras, Colin. *The Performing Arts in Contemporary China.* London: Routledge and Kegan Paul, 1981.

Chinese Literature for the 1980s: The Fourth Congress of Writers and Artists. Edited by Howard Goldblatt. Armonk, NY: M. E. Sharpe, 1982.

Modern Chinese Women Writers: Critical Appraisals. Edited by Michael S. Duke. Armonk, NY: M. E. Sharpe, 1989.

Worlds Apart: Recent Chinese Writing and its Audiences. Edited by Howard Goldblatt. Armonk, NY: M. E. Sharpe, 1990. (Studies on PRC and Taiwan literature.)

Perspectives on Chinese Cinema. Edited by Chris Berry. London: British Film Institute, 1991.

Su, Xiaokang and Wang Luxiang. *Deathsong of the River: A Reader's Guide to the Chinese TV Series Heshang.* Translated by Richard W. Bodman and Pin P. Wang. Cornell East Asia Series. Ithaca: East Asia Program, Cornell University, 1991.

Leung, Laifong. *Morning Sun: Interviews with Post-Mao Chinese Writers.* Armonk, NY: M. E. Sharpe, 1992.

Hagenaar, Elly. *Stream of Consciousness and Free Indirect Discourse in Modern Chinese Literature.* Leiden: Center of Non-Western Studies, 1992.

Inside Out: Modernism and Postmodernism in Chinese Literary Culture. Edited by Wendy Larson and Anna Wedell-Wedellsborg. Åarhus: Åarhus University Press, 1993.

The Lost Boat: Avant Garde Fiction from China. Edited by Henry Zhao. London: Wellsweep, 1993

Film in Contemporary China: Critical Debates, 1979-1989. Edited by George S. Semsel, Chen Xihe, and Xia Hong. Westport: Praeger, 1993.

New Chinese Cinemas, Forms, Identities, Politics. Edited by Nick Brown et al. Cambridge: Cambridge University Press, 1994.

Cinematic Landscapes: Observations on the Visual Arts of China and Japan. Edited by Linda C. Ehrlich and David Desser. Austin: University of Texas Press, 1994.

Chen, Xiaomei. *Occidentalism, A Theory of Counter-Discourse in Post-Mao China.* New York: Oxford University Press, 1995.

Lu, Tonglin. *Misogyny, Cultural Nihilism, and Oppositional Politics: Contemporary Chinese Experimental Fiction.* Stanford: Stanford University Press, 1995.

Chow, Rey. *Primitive Passions: Visuality, Sexuality, Ethnography, and Contemporary Chinese Cinema.* Film and Culture Series. New York: Columbia University Press, 1995.

Individual authors
Bai Hua
The Remote Country of Women. Translated by Qingyun Wu and Thomas O. Beebee. Honolulu: University of Hawaii Press, 1994.

Bei Dao (Zhao Zhenkai)
Notes from the City of the Sun: Poems by Bei Dao. Translated by Bonnie S. McDougall. Ithaca: China-Japan Program, Cornell University, 1983.

Waves: Stories. Edited by Bonnie S. McDougall and Susette Ternent Cooke. Hong Kong: Chinese University Press, 1985.

Bei Dao. *Old Snow: Poems.* Translated by Bonnie S. McDougall and Chen Maiping. New York: New Directions, 1991.
Forms of Distance: Poems. Translated by David Hinton. New York: New Directions, 1994.

Can Xue
Can Xue. *Dialogues in Paradise.* Translated by Ronald R. Janssen and Jian Zhang. Evanston, IL: Northwestern University Press, 1989.
———. *Old Floating Clouds: Two Novellas.* Translated by Ronald R. Janssen and Jian Zhang. Evanston, IL: Northwestern University Press, 1991.

Dai Houying
Dai Houying. *Stones of the Wall.* Translated by Frances Wood. London: Joseph, 1985.

Duoduo
Duoduo. *Looking Out From Death: From the Cultural Revolution to Tiananmen Square.* Translated by Gregory Lee and John Cayley. London: Bloomsbury, 1989.
Crevel, Maghiel van. *Language Shattered: Contemporary Chinese Poetry and Duoduo.* Leiden: CNWS Publications, 1996.

Feng Jicai
Feng Jicai. *The Three-Inch Golden Lotus.* Translated by David Wakefield. Honolulu: University of Hawaii Press, 1994.

Gu Cheng
Gu Cheng. *Selected Poems.* Edited by Seán Golden and Chu Chiyu. Hong Kong: Renditions Paperbacks, 1990.
Gu Cheng and Lei Mi. *Ying'er: The Kingdom of Daughters.* Translated by Li Xia. Dortmund: Projekt Verlag, 1995.

Gu Hua
Gu Hua. *Virgin Widows.* Translated by Howard Goldblatt. Honolulu: University of Hawaii Press, 1996.

Han Shaogong
Han Shaogong. *Homecoming? and Other Stories.* Translated by Martha Cheung. Hong Kong: Chinese University of Hong Kong, 1992.

Jia Pinghua
Jia Pinghua. *Turbulence.* Translated by Howard Goldblatt. Baton Rouge: Louisiana State University Press, 1991.

Li Cunbao
Li Cunbao. *The Wreath at the Foot of the Monument.* Translated by Chen Hanming and James O. Belcher. New York: Garland Publishing, 1991.

Liu Binyan
Liu Binyan. *People or Monsters? and Other Stories and Reportage from China after Mao.* Edited by Perry Link. Bloomington: Indiana University Press, 1983.

————. *A Higher Kind of Loyalty.* Translated by Zhu Hong. New York: Pantheon Books, 1990. (Autobiography.)

Liu Heng

Liu Heng. *Black Snow: A Novel of the Beijing Demimonde.* Translated by Howard Goldblatt. New York: Atlantic Monthly Press, 1993.

Liu Suola

Liu Sola. *Blue Sky Green and Other Stories.* Translated by Martha Cheung. Hong Kong: Renditions Paperbacks, 1993.

————. *Chaos and All That: An Irreverent Novel.* Translated by Richard King. Honolulu: University of Hawaii Press, 1995.

Mo Yan

Mo Yan. *Red Sorghum.* Translated by Howard Goldblatt. New York: Viking Penguin, 1993.

————. *The Garlic Ballads.* Translated by Howard Goldblatt. New York: Viking, 1995.

Su Tong

Su Tong. *Raise the Red Lantern: Three Novellas.* Translated by Michael Duke. New York: William Morrow, 1993.

————. *Rice.* Translated by Howard Goldblatt. New York: William Morrow, 1995.

Wang Anyi

Wang Anyi. *Brocade Valley.* Translated by Bonnie McDougall and Chen Maiping. New York: New Directions, 1992.

Wang Meng

Wang Meng. *Bolshevik Salute: A Modernist Chinese Novel.* Translated, with introduction and critical essay, by Wendy Larson. Seattle: University of Washington Press, 1989.

————. *Alienation.* Translated by Nancy T. Lin and Tong Qi Lin. Hong Kong: Joint Publishing, 1993.

————. *The Stubborn Porridge and Other Stories.* Introduction by Zhu Hong. New York: George Braziller, 1994.

Wang Ruowang

Wang Ruowang. *Hunger Trilogy.* Translated by Kyna Rubin with Ira Krasoff. Armonk, NY: M. E. Sharpe, 1991.

Yang Jiang

Yang, Chiang. *A Cadre School Life: Six Chapters.* Translated by Geremie Barme with Bennett Lee. Hong Kong: Joint Publishing Co., 1982.

————. *Six Chapters from My Life 'Downunder'.*. Translated by Howard Goldblatt. Hong Kong: Chinese University Press, 1983.

————. *Six Chapters of Life in a Cadre School: Memoirs from China's Cultural Revolution.* Translated and annotated by Djang Chu. Boulder: Westview Press, 1986.

Yang Lian

Yang Lian. *Masks and Crocodiles: A Contemporary Chinese Poet and his Poetry.* Translated by Mabel Lee. Broadway, N.S.W., Australia: Wild Peony, 1990.
————. *Non-Person Singular.* Translated by Brian Holton. London: Wellsweep, 1994.

Yu Hua

Yu Hua. *The Past and the Punishments: Eight Stories.* Translated by Andrew F. Jones. Honolulu: University of Hawaii Press, 1996.

Yu Luojin

Yu Luojin. *A Chinese Winter's Tale: An Autobiographical Fragment.* Translated by Rachel May and Zhu Zhiyu. Hong Kong: Research Centre for Translation, Chinese University of Hong Kong, 1986, rpt. 1988.

Zhang Jie

Zhang Jie. *Love Must Not Be Forgotten.* Translated by Gladys Yang et al. Peking: Panda Books, 1986.

Zhang Xianliang

Zhang Xianliang. *Man is Half a Woman.* Translated by Martha Avery. New York: Viking, 1987.
————. *Getting Used to Dying.* Translated and edited by Martin Avery. London: Collins, 1991.
————. *Grass Soup.* Translated by Martha Avery. London: Secker and Warburg, 1994.

Zhang Xinxin

Zhang Xinxin. *The Dream of Our Generation and Selections from Beijing People.* Edited and translated by Edward Gunn and D. Jung. Ithaca: Cornell University Press, 1986.

Theater

Drama in the People's Republic of China. Edited by Constantine Tung and Colin Mackerras. Albany: State University of New York Press, 1987.

Chinese literature in Taiwan since 1949

The Muse of China: A Collection of Prose and Short Stories by Contemporary Chinese Women Writers. 2 volumes. Taipei: Chinese Women Writers' Association, 1974-78.
An Anthology of Contemporary Chinese Literature, Taiwan: 1949–1974. Vol. I, *Poems and Essays,* idem, Vol. II, Short Stories. Edited by Pang-yuan Chi et al. Taipei: National Institute for Compilation & Translation, 1975.
New Voices: Stories and Poems by Young Chinese Writers. 2nd edition. Translated by Nancy Ing. San Francisco: N.p., 1980.

Fiction

Chinese Stories from Taiwan: 1960–1970. Edited by Joseph S. M. Lau and Timothy A. Ross. New York: Columbia University Press, 1976.
Chinese Fiction from Taiwan: Critical Perspectives. Edited by Jeanette L. Faurot. Bloomington: Indiana University Press, 1980.

Winter Plum: Contemporary Chinese Fiction. Edited by Nancy Ing. San Francisco: Chinese Materials Centre, 1982.

Carver, Ann C. and Song-sheng Yvonne Chang. *Bamboo Shoots After the Rain: Contemporary Stories of Women Writers of Taiwan.* New York: Feminist Press at the City University of New York, 1991.

Modernism and the Nativist Resistance: Contemporary Chinese Fiction from Taiwan. Edited by Yvonne Sung-cheng Chang. Durham: Duke University Press, 1993.

Death in a Cornfield and Other Stories from Contemporary Taiwan. Edited by Ching-hsi Peng and Chiu-kuei Wang. Hong Kong, Oxford, New York: Hong Kong University Press, 1994.

Oxcart: Nativist Stories from Taiwan, 1934–1977. Translated by Rosemary M. Haddon. Dortmund: Projekt Verlag, 1996.

Poetry: General

New Chinese Poetry. Edited and translated by Kwang-chung Yu. Taipei: Heritage Press, 1960.

Modern Chinese Poetry. Twenty Poets from the Republic of China 1955–1965. Translated by Wai-lim Yip. Iowa City: University of Iowa Press, 1970.

Modern Verse from Taiwan. Translated by Angela Jung Palandri. Berkeley: University of California Press, 1972.

Summer Glory: A Collection of Contemporary Chinese Poetry. Translated by Nancy Ing. San Francisco: Chinese Materials Centre, 1982.

Lin, Julia C. *Essays on Contemporary Chinese Poetry.* Athens: Ohio, 1985.

The Isle Full of Noises: Modern Chinese Poetry from Taiwan. Edited and translated by Dominic Cheung. New York: Columbia University Press, 1987.

Individual authors
Bai Xianyong

Pai Hsien-yung (Bai Xianyong). *Wandering in the Garden, Waking from a Dream: Tales of Taipei Characters.* Bloomington: Indiana University Press, 1982.

Pai Hsien-yung. *Crystal Boys.* Translated by Howard Goldblatt. San Francisco: Gay Sunshine Press, 1990.

Bo Yang

Bo Yang. *Secrets.* Translated by David Deterding. Boston: Cheng and Tsui, 1985.

Chen Ruoxi

Chen Jo-hsi. *The Execution of Mayor Yin: and Other Stories from the Great Proletarian Cultural Revolution.* Translated by Nancy Ing and Howard Goldblatt. Bloomington: Indiana University Press, 1978.

———. *The Old Man and Other Stories.* Hong Kong: Research Centre for Translation, Chinese University of Hong Kong, 1986.

Chen Yingzhen

Exiles at Home: Short Stories by Ch'en Ying-chen. Translated by Lucien Miller. Ann Arbor: Center for Chinese Studies, University of Michigan, 1986.

Gao Yang

Gao Yang. *Stories by Gao Yang: 'Rekindled Love' and 'Purple Jade Hairpin'.* Translated by Chan Sin-wai. Hong Kong: Chinese University of Hong Kong, 1989.

Huang Chunming
Hwang Chun-ming. *The Drowning of an Old Cat and Other Stories.* Translated by Howard
   Goldblatt. Bloomington: Indiana University Press, 1980.

Jiang Gui
Ross, Timothy A. *Chiang Kuei.* New York: Twayne, 1974.
Chiang Kuei. *The Whirlwind.* Translated by Timothy A. Ross. San Francisco: Chinese
   Materials Center, 1977.

Li Ang
Li Ang. *The Butcher's Wife (Shafu).* Translated by Howard Goldblatt and Ellen Yeung. San
   Francisco: North Point Press, 1986.
Li Ang. *Butcher.* Translated by Fan Wen-mei. Hong Kong: Chinese University of Hong
   Kong, 1988.

Luo Fu
Luo Fu. *Death of a Stone Cell.* Translated by John Balcom. Monterey: Taoran Press, 1993.

Luo Qing
Forbidden Games and Video Poems: The Poetry of Yang Mu and Lo Ch'ing. Translated by Joseph
   Roe Allen III. Seattle: University of Washington Press, 1993.

Nie Hualing
Nieh Hualing. *Mulberry and Peach: Two Women of China.* Translated by Jane Parish Yang with
   Linda Lappin. Boston: Beacon Press, 1988.

Shang Qin
Shang Ch'in. *The Frozen Torch: Selected Prose Poems.* Translated by N. G. D. Malmqvist.
   London: Wellsweep, 1992.

Wang Wenxing
Wang Wen-hsing. *A Family Catastrophe.* Translated from the Chinese by Susan Wan Dolling.
   Honolulu: University of Hawaii Press, 1995.

Xie Fengzheng
Hsieh Fengcheng. *After the Death of Younger Werther: Poems.* Translated by Howard Goldblatt.
   Santa Barbara: Fithian Press, 1990.

Yang Mu
Forbidden Games and Video Poems: The Poetry of Yang Mu and Lo Ch'ing. Translated by Joseph R.
   Allen. Seattle: University of Washington Press, 1993.

Hong Kong and the "diaspora"
Chang Ai-ling. *Naked Earth.* Hong Kong: Union Press, 1956. (The author's own translation
   of her novel *Chidi zhi lian.*)
———. *The Rice-Sprout Song.* Hong Kong, 1963. (The author's own translation of her novel
   Yangge.)

Chinese Literature Today. Special Issue. *Renditions* 19-20 (Spring-Autumn 1983).

Xi Xi. *A Girl Like Me and Other Stories.* Translated by Rachel May et al. Hong Kong: Research Centre for Translation, Chinese University of Hong Kong, 1986.

Hong Kong. Special issue. *Renditions* 29-30 (Spring-Autumn 1988).

Nativism Overseas: Contemporary Chinese Women Writers. Edited by C. Hsing-sheng Kao. Albany: State University of New York Press, 1993.

Lee, Lilian (Li Pik-wah). *Farewell to My Concubine.* Translated by Andrea Lingenfelter. London: Penguin, 1993.

Eileen Chang. Special issue. *Renditions* 45 (Spring 1996).

GLOSSARY–INDEX